Child Development

A Developmentally Appropriate Curriculum Approach

Darrell Meece

CONTENTS

Learning Objectives	NAEYC Standard
At the completion of this course, students will be able to:	
1. Describe the biological and environmental factors that influence the physical, cognitive, social and emotional development of the young child during infancy, toddlerhood, preschool, middle childhood, and early adolescence periods.	1(a), 1(b), 1(c)
2. Recognize the importance of understanding culture in understanding children's development.	2 (a), 2 (b), 2 (c),4 (a), 4 (c), 4 (d)
3. Decribe the the scientific study of children and the major theories of child development.	1(a), 1(b), 1(c), 2 (a)
4. Describe the physical development of young children during infancy, toddlerhood, preschool, middle childhood, and early adolescence.	1(a), 1(b), 1(c), 5 (a)
5. Describe cognitive development in children and how early experiences contribute to individual differences in cognitive development.	1(a), 1(b), 1(c), 5 (a)
6. Describe communication, speech and language development---both receptive and expressive---from birth through early adolescence, with attention to diverse cultures.	1(a), 1(b), 1(c), 2(a), 5 (a)
7. Describe the social and emotional development of children.	1(a), 1(b), 1(c), 2(a)
8. Recognize the importance of play in sensory and motor development and cognitive, language, social and emotional development.	1(a), 1(b), 1(c), 4 (a), 4 (c), 5 (a), 6(b)
9. Describe the basic health needs of infants, toddlers, preschoolers, middle childhood children and early adolescents.	1(a), 1(b), 1(c), 2(a), 2(b), 2(c), 5 (a)
10. Observe and record behavior of children and demonstrate the ability to integrate observational data with existing knowledge of child development and communicate findings.	3(c), 4(c), 4 (d), 6 (b), 6(d)
11. Recognize signs of emotional distress and child abuse in children.	1(a),1(c), 4(a), 5 (a), 6(b), 6(d)

1. WAYS OF THINKING ABOUT CHILDREN

Learning Objectives At the completion of this chapter, students will be able to:	Related Course Objective
1-1 Describe the scientific method in child development.	3
1-2 Recognize that a developmentally appropriate approach to child development acknowledges that context and environment impact development as well as biological factors.	1
1-2 Recognize that risk factors and foster protective factors influence development.	1
1-3 Recall current demographic information describing children in the United States.	2

My intention is for this book to serve as a foundation in basic knowledge about how children develop – that is, how children grow and change over time. My focus here is on children from birth through around age 12 or so – it is difficult to state an exact age because different areas of research may focus on different age ranges, but I mean to about the age of early adolescence, the onset of puberty, the transition from elementary school to middle school. My goal is for this book to be useful for students embarking on plans of study that will equip them to work with children and families in a variety of careers, such as teaching, child and family services, social work, nursing, outdoor and recreational programs, and so on. It is impossible for me to include all the information that one would need to competently engage in all these tasks in a single course; my focus here is to provide basic knowledge of "Child Development" as a subject of content.

The book is segmented in to weekly chapters focusing on biological and physical aspects of development, cognitive development, language development, emotional development, and social development. The truth of the matter is, though, that development does not occur in isolation in these separate domains – what happens in cognitive development impacts what happens in language development, and what happens in language development impacts what happens in social development, and what happens in social development impacts what happens in cognitive development, and on and on. The way that I am "breaking" these subjects up in to domains is artificial, something that I am just making up, as a way to communicate to you a large amount of information in "chunks" that are manageable for both of us.

Developmental Period	Age range
Prenatal	Conception to birth
Infancy	Birth to 18-24 months
Toddler	~18 months to ~30 months
Early Childhood (preschool years)	24 months to 5-6 years
Middle / Late Childhood (elementary school years)	6 years to 11 years
Early Adolescence	About 10-12 years; onset of puberty and transition to middle school
Adolescence	10-12 years to 18-22 years

Before we begin discussing those different domains, though, I am going to start with a question that will probably seem odd to you. A moment ago, I wrote "The truth of the matter is..." Now, stop and think for a second. When you read that, did you question if the following statement was "true?" Or, did you accept it is a "true" because it was written and seemed to make sense as you read through it? There is really a deeper question here, and that is *"How do we know that something is true?"*

How would you answer this question?

One of the central issues in the Study of Child Development – and this book – is the need to think critically about our observations of children. This is difficult, because we were all children and have preconceived ideas about what is right or what isn't. Will return to this idea in Chapter 2.

"Kids are Kids"

When I was an undergraduate college student, I had a summer job as a camp counselor at a residential summer camp in central Alabama. Several comments were made suggesting that staff should be extra "strict" during a week of camp that would be attended by children who lived in poverty, because "*those* children will take a mile if you give them an inch." The water front director calmly looked at one of the life guards making these claims and said "I don't know about that, to me kids are kids."

That line stuck with me, and has for the past 30 years. "Kids are kids." I think that what he meant by that was that children from all backgrounds can do "typical kid things." I have heard the same sort of argument that the lifeguard was making at that lake in Alabama made again and again. For example, in Michigan during discussions of discipline using positive guidance strategies, I have heard adults argue "that might work with middle class children, but it won't work with *these* kids, because poor kids are not used to people talking to them like that, they are used to people being strict with them and telling them what to do." I have heard it in terms of giving children opportunities to make choices in their learning "that might work with *those* middle class kids because they are used to adults giving them choices, but it won't work with *these* kids." I have seen it in Tennessee when visiting different schools; for example, at schools in middle class communities where children amble and chatter as they walk down the halls, in contrast to schools zoned for areas high in poverty in which children are required to walk the halls silently in straight lines. Over time I have realized that my "alarm" goes off when I hear phrases about "*these* children, and *those* children."

During those 30 years I worked with children in a variety of ages in a variety of settings. From preschoolers in University-sponsored laboratory schools, to their similar-aged peers in Head Start classrooms, to middle-childhood children in YMCA after-school programs, to adolescents in residential mental health treatment centers, to children from all backgrounds in Girl and Boy Scouts, and so on. Intuitively, it has always made sense to me that "kids are kids." And as I learned more about child development, I learned more examples to support that. For example, I "know" how a typical three-year-old will hold and cut with scissors. I "know" that somewhere in a preschool serving upper middle-class four-year-olds, and also in a Head Start classroom serving four-year-olds in a rural community who live in poverty, a child will say "You can't be my friend, because she is my friend." I "know" that if I went to lunch today at either a school in the poorest downtown neighborhood or a school in the upper-middle class suburbs, that when the second-graders are having lunch there will be tables full of girls only and tables full of boys only. I know that if I watched children on a school playground in Minnesota and children on a school playground in Miami the biggest difference in my observations will be the amount of winter clothes they are wearing.

To me, it makes perfect sense that "Kids are Kids."

Human Ecology

A couple of years after that summer I began graduate school. I remember the "main idea" of that first semester, that was repeated in every course, was the importance of "Human Ecology." Human Ecology is the study of human beings are impacted by the world around them, including not only the physical aspects of the environment, but also the social and relationship aspects of our environment. As human beings, we are "social creatures." We do not grow and develop alone or in isolation. Instead, as children we depend on others to care for us. As children develop, they take part in many social systems, including their family, their school, their peers, their neighborhood and so on. Their development is impacted by many aspects of the social world that they are enmeshed in. They learn the "rules" of their culture. They are impacted by how society treats different ethnic, religious, and racial groups. They are impacted by both the "content" of what their interactions with parents as well as the "style" of the quality of the relationship they have with their parents. They are impacted by their experiences in schools and in neighborhoods.

Intuitively, this made such perfect sense to me that it seemed like believing that people live on a planet and breath air. Of course we are influenced by the people around us, by are families, by our culture, by the media. Of course, I thought, that must be the case!

To me, it makes perfect sense that development is shaped by *Human Ecology.*

The Dilemma

Have you seen the dilemma here? Two things intuitively made sense to me: "Kids are Kids" and "Human Ecology." If I thought of either, I thought that they must be true. However, the two are contradictory if you think about it. If "kids are kids" and all children "do kid things" regardless of their background, then how was their human ecology important? If, on the other hand, all children are influenced and shaped by the social world around them, and their development is the outcome of their experiences in social relationships, families, and culture, then how could it be that "kids are kids?" The two just do not seem to fit together. In some ways, this is a reflection of perhaps the oldest and most central argument about how children develop, the contrast of "Nature vs. Nurture." Have you heard the expression "Nature vs.

Nurture?" This question asks what is most important for the development of the traits that make each of us unique human beings. Is it "nature," the biological underpinnings contained in our genes and chromosomes? Or is it "nurture," the impact of the social world that we live in as we develop? The "nature" point of view, being that the way we develop is influenced by our biology, is more aligned with the view of "Kids are Kids." On the other hand, the "nurture" view, that our development is shaped by our experience with the world around us, is more aligned with the "Human Ecology" view.

And here I was, intuitively "knowing" that both views were "true." How could I make sense of this?

Developmentally Appropriate Practice

As I continued in my graduate work, my interests leaned most heavily on children's social development and especially peer relations, and I began working on two areas of emphasis for my doctorate study: statistics, and early childhood education. That combination gave me two tools to help me think about my "dilemma" concerning that nature of human development.

First, I learned through the study of statistics I learned that scientists try to think in ways that are as un-biased as possible. This is particularly difficult in the study of child development because we all were once children and we tend to remember our own childhoods as the "right way" (or the "wrong way") that things should be, and so it is difficult to take our personal feelings, memories and beliefs out of our understanding of how humans develop. Second, I learned that when we talk about human development, and human behavior, emotions and cognitions, there are rarely "single" variables that "cause" any particular outcome. Instead, human development is complex, and it is comprised of multiple influences that interact in complex ways. In other words, there does not tend to be simple explanations for human development.

Second, from the study of early childhood education I learned about the phrase "Developmentally Appropriate Practice," often abbreviated as "DAP." DAP is a way of thinking that impacts how professionals interact with children and families. DAP applies to a wide range of activities, from how a professional engages a child in direct conversation, to the types of lessons a teacher plans for a classroom, the type of curriculum that a community selects for the schools, to the types of policies that administrators enact for a state or nation.

The key to the DAP model is that each child must be considered as an individual. For each child, we must consider age-related expectations. For example, I know how a typical three-year-old holds scissors. This age-related expectation is equivalent to the idea of "kids are Kids." However, I know that not every three-year-old will hold scissors in the same way; some have had many opportunities to use scissors and have been encouraged to use scissors by those around them. These children may hold the scissors in a way that is more like what is typical for a four-year-old. Other children may never have used scissors before, or used them only a few times. This children might hold the scissors in ways more common for a two-year-old. Thus, to understand a child we must consider there experience, their culture, the contexts around them. This is equivalent to human ecology. Finally, the third component of DPA is individual differences in the child themselves, such as inborn, biologically based traits. DAP calls for attending to all three components in a given child. In this way, DAP is a tool that helps to consider how both "kids are kids" and "human ecology" both interact.

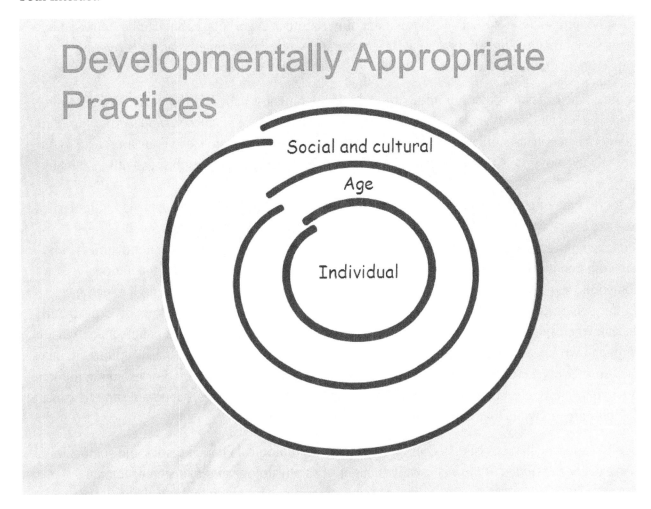

Components of DAP

Social and Cultural Influence

Social and cultural Contexts are the settings in which development occurs. These form the outer layer of the DAP model. These include *historical contexts* which relate to the time period in which children live. For example, think of the different life experiences that a child growing up in Chattanooga, Tennessee during the great depression and another child growing up in the same neighborhood during the civil rights movement, and a third child growing up in the same neighborhood today would be exposed to.

Another type of context that influences development involves social contexts. These are the direct relationships that a child experiences, including interactions with the family, their peers, their teachers, other adults and others in their community. Sometimes social contexts directly impact the child, whereas other social contexts indirectly impact the child. For example, a child may never directly participate in the social environment of her mother's workplace, but can be impacted by those social relationships if the mother has a stressful work environment that spills over by impacting her behavior at home.

A third type of context that can influence child development is *economic contexts*. In our country, there is a wide range of economic realities for families. The term *socioeconomic status* is used to categorize people as similar or different in income, occupational status, and education levels. As we will see, poverty is a major "risk factor" for children, because poverty brings with it so many challenges.

A fourth type of context that can influence child is *culture*. Culture is multifaceted, and impacts the way we interact with each other. Culture can be based on a number of factors, such as race, language, religion and ethnicity. As you can see, these elements of culture are not distinct from each other and can overlap and interact. Culture is passed from generation to generation, sometimes explicitly taught and other times simply indirectly "picked up" through experience. Culture gives rules for behavior patterns. For example, in some cultures children are expected to "speak when spoken to" and show reverence for elders. Culture also impacts beliefs about what is right and wrong, and what is expected from individuals in different roles. Finally, culture includes the "stuff" - objects that are special to that culture, types of dress and so on. For example, think of how your family celebrates winter holidays. Items like Christmas Trees, Menorahs, and Kwanzaa Candles are materials that reflect cultural practices and traditions.

Sex is a special characteristic, because it involves both biological characteristics and sociocultural contexts. *Sex assigned at birth* is usually thought of as physiological dimension of human development. This physiological aspect of sex is determined by many biological characteristics, including the types of chromosomes, hormones, genitalia and secondary sexual characteristics. As these physical characteristics are interpreted at birth, children are typically classified as either male or female. *Gender* is the psychological and sociological experience of the meaning of the sex assigned at birth. Children become aware of societal expectations for their sex, and determine psychological meaning of those social expectations. In this way, the sex the child is assigned at birth interacts with the child's social cultural contexts to impact the child's experiences.

Age

Age related expectations are the second layer of the DAP model. This layer appears below the Social and Cultural expectations layer because age-related expectations are impacted by social and cultural expectations. For example, in modern-day China it is considered "dirty" to put children on the floor. Children are expected to walk at a later age than the expectation of parents in North America. In fact, infants in China do walk, on average, at later ages than infants in North America. In contrast, Jamaican parents report the belief that the expected age that an infant should begin to walk is earlier than that expected by parents in North America. When observed, Jamaican mothers exercise their babies legs and practice them walking earlier than do North American mother's. In turn, Jamaican infants do begin to walk, on average, at a slightly younger age than infants in North America. In all three cases, culturally-based expectations influenced parental behavior, and in each case that resulted in different timing of the outcomes for children. However, all typically developing infants in China, North America, and Jamaica do begin to walk, and, even though there are small differences in the timing related to the cultural practices, all begin to walk within a "normal range" of timing; Jamaican infants walk earlier, Chinese infants walk later, and all fall within in the expected range of ages for beginning to walk (which is about 10- to 14- months).

Because the timing of different behaviors can be influences by cultural practices, some experts suggest that age-related expectations should not be considered. However, the DAP approach allows for taking age-related expectations into account while remembering that these can be impacted by cultural experiences.

Individual

The third element of the DAP model is the individual. This includes all the unique characteristics that make up an individual child. These can be biological differences that are rooted in our DNA. For example, the biological aspect of sex assigned at birth is an individual trait. This can also include aspects of a child's temperament and personality.

For an example of DAP, consider three-year-old children using scissors. I have an idea of how three-year-olds "typically" hold scissors (we will read about this in the small motor chapter). However, some three-year-olds come from families that have not encouraged using scissors and may never have held scissors before. These children might look more like what is typically expected of two-years-old. Other children may have grown in a home environment where arts and crafts are valued and stressed and so they may have used scissors many times. These children might look more like what is expected from four-year-olds with scissors. But there are other individual differences. One child may have been born with genes that allowed for the development of excellent fine motor skills. Another child may have experienced a lack of oxygen at birth that resulted in delayed motor skills.

To turn back to the idea of "Nature vs. Nurture," the DAP model suggests that, not only are "nature" and "nurture" both important, the two interact in complex ways over time.

A word about "risk factors"

As you will see, much of the research in child development has been conducted with the idea that results could benefit children and society by improving the likelihood that children will have positive outcomes over time. Many times, the idea is "if we can identify factors that put children at increased risk for negative outcomes, we can help them to avoid it." Unfortunately, this means that much of the research in child development has a sort of negative view – what factors are negative and should be avoided to prevent negative outcomes? The key thing to remember about "risk factors" is that they are identified from research based upon large groups of children. The goal is to examine large groups of children and identify factors that are correlated with negative outcomes. This means that we can not use this information to make predictions about any given individual child – the statistics concerning risk factors do not work that way. So, for example, we know that being a child of a single, teen-age mother is a "risk factor." We know this, because in large studies, children who have a single teen-age mother are more likely than other children to experience a negative outcome. But not all of the children with a teen-age mother will have a negative outcome, and many children who do not have a teen-age single mother will have a negative outcome. All the risk factor means is that children with single-parent mothers are more likely to have a negative outcome. Think of the example of gambling on a horse race. Knowing certain information – the performance of the horse before on a certain type of track in certain weather at certain distances – might help to make a better guess about which horse will win. But it will still be a guess. Risk factors help to predict outcomes at a group level, but they do not help us to predict outcomes for any individual because there are always individuals who do not follow that pattern. Another example might be car insurance. With all other things equal, a male will pay more for car insurance than a female. This is because males are statistically more likely to file an insurance claim. But we can not pick any one female and one male and conclude that this female is a better driver than this male.

The unfortunate side of identifying risk factors is that it tends to lead to a "deficit approach" type of view. By cataloging risk factors associated with negative outcomes, we begin to think of individuals and groups as having deficits, instead of thinking about what positives they possess. Many risk factors have been identified. Being born low-birth weight and / or prematurely is a risk factor. So is having a teen mother and a single mother. So are health conditions, living in a neighborhood with a zip code that has a high crime rate, not having health insurance, attending a poorly performing school, having a parent who is incarcerated, having a parent who is a substance abuser, and poor nutrition, to name a few. As you can see, there are many risk factors of many different types. Poverty is probably the single-biggest overall risk factor, because poverty brings with the likelihood of experiencing so many other risk factors.

One example of this type of approach is known by the phrase "Adverse Childhood Experience." According to the CDC, Adverse Childhood Experiences, or ACEs, are potentially traumatic events that occur in childhood (0-17 years) such as experiencing violence, abuse, or neglect; witnessing violence in the home; and having a family member attempt or die by suicide. Also included are aspects of the child's environment that can undermine their sense of safety, stability, and bonding such as growing up in a household with substance misuse, mental health problems, or instability due to parental separation or incarceration of a parent, sibling, or other member of the household.

Adverse Childhood Experiences have been linked to

- risky health behaviors,

- chronic health conditions,

- low life potential, and

- early death.

As the number of ACEs increases, so does the risk for these outcomes.

One limitation to a deficit-type approach is that sometimes research and policy are biased from a middle-class perspective, and tend to assume that what is prevalent in middle-class culture is "best" or "right." This can lead to the view that practices in other cultures, which may have different meanings or goals, are a at a deficit. It may be that these experiences are only "different" not more negative. Having a deficit approach can sometimes blind us to the "protective factors" that children experience. Protective factors are variables that are associated with increased possibilities of positive outcomes. For example, having a parent who is responsive and warm is a protective factor. So is a positive and supportive relationship with a teacher. Positive self-esteem and a positive ethnic identity are both protective factors. There are many children who experience a number of risk factors who turn out great, and many more that turn out just fine and live happy and productive lives. The term "resilience" is used to describe the characteristics that account for positive outcomes in the face of adversity. A view of child development focused on resilience can lead to a more positive outlook that one based on identifying deficits.

Following are some descriptive data about Children in the U.S. The first is a map of the U.S. that displays the percentage of school-age children in each state who are learning English. There are about 6.5 million children in the U.S. who are learning the English language.

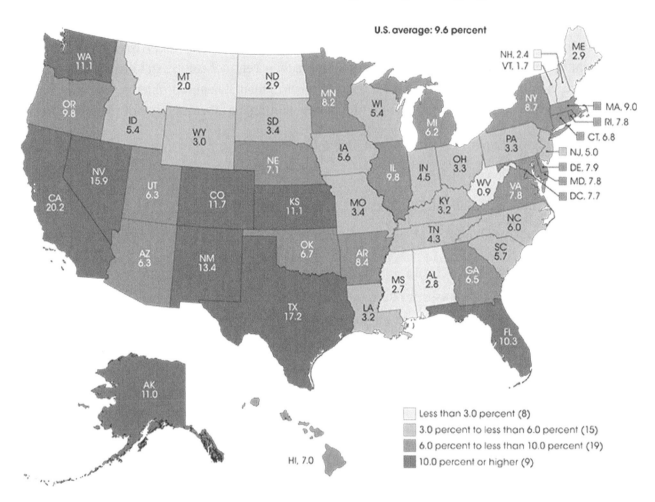

Percentage of public school students who were English language learners, by state: Fall 2016SOURCE: U.S. Department of Education, National Center for Education Statistics, Common Core of Data (CCD), "Local Education Agency Universe Survey," 2016–17.

The following charts are from U.S. Census Bureau data. There are about 67.9 million children under the age of 18 living in the U.S. About 25% of them live with a single mother, but the majority live in two parent-households.

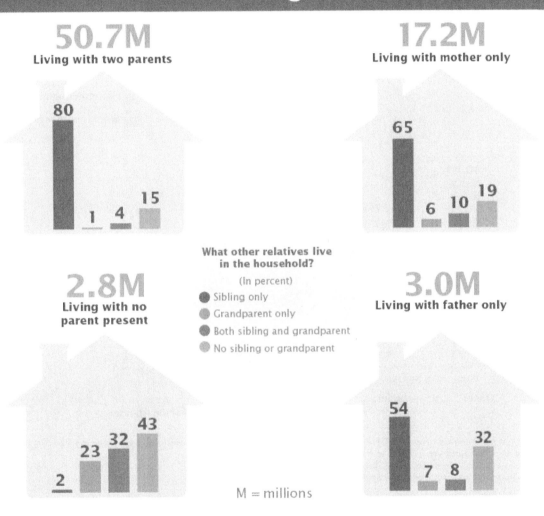

This chart shows the percentage of children living in poverty. Overall, about 8.4% of the children living in two-parent households are living in poverty. Among children living in single-parent households, the percentage is substantially higher, 40.7%. There is also a difference in the percentage of children in poverty based upon ethnicity. Children in white and in Asian American households are less likely to live in poverty compared to children in African American and Hispanic households.

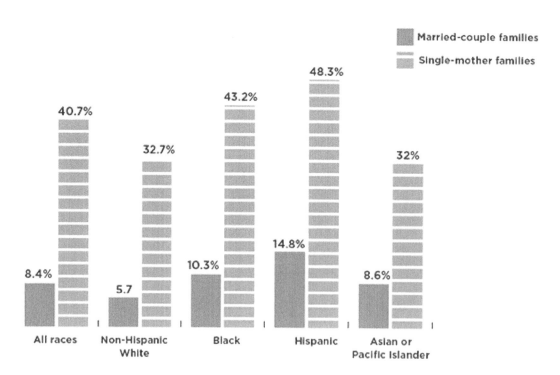

Percentage of Children in Poverty, by Family Structure and Race/Hispanic Origin: 2017

Note: Estimates reflect the new OMB race definitions, and include only those who are identified with a single race. Hispanics may be of any race.
Source: U.S. Census Bureau. CPS Table Creator (online tool), available at: http://www.census.gov/cps/data/cpstablecreator.html.

childtrends.org

Although the birth rate in the U.S. has been going down since the "baby boomer" generation, the U.S. population remains stable, and has even grown, due to immigration. The percentage of children in the U.S. that are Native American and African American has remained about the same. On the other hand, the percentage of children who are Hispanic and who are Asian American has been growing. The percentage of children from European American ancestry has declined. Think about this question: what is the fastest growing Ethnic group in the U.S.? One way to answer that question is "Hispanic." Between 1980 and 2020, the Hispanic group of children grew from about 10% of the population to about 20%. Another way to answer the question is "Asian American." Between 1980 and 2020, the population of Asian American children has grown from less than 5% to more than 10%. Both answers are a correct way of answering the question – the Hispanic group is "fastest growing" in terms of overall number, the Asian American group is "fastest growing" in terms of rate of population increase.

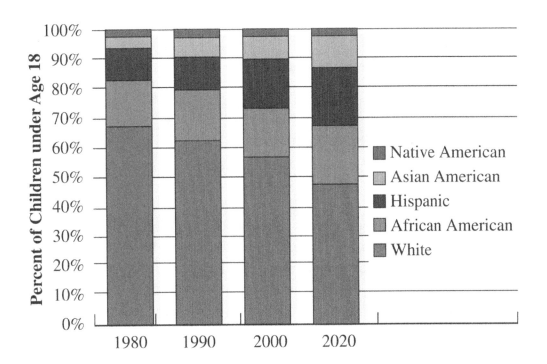

2 RESEARCH METHODS IN CHILD DEVELOPMENT

Learning Objectives At the completion of this chapter, students will be able to:	Related Course Objective
2-1 Describe methods of scientific research in child development.	3
2-2 Describe types of developmental research designs.	3

Research Methods

An important part of learning any science is having a basic knowledge of the techniques used in gathering information. The hallmark of scientific investigation is that of following a set of procedures designed to keep questioning or skepticism alive while describing, explaining, or testing any phenomenon. Some people are hesitant to trust academicians or researchers because they always seem to change their story. That, however, is exactly what science is all about; it involves continuously renewing our understanding of the subjects in question and an ongoing investigation of how and why events occur. Science is a vehicle for going on a never-ending journey. In the area of development, we have seen changes in recommendations for nutrition, in explanations of psychological states as people age, and in parenting advice. So think of learning about human development as a lifelong endeavor.

Remember in the first chapter I raised the question, *"How do we know that something is true?"* This question is central to the study of Child Development as *Science*. A scientific study of Child Development uses the *Scientific Method*. This involves thinking critically about observations that we make by trying to be objective. It is particularly difficult to be objective in the discussion of child development because we all have emotional connections and prior beliefs about the nature of children.

"I love children...I was one once myself."

Each of us is biased by our own past experiences and memories. We may tend to believe that our experiences are most typical, or that the ways our families interacted were the "correct" or "best" ways. It is very difficult to separate our own experiences and values from the way we interpret our observations.

Take a moment to write down two things that you know about childhood. Now, how do you know? Chances are you know these things based on your own history (experiential reality) or based on what others have told you or cultural ideas (agreement reality) (Seccombe and Warner, 2004). There are several problems with personal inquiry. Read the following sentence aloud:

Paris in the

the spring

Are you sure that is what it said? Read it again:

Paris in the

the spring

If you read it differently the second time (adding the second "the") you just experienced one of the problems with personal inquiry; that is, the tendency to see what we believe. Our assumptions very often guide our perceptions, consequently, when we believe something, we tend to see it even if it is not there. This problem may just be a result of cognitive 'blinders' or it may be part of a more conscious attempt to support our own views. Confirmation bias is the tendency to look for evidence that we are right and in so doing, we ignore contradictory evidence. Popper suggests that the distinction between that which is scientific and that which is unscientific is that science is falsifiable; scientific inquiry involves attempts to reject or refute a theory or set of assumptions (Thornton, 2005). Theory that cannot be falsified is not scientific. And much of what we do in personal inquiry involves drawing conclusions based on what we have personally experienced or validating our own experience by discussing what we think is true with others who share the same views.

Science offers a more systematic way to make comparisons guard against bias.

The steps in the scientific method can vary a little depending on the field that is being studied, but in general, the steps involved are these:

1. **Formulate a question.** The question seeks to understand something that has been observed, for example "How do children learn to speak?"

2. **Review Previous Studies** on the topic. What do we know? This is sometimes called a "literature review."

2. **From a hypothesis.** The hypothesis is a guess, based on what has been observed, that is testable.

3. **Make a prediction.** The prediction is designed to differentiate between observations that support the hypothesis and observations that do not.

4. **Gather data that test the prediction**. In child development, the data could come from sources such as observations of children, questionnaires or interviews, physiological measures, standardized tests, or experiments.

5. **Analyze these data**. The data are analyzed to determine if they support the hypothesis or not. At this point, the hypotheses may be rejected, altered, or expanded.

6. **Draw conclusions**; stating limitations of the study and suggestions for future research.

7. **Make your findings available** to others (both to share information and to have your work scrutinized by others)

Here is a graphic of the Scientific Process that is a part of the creative commons on wikimedia.

https://commons.wikimedia.org/wiki/File:The_Scientific_Method_as_an_Ongoing_Process.svg

The important thing to note is that the scientific method is a *recursive* process – this means that our findings may result in the hypotheses being refined and retested through gathering new data.

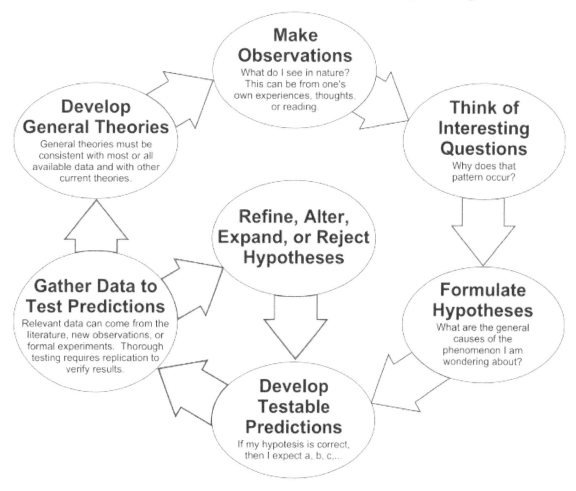

The Scientific Method as an Ongoing Process

Your findings can then be used by others as they explore the area of interest and through this process a literature or knowledge base is established. This model of scientific investigation presents research as a linear process guided by a specific research question. And it typically involves quantifying or using statistics to understand and report what has been studied. Many academic journals publish reports on studies conducted in this manner.

Another model of research referred to as qualitative research may involve steps such as these:

1. Begin with a broad area of interest

2. Gain entrance into a group to be researched

3. Gather field notes about the setting, the people, the structure, the activities or other areas of interest

4. Ask open ended, broad "grand tour" types of questions when interviewing subjects

5. Modify research questions as study continues

6. Note patterns or consistencies

7. Explore new areas deemed important by the people being observed

8. Report findings

In this type of research, theoretical ideas are "grounded" in the experiences of the participants. The researcher is the student and the people in the setting are the teachers as they inform the researcher of their world (Glazer & Strauss, 1967). Researchers are to be aware of their own biases and assumptions, acknowledge them and bracket them in efforts to keep them from limiting accuracy in reporting. Sometimes qualitative studies are used initially to explore a topic and more quantitative studies are used to test or explain what was first described.

Research Methods

Let's look more closely at some techniques, or research methods, used to describe, explain, or evaluate. Each of these designs has strengths and weaknesses and is sometimes used in combination with other designs within a single study.

Observational Studies

Observational studies involve watching and recording the actions of participants. This may take place in the natural setting, such as observing children at play at a park, or behind a one-way glass while children are at play in a laboratory playroom. The researcher may follow a checklist and record the frequency and duration of events (perhaps how many conflicts occur among 2-year-olds) or may observe and record as much as possible about an event (such as observing children in a classroom and capturing the details about the room design and what the children and teachers are doing and saying). In general, observational studies have the strength of allowing the researcher to see how people behave rather than relying on self-report. What people do and what they say they do are often very different. A major weakness of observational studies is that they do not allow the researcher to explain causal relationships. Yet, observational studies are useful and widely used when studying children, because children may not be very verbal to ask questions in an interview or through a written survey.

There are two main types of observational studies. *Laboratory observations* are conducted in controlled settings, such as a laboratory space behind a one-way mirror. The advantage to these types of observations is that the experimenters can control the situation and environment. Every participant is observed in the same setting. This gives the experimenter control over the events that they will observe. However, children tend to change their behavior when they know they are being watched (known as the Hawthorne effect), and so laboratory observations may miss actions that would have been observed in the real world.

Consider this study. Researchers at the Museum of Natural History were interested in how parents might talk differently to girls and boys about science-related concepts. In the study, researchers sat at a display of the fossil of a giant ground sloth, writing notes on a clipboard so as to appear to be studying the display itself. Instead, the observers were listening to the conversations that parents held with children and recording if the parents explained the science concepts to their sons and daughters. Their data are presented in this figure:

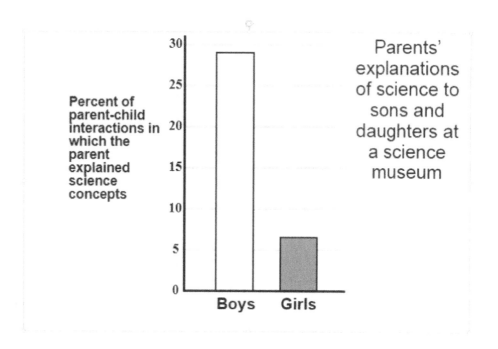

Now imagine that these researchers had conducted their observations in a laboratory-based setting. The researchers might invite the parents and their children to their lab on a college campus, and tell them that they are interested in how parents and children discuss things. The researchers might then give the parents toys, such as a box of dinosaur models, and observe as the parents discussed the toys with their children. If they had followed this procedure, do you think that the results showing a difference between how parents talk to boys and girls would have been found?

Case Studies

Case studies involve exploring a single case or situation in great detail. Information may be gathered with the use of observation, interviews, testing, or other methods to uncover as much as possible about a person or situation. Case studies are helpful when investigating unusual situations such as brain trauma or children reared in isolation. And they are often used by clinicians who conduct case studies as part of their normal practice when gathering information about a client or patient coming in for treatment. Case studies can be used to explore areas about which little is known and can provide rich detail about situations or conditions. However, each individual is genetically unique and so caution must be taken when generalizing to others. The findings can not be duplicated or tested in others and so the findings from case studies cannot be generalized or applied to larger populations; this is because cases are not randomly selected and no control group is used for comparison. Because the case study involves judgment, the reliability of the information – how the information can relate to others – can not be determined.

Surveys

Surveys are familiar to most people because they are so widely used. Surveys enhance accessibility to subjects because they can be conducted in person, over the phone, through the mail, or online. A survey involves asking a standard set of questions to a group of subjects. In a highly structured survey, subjects are forced to choose from a response set such as "strongly disagree, disagree, undecided, agree, strongly agree"; or "0, 1-5, 6-10, etc." This is known as **Likert Scale**. Surveys are commonly used by sociologists, marketing researchers, political scientists, therapists, and others to gather information on many independent and dependent variables in a relatively short period of time. Surveys typically yield surface information on a wide variety of factors, but may not allow for in-depth understanding of human behavior.

Of course, surveys can be designed in a number of ways. They may include forced choice questions and semi-structured questions in which the researcher allows the respondent to describe or give details about certain events. One of the most difficult aspects of designing a good survey is wording questions in an unbiased way and asking the right questions so that respondents can give a clear response rather than choosing "undecided" each time. Knowing that 30% of respondents are undecided is of little use! So a lot of time and effort should be placed on the construction of survey items. One of the benefits of having forced choice items is that each response is coded so that the results can be quickly entered and analyzed using statistical software. Analysis takes much longer when respondents give lengthy responses that must be analyzed in a different way. Surveys are useful in examining stated values, attitudes, opinions, and reporting on practices. However, they are based on self-report or what people say they do rather than on observation and this can limit accuracy.

Interviews

Interviews are similar to surveys in that they ask participants a set of questions. However, interviews are conducted by a real person in real time, either face-to-face or over the phone. This means that the scripts for interviews can be individualized to offer branching trees of questions based upon each participants answers to scripted prompts. It is important for both surveys and interviews present clear, unbiased questions. One major threat to critical evaluation of results is obtaining data through asking questions that are intended to "lead" the participants to certain answers.

Standardized Tests

Standardized tests evaluate participants through a standard set of questions presented through a standard procedure. Thus, these types of tests have uniform procedures for administration and scoring. Responses can be statistically "standardized" by comparing one participant's responses to all other participant's responses, yielding standardized scores that can be reported in percentiles.

Psychophysiological Measures

Researchers can make direct measurement of biological responses. This can include things such as heart rate, blood pressure or galvanic skin response (e.g., sweating). For example, researchers might measure children's heart rates during the presentation of violent and non-violent cartoons. Researchers can also measure the presence of hormones, such as cortisol which is an indicator of stress. Direct measurements of brain functioning can also be performed through magnetic resonance imaging (MRI) and Electroencephalograms (EEG).

Research Designs

There are two main categories of research design. First, *Quantitative* designs use numbers to measure and assign value to variables of interest, in order to use statistical methods to arrive at conclusions about the data. In the second type, *Qualitative* designs, researchers do not try to assign numerical values to the data. There are two types of quantitative methods: descriptive designs, were the goal is to describe a variable, and inferential designs, were the goal is to investigate relationships among variables. There are two types of inferential designs, experimental and correlational designs. The next sections will describe descriptive designs, then correlational and experimental designs, and then qualitative methods.

Descriptive Designs

Descriptive designs allow researchers to observe and record behavior in order to describe the who, what, when and where of a given variable or phoneme. Descriptive designs answer questions such as how many? What percent? What is the average? The maximum? The minimum? Descriptive designs do not try to look at how variables may be related to each other. Examples of descriptive designs include mean, standard deviation, median, mode, and range. Frequencies or percentages displayed in bar graphs and pie charts are representations of descriptive statistics.

Inferential Designs

In contrast to descriptive designs, inferential designs *do* try to examine if two or more variables are related. Thus the purpose is to use one variable to "make an inference" about the other. Inferential designs use statistical methods to examine the probability of observed associations. There are two main categories: correlational designs and experimental designs.

Correlational Designs

Correlational research examines the strength of association between two or more events or characteristics. This type of research seeks to answer the question, "if one variable changes, is it likely that another will?" For example, a researcher may wonder if there is a correlation between height and shoe size. There are two variables here, height and shoe size. The researcher could measure these two variables among a group of people and determine if there is a relationship between the two variables. As height goes up is it likely that shoe size would also go up? A correlation can also be negative, meaning that when one variable goes up, the other goes down. For example, there might be a negative correlation between the time that high schoolers spend on social media and their grades: more time on social media might be associated with lower grades.

A correlation does not equal causation. This is the most important critical thinking issue concerning correlational research. A significant correlation between variable X and variable Y does not mean that variable X necessarily causes variable Y. It could be that variable Y actually causes variable X. Or, it could be that another variable that was not measured, let's call it variable Z actually causes both variable X and Y. So, a change in variable X happens along with a change in variable Y, but it was because of this unmeasured variable (this variable is often called an extraneous variable). In the above example, the researcher might find a positive correlation between shoe size and height, but this does not mean that shoe size causes height. It also does not mean that height causes shoe size. Something else (genes, nutrition, etc.) causes both height and shoe size. Consider the following figure:

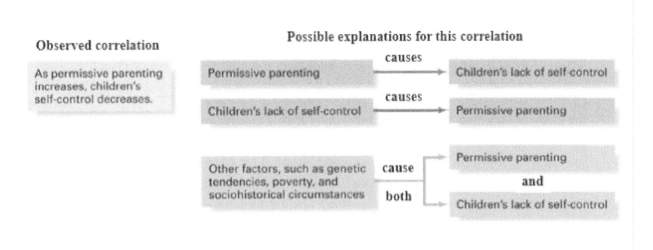

Experiments

Experiments are designed to test hypotheses (or specific statements about the relationship between variables) in a controlled setting in efforts to explain how certain factors or events produce outcomes. A variable is anything that changes in value. Concepts are operationalized or transformed into variables in research, which means that the researcher must specify exactly what is going to be measured in the study. An experiment: carefully regulated procedure in which one or more factors is manipulated while all other factors are held constant (cause and effect).

Independent Variables are the variables that the researcher intentionally manipulates.

Dependent Variables are the variables that the researcher measures to determine if the Independent Variable has an effect.

In the most simple experimental design, there are two groups, an experimental (or treatment) group and a control group. For example, a researcher may wonder if a flu vaccine is effective. The experimental group receives the vaccine, the control group does not. The experimental group vs. treatment group is synonymous with the independent variable (presence or absence of flu vaccine). The dependent variable is whether or not the participants got the flu. If the participants in the control group get the flu, and those in the experimental group do not, and *all other extraneous variables are controlled* (e.g., "all other things are equal") then the researcher can conclude that the relationship between the vaccine and the flu was causal.

Three conditions must be met in order to establish cause and effect. Experimental designs are useful in meeting these conditions.

1. The independent and dependent variables must be related. In other words, when one is altered, the other changes in response. (The independent variable is something altered or

introduced by the researcher. The dependent variable is the outcome or the factor affected by the introduction of the independent variable. For example, if we are looking at the impact of exercise on stress levels, the independent variable would be exercise; the dependent variable would be stress.)

2. The cause must come before the effect. Experiments involve measuring subjects on the dependent variable before exposing them to the independent variable (establishing a baseline). So we would measure the subjects' level of stress before introducing exercise and then again after the exercise to see if there has been a change in stress levels. (Observational and survey research does not always allow us to look at the timing of these events, which makes understanding causality problematic with these designs.)

3. The cause must be isolated. The researcher must ensure that no outside, perhaps unknown variables are actually causing the effect we see. The experimental design helps make this possible. In an experiment, we would make sure that our subjects' diets were held constant throughout the exercise program. Otherwise, diet might really be creating the change in stress level rather than exercise.

A basic experimental design involves beginning with a sample (or subset of a population) and randomly assigning subjects to one of two groups: the experimental group or the control group. The experimental group is the group that is going to be exposed to an independent variable or condition the researcher is introducing as a potential cause of an event. The control group is going to be used for comparison and is going to have the same experience as the experimental group but will not be exposed to the independent variable. After exposing the experimental group to the independent variable, the two groups are measured again to see if a change has occurred. If so, we are in a better position to suggest that the independent variable caused the change in the dependent variable.

The major advantage of the experimental design is that of helping to establish cause and effect relationships. A disadvantage of this design is the difficulty of translating much of what happens in a laboratory setting into real life. Consider this figure depicting the design of Bandura's "bobo doll" experiment:

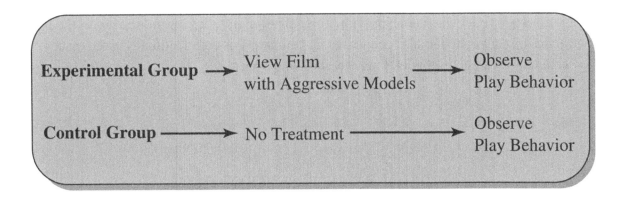

Developmental Designs

Developmental designs are techniques used in developmental research (and other areas as well). These techniques try to examine how age, cohort, gender, and social class impact development. The importance here is the element of *TIME* in the research design.

Longitudinal Research

Longitudinal research involves beginning with a group of people who may be of the same age and background, and measuring them repeatedly over a long period of time. One of the benefits of this type of research is that people can be followed through time and be compared with them when they were younger.

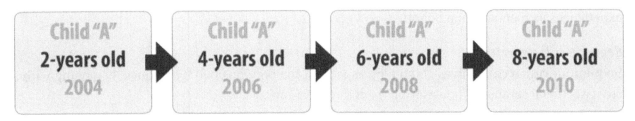

Figure – A longitudinal research design.[1]

A problem with this type of research is that it is very expensive and subjects may drop out over time. The Perry Preschool Project which began in 1962 is an example of a longitudinal study that continues to provide data on children's development.

Cross-sectional Research

Cross-sectional research involves beginning with a sample that represents a cross-section of the

---

[1]   Image by NOBA is licensed under CC BY-NC-SA 4.0

population. Respondents who vary in age, gender, ethnicity, and social class might be asked to complete a survey about television program preferences or attitudes toward the use of the Internet. The attitudes of males and females could then be compared, as could attitudes based on age. In cross-sectional research, respondents are measured only once.

Year of Study - 2004

Cohort A - 2-year-olds

Cohort B - 6-year-olds

Cohort C - 8-year-olds

Figure – a cross-sectional research design

A This method is much less expensive than longitudinal research but does not allow the researcher to distinguish between the impact of age and the cohort effect. Different attitudes about the use of technology, for example, might not be altered by a person's biological age as much as their life experiences as members of a cohort.

Sequential Research
Sequential research involves combining aspects of the previous two techniques; beginning with a cross-sectional sample and measuring them through time.

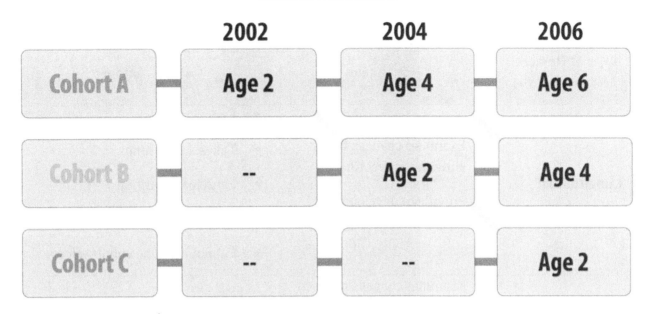

Figure - A sequential research design.[2]

This is the perfect model for looking at age, gender, social class, and ethnicity. But the drawbacks of high costs and attrition are here as well.[3]

Table Advantages and Disadvantages of Different Research Designs[4]

Type of Research Design	Advantages	Disadvantages
Longitudinal	• Examines changes within individuals over time • Provides a developmental analysis	• Expensive • Takes a long time • Participant attrition • Possibility of practice effects • Cannot examine cohort effects
Cross-sectional	• Examines changes between participants of different ages at the same point in time • Provides information on age-related change	• Cannot examine change over time • Cannot examine cohort effects
Sequential	• Examines changes within individuals over time • Examines changes between participants of different ages at the same point in time • Can be used to examine cohort effects	• May be expensive • Possibility of practice effects

Reliability and Validity

Reliability refers to the consistency or precision of a measurement when repeated under similar circumstances. Does the measurement always get the same results? If you can depend on your measure reliably assessing the variable then you can not trust the results. Validity of a measure refers to whether or not it provides an accurate measure of the phenomenon being studied. Validity asks whether or not the researcher is actually measuring what they say they are.

---

[4] Research Methods in Developmental Psychology by Angela Lukowski and Helen Milojevich is licensed under a CC BY-NC-SA 4.0

Action Research and Qualitative Research

Action research is carried out by teachers, administrators, and other change agents in the school to improve the educational environment for their students. In action research, the researcher uses data that are collected to inform and revise the research questions as they go. This figure depicts action research:

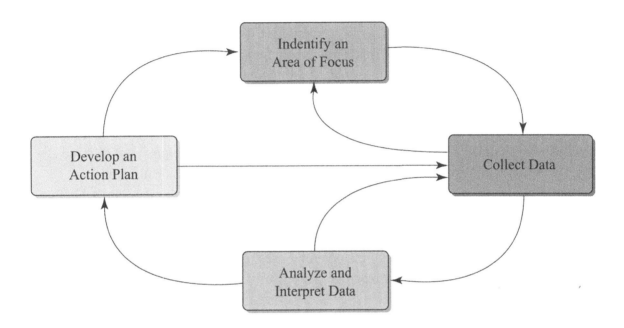

Qualitative Studies

Qualitative Studies do not attempt to "quantify" data by assigning numbers to variables, instead text descriptions are used. This allows for a more full description of phenomenon, but makes it difficult to compare one instance to another. Consider how difficult it would be to compare the performance of two schools based upon written reports of each school, versus comparing the two schools on the basis of standardized test scores. The written reports would certainly give you more information, more detail and a more contextualized understanding. On the other hand, it would be more difficult to communicate your findings to others in ways that everyone could agree.

In this way, results from qualitative studies are 'thick descriptions' of children's development that capture all aspects of their lives. Qualitative studies provide rich and detailed narratives that illustrate children's development. The purpose is to describe individual behavior or development within a particular context. Through qualitative studies, patterns or trends in behavior can be identified.

One type of qualitative study is an *Ethnographic Study.* Ethnographic studies are a type of qualitative research that uses methods from anthropology to study development with a particular group. Ethnographic studies capture the rich complexity of the individual, their culture and their context. These give us the most complete picture of development with a particular culture.

How do quantitative and qualitative methods differ? In quantitative methods, behaviors are counted or rated numerically. This can capture trends in behavior among large groups of individuals. It also makes the results easier to communicate and understand. However, quantitative studies do not provide the rich detail of qualitative and ethnographic approaches. Quantitative studies may not take into account cultural context, or may not capture the important details of an individual child's experience.

Consent and Ethics in Research

Research should, as much as possible, be based on participants' freely volunteered informed consent. For minors, this also requires consent from their legal guardians. This implies a responsibility to explain fully and meaningfully to both the child and their guardians what the research is about and how it will be disseminated. Participants and their legal guardians should be aware of the research purpose and procedures, their right to refuse to participate; the extent to which confidentiality will be maintained; the potential uses to which the data might be put; the foreseeable risks and expected benefits; and that participants have the right to discontinue at any time.

Sometimes it is necessary for the research design for the experimenter to hide the nature of the study from participants. This occurs when it is possible that knowing the goals of the study might influence or change participants behavior. For example, a researcher might be concerned that telling participants that a study is on the impact on music on studying might cause all participants to study more (or less). Thus, the researcher might tell the participants the study is about "how students use their time." In cases of deception such as this, the researcher must first justify the deception to an Internal Review Board (IRB) and then must debrief all participants afterwords to explain the deception.

But consent alone does not absolve the responsibility of researchers to anticipate and guard against potential harmful consequences for participants.[5] It is critical that researchers protect all rights of the participants including confidentiality. This means that participants privacy is maintained and no identifying information is released. The safety of participants – physical and emotional – is the

---

[5] Confidentiality and Informed Consent: Issues for Consideration in the Preservation of and Provision of Access to Qualitative Data Archives by Louise Corti, Annette Day & Gill BackhouseSource is licensed under CC BY 4.0 (modified by Jennifer Paris); "No thank you, not today": Supporting Ethical and Professional Relationships in Large Qualitative Studies by Lisa J. Blodgett, Wanda Boyer & Emily TurkSource is licensed under CC BY 4.0 (modified by Jennifer Paris)

primary first concern. Researchers should follow the "do no harm" rule – that no harm will come from participation in the research. Sometimes there may be potential risks associated with research (such as testing a new drug) and these must be out weighed by potential benefits.

It is important to think critically about research findings that you might read in the media. One factor to consider is if the research is published in a peer-reviewed journal. This means that the research was evaluated by other experts in the topic before it was published. Be cautious when reading about research in the media or the internet. Consider if the organization that is presenting the information might have an intentional agenda that influences how the information is presented. Always consider the source of the information. Be careful not to accept the results of only a single study; when studies are *replicated*, meaning they are repeated with different participants, and the same results are obtained we grow in confidence about the findings. Finally, always remember that "correlation does not mean causation." It is very common to read reports in the popular media that confuse the two.

Child development is a fascinating field of study – but care must be taken to ensure that researchers use appropriate methods to examine infant and child behavior, use the correct experimental design to answer their questions, and be aware of the special challenges that are part-and-parcel of developmental research. Hopefully, this information helped you develop an understanding of these various issues and to be ready to think more critically about research questions that interest you. There are so many interesting questions that remain to be examined by future generations of developmental scientists – maybe you will make one of the next big discoveries![6]

---

[6] Research Methods in Developmental Psychology by Angela Lukowski and Helen Milojevich is licensed under a CC BY-NC-SA 4.0

3 THEORIES OF CHILD DEVELOPMENT

Learning Objectives At the completion of this module, students will be able to:	Related Course Objective
3-1 Describe major concepts of Behaviorism and Learning Theories.	1 3 5
3-2 Describe major concepts of Piget's theory of cognitive development and Vygotsky's sociocultural theory and Information Processing Theories	1 3 5
3-3 Describe major concepts of Psychoanalytic Theory.	1 3 5
3-4 Describe major concepts of Ethological Theories and Ecological Theories.	1 3 5
3-5 Explain similarities and differences among the theories presented	1 3 5

What is a theory?

Students sometimes feel intimidated by the word "theory;" even the phrase, "Now we are going to look at some theories…" is met with blank stares and other indications that the audience is now lost. But theories are valuable tools for understanding human behavior; in fact they are proposed explanations for the "how" and "whys" of development. Have you ever wondered, "Why is this 3 year old so inquisitive?" or "Why are some fifth graders rejected by their classmates?" Theories can help explain these and other occurrences. Developmental theories offer explanations about how we develop, why we change over time and the kinds of influences that impact development.

A theory guides and helps us interpret research findings as well. It provides the researcher with a blueprint or model to be used to help piece together various studies. Think of theories as guidelines much like directions that come with an appliance or other object that requires assembly. The instructions can help one piece together smaller parts more easily than if trial and error are used.

A theory is an attempt to describe reality. When a person forms a theory, they are trying to make sense of observations they have made of the world in a way that they can communicate with others. Predictions about what might be observed in the future can be made based upon the theory.

In the study of child development, many theories are based upon identifying risk factors. Risk factors are circumstances that make a challenging or difficult adaptation in the future more likely. For example, being born low birth weight is considered a risk factor. This is because there is a correlation between low birth weight and difficult adjustment later in childhood. Remember, though, that correlation does not mean causation. Moreover, we can not make predictions about any one individual made from observations of a group. This means that, although being low birth weight is a risk factor that predicts increased chance of difficulty later, we can not look at any single low birth weight infant and know that the child will have difficulty. Many children with a variety of risk factors in their lives do not suffer from later adaptation issues. Some additional risk factors include: being born pre-term, being from a single-parent home, having a teenage parent, having parents who are substance abusers, having a parent who is incarcerated, having a parent who did not complete high school, living in a neighborhood with a high crime rate, spending time unsupervised with peers, and environmental hazards (such as levels of lead in the environment). Poverty is the single biggest risk factor, because so many risk factors come hand-in-hand with poverty.

On the other hand, some life circumstances lower the risk of maladaption. These factors lower the statistical probability that risk factors will negatively impact a child. For example, having a warm and supportive relationship with parents can serve as a buffer for the risk of living in a dangerous neighborhood. Together, risk and protective factors reflect the cumulative negative and positive influences on development.

When theorists developed their theories, they were trying to explain the world that they saw and lived in. They were trying to explain why factors that they observed might impact children. Some theorists focused on how children learn and think. Others focused on the impact of social interaction. In the sections below, there are three presentations that give an overview of various Theories of child development. Following each of the presentations are a couple of additional videos focused on the topics of the presentation.

Theories can be developed using induction in which a number of single cases are observed and after patterns or similarities are noted, the theorist develops ideas based on these examples. Established theories are then tested through research; however, not all theories are equally suited to scientific investigation. Some theories are difficult to test but are still useful in stimulating debate or providing concepts that have practical application. Keep in mind that theories are not facts; they are guidelines for investigation and practice, and they gain credibility through research that fails to disprove them[7].

Let's take a look at some key theories in Child Development. We have already been introduced to the concept of "Developmentally Appropriate Practice," the concept that each child must be viewed as the interaction between individual characteristics, age-related expectations, and ecological characteristics such as context and culture. In the following section we will examine:

1. Psychoanalytic Perspectives

2. Learning Theory and Behaviorism

3. Cognitive Theories

4. Biological Theories

5. Ecological Theories

Psychoanalytic Theories

Focus on developmental changes in the self and personality. Psychoanalytic Theories describe development as:

- Primarily unconscious
- Heavily colored by emotion
- Behavior is surface characteristic
- Analyze symbolic workings of mind
- Emphasize early experiences
- Biological process important here

Sigmund Freud's Psychosexual Theory

We begin with the often controversial figure, Sigmund Freud (1856-1939). Freud has been a very influential figure in the area of development; his view of development and psychopathology dominated the field of psychiatry until the growth of behaviorism in the 1950s. His assumptions that personality forms during the first few years of life and that the ways in which parents or other caregivers interact with children have a long-lasting impact on children's emotional states have guided parents, educators, clinicians, and policy-makers for many years. We have only recently begun to recognize that early childhood experiences do not always result in certain personality traits or emotional states. There is a growing body of literature addressing resilience in children who come from harsh backgrounds and yet develop without damaging emotional scars (O'Grady and Metz, 1987). Freud has stimulated an enormous amount of research and generated many ideas. Agreeing with Freud's theory in its entirety is hardly necessary for appreciating the contribution he

---

[7]Introduction to Developmental Theories by Lumen Learning is licensed under CC BY 4.0

has made to the field of development.

Freud's theory of self suggests that there are three parts of the self.

The *id* is the part of the self that is inborn. It responds to biological urges without pause and is guided by the principle of pleasure: if it feels good, it is the thing to do. A newborn is all id. The newborn cries when hungry, defecates when the urge strikes.

The *ego* develops through interaction with others and is guided by logic or the reality principle. It has the ability to delay gratification. It knows that urges have to be managed. It mediates between the id and superego using logic and reality to calm the other parts of the self. The *superego* represents society's demands for its members. It is guided by a sense of guilt. Values, morals, and the conscience are all part of the superego.

Three structures of personality:

- Id: immediate gratification, hedonistic

- Superego - messages from others internalized

- Ego - what is actually expressed, compromise between id and superego

Freud's Stages
Oral: Birth to 18 months
Anal: 18 months to 3 years
Phallic: 3 to 6 years (Oedipus complex)
Latency: 6 years to puberty
Genital: puberty onward

In Freud's view, the personality is thought to develop in response to the child's ability to learn to manage biological urges. Parenting is important here. If the parent is either overly punitive or lax, the child may not progress to the next stage. Here is a brief introduction to Freud's stages

Name of Stage	Descriptions of Stage
Oral Stage	The oral stage lasts from birth until around age 2. The infant is all id. At this stage, all stimulation and comfort is focused on the mouth and is based on the reflex of sucking. Too much indulgence or too little stimulation may lead to fixation.
Anal Stage	The anal stage coincides with potty training or learning to manage biological urges. The ego is beginning to develop in this stage. Anal fixation may result in a person who is compulsively clean and organized or one who is sloppy and lacks self-control.
Phallic Stage	The phallic stage occurs in early childhood and marks the development of the superego and a sense of masculinity or femininity as culture dictates.
Latency	Latency occurs during middle childhood when a child's urges quiet down and friendships become the focus. The ego and superego can be refined as the child learns how to cooperate and negotiate with others.
Genital Stage	The genital stage begins with puberty and continues through adulthood. Now the preoccupation is that of sex and reproduction.

Strengths and Weaknesses of Freud's Theory

Freud's theory has been heavily criticized for several reasons. One is that it is very difficult to test scientifically. How can parenting in infancy be traced to personality in adulthood? Are there other variables that might better explain development? The theory is also considered to be sexist in suggesting that women who do not accept an inferior position in society are somehow psychologically flawed. Freud focuses on the darker side of human nature and suggests that much of what determines our actions is unknown to us. So why do we study Freud? As mentioned above, despite the criticisms, Freud's assumptions about the importance of early childhood experiences in shaping our psychological selves have found their way into child development, education, and parenting practices. Freud's theory has heuristic value in providing a framework from which to elaborate and modify subsequent theories of development. Many later theories, particularly behaviorism and humanism, were challenges to Freud's views.[8]

---

[8]Psychodynamic Theory by Lumen Learning is licensed under CC BY 4.0; Lecture Transcript: Developmental

Main Points to Note About Freud's Psychosexual Theory
Freud believed that:

- Development in the early years has a lasting impact.

- There are three parts of the self: the id, the ego, and the superego

- People go through five stages of psychosexual development: the oral stage, the anal stage, the phallic stage, latency, and the genital stage

We study Freud because his assumptions about the importance of early childhood experience provide a framework for later theories (that both elaborated and contradicted/challenged his work).

Erik Erikson's Psychosocial Theory

Now, let's turn to a less controversial theorist, Erik Erikson. Erikson (1902-1994) suggested that our relationships and society's expectations motivate much of our behavior in his theory of psychosocial development. Erikson was a student of Freud's but emphasized the importance of the ego, or conscious thought, in determining our actions. In other words, he believed that we are not driven by unconscious urges. We know what motivates us and we consciously think about how to achieve our goals. He is considered the father of developmental psychology because his model gives us a guideline for the entire life span and suggests certain primary psychological and social concerns throughout life.

Erikson expanded on his Freud's theory by emphasizing the importance of culture in parenting practices and motivations and adding three stages of adult development (Erikson, 1950; 1968). He believed that we are aware of what motivates us throughout life and the ego has greater importance in guiding our actions than does the id. We make conscious choices in life and these choices focus on meeting certain social and cultural needs rather than purely biological ones. Humans are motivated, for instance, by the need to feel that the world is a trustworthy place, that we are capable individuals, that we can make a contribution to society, and that we have lived a meaningful life. These are all psychosocial problems. Erikson divided the lifespan into eight stages. In each stage, we have a major psychosocial task to accomplish or crisis to overcome. Erikson believed that our personality continues to take shape throughout our lifespan as we face these challenges in living. Here is a brief overview of the eight stages:

Erik Erikson's Psychosocial Theory

Name of Stage	Description of Stage
Trust vs. mistrust (0-1)	The infant must have basic needs met in a consistent way in order to feel that the world is a trustworthy place.
Autonomy vs. shame and doubt (1-2)	Mobile toddlers have newfound freedom they like to exercise and by being allowed to do so, they learn some basic independence.
Initiative vs. Guilt (3-5)	Preschoolers like to initiate activities and emphasize doing things "all by myself."
Industry vs. inferiority (6-11)	School aged children focus on accomplishments and begin making comparisons between themselves and their classmates
Identity vs. role confusion (adolescence)	Teenagers are trying to gain a sense of identity as they experiment with various roles, beliefs, and ideas.
Intimacy vs. Isolation (young adulthood)	In our 20s and 30s we are making some of our first long-term commitments in intimate relationships.
Generativity vs. stagnation (middle adulthood)	The 40s through the early 60s we focus on being productive at work and home and are motivated by wanting to feel that we've made a contribution to society.
Integrity vs. Despair (late adulthood)	We look back on our lives and hope to like what we see-that we have lived well and have a sense of integrity because we lived according to our beliefs.

These eight stages form a foundation for discussions on emotional and social development during the life span. Keep in mind, however, that these stages or crises can occur more than once. For instance, a person may struggle with a lack of trust beyond infancy under certain circumstances. Erikson's theory has been criticized for focusing so heavily on stages and assuming that the completion of one stage is prerequisite for the next crisis of development. His theory also focuses on the social expectations that are found in certain cultures, but not in all. For instance, the idea that adolescence is a time of searching for identity might translate well in the middle-class culture of the United States, but not as well in cultures where the transition into adulthood coincides with puberty through rites of passage and where adult roles offer fewer choices.[9]

Erikson's Life-Span Stages

Infancy: 1st year of life	Trust vs. mistrust
Infancy: 1 to 3 years	Autonomy vs. shame and doubt
Early childhood	Initiative vs. guilt
Middle and late childhood	Industry vs. inferiority
Adolescence	Identity vs. identity confusion
Early adulthood	Intimacy vs. isolation
Middle adulthood	Generativity vs. stagnation
Late adulthood	Integrity vs. despair

Main Points to Note About Erikson's Psychosocial Theory

Erikson was a student of Freud but focused on conscious thought.

- His stages of psychosocial development address the entire lifespan and suggest primary psychosocial crisis in some cultures that adults can use to understand how to support children's social and emotional development.

- The stages include: trust vs. mistrust, autonomy vs. shame and doubt, initiative vs. guilt, industry vs. inferiority, identity vs. role confusion, intimacy vs. isolation, generativity vs. stagnation, and integrity vs. despair.

---

[9]Psychosocial Theory by Lumen Learning is licensed under CC BY 4.0

Evaluating the Psychoanalytic Theories

Contributions:

- Early experiences
- Family relationships
- Development view of personality
- Unconscious
- Adult changes

Criticisms:

- Difficult to test
- Sexual underpinnings
- Unconscious too important
- Negative view
- Culture- and gender- biased

Behaviorism

While Freud and Erikson looked at what was going on in the mind, behaviorism rejected any reference to mind and viewed overt and observable behavior as the proper subject matter of psychology. Through the scientific study of behavior, it was hoped that laws of learning could be derived that would promote the prediction and control of behavior.[1]

Behaviorists focus on observable and measurable behaviors and do not focus on internal mental states or emotions that can not be observed. Observations are made in controlled laboratory settings. Behavior is believed to be learned from the environment.

Ivan Pavlov

Ivan Pavlov (1880-1937) was a Russian physiologist interested in studying digestion. As he recorded the amount of salivation his laboratory dogs produced as they ate, he noticed that they actually began to salivate before the food arrived as the researcher walked down the hall and toward the cage. "This," he thought, "is not natural!" One would expect a dog to automatically salivate when food hit their palate, but BEFORE the food comes? Of course, what had happened was . . . you tell me. That's right! The dogs knew that the food was coming because they had learned to associate the footsteps with the food. The key word here is "learned." A learned response is called a "conditioned" response.

Pavlov's Classical conditioning: Neutral stimulus paired with active stimulus to produce response.

Pavlov began to experiment with this concept of classical conditioning. He began to ring a bell, for instance, prior to introducing the food. Sure enough, after making this connection several times, the dogs could be made to salivate to the sound of a bell. Once the bell had become an event to which the dogs had learned to salivate, it was called a conditioned stimulus. The act of salivating to a bell was a response that had also been learned, now termed in Pavlov's jargon, a conditioned response. Notice that the response, salivation, is the same whether it is conditioned or unconditioned (unlearned or natural). What changed is the stimulus to which the dog salivates. One is natural (unconditioned) and one is learned (conditioned).

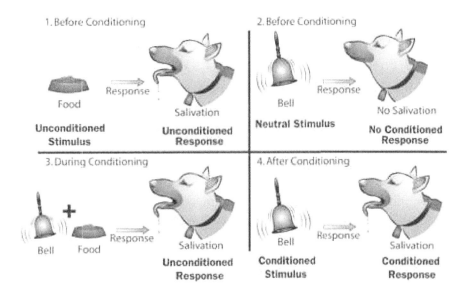

Let's think about how classical conditioning is used on us. One of the most widespread applications of classical conditioning principles was brought to us by the psychologist, John B. Watson.

John B. Watson

John B. Watson (1878-1958) believed that most of our fears and other emotional responses are classically conditioned. He had gained a good deal of popularity in the 1920s with his expert advice on parenting offered to the public.

He tried to demonstrate the power of classical conditioning with his famous experiment with an 18 month old boy named "Little Albert." Watson sat Albert down and introduced a variety of seemingly scary objects to him: a burning piece of newspaper, a white rat, etc. But Albert remained curious and reached for all of these things. Watson knew that one of our only inborn fears is the fear of loud noises so he proceeded to make a loud noise each time he introduced one of Albert's favorites, a white rat. After hearing the loud noise several times paired with the rat, Albert soon came to fear the rat and began to cry when it was introduced. Watson filmed this experiment for posterity and used it to demonstrate that he could help parents achieve any outcomes they desired, if they would only follow his advice. Watson wrote columns in newspapers and in magazines and gained a lot of popularity among parents eager to apply science to household order.

<u>Watson: little Albert and a white rat</u>

Generalizing fear as a involuntary response

Focus on behavior, not inner motives.

<u>Skinner's Operant Conditioning</u>

Operant conditioning looks at the way the consequences of a behavior increase or decrease the likelihood of a behavior occurring again. Skinner proposed that the consequences of behavior change the probability of behavior's occurrence; Skinner believed that the use of punishments and rewards could make a behavior less or more likely to be repeated.[10]

B.F. Skinner and Operant Conditioning

<u>B. F. Skinner</u> (1904-1990), who brought us the principles of operant conditioning, suggested that reinforcement is a more effective means of encouraging a behavior than is criticism or punishment. By focusing on strengthening desirable behavior, we have a greater impact than if we emphasize what is undesirable. Reinforcement is anything that an organism desires and is motivated to obtain.

A reinforcer is something that encourages or promotes a behavior. Some things are natural rewards. They are considered intrinsic or primary because their value is easily understood. Think of what kinds of things babies or animals such as puppies find rewarding.

Extrinsic or secondary reinforcers are things that have a value not immediately understood. Their value is indirect. They can be traded in for what is ultimately desired.

The use of positive reinforcement involves adding something to a situation in order to encourage a behavior. For example, if I give a child a cookie for cleaning a room, the addition of the cookie makes cleaning more likely in the future. Think of ways in which you positively reinforce others.

Negative reinforcement occurs when taking something unpleasant away from a situation encourages behavior. For example, I have an alarm clock that makes a very unpleasant, loud sound when it goes off in the morning. As a result, I get up and turn it off. By removing the noise, I am reinforced for getting up. How do you negatively reinforce others?

---

[10]<u>History of Psychology</u> by <u>David B. Baker and Heather Sperry</u> is licensed under <u>CC BY-NC-SA 4.0</u>

Punishment is an effort to stop a behavior. It means to follow an action with something unpleasant or painful. Punishment is often less effective than reinforcement for several reasons. It doesn't indicate the desired behavior, it may result in suppressing rather than stopping a behavior, (in other words, the person may not do what is being punished when you're around, but may do it often when you leave), and a focus on punishment can result in not noticing when the person does well.

Not all behaviors are learned through association or reinforcement. Many of the things we do are learned by watching others. This is addressed in social learning theory.

Social Cognitive Theories

<u>Bandura's Social Cognitive Theory</u>

Early work: Modeling

Observational learning: use imitation or modeling to adopt behaviors

Social Learning Theory

<u>Albert Bandura</u> (1925-) is a leading contributor to social learning theory. He calls our attention to the ways in which many of our actions are not learned through conditioning; rather, they are learned by watching others (1977). Young children frequently learn behaviors through imitation. Bandura (et als. 1963) began a series of studies to look at the impact of television, particularly commercials, on the behavior of children. Are children more likely to act out aggressively when they see this behavior modeled? What if they see it being reinforced? Bandura began by conducting an experiment in which he showed children a film of a woman hitting an inflatable clown or "bobo" doll. Then the children were allowed in the room where they found the doll and immediately began to hit it. This was without any reinforcement whatsoever. Not only that, but they found new ways to behave aggressively. It's as if they learned an aggressive role.

Sometimes, particularly when we do not know what else to do, we learn by modeling or copying the behavior of others. A kindergartner on his or her first day of school might eagerly look at how others are acting and try to act the same way to fit in more quickly. Adolescents struggling with their identity rely heavily on their peers to act as role-models. Sometimes we do things because we've seen it pay off for someone else. They were operantly conditioned, but we engage in the behavior because we hope it will pay off for us as well. This is referred to as vicarious reinforcement (Bandura, Ross and Ross, 1963).

Bandura (1986) suggests that there is interplay between the environment and the individual. We are not just the product of our surroundings, rather we influence our surroundings. Parents not only influence their child's environment, perhaps intentionally through the use of reinforcement, etc., but children influence parents as well. Parents may respond differently with their first child than with their fourth. Perhaps they try to be the perfect parents with their firstborn, but by the time their last child comes along they have very different expectations both of themselves and their child. Our environment creates us and we create our environment.[11]

---

[11]<u>Exploring Behavior</u> by <u>Lumen Learning</u> is licensed under <u>CC BY 4.0</u> ; <u>Lecture Transcript: Developmental Theories</u> by <u>Lumen Learning</u> is licensed under <u>CC BY 4.0</u>

Main Points to Note About Behaviorism

Behaviorists look at observable behavior and how it can be predicted and controlled.

- Pavlov experimented with classical conditioning, the process of conditioning a response to stimulus (the dog's salivating to the bell).

- Watson offered advice to parents to show them how classical conditioning can be used. His most famous experiment was conditioning Little Albert to fear a white rate.

- Skinner believed that reinforcing behavior is the most effective way of increasing desirable behavior. This is done through operant conditioning.

- Bandura noted that many behaviors are not learned through any type of conditioning, but rather through imitation. And he believed that people are not only influenced by their surroundings, but that they also have an impact on their surroundings.

Evaluating the Behavioral and Social Cognitive Theories

Contributions:

- Scientific research
- Environmental determinants
- Observational learning
- Person and cognitive factors

Criticisms:

- Lack focus on cognition
- Overemphasize environmental determinants
- Too little attention to developmental changes, creativity, and spontaneity

Cognitive Theories

Theories also explore cognitive development and how mental processes change over time. Cognitive Theories focus on the ways children construct their own understandings of their environment.

Jean Piaget's Theory of Cognitive Development

Jean Piaget (1896-1980) is one of the most influential cognitive theorists. Piaget was inspired to explore children's ability to think and reason by watching his own children's development. He was one of the first to recognize and map out the ways in which children's thought differs from that of adults. His interest in this area began when he was asked to test the IQ of children and began to notice that there was a pattern in their wrong answers. He believed that children's intellectual skills change over time through maturation. Children of differing ages interpret the world differently.

Piaget's Cognitive Developmental Theory

Piaget believed that children actively construct their understanding of the world. Piaget believed our desire to understand the world comes from a need for cognitive equilibrium. This is an agreement or balance between what we sense in the outside world and what we know in our minds. If we experience something that we cannot understand, we try to restore the balance by either changing our thoughts or by altering the experience to fit into what we do understand. Perhaps you meet someone who is very different from anyone you know. How do you make sense of this person? You might use them to establish a new category of people in your mind or you might think about how they are similar to someone else. A schema or schemes are categories of knowledge. They are like mental boxes of concepts. A child has to learn many concepts. They may have a scheme for "under" and "soft" or "running" and "sour". All of these are schema. Our efforts to understand the world around us lead us to develop new schema and to modify old ones.
One way to make sense of new experiences is to focus on how they are similar to what we already know. This is assimilation. So the person we meet who is very different may be understood as being "sort of like my brother" or "his voice sounds a lot like yours." Or a new food may be assimilated when we determine that it tastes like chicken!

Another way to make sense of the world is to change our mind. We can make a cognitive accommodation to this new experience by adding new schema. This food is unlike anything I've tasted before. I now have a new category of foods that are bitter-sweet in flavor, for instance. This is accommodation. Do you accommodate or assimilate more frequently? Children accommodate more frequently as they build new schema. Adults tend to look for similarity in their experience and assimilate. They may be less inclined to think "outside the box."Piaget suggested different ways of understanding that are associated with maturation. He divided this into four stages:

Piaget's Theory of Cognitive Development

Name of Stage	Description of Stage
Sensorimotor Stage	During the sensorimotor stage children rely on use of the senses and motor skills. From birth until about age 2, the infant knows by tasting, smelling,

Name of Stage	Description of Stage
	touching, hearing, and moving objects around. This is a real hands on type of knowledge.
Preoperational Stage	In the preoperational stage, children from ages 2 to 7, become able to think about the world using symbols. A symbol is something that stands for something else. The use of language, whether it is in the form of words or gestures, facilitates knowing and communicating about the world. This is the hallmark of preoperational intelligence and occurs in early childhood. However, these children are preoperational or pre-logical. They still do not understand how the physical world operates. They may, for instance, fear that they will go down the drain if they sit at the front of the bathtub, even though they are too big.
Concrete Operational	Children in the concrete operational stage, ages 7 to 11, develop the ability to think logically about the physical world. Middle childhood is a time of understanding concepts such as size, distance, and constancy of matter, and cause and effect relationships. A child knows that a scrambled egg is still an egg and that 8 ounces of water is still 8 ounces no matter what shape of glass contains it.
Formal Operational	During the formal operational stage children, at about age 12, acquire the ability to think logically about concrete and abstract events. The teenager who has reached this stage is able to consider possibilities and to contemplate ideas about situations that have never been directly encountered. More abstract understanding of religious ideas or morals or ethics and abstract principles such as freedom and dignity can be considered.

Assimilation: incorporation of new information into existing knowledge

Accommodation: adjusting knowledge to fit new information and experience

Piaget's Four Stages of Cognitive Development

Sensorimotor Stage	Coordinate sensory experiences#with physical actions (0–2 years)
Preoperational Stage	Represent world with words, images, drawings (2–7 years)
Concrete Operational Stage	Perform operations; logical thought replaces intuitive (7–11 years)
Formal Operational Stage	Think in abstract and more logical terms (11 years–adulthood)

We will discuss Piaget's theory and stages in more detail when we discuss Cognitive Development.

Criticisms of Piaget's Theory

Piaget has been criticized for overemphasizing the role that physical maturation plays in cognitive development and in underestimating the role that culture and interaction (or experience) plays in cognitive development. Looking across cultures reveals considerable variation in what children are able to do at various ages. Piaget may have underestimated what children are capable of given the right circumstances.[12]

Main Points To Note About Piaget's Theory of Cognitive Development

Piaget, one of the most influential cognitive theorists, believed that

- Understanding is motivated by trying to balance what we sense in the world and what we know in our minds.

- Understanding is organized through creating categories of knowledge. When presented with new knowledge we may add new schema or modify existing ones.

Children's understanding of the world of the world changes are their cognitive skills mature through 4 stages: sensorimotor stage, preoperational stage, concreate operational stage, and formal operational stage.

Vygotsky's Sociocultural Cognitive Theory

---

[12]Exploring Cognition by Lumen Learning is licensed under CC BY 4.0

Lev Vygotsky (1896-1934) was a Russian psychologist who wrote in the early 1900s but whose work was discovered in the United States in the 1960s but became more widely known in the 1980s. Vygotsky differed with Piaget in that he believed that a person not only has a set of abilities, but also a set of potential abilities that can be realized if given the proper guidance from others. His sociocultural theory emphasizes the importance of culture and interaction in the development of cognitive abilities. He believed that through guided participation known as scaffolding, with a teacher or capable peer, a child can learn cognitive skills within a certain range known as the zone of proximal development. His belief was that development occurred first through children's immediate social interactions, and then moved to the individual level as they began to internalize their learning.[13]

Have you ever taught a child to perform a task? Maybe it was brushing their teeth or preparing food. Chances are you spoke to them and described what you were doing while you demonstrated the skill and let them work along with you all through the process. You gave them assistance when they seemed to need it, but once they knew what to do-you stood back and let them go. This is scaffolding and can be seen demonstrated throughout the world. This approach to teaching has also been adopted by educators. Rather than assessing students on what they are doing, they should be understood in terms of what they are capable of doing with the proper guidance. You can see how Vygotsky would be very popular with modern day educators.

Main Points to Note About Vygotsky's Sociocultural Theory

Vygotsky concentrated on the child's interactions with peers and adults. He believed that the child was an apprentice, learning through sensitive social interactions with more skilled peers and adults.

Comparing Piaget and Vygotsky

Vygotsky concentrated more on the child's immediate social and cultural environment and his or her interactions with adults and peers. While Piaget saw the child as actively discovering the world through individual interactions with it, Vygotsky saw the child as more of an apprentice, learning through a social environment of others who had more experience and were sensitive to the child's needs and abilities.2Vygotsky believed that culture and social interaction guide cognitive development. Social interaction with more-skilled adults and peers advances cognitive development through the child learning to adapt. Memory, attention, and reasoning involves learning to use society's inventions (e.g., math and language). In Vygotsky's view, knowledge is

---

[13] <u>Children's Development</u> by Ana R. Leon is licensed under <u>CC BY 4.0</u>

best advanced in cooperative activities

Information-Processing Theory

There is not one single information processing theory or theorist, rather it is a collection of "mini theories" that share certain characteristics. Information processing theories use the language of computer science to compare the human brain to the ways that a computer works. Information processing theorists do not believe that the brain actually works like a computer, but are using computers as a metaphor for how the brain functions. In this type of metaphor, "hardware" is analogous to the brain while software is analogous to cognition. Information Processing emphasizes how individuals manipulate information, monitor it, and strategize about it.One information processing theorist is Juan Pascual-Leone, who studies working memory. Another is Robbie Case who studied cognitive processing efficiency. Some information processing theoriests are sometimes called "neo-Piagetians," because they believe that Piaget was correct in the gist of his observations but made mistakes in his beliefs about the nature of thought. We will discuss information processing theories in more detail when we discuss Cognition.

Evaluating the Cognitive Theories

Contributions:

- Positive view
- Active construction of understanding
- Importance of developmental changes
- Detailed descriptions

Criticisms:

- Pureness of Piaget’s stages
- Lack individual variations
- Info-processing theory lacks description
- no focus on Unconscious

Biological Theories

Biological theories maintain that aspects of human development are rooted in our biology. For example, the idea that some traits or behaviors may have a genetic basis is an aspect of Biological Theories. Biological Theories have been used to explain changes in height, weigh, language, mental abilities, motor skills, and many other characteristics.

Ethological Theory

Ethology is based upon studies of animal behavior. This means that this view brings a strong influence of biology and evolution. In ethological theory, development is characterized by critical or sensitive periods for some experiences.

Konrad Lorenz (1903-1989) was an Austrian zoologist, ethologist, and ornithologist. He is regarded as one of the founders of ethology, the study study of animal behavior. Lorenz studied inborn, instinctive behavior in animals such as geese. In a famous experiment, Lorenz found that geese imprinted on the first being they saw after hatching. He theorized that this behavior was an in-born instinct that existed because it helped geese to survive. Geese that imprinted stayed close to a mother goose and lived to adulthood, and passed the trait to their off spring. Geese that did not imprint did not survive to adulthood and had no offspring. Thus, imprinting became a characteristic of the species of geese. In Lorenz's view, imprinting is rapid, innate learning within a critical period of time (if the geese do not imprint during this critical period, they will never imprint).

Bowlby's view of attachment

John Bowlby (1907-1990) was a British Psychiatrist who was influenced by both the psychoanalytic theory and ethological theory. Bowlby developed a theory of Attachment that states that human infants develop an attachment relationship with their caregivers over time. Bowlby believed that this was an innate aspect of development that helped babies to survive. We will discuss attachment theory more when we discuss self and emotional development.

Evaluating Ethological Theory

Contributions:

- •Biological and evolutionary
- •Careful observations
- •Sensitive periods of development

Criticisms:

- •Too rigid on critical and sensitive periods

- •Emphasis on biological foundations
- •Inadequate attention to cognition
- •Animal research

Contextual Theories

In the classic debate of Nature vs. Nurture, biological and ethological theories represent the extreme of the "Nature" view point. On the other end of the spectrum, contextual theories represent the extreme of the "nurture" view point. Contextual theories focus on the influence of the social and cultural context on children's development. The theory of Lev Vygotsky, who was discussed under cognitive theories, could also be considered a contextual theory.

Ecological Theories

Urie Bronfenbrenner's Ecological Systems Model

Urie Bronfenbrenner (1917-2005) offers us one of the most comprehensive theories of human development. Bronfenbrenner studied Freud, Erikson, Piaget, and learning theorists and believed that all of those theories could be enhanced by adding the dimension of context. What is being taught and how society interprets situations depends on who is involved in the life of a child and on when and where a child lives.

Bronfenbrenner's ecological systems model explains the direct and indirect influences on an individual's development.

Table: Urie Bronfenbrenner's Ecological Systems Model

Name of System	Description of System
Microsystems	Microsystems impact a child directly. These are the people with whom the child interacts such as parents, peers, and teachers. The relationship between individuals and those around them need to be considered. For example, to appreciate what is going on with a student in math, the relationship between the student and teacher should be known.
Mesosystems	Mesosystems are interactions between those surrounding the individual. The relationship between parents and schools, for example will indirectly affect the child.
Exosystem	Larger institutions such as the mass media or the healthcare system are

Name of System	Description of System
	referred to as the exosystem. These have an impact on families and peers and schools who operate under policies and regulations found in these institutions.
Macrosystems	We find cultural values and beliefs at the level of macrosystems. These larger ideals and expectations inform institutions that will ultimately impact the individual.
Chronosystem	All of this happens in an historical context referred to as the chronosystem. Cultural values change over time, as do policies of educational institutions or governments in certain political climates. Development occurs at a point in time.

For example, in order to understand a student in math, we can't simply look at that individual and what challenges they face directly with the subject. We have to look at the interactions that occur between teacher and child. Perhaps the teacher needs to make modifications as well. The teacher may be responding to regulations made by the school, such as new expectations for students in math or constraints on time that interfere with the teacher's ability to instruct. These new demands may be a response to national efforts to promote math and science deemed important by political leaders in response to relations with other countries at a particular time in history.

Bronfenbrenner's view that development influenced by five environmental systems:

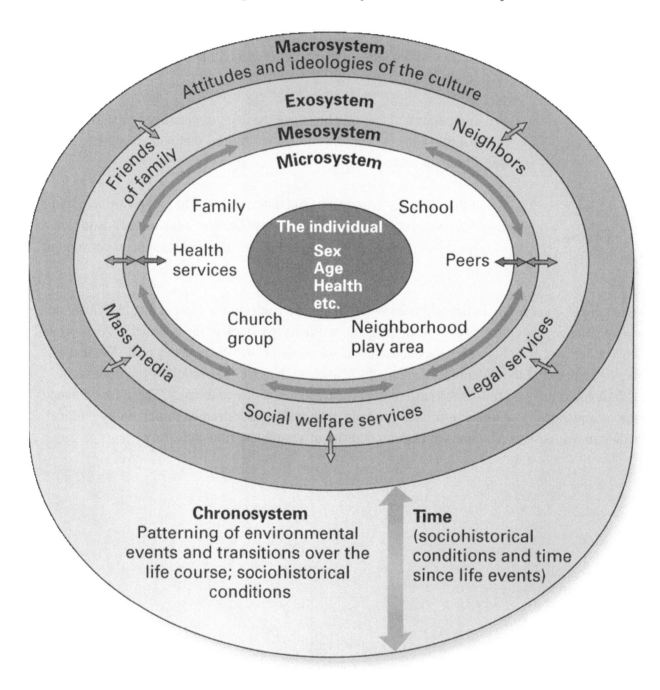

Bronfenbrenner's ecological systems model challenges us to go beyond the individual if we want to understand human development and promote improvements.[14]

14

Main Points to Note About Bronfenbrenner's Ecological Model

After studying all of the prior theories, Bronfenbrenner added an important element of context to the discussion of influences on human development.

- He believed that the people involved in children's lives and when and where they live are important considerations.

- He created a model of nested systems that influence the child (and are influenced by the child) that include: microsystems, mesosystems, the exosystem, macrosystems, and chronosystems.

Bronfenbrenner updated the theory to become a "bioecological" theory, by including elements such as an individual's age and sex in the center of the model. However, this theory remains primarily ecological.

An example of Ecological Theory is the following list of mesosystem connections between organizations and families in caring for children:

- Provide assistance to families
- Encourage parents to volunteer
- Involve families in learning at home
- Include families in school decisions
- Coordinate community collaboration

Evaluating Ecological Theory

Contributions:

- Macro and micro dimensions
- Connections of environments
- Sociohistorical influences

Criticisms:

- Lacks emphasis on biological foundations
- Inadequate attention to cognitive processes

Dynamic systems perspective

This perspective is an emerging area of theory. Dynamic systems describes the self-organizing nature of development over time. One example involves studies by Ester Thelen (1941-2004) of infant's reaching behavior. Thelen concluded that different pathways can lead to similar developmental outcomes. Thelen's work is linked to recent important changes in children's environments.

An Eclectic Theoretical Orientation

In this chapter we examined several major theories of development. There are many theories of child development that are often based on competing assumptions about the nature of human development and so do not always fit together. It is best to follow an orientation that does not follow any one particular theoretical approach and instead view theories as tools to help you understand different aspects of human behavior and human development. In any given situation, select whatever is considered the best in each theory.

4 BIOLOGICAL BASIS OF DEVELOPMENT

Learning Objectives At the completion of this module, students will be able to:	Related Course Objective
4-1 Describe Genes, chromosomes, and DNA.	1
4-2 Explain genotype, phenotype and inheritance patterns.	1
4-3 Describe the course of prenatal development.	1
4-4 Define and give examples of teratogens.	1
4-5 List common chromosomal abnomalities	1

One famous study of twins was conducted at the University of Minnesota. The Jim and Jim twins were identical twins who were separated after birth and raised by different adoptive families. When they were reunited 39 years later, they had a number of remarkable coincidences in their lives. They were part of the Minnesota Study of Twins Reared Apart; other twin sets in the study had similar outcomes but none were as dramatic as Jim and Jim. As "identical" twins, the Jims shared exactly the same DNA. The story of these twins makes us wonder how much of our life stories are written in our genetic code?

Natural Selection and Adaptive Behavior

The term *Natural selection* suggests that evolutionary processes favor individuals best adapted to survive and reproduce. In this view, an organism that has adaptations that allow it to survive in it's environment long enough to reproduce passes along those genetic traits to its offspring. Thus, the traits that best promote survival in a given niche of a particular environment are naturally selected over time. In terms of human beings, the field of *Evolutionary psychology* emphasizes the role of adaptation, reproduction, and "survival of the fittest" in shaping human behavior. An evolutionary view of human development is termed *"Evolutionary Developmental Psychology."* The main idea of this view is that in humans an extended "juvenile" period evolved that benefits our species in survival. In this view, aspects of childhood are thought to be important for survival because they prepare us for adulthood. Additionally, some childhood characteristics are adaptive at specific points in life; for example, staying close to her mother may help a two-year-old survive long enough to grow up and have offspring, but on the other hand staying close to her mother probably would not aid a 20-year-old in having offspring.

In this evolutionary view, the human brain is seen as one of the main factors that benefits human survival. Our large brains allow us to communicate and work together, to use tools, and to teach each other to use tools. It is thought that our extended "juvenile period" - childhood - developed because our large human brains take time to develop.

Evaluating Evolutionary Psychology

Evolution has produced our genetic makeup that allows for bodily structures and biological potentials; however, evolution can not account for all complex human behavior. Our biology allows broad range of potentials, but our cultural experience allow various possibilities in how these are expressed. Let us think about how our biology and our environment interact before we more closely examine our biological underpinnings.

Nature *and* Nurture

Most scholars agree that there is a constant interplay between nature (heredity) and nurture (the environment). It is difficult to isolate the root of any single characteristic as a result solely of nature or nurture, and most scholars believe that even determining the extent to which nature or nurture impacts a human feature is difficult to answer. In fact, almost all human features are polygenic (a result of many genes) and multifactorial (a result of many factors, both genetic and environmental). It's as if one's genetic make-up sets up a range of possibilities, which may or may not be realized depending upon one's environmental experiences. For instance, a person might be genetically predisposed to develop diabetes, but the person's lifestyle may determine whether or not they actually develop the disease.

This bidirectional interplay between nature and nurture is the epigenetic framework, which suggests that the environment can affect the expression of genes just as genetic predispositions can impact a person's potentials. And environmental circumstances can trigger symptoms of a genetic disorder.[15]

Environment Correlations

Environment Correlations refer to the processes by which genetic factors contribute to variations in the environment (Plomin, DeFries, Knopik, & Neiderhiser, 2013). There are three types of genotype-environment correlations:

1. *Passive genotype-environment* correlation occurs when children passively inherit the genes and the environments their family provides. Certain behavioral characteristics, such as being athletically inclined, may run in families. The children have inherited both the genes that would enable success at these activities, and given the environmental encouragement to engage in these actions.[16]

2. *Evocative genotype-environment* correlation refers to how the social environment reacts to individuals based on their inherited characteristics.This occurs when a child's genotype (genetic potential) elicits certain responses from the environment. For example, whether one has a more outgoing or shy temperament will affect how he or she is treated by others.

3. *Active genotype-environment* correlation occurs when individuals seek out environments that support their genetic tendencies. This is also referred to as *niche picking*. For example, children who are musically inclined seek out music instruction and opportunities that facilitate their natural musical ability.

Conversely, Genotype-Environment Interactions involve genetic susceptibility to the environment. Adoption studies provide evidence for genotype-environment interactions. For example, the Early Growth and Development Study (Leve, Neiderhiser, Scaramella, & Reiss, 2010) followed 360 adopted children and their adopted and biological parents in a longitudinal study. Results have shown that children whose biological parents exhibited psychopathology, exhibited significantly fewer behavior problems when their adoptive parents used more structured parenting than unstructured. Additionally, elevated psychopathology in adoptive parents increased the risk for the children's development of behavior problems, but only when the biological parents' psychopathology was high. Consequently, the results show how environmental effects on behavior differ based on the genotype, especially stressful environments on genetically at-risk children Heredity-environment interaction has complexities. Individuals influence their environments, yet individuals "inherit" environments. The three genotype-environment correlations change as children grow, as heredity and environment continue to mutually influence each other.

---

[15]Lifespan Development - Module 3: Prenatal Development by Lumen Learning references Psyc 200 Lifespan Psychology by Laura Overstreet, licensed under CC BY 4.0

[16]Lifespan Development: A Psychological Perspective (page 40) by Martha Lally and Suzanne Valentine-French is licensed under CC BY-NC-SA 3.0

The Genetic Process

Now, let's look more closely at "just nature." Nature refers to the contribution of genetics to one's development. The basic building block of the nature perspective is the gene. Genes are recipes for making proteins, while proteins influence the structure and functions of cells. Genes are located on the chromosomes and there are an estimated 20,500 genes for humans, according to the Human Genome Project (NIH, 2015).

DNA and the Collaborative Gene

Life begins as a single cell. That one cell has the full DNA that provides a blue print for the development of every physical aspect of the individual. Each further cell that develops across that individual's life time contains a replica of this original code. Typically developing human cells contain 46 chromosomes, threadlike structures that composed of DNA molecules. Human chromosomes come in 23 pairs (e.g., the total of 46), with one member of each pair coming from each parent.

The Genetic Process

DNA: The Collaborative Gene

DNA is a complex molecule that contains genetic information. Genes are the units of hereditary information composed of DNA; each has its own function but each works collaboratively with other genes. Genes do not work in isolation, but in "patterns." The center of the cell, the nucleus contains chromosomes and genes

Each gene is a segment of DNA (spiraled double chain) containing the hereditary code. Chromosomes are threadlike structures composed of DNA molecules. We know from the Human Genome Project that humans have about 25,000 genes. This is enough genes to account for human diversity because each gene does not work alone, they are dependent on and collaborative with other genes.

After conception, most cells of the body are created by a process called mitosis. Mitosis is defined as the cell's nucleus making an exact copy of all the chromosomes and splitting into two new cells.

However, the cells used in sexual reproduction, called the gametes (sperm or ova), are formed in a process called meiosis. In meiosis, the gamete's chromosomes duplicate, and then divide twice resulting in four cells containing only half the genetic material of the original gamete. Thus, each sperm and egg possesses only 23 chromosomes and combine to produce the typical 46.

Table - Mitosis & Meiosis[17]

Type of Cell Division	Explanation	Steps
Mitosis	All cells, except those used in sexual reproduction, are created by mitosis	1. Chromosomes make a duplicate copy 2. Two identical cells are created
Meiosis	Cells used in sexual reproduction are created by meiosis	1. Exchange of gene between the chromosomes (crossing over) 2. Chromosomes make a duplicate 3. First cell division 4. Second cell division

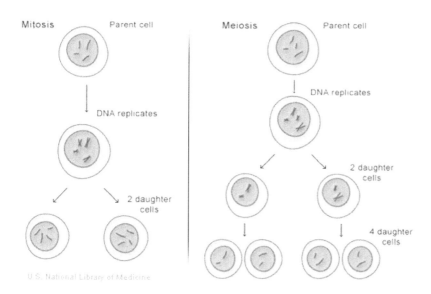

[17]Lifespan Development: A Psychological Perspective (page 34) by Martha Lally and Suzanne Valentine-French is licensed under CC BY-NC-SA 3.0 Image by U.S. National Laboratory of Medicine is in public domain

Given the amount of genes present and the unpredictability of the meiosis process, the likelihood of having offspring that are genetically identical (and not twins) is one in trillions (Gould & Keeton, 1997).

Of the 23 pairs of chromosomes created at conception, 22 pairs are similar in length. These are called autosomes. The remaining pair, or sex chromosomes, may differ in length. If a child receives the combination of XY, the child will be genetically male. If the child receives the combination XX, the child will be genetically female.[18]

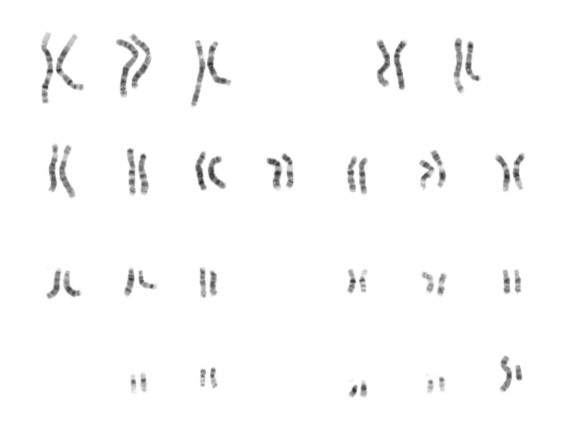

Here is a public domain image (called a karyogram) of what the 23 pairs of chromosomes look like. Notice the the 23rd pair. Is this individual male or female?

Twins and Multiples

---

[18]Lifespan Development: A Psychological Perspective (page 34-35) by Martha Lally and Suzanne Valentine-French is licensed under CC BY-NC-SA 3.0

Monozygotic or identical twins occur when a fertilized egg splits apart in the first two weeks of development. One egg, one sperm. The result is the creation of two separate, but genetically identical offspring. That is, they possess the same genotype and often the same phenotype. About one-third of twins are monozygotic twins.

Sometimes, however, two eggs or ova are released and fertilized by two separate sperm. The result is dizygotic or fraternal twins. These two individuals share the same amount of genetic material as would any two children from the same mother and father. In other words, they possess a different genotype and phenotype.

Older mothers are more likely to have dizygotic twins than are younger mothers, and couples who use fertility drugs are also more likely to give birth to dizygotic twins.[1]Multiple births are more likely to be preterm and have a higher risk for health problems. In the US today, 3% of live births are twins or multiples. The rate of dizyotic twins, but not monozygotic, increases with artificial reproductive technology, such as fertility medications that increase the release of ovum.

Prenatal Development

Now we turn our attention to prenatal development which is divided into three periods: The germinal period, the embryonic period, and the fetal period. The three periods of prenatal development are not equal in length and are not the same as "the three trimesters of pregnancy." When someone says "three trimesters" they are describing periods of equal length, about three months each. While this makes sense to those around the pregnant woman, they do not correspond to physical changes and the developing organism. The three periods of prenatal development are based on physiological changes, and so they do not form equal time periods. The following is an overview of some of the changes that take place during each period.

The Germinal Period

The *germinal period* (about 14 days in length) is the first period of prenatal development and lasts from conception to implantation of the fertilized egg in the lining of the uterus. At ejaculation millions of sperm are released into the vagina, but only a few reach the egg and typically only one fertilizes the egg. Once a single sperm has entered the wall of the egg, the wall becomes hard and prevents other sperm from entering. After the sperm has entered the egg, the tail of the sperm breaks off and the head of the sperm, containing the genetic information from the father, unites with the nucleus of the egg. It is typically fertilized in the top section of the fallopian tube and continues its journey to the uterus. As a result, a new cell is formed. This cell, containing the combined genetic information from both parents, is referred to as a zygote.
During this time, the organism begins cell division through mitosis. After five days of mitosis there are 100 cells, which is now called a blastocyst. The blastocyst consists of both an inner and outer

group of cells. The inner group of cells, or embryonic disk will become the embryo, while the outer group of cells, or trophoblast, becomes the support system which nourishes the developing organism. This stage ends when the blastocyst fully implants into the uterine wall (U.S. National Library of Medicine, 2015).

Germinal period

- First two weeks after conception
- Creation of zygote
- Rapid cell division forming blastocyst
- Hollow ball with inner and outer layers
- Has projections (villi) to attach to uterine lining
- Differentiation starts
- Cells organize into organs and systems
- Germinal period starts with fertilization and ends with attachment to uterine wall (implantation)

Parts of the Zygote:

Blastocyst: inner layer of cells that develops during the germinal periodLater develops into embryo

Trophoblast: outer layer of cells that develops during germinal periodProvides embryo nutrition and support

---

Mitosis is a fragile process and fewer than one half of all zygotes survive beyond the first two weeks (Hall, 2004). Some of the reasons for this include: the egg and sperm do not join properly, thus their genetic material does not combine, there is too little or damaged genetic material, the zygote does not replicate, or the blastocyst does not implant into the uterine wall. The failure rate is higher for in vitro conceptions. The figure below illustrates the journey of the ova from its release to its fertilization, cell duplication, and implantation into the uterine lining. The following picture displays the track of the zygote during the germinal period from fertilization to implantation. [19]

---

[19] Image is public domain

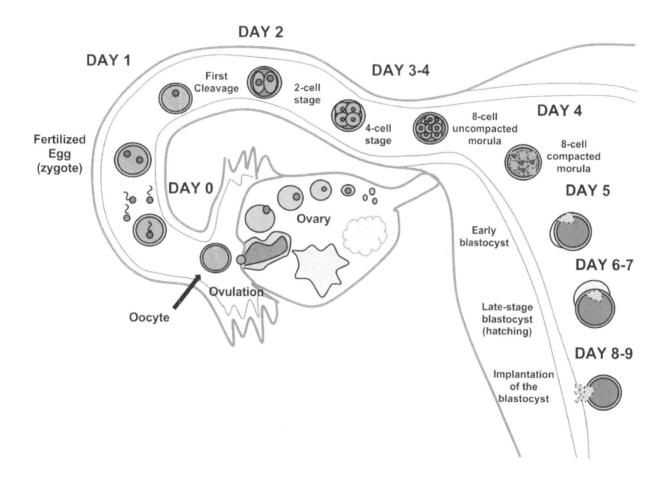

The Embryonic Period

Starting the third week, the blastocyst has implanted in the uterine wall. Upon implantation this multi-cellular organism is called an embryo. Now blood vessels grow forming the placenta. The placenta is a structure connected to the uterus that provides nourishment and oxygen from the mother to the developing embryo via the umbilical cord.

During this period, cells continue to differentiate. Growth during prenatal development occurs in two major directions: from head to tail called cephalocaudal development and from the midline outward referred to as proximodistal development. This means that those structures nearest the head develop before those nearest the feet and those structures nearest the torso develop before those away from the center of the body (such as hands and fingers). You will see that this pattern continues after birth.

The head develops in the fourth week and the precursor to the heart begins to pulse. In the early stages of the embryonic period, gills and a tail are apparent. However, by the end of this stage they disappear and the organism takes on a more human appearance.

The following figure depicts a human embryo at five stages.[20]

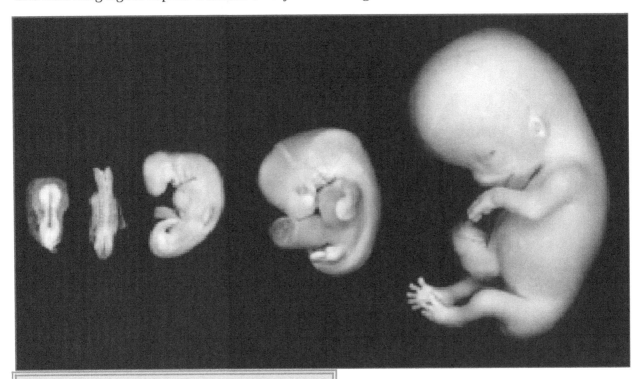

The Embryonic Period

- Two to eight weeks after conception
- Rate of cell differentiation intensifies
- Support systems for cells form
- Organogenesis: organ formation
- Embryo has three layers of cells

About 20 percent of organisms fail during the embryonic period, usually due to gross chromosomal abnormalities, often before the mother even knows that she is pregnant. It is during this stage that the major structures of the body are taking form, making the embryonic period the

_____

[20] Image is public domain

time when the organism is most vulnerable to the greatest amount of damage if exposed to harmful substances. Prospective mothers are not often aware of the risks they introduce to the developing embryo during this time. The embryo is approximately 1 inch in length and weighs about 4 grams at the end of eight weeks. The embryo can move and respond to touch at this time.[21]

Parts of the Embryo:

Endoderm: inner layer of cells forming digestive and respiratory systems

Mesoderm: middle layer of cells forming circulatory system, bones, muscles, excretory and reproductive systems

Ectoderm: outermost layer of cells forming nervous system, sensory receptors, and skin parts

---

The Fetal Period

From the ninth week until birth (which is forty weeks for a full-term pregnancy - lasts about 7 months), the organism is referred to as a fetus. Physiologically, the change to the fetal stage begins when the placenta has developed to provide the organism life support. During this stage, the major structures are continuing to develop. This period is the time of the largest prenatal size and weight gains. Fingers, toes, skin, features, lungs, other structures, and reflexes all develop to prepare for birth.By the third month, the fetus has all its body parts including external genitalia. The fetus is about 3 inches long and weighs about 28 grams. In the following weeks, the fetus will develop hair, nails, teeth and the excretory and digestive systems will continue to develop.

Placenta: intertwines but does not join mother and baby

- Carries off waste products
- Provides nutrients and oxygen
- Produces human gonadotrophin (hCG)
- Alerts mother's body to the pregnancy
- Umbilical cord: connects fetus to placenta
- Amnion and amniotic fluid: provides fetus's environment

During the 4th - 6th months, the eyes become more sensitive to light and hearing develops. The respiratory system continues to develop, and reflexes such as sucking, swallowing and hiccupping,

---

[21]Chapter 3: Prenatal Development – Environmental Risks references Psyc 200 Lifespan Psychology by Laura Overstreet, which is licensed under CC BY 4.0

develop during the 5th month. Cycles of sleep and wakefulness are present at this time as well. The first chance of survival outside the womb, known as the age of viability is reached at about 24 weeks (Morgan, Goldenberg, & Schulkin, 2008). Many practitioners hesitate to resuscitate before 24 weeks. The majority of the neurons in the brain have developed by 24 weeks, although they are still rudimentary, and the glial or nurse cells that support neurons continue to grow. At 24 weeks the fetus can feel pain (Royal College of Obstetricians and Gynecologists, 1997).

Between the 7th - 9th months, the fetus is primarily preparing for birth. It is exercising its muscles and its lungs begin to expand and contract. The fetus gains about 5 pounds and 7 inches during this last trimester of pregnancy, and during the 8th month a layer of fat develops under the skin. This layer of fat serves as insulation and helps the baby regulate body temperature after birth.At around 36 weeks the fetus is almost ready for birth. It weighs about 6 pounds and is about 18.5 inches long. By week 37 all of the fetus's organ systems are developed enough that it could survive outside the mother's uterus without many of the risks associated with premature birth. The fetus continues to gain weight and grow in length until approximately 40 weeks. By then the fetus has very little room to move around and birth becomes imminent. The progression through the stages is shown in the following figure.[22]

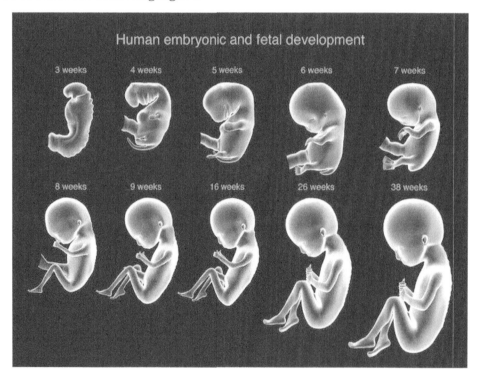

---

[22] Image is public domain

Confirming the Pregnancy and Calculating the Due Date:

Pregnancy test checks for human chorionic gonadotropin (HCG)

Pregnancy calculated from first day of the woman's last menstrual period

Lasts about 280 days or 40 weeks - 38 weeks considered "full term" medically

At birth, the average baby in the US weighs about 7.5 pounds and is about 20 inches long.

Teratogens

Good prenatal care is essential to protect against maternal and fetal/infant mortality and birth complications. The embryo and fetus is most at risk for some of the most severe problems during the first three months of development. Unfortunately, this is a time at which many mothers are unaware that they are pregnant. Today, we know many of the factors that can jeopardize the health of the developing child. The study of factors that contribute to birth defects is called teratology. Teratogens are environmental factors that can contribute to birth defects, and include some maternal diseases, pollutants, drugs and alcohol.Factors influencing prenatal risks: There are several considerations in determining the type and amount of damage that might result from exposure to a particular teratogen (Berger, 2005). These include:

•The timing of the exposure: Structures in the body are vulnerable to the most severe damage when they are forming. If a substance is introduced during a particular structure's critical period (time of development), the damage to that structure may be greater. For example, the ears and arms reach their critical periods at about 6 weeks after conception. If a mother exposes the embryo to certain substances during this period, the arms and ears may be malformed. (see figure below)

•The amount of exposure: Some substances are not harmful unless the amounts reach a certain level. The critical level depends in part on the size and metabolism of the mother.

•The number of teratogens: Fetuses exposed to multiple teratogens typically have more problems than those exposed to only one.

•Genetics: Genetic makeup also plays a role on the impact a particular teratogen might have on the child. This is suggested by fraternal twins exposed to the same prenatal environment, but they do not experience the same teratogenic effects. The genetic makeup of the mother can also have an effect; some mothers may be more resistant to teratogenic effects than others.

• Being male or female: Males are more likely to experience damage due to teratogens than are females. It is believed that the Y chromosome, which contains fewer genes than the X, may have an impact.[23]

There are four categories of teratogens:

1. Physical teratogens: These could be saunas, hot tubs, or infections that raise a pregnant woman's body temperature to 102 degrees Fahrenheit or higher. This is associated with neural tube defects, spontaneous abortions, and various cardiovascular abnormalities.

2. Metabolic conditions affecting pregnant females: Metabolic conditions are abnormalities in the chemical process of producing energy from food, and thereby affect the development and function of the body. If a pregnant woman is malnourished, then her fetus likely lacks the nutrients essential for its development. These include: malnutrition, diabetes, and thyroid disorders.

3. Infections: Different maternal infections, including rubella virus, herpes simplex virus, and syphilis can cause congenital abnormalities in fetuses.

4. Drugs and chemicals: When pregnant females ingest or absorb these, they may cause a variety of different effects based on specific agent, amount of exposure, and timing. This category includes: radiation, heavy metals (including lead), insecticides and herbicides, prescription and over the counter drugs, illicit and recreational drugs, alcohol, cigarettes, nicotine, caffeine, and even some vitamins.[24]

While there are many, many potential teratogens, the following tables look at the effects of some different types of teratogens. The risks of exposure vary based on lifestyle and health. The effects may vary greatly depending on the factors mentioned previously. Protection and prevention will vary based on the method of exposure.

Table – Drugs as Teratogens

Teratogen	Potential Effects
Caffeine	Moderate amounts of caffeine (200 mg or around 12 ounces of coffee) appear to be safe during pregnancy. Some studies have shown a link between higher amounts of caffeine and miscarriage and preterm birth.[25]
Tobacco	Tobacco use has been associated with low birth weight, placenta

---

[23]Lifespan Development: A Psychological Perspective (pages 52-55) by Martha Lally and Suzanne Valentine-French is licensed under CC BY-NC-SA 3.0

[24]Staying healthy and safe by OWH is in the public domain

Teratogen	Potential Effects
	previa, preterm delivery, fetal growth restriction, sudden infant death syndrome, cleft lip or palate, and later health problems (such as high blood pressure and diabetes).
Alcohol	There is no safe amount of alcohol a woman can drink while pregnant. Alcohol can slow down the baby's growth, affect the baby's brain, and cause birth defects, and may results in fetal alcohol spectrum disorder (FASD). The effects can be mild to severe. Children born with a severe form of FASD can have abnormal facial features, severe learning disabilities, behavioral problems, and other problems.
Cocaine	Cocaine use has connected with low birth weight, stillbirths, spontaneous abortion, placental abruption, premature birth, miscarriage, and neonatal abstinence syndrome (fetal addiction leads the newborn to experiences withdrawal).
Marijuana	No amount of marijuana has been proven safe to use during pregnancy. Heavy use has been associated with brain damage, premature birth, and stillbirth.
Heroin	Using heroin during pregnancy can cause birth defects, placental abruption, premature birth, low birthweight, neonatal abstinence syndrome, still birth, and sudden infant death syndrome.[26]
Over-the-Counter (OTC) medication	Some OTC medications are safe to use during pregnancy and others may cause health problems during pregnancy. Pregnant women should consult their health care provider before using OTC medications.
Prescription drugs	Some prescription drugs can cause birth defects that change the

[25]Chapter 3: Prenatal Development – Environmental Risks references Psyc 200 Lifespan Psychology by Laura Overstreet, which is licensed under CC BY 4.0;Prescription drugs, over-the-counter drugs, supplements and herbal products (n.d.). Retrieved from: https://www.marchofdimes.org/pregnancy/prescription-drugs-over-the-counter-drugs-supplements-and-herbal-products.aspx

[26]Chapter 3: Prenatal Development – Environmental Risks references Psyc 200 Lifespan Psychology by Laura Overstreet, which is licensed under CC BY 4.0;Prescription drugs, over-the-counter drugs, supplements and herbal products (n.d.). Retrieved from: https://www.marchofdimes.org/pregnancy/prescription-drugs-over-the-counter-drugs-supplements-and-herbal-products.aspx

Teratogen	Potential Effects
	shape or function of one or more parts of the body that can affect overall health. Pregnant women should consult their health care provider before discontinuing or starting new medications.
Herbal or dietary supplements	Except for some vitamins, little is known about using herbal or dietary supplements while pregnant. Most often there are no good studies to show if the herb can cause harm to you or your baby. Also, some herbs that are safe when used in small amounts as food might be harmful when used in large amounts as medicines.

Table - Environmental Teratogens

Teratogen	Potential Effects
Lead	Exposure to high levels of lead before and during pregnancy can lead to high blood pressure, problems with fetal brain and nervous system development, premature birth, low birthweight, and miscarriage.[27]
Mercury	Exposure to mercury in the womb can cause brain damage and hearing and vision problems.
Radiation	Exposure to radiation during pregnancy (especially between 2 and 18 weeks of pregnancy) can slow growth, cause birth defects, affect brain development, cause cancer, and cause miscarriage.
Solvents	These chemicals include degreasers, paint thinners, stain and varnish removers, paints, and more Maternal inhalation of solvents can cause fetal exposure than may cause miscarriage, slow fetal growth, premature birth, and birth defects.

Table - Maternal Infections as Teratogens

---

[27] Chapter 3: Prenatal Development – Environmental Risks references Psyc 200 Lifespan Psychology by Laura Overstreet, which is licensed under CC BY 4.0

Teratogen	Potential Effects
Rubella	Congenital infection (becoming infected while in the womb) can damage the development of the eyes, ears, heart, and brain and result in deafness.[28]
Zika	Congenital infection can cause microcephaly and other severe brain abnormalities.[29]
Varicella (chicken pox)	Congenital infection can cause a severe form of the infection affecting the eyes, limbs, skin, and central nervous system.[30]
Sexually transmitted infections	Infections such as HIV, gonorrhea, syphilis, and chlamydia can be passed from the mother during pregnancy and/or delivery.[31]
Listeria	Pregnant women are more susceptible to this food-borne illness. Congenital infection can cause miscarriage, stillbirth, premature labor, and neonatal sepsis.[32]

Table Teratogens from Animals/Pets

Teratogen	Potential Effects
Toxoplamosis	This parasite can be passed through cat feces and undercooked meat (especially pork, lamb, or deer meet). If the fetus is infected it can cause miscarriage, stillbirth, hydrocephalus, macro or microcephalus, vision issues, and damage to the nervous system.
Lymphocytic	This virus carried by rodents including mice, hamsters, and guinea pigs.

[28] Chapter 3: Prenatal Development – Environmental Risks references Psyc 200 Lifespan Psychology by Laura Overstreet, which is licensed under CC BY 4.0

[29] Protocols on prenatal care for pregnant women with Zika infection and children with microcephaly: nutritional approach by Rachel de Sá Barreto Luna Callou Cruz, Malaquias Batista Filho, Maria de Fátima Costa Caminha, and Edvaldo da Silva Souza is licensed under CC BY 4.0

[30] Congenital Varicella syndrome by WikiDoc is licensed under CC BY-SA 3.0

[31] Chapter 3: Prenatal Development – Environmental Risks references Psyc 200 Lifespan Psychology by Laura Overstreet, which is licensed under CC BY 4.0

[32] https://www.ncbi.nlm.nih.gov/pmc/articles/PMC2860824/

Teratogen	Potential Effects
choriomeningitis	If an infected mother passes it to her fetus it can cause issues with brain development, long-term neurological and/or visual impairment, and higher mortality rates after birth.

Prenatal Assessment

A number of assessments are suggested to women as part of their routine prenatal care to find conditions that may increase the risk of complications for the mother and fetus (Eisenberg, Murkoff, & Hathaway, 1996). These can include blood and urine analyses and screening and diagnostic tests for birth defects.

Ultrasound is one of the main screening tests done in combination with blood tests. The ultrasound is a test in which sound waves are used to examine the fetus. There are two general types. Transvaginal ultrasounds are used in early pregnancy, while transabdominal ultrasounds are more common and used after 10 weeks of pregnancy (typically, 16 to 20 weeks).

Ultrasounds are used to check the fetus for defects or problems. It can also find out the age of the fetus, location of the placenta, fetal position, movement, breathing and heart rate, amount of amniotic fluid in the uterus, and number of fetuses. Most women have at least one ultrasound during pregnancy, but if problems are noted, additional ultrasounds may be recommended.

When diagnosis of a birth defect is necessary, ultrasounds help guide the more invasive diagnostic tests of amniocentesis and chorionic villus sampling. Amniocentesis is a procedure in which a needle is used to withdraw a small amount of amniotic fluid and cells from the sac surrounding the fetus and later tested.

Chorionic Villus Sampling is a procedure in which a small sample of cells is taken from the placenta and tested. Both amniocentesis and chorionic villus sampling have a risk of miscarriage, and consequently they are not done routinely.[33]

Maternal Factors

There are additional factors that affect the outcome of pregnancy for both mother and child. Let's look at these next.

---

[33]Chapter 3: Prenatal Development – Environmental Risks references Psyc 200 Lifespan Psychology by Laura Overstreet, which is licensed under CC BY 4.0

Penatal care

Adequate prenatal care is one of the most important factors in healthy pregnancies. The U.S. does not provide uniform prenatal care. Prenatal care may also be poor In developing countries, especially when poverty is high. When the health and nutrition of mothers is poor, the percentage of low birthweight reaches 50%. Monthly to weekly visits to assess mother's health and weight and the health of the fetus are beneficial. Prenatal is also important for detecting any medical conditions or the presence of complications. Reasons for not seeking prenatal care include lack of health insurance, inability to pay for medical care, psychological problems, family problems, and negative feelings about the pregnancy. Teen mothers are mothers in poverty are less likely to receive adequate prenatal care Most U.S. women do receive adequate care.

Mothers over 35

Most women over 35 who become pregnant are in good health and have healthy pregnancies. However, according to the March of Dimes (2016d), women over age 35 are more likely to have an increased risk of:

- Fertility problems
- High blood pressure
- Diabetes
- Miscarriages
- Placenta Previa
- Cesarean section
- Premature birth
- Stillbirth
- A baby with a genetic disorder or other birth defects

Because a woman is born with all her eggs, environmental teratogens can affect the quality of the eggs as women get older. Also, a woman's reproductive system ages which can adversely affect the pregnancy. Some women over 35 choose special prenatal screening tests, such as a maternal blood screening, to determine if there are any health risks for the baby.
Although there are medical concerns associated with having a child later in life, there are also many positive consequences to being a more mature parent. Older parents are more confident, less stressed, and typically married, providing family stability. Their children perform better on math and reading tests, and they are less prone to injuries or emotional troubles (Albert, 2013). Women who choose to wait are often well educated and lead healthy lives. According to Gregory (2007),

older women are more stable, demonstrate a stronger family focus, possess greater self-confidence, and have more money. Having a child later in one's career equals overall higher wages. In fact, for every year a woman delays motherhood, she makes 9% more in lifetime earnings. Lastly, women who delay having children actually live longer.

Teenage Pregnancy

A teenage mother is at a greater risk for having pregnancy complications including anemia, and high blood pressure. These risks are even greater for those under age 15. Infants born to teenage mothers have a higher risk for being premature and having low birthweight or other serious health problems. Premature and low birthweight babies may have organs that are not fully developed which can result in breathing problems, bleeding in the brain, vision loss, serious intestinal problems, and higher likelihood of dying. Reasons for these health issues include that teenagers are the least likely of all age groups to get early and regular prenatal care and they may engage in negative behaviors including eating unhealthy food, smoking, drinking alcohol, and taking drugs.

Gestational Diabetes

Seven percent of pregnant women develop gestational diabetes (March of Dimes, 2015b). Diabetes is a condition where the body has too much glucose in the bloodstream.[34]Most pregnant women have their glucose level tested between 24 to 28 weeks of pregnancy. Gestational diabetes usually goes away after the mother gives birth, but it might indicate a risk for developing diabetes later in life. If untreated, gestational diabetes can cause premature birth, stillbirth, the baby having breathing problems at birth, jaundice, or low blood sugar. Babies born to mothers with gestational diabetes can also be considerably heavier (more than 9 pounds) making the labor and birth process more difficult. For expectant mothers, untreated gestational diabetes can cause preeclampsia (high blood pressure and signs that the liver and kidneys may not be working properly) discussed later in the chapter.

Risk factors for gestational diabetes include age (being over age 25), being overweight or gaining too much weight during pregnancy, family history of diabetes, having had gestational diabetes with a prior pregnancy, and race and ethnicity (African-American, Native American, Hispanic, Asian, or Pacific Islander have a higher risk). Eating healthy and maintaining a healthy weight during pregnancy can reduce the chance of gestational diabetes. Women who already have diabetes and become pregnant need to attend all their prenatal care visits, and follow the same advice as those for women with gestational diabetes as the risk of preeclampsia, premature birth, birth defects, and stillbirth are the same.

---

[34]Chapter 3: Prenatal Development – Environmental Risks references Psyc 200 Lifespan Psychology by Laura Overstreet, which is licensed under CC BY 4.0

High Blood Pressure (Hypertension)

Hypertension is a condition in which the pressure against the wall of the arteries becomes too high. There are two types of high blood pressure during pregnancy, gestational and chronic. Gestational hypertension only occurs during pregnancy and goes away after birth. Chronic high blood pressure refers to women who already had hypertension before the pregnancy or to those who developed it during pregnancy and it did not go away after birth.[35]

According to the March of Dimes (2015c), about 8 in every 100 pregnant women have high blood pressure. High blood pressure during pregnancy can cause premature birth and low birth weight (under five and a half pounds), placental abruption, and mothers can develop preeclampsia.

Rh Disease

Rh is a protein found in the blood. Most people are Rh positive, meaning they have this protein. Some people are Rh negative, meaning this protein is absent. Mothers who are Rh negative are at risk of having a baby with a form of anemia called Rh disease (March of Dimes, 2009). A father who is Rh-positive and mother who is Rh-negative can conceive a baby who is Rh-positive. Some of the fetus's blood cells may get into the mother's bloodstream and her immune system is unable to recognize the Rh factor.

The immune system starts to produce antibodies to fight off what it thinks is a foreign invader. Once her body produces immunity, the antibodies can cross the placenta and start to destroy the red blood cells of the developing fetus. As this process takes time, often the first Rh positive baby is not harmed, but as the mother's body will continue to produce antibodies to the Rh factor across her lifetime, subsequent pregnancies can pose greater risk for an Rh positive baby. In the newborn, Rh disease can lead to jaundice, anemia, heart failure, brain damage and death.

Weight Gain during Pregnancy

According to March of Dimes (2016f), during pregnancy most women need only an additional 300 calories per day to aid in the growth of the fetus. Gaining too little or too much weight during pregnancy can be harmful. Women who gain too little may have a baby who is low-birth weight, while those who gain too much are likely to have a premature or large baby. There is also a greater risk for the mother developing preeclampsia and diabetes, which can cause further problems during the pregnancy.

The table below shows the healthy weight gain during pregnancy. Putting on the weight slowly is best. Mothers who are concerned about their weight gain should talk to their health care provider.

---

[35] Chapter 3: Prenatal Development -- Environmental Risks references Psyc 200 Lifespan Psychology by Laura Overstreet, which is licensed under CC BY 4.0

Table - Weight Gain during Pregnancy

If you were a healthy weight before pregnancy:	If you were underweight before pregnancy:	If you were overweight before pregnancy:	If you were obese before pregnancy:
• Gain 25-35 pounds • 1-4½ pounds in the 1st trimester • 1 pound per week in the 2nd and 3rd trimesters	• Gain 28-30 pounds • 1-4½ pounds in the 1st trimester • A little more than 1 pound per week thereafter	• Gain 12-25 pounds • 1-4½ pounds in the 1st trimester • A little more than ½ pound per week in 2nd and 3rd trimesters	• 11-20 pounds • 1-4½ pounds in the 1st trimester • A little more than ½ pound per week in 2nd and 3rd trimesters
Mothers of twins or higher order multiples need to gain more in each category.			

Exercise During Pregnancy:

- Exercise for shorter time intervals
- Decrease intensity as pregnancy progresses
- Avoid prolonged overheating
- Avoid high-risk activities
- Warm up, stretch, cool down
- After exercise, lie on left side 10 minutes
- Wear supportive shoes and bra
- Reduce exercise significantly in the last four weeks

Nutrition: Need for protein, iron, vitamin D, calcium, phosphorus, magnesium increases 50 percent, water is essential

Weight Gain: average 25 to 35 pounds weight gain associated with best reproductive outcomes.

Maternal obesity adversely impacts pregnancy outcomes; carries risks of Hypertension, Diabetes, Respiratory complications.

Stress

Feeling stressed is common during pregnancy, but high levels of stress can cause complications including having a premature baby or a low-birthweight baby. Babies born early or too small are at an increased risk for health problems. Stress-related hormones may cause these complications by affecting a woman's immune systems resulting in an infection and premature birth. Additionally, some women deal with stress by smoking, drinking alcohol, or taking drugs, which can lead to problems in the pregnancy. High levels of stress in pregnancy have also been correlated with problems in the baby's brain development and immune system functioning, as well as childhood problems such as trouble paying attention and being afraid (March of Dimes, 2012b).

Depression

Depression is a significant medical condition in which feelings of sadness, worthlessness, guilt, and fatigue interfere with one's daily functioning. Depression can occur before, during, or after pregnancy, and 1 in 7 women are treated for depression sometime between the year before pregnancy and year after pregnancy (March of Dimes, 2015a). Women who have experienced depression previously are more likely to have depression during pregnancy. Consequences of depression include the baby being born premature, having a low birthweight, being more irritable, less active, less attentive, and having fewer facial expressions.

About 13% of pregnant women take an antidepressant during pregnancy. It is important that women taking antidepressants during pregnancy discuss the medication with a health care provider as some medications can cause harm to the developing organism.

Paternal Impact

The age of fathers at the time of conception is also an important factor in health risks for children. According to Nippoldt (2015), offspring of men over 40 face an increased risk of miscarriages, autism, birth defects, achondroplasia (bone growth disorder) and schizophrenia. These increased health risks are thought to be due to accumulated chromosomal aberrations and mutations during the maturation of sperm cells in older men (Bray, Gunnell, & Smith, 2006). However, like older women, the overall risks are small.

In addition, men are more likely than women to work in occupations where hazardous chemicals, many of which have teratogenic effects or may cause genetic mutations, are used (Cordier, 2008). These may include petrochemicals, lead, and pesticides that can cause abnormal sperm and lead to miscarriages or diseases. Men are also more likely to be a source of second hand smoke for their developing offspring. As noted earlier, smoking by either the mother or around the mother can hinder prenatal development.[36]

Complications of Pregnancy

There are a number of common side effects of pregnancy. Not everyone experiences all of these, nor to the same degree. And although they are considered "minor", this is not to say that these problems are not potentially very uncomfortable. These side effects include nausea (particularly during the first 3-4 months of pregnancy as a result of higher levels of estrogen in the system), heartburn, gas, hemorrhoids, backache, leg cramps, insomnia, constipation, shortness of breath or varicose veins (as a result of carrying a heavy load on the abdomen). These are minor issues. But there are also serious complications of pregnancy which can pose health risks to mother and child and that often require hospitalization.

Hyperemesis gravidarum is characterized by severe nausea, vomiting, weight loss, and possibly dehydration. Signs and symptoms may also include vomiting many times a day and feeling faint. The exact causes of hyperemesis gravidarum are unknown. Risk factors include the first pregnancy, multiple pregnancy, obesity, prior or family history of HG, trophoblastic disorder, and a history of eating disorders. Treatment includes drinking fluids and a bland diet. Medication, intravenous fluids, and hospitalization may be required. Hyperemesis gravidarum is estimated to affect 0.3–2.0% of pregnant women. Those affected have a low risk of miscarriage but a higher risk of premature birth.

Miscarriage is experienced in an estimated 20-40 percent of undiagnosed pregnancies and in another 10 percent of diagnosed pregnancies. Usually the body aborts due to chromosomal abnormalities, and this typically happens before the 12th week of pregnancy. Cramping and bleeding result and normal periods return after several months. Some women are more likely to have repeated miscarriages due to chromosomal, amniotic, or hormonal problems, but miscarriage can also be a result of defective sperm (Carrell et. al., 2003).

Preeclampsia, also known as Toxemia, is characterized by a sharp rise in blood pressure, a leakage of protein into the urine as a result of kidney problems, and swelling of the hands, feet, and face during the third trimester of pregnancy. Preeclampsia is the most common complication of pregnancy. When preeclampsia causes seizures, the condition is known as eclampsia, which is the second leading cause of maternal death in the United States. Preeclampsia is also a leading cause of fetal complications, which include low birth weight, premature birth, and stillbirth. Treatment is typically bed rest and sometimes medication. If this treatment is ineffective, labor may be induced.

---

[36]Chapter 3: Prenatal Development – Environmental Risks references Psyc 200 Lifespan Psychology by Laura Overstreet, which is licensed under CC BY 4.0

Maternal Mortality: Approximately 1000 women die in childbirth around the world each day (World Health Organization, 2010). Rates are highest in Sub-Saharan Africa and South Asia, although there has been a substantial decrease in these rates. The campaign to make childbirth safe for everyone has led to the development of clinics accessible to those living in more isolated areas and training more midwives to assist in childbirth.[37]

Ectopic Pregnancy occurs when the zygote becomes attached to the fallopian tube before reaching the uterus. About 1 in 50 pregnancies in the United States are tubal pregnancies and this number has been increasing because of the higher rates of pelvic inflammatory disease and Chlamydia (Carroll, 2007). Abdominal pain, vaginal bleeding, nausea and fainting are symptoms of ectopic pregnancy.

Infertility

When a couple has failed to conceive a child in a year of trying, they receive the diagnosis of infertility. Infertility affects about 10 to 15 percent of couples in the United States (Mayo Clinic, 2015). Male factors create infertility in about a third of the cases. For men, the most common cause is a lack of sperm production or low sperm production.
Female factors cause infertility in another third of cases. For women, one of the most common causes of infertility is the failure to ovulate. Another cause of infertility in women is Pelvic Inflammatory Disease (PID), which is an infection of a woman's reproductive organs (Carroll, 2007). Both male and female factors contribute to the remainder of cases of infertility.[38]

Options for Building Families

There are numerous options to pursue parenthood and building families. Let's briefly explore some of these.

Assisted Reproductive Technology

Assisted reproductive technology (ART) is the technology used to achieve pregnancy in procedures such as fertility medication (to stimulate ovulation), surgical procedures, artificial insemination IUI), in vitro fertilization (IVF) and surrogacy. In the US in 2002, over 100,00 ART procedures resulted in 45,000 births (1% of all births). These options are available for people who are experiencing infertility or cannot conceive children naturally (which also includes single

---

[37] Chapter 3: Prenatal Development – Environmental Risks references Psyc 200 Lifespan Psychology by Laura Overstreet, which is licensed under CC BY 4.0

[38] Chapter 3: Prenatal Development – Environmental Risks references Psyc 200 Lifespan Psychology by Laura Overstreet, which is licensed under CC BY 4.0

parents, and gay/lesbian couples).[39]

[40]*Intrauterine insemination*: (IUI) as a type of artificial insemination involves the placement of sperm directly into the uterus at the time of ovulation, either in a natural menstrual cycle or following ovarian stimulation.[41]

[42]*In vitro fertilization (IVF)*: IVF generally starts with stimulating the ovaries to increase egg production. Most fertility medications are agents that stimulate the development of follicles in the ovary. Examples are gonadotropins and gonadotropin releasing hormone. After stimulation, the physician surgically extracts one or more eggs from the ovary, and unites them with sperm in a laboratory setting, with the intent of producing one or more embryos. Fertilization takes place outside the body, and the fertilized egg is reinserted into the woman's reproductive tract, in a procedure called embryo transfer.[43]

ART Techniques:

- In vitro fertilization (IVF) ova and sperm are combined in lab, fertilized ovum returned to uterus
- Gamete intrafallopian transfer (GIFT) sperm and ova are transferred to fallopian tubes
- Zygote intrafallopian transfer (ZIFT) ova and sperm are combined in lab, fertilized ovum returned to fallopian tubes.

Donor Gametes & Embryos: People can also use sperm, ova (eggs), and embryos from donors in conjunction with ART. These donations take place through agencies and donor banks or between private individuals. In the U.S., donors can be compensated for their donations.

Surrogacy: In surrogacy, one woman (surrogate mother) carries a child for another person/s (commissioning person/couple), based on a legal agreement before conception requiring the child to be relinquished to the commissioning person/couple following birth. There are different types of surrogacy which relate to whether or not the ova used to conceive the child are her own (traditional surrogacy) or not (gestational surrogacy).

Adoption: People can also choose to pursue adoption to build their families (with or without

---

[39]Development: A Psychological Perspective (page 57) by Martha Lally and Suzanne Valentine-French is licensed under CC BY-NC-SA 3.0

[40]Reproductive Technology by Fertilitypedia is licensed under CC BY-SA 4

[41]Insemination by Fertilitypedia is licensed under CC BY-SA 4.0

[42]Reproductive Technology by Fertilitypedia is licensed under CC BY-SA 4.

[43]Fertilitypedia is licensed under CC BY-SA 4.0

experiencing infertility). Adoption can take place through the foster care system, privately, or through agencies. Adoptions can be domestic (within the U.S.) or international. And they can be open (with differing amounts of contact between biological/birth families and adoptive families) or closed.

Preparing for Childbirth

After around 266 days of developing inside the womb (for a full-term pregnancy), comes the arduous process of childbirth. After birth, newborns have to regulate their own body temperature, breathe for themselves, and take in all of their nutrition through feeding. Let's look at both the process of birth and some attributes of the newborn.

Prepared childbirth refers to being not only in good physical condition to help provide a healthy environment for the baby to develop, but also helping individuals to prepare to accept their new roles as parents. Additionally, parents can receive information and training that will assist them for delivery and life with the baby. The more future parents can learn about childbirth and the newborn, the better prepared they will be for the adjustment they must make to a new life.

Approaches to Childbirth

There are many different approaches to childbirth that influence how expectant parents prepare. The following table describes a few of these:

Table - Approaches to Childbirth

Method	Description
The Lamaze Method	The emphasis of this method is on teaching the woman to be in control in the process of delivery. It includes learning muscle relaxation, breathing through contractions, having a focal point (usually a picture to look at) during contractions and having a support person who goes through the training process with the mother and serves as a coach during delivery.
The Leboyer Method	This method involves giving birth in a quiet, dimly lit room and allowing the newborn to lie on the mother's stomach with the umbilical cord intact for several minutes while being given a warm bath.
Dick-Read Method / Mongan Method /	This method comes from the suggestion that the fear of childbirth increases tension and makes the process of childbearing more painful.

Method	Description
Hypnobirthing	It emphasizes the use of relaxation and proper breathing with contractions as well as family support and education.
Bradley Method	"The Bradley Method focuses on preparing the mother for a natural childbirth coached by her partner. They learn techniques to reduce the perception of pain and stay relaxed. The emphasis is on being prepared for an unassisted vaginal birth without medication."
Alexander Technique	This is a technique that can be used during childbirth that involves training to stop habitual reactions to pain, such as tensing muscles and increase conscious awareness and control over posture and movement. This involves being able to move freely and stay upright during labor and using body positioning that is beneficial to the labor process.
Waterbirth	Involves immersion in warm water. Proponents believe this method is safe and provides many benefits for both mother and infant, including pain relief and a less traumatic birth experience for the baby. However, critics argue that the procedure introduces unnecessary risks to the infant such as infection and water inhalation.
Lotus Birth	Or umbilical cord nonseverance – UCNS, is the practice of leaving the umbilical cord uncut after childbirth so that the baby is left attached to the placenta until the cord naturally separates at the umbilicus. This usually occurs within 3–10 days after birth. The practice is performed mainly for spiritual purposes of the parents, including for the perceived spiritual connection between placenta and newborn.
Silent Birth	Sometimes known as quiet birth, is a birthing procedure advised by L. Ron Hubbard and advocated by Scientologists in which "everyone attending the birth should refrain from spoken words as much as possible."
Medicated Childbirth	Health care providers can provide pain relief during labor with different types of medication, including epidurals, spinal blocks, combined spinal-epidurals, and systemic and local analgesia. There are

Method	Description
	benefits and side effects of each.

<u>Choosing Location of Childbirth & Who Will Deliver</u>

The vast majority of births occur in a hospital setting. However, one percent of women choose to deliver at home (Martin, Hamilton, Osterman, Curtin, & Mathews, 2015). Women who are at low risk for birth complications can successfully deliver at home. More than half (67%) of home deliveries are by certified nurse midwives. Midwives are trained and licensed to assist in delivery and are far less expensive than the cost of a hospital delivery. However, because of the potential for a complication during the birth process, most medical professionals recommend that delivery take place in a hospital. In addition to home births, one-third of out-of-hospital births occur in freestanding clinics, birthing centers, in physician's offices, or other locations.

Childbirth

<u>Onset of Labor</u>

Childbirth typically occurs within a week of a woman's due date, unless the woman is pregnant with more than one fetus, which usually causes her to go into labor early. As a pregnancy progresses into its final weeks, several physiological changes occur in response to hormones that trigger labor.

A common sign that labor is beginning is the so-called "bloody show." During pregnancy, a plug of mucus accumulates in the cervical canal, blocking the entrance to the uterus. Approximately 1–2 days prior to the onset of true labor, this plug loosens and is expelled, along with a small amount of blood.

As labor nears, the mothers' pituitary gland produces oxytocin. This begins to stimulate stronger, more painful uterine contractions, which—in a positive feedback loop—stimulate the secretion of prostaglandins from fetal membranes. Like oxytocin, prostaglandins also enhance uterine contractile strength. The fetal pituitary gland also secretes oxytocin, which increases prostaglandins even further.

And the stretching of the cervix by a full-term fetus in the head-down position is regarded as a stimulant to uterine contractions. Combined, these stimulate true labor.

Stages of Birth for Vaginal Delivery

<u>The First Stage</u>

Uterine contractions signify that the first stage of labor has begun. These contractions may initially last about 30 seconds and be spaced 15 to 20 minutes apart. These increase in duration and frequency to more than a minute in length and about 3 to 4 minutes apart. Typically, doctors advise that they be called when contractions are coming about every 5 minutes. Some women experience false labor or Braxton-Hicks Contractions, especially with the first child. These may come and go. They tend to diminish when the mother begins walking around. Real labor pains tend to increase with walking. In one out of 8 pregnancies, the amniotic sac or water in which the fetus is suspended may break before labor begins. In such cases, the physician may induce labor with the use of medication if it does not begin on its own in order to reduce the risk of infection. Normally this sac does not rupture until the later stages of labor.

The first stage of labor is typically the longest. During this stage the cervix or opening to the uterus dilates to 10 centimeters or just under 4 inches. This may take around 12-16 hours for first children or about 6-9 hours for women who have previously given birth. Labor may also begin with a discharge of blood or amniotic fluid.

<u>The Second Stage</u>

The passage of the baby through the birth canal is the second stage of labor. This stage takes about 10-40 minutes. Contractions usually come about every 2-3 minutes. The mother pushes and relaxes as directed by the medical staff. Normally the head is delivered first. The baby is then rotated so that one shoulder can come through and then the other shoulder. The rest of the baby quickly passes through. At this stage, an episiotomy, or incision made in the tissue between the vaginal opening and anus, may be performed to avoid tearing the tissue of the back of the vaginal opening (Mayo Clinic, 2016). The baby's mouth and nose are suctioned out. The umbilical cord is clamped and cut.

<u>The Third Stage</u>

The third and final stage of labor is relatively painless. During this stage, the placenta or afterbirth is delivered. This is typically within 20 minutes after delivery. If an episiotomy was performed it is stitched up during this stage.

Additional Considerations

More than 50% of women giving birth at hospitals use an epidural anesthesia during delivery (American Pregnancy Association, 2015). An epidural block is a regional analgesic that can be used during labor and alleviates most pain in the lower body without slowing labor. The epidural block can be used throughout labor and has little to no effect on the baby. Medication is injected into a small space outside the spinal cord in the lower back. It takes 10 to 20 minutes for the medication to take effect. An epidural block with stronger medications, such as anesthetics, can be used shortly before a Cesarean Section or if a vaginal birth requires the use of forceps or vacuum extraction.

Women giving birth can also receive other pain medications (although medications given through injection can have negative side effects on the baby). In emergency situations (such as the need for a C-section), women may be given general anesthesia. They can also choose not to utilize any pain medications. That is often referred to as natural childbirth.

Women can also use alternate positions (including standing, squatting, being on hands and knees, and using a birthing stool) and laboring, and even delivering in tubs of warm water to help relieve the pain of childbirth.

Medical Interventions in Childbirth

Sometimes women cannot go into labor on their own and/or deliver vaginally. Let's look at induction of labor and Cesarean Sections.

Sometimes a baby's arrival may need to be induced before labor begins naturally. Induction of labor may be recommended for a variety of reasons when there is concern for the health of the mother or baby. For example:

- The mother is approaching two weeks beyond her due date and labor has not started naturally

- The mother's water has broken, but contractions have not begun

- There is an infection in the mother's uterus

- The baby has stopped growing at the expected pace

- There is not enough amniotic fluid surrounding the baby

- The placenta peels away, either partially or completely, from the inner wall of the uterus before delivery

- The mother has a medical condition that might put her or her baby at risk, such as high blood pressure or diabetes (Mayo Clinic, 2014).

A Cesarean Section (C-section) is surgery to deliver the baby by being removed through the mother's abdomen. In the United States, about one in three women have their babies delivered this way (Martin et al., 2015). Most C-sections are done when problems occur during delivery unexpectedly. These can include:

•Health problems in the mother

•Signs of distress in the baby

•Not enough room for the baby to go through the vagina

•The position of the baby, such as a breech presentation where the head is not in the downward position.

C-sections are also more common among women carrying more than one baby. Although the surgery is relatively safe for mother and baby, it is considered major surgery and carries health risks. Additionally, it also takes longer to recover from a C-section than from vaginal birth. After healing, the incision may leave a weak spot in the wall of the uterus. This could cause problems with an attempted vaginal birth later. In the past, doctors were hesitant to allow a vaginal birth after a C-section. However, now more than half of women who have a C-section go on to have a vaginal birth later. This is referred to as a Vaginal Birth After Cesarean (VBAC).

5 Children with Disabilities

Learning Objectives At the completion of this module, students will be able to:	Related Course Objective
5-1 Name the major categories of childhood disabilities recognized by the US Department of Education. 5-2 Define the terms "Least Restrictive Environment" and "Inclusion."	1 2 4 5 6 7 9

In the first chapter we discussed the Developmental Appropriate Practices model. You will remember that the DAP model includes three elements to consider in our interactions with a child – age-related expectations, the impact of culture and context, and individual differences. One source of individual differences in children is differences in ability. There are many ways that we could define children with special needs or children with disabilities. For example, we could organize them according to groups based upon medical diagnosis. Instead, I will use the categories defined by the U.S. Department of Education as an organizational scheme. About 10% of U.S. children receive special education or related services. Let us briefly explore U.S. policy about education for children with disabilities.

Since the 1970s political and social attitudes have moved increasingly toward including people with disabilities into a wide variety of "regular" activities. In the United States, the shift is illustrated clearly in the Federal legislation that was enacted during this time. Three major laws were passed that guaranteed the rights of persons with disabilities, and of children and students with disabilities in particular. The third law has had the biggest impact on education.

The Rehabilitation Act of 1973, Section 504
This law, the first of its kind, required that individuals with disabilities be accommodated in any program or activity that receives Federal funding (PL93-112, 1973). Although this law was not

intended specifically for education, in practice it has protected students' rights in some extra-curricular activities (for older students) and in some childcare or after-school care programs (for younger students). If those programs receive Federal funding of any kind, the programs are not allowed to exclude children or youths with disabilities, and they have to find reasonable ways to accommodate the individuals' disabilities.

Americans with Disabilities Act of 1990 (or ADA)

This legislation also prohibited discrimination on the basis of disability, just as Section 504 of the Rehabilitation Act had done (PL 101-336, 1990). Although the ADA also applies to all people (not just to students), its provisions are more specific and "stronger" than those of Section 504. In particular, ADA extends to all employment and jobs, not just those receiving Federal funding. It also specifically requires accommodations to be made in public facilities such as with buses, restrooms, and telephones. ADA legislation is therefore responsible for some of the "minor" renovations in schools that you may have noticed in recent years, like wheelchair-accessible doors, ramps, and restrooms, and public telephones with volume controls.

Individuals with Disabilities Education Act (or IDEA)

As its name implied this legislation was more focused on education than either Section 504 or ADA. It was first passed in 1975 and has been amended several times since, including most recently in 2004 (PL 108-446, 2004).

In 1975 Public Law 94-142 (the Education for All Handicapped Children Act) was passed. This law required that that all children with disabilities had the right to access a free and appropriate public education. This right is now sometimes abbreviated "FAPE." Since 1975, laws have been updated and re-authorized, and today each child's access to a free and appropriate public education is guaranteed by both the Individuals with Disabilities Education Act (IDEA) and section 504 of the Rehabilitation Act.

The 1990 re-authorization changed the name to the Individuals with Disabilities Act or IDEA. Notice the change to "*People first language*." The law moved from the "All Handicapped Children..." to the "Individuals with Disabilties...." This reflects using language by always stating the person before the conditioning label. This is to emphasize that the individual is a person who happens to have the disabling condition, not labeled by the disabling condition itself. All professionals who work with children and families should practice and become accustomed to using people first language. For example, rather than "An autistic girl," we say "A girl on the Autism spectrum." Rather than saying "that deaf child" we say "the child with a hearing impairment." Notice that we always place the child before the disabling condition.

IDEA was further amended in 1997 to include the use of *instructional technology* and *assistive technology*. Instructional technology (or Educational technology) includes any piece of technology that educators integrate into their instructional practice to engage students and enhance students' learning, for example, tablets, interactive whiteboards, clickers or smart phone apps, and so on. Instructional technology: hardware and software to accommodate students' learning needs. Assistive technology includes any piece of technology that helps a student with or without a disability to increase or maintain his/her level of functioning, for example, speech-to-text software, word processors, adapted keyboards, and so on. Assistive technology includes various services and devices to help children with disabilities function in the educational environment. For a child with a disability, assistive technology could be high-tech, such as screen reading software for a child with a visual impairment, or low-tech, such as a wheel chair for a child with mobility difficulties.

In its current form, the law guarantees the following rights related to education for anyone with a disability from birth to age 21. The first two rights influence schooling in general, but the last three affect the work of classroom teachers rather directly:

Free, appropriate education: An individual or an individual's family should not have to pay for education simply because the individual has a disability, and the educational program should be truly educational; i.e., not merely caretaking or babysitting.

Due process: In case of disagreements between an individual with a disability and the schools or other professionals, there must be procedures for resolving the disagreements that are fair and accessible to all parties, including the person himself or herself or the person's representative.

Fair evaluation of performance in spite of disability: Tests or other evaluations should not assume test taking skills that a person with a disability cannot reasonably be expected to have, such as holding a pencil, hearing or seeing questions, working quickly, or understanding and speaking orally. Evaluation procedures should be modified to allow for these differences. This provision of the law applies both to evaluations made by teachers and to school-wide or "high-stakes" testing programs.

Education in the "least restrictive environment": Education for someone with a disability should provide as many educational opportunities and options for the person as possible, both in the short term and in the long term. In practice, this requirement has meant including students in regular classrooms and school activities as much as possible.

An Individualized Educational Plan (IEP): Given that every disability is unique, instructional planning for a person with a disability should be unique or individualized as well. In practice, this provision has led to classroom teachers planning individualized programs jointly with other professionals (like reading specialists, psychologists, or medical personnel) as part of a team.[44]

For children from birth to age 3, a child with a disability qualifies for the development of an "Individualized Family Services Plan" or "IFSP." At this age, the plan is geared towards the family as a whole. From age 4 to age 21, a child with a disability qualifies for the development of an IEP. The IEP should be a written statement that spells out a unique program tailored to the individual child with a disability. The IEP team develops the plan related to the child's learning capacity, designed to meet the child's individual needs and to provide educational benefits. The IEP includes a statement about the child's present level of functioning and annual goals for the child, as well as specific benchmarks and short-term goals related to reaching the annual goals. The IEP states the specific education and related services and supplementary aids to be provided to the child, and a statement of program modifications or supports for school personnel that will be provided. The term "accomodation" refers to changes that allow for the child to succeed, such as extended time to take a test, or a reader to read questions aloud. The term "modifications" relates to changes in the curriculum standards themselves.

An IEP also includes an explanation of the extent, if any, that the child will not participate with children who are typically developing in the general education classroom. In previous generations, children with disabilities routinely spent their day in specialized classrooms, segregated from the typical general education classrooms. Today, the law requires that all children with disabilities must be educated in settings as similar as possible to the ones in which children without disabilities are educated. This is called the Least Restrictive Environment (LRE) in which the child can reach their educational goals. During the years in which children with disabilities were first included iin the typical classroom, it was commonly called "mainstreaming." Today this term is no longer used, because "mainstreaming" implied that that the focus was on fitting the child with the disability in to the general education environment. Instead, today the term used is "inclusion," because this implies that the classroom environment is established in such a way that it includes everyone. Inclusion means that children with special needs participate fully in the general education classroom - children with differing abilities are included in the social, recreational and educational activities that other children experience.

Inclusion is beneficial for all children. Inclusive environments provide a host of benefits for children with disabilities. For example, children with intellectual disabilities who participate in general education classrooms are doing better academically, with language and reading, and with daily living skills than are children with intellectual disabilities who are in segregated classrooms. One of the major benefits of inclusion is to enhance their social competence so that they may later

---

[44] Lifespan Development: A Psychological Perspective by Martha Lally and Suzanne Valentine-French is licensed under CC BY-NC-SA 3.0

live more comfortably and successfully in the mainstream of society.

Inclusion is also beneficial for children who do not have disabilities. The value is to promote the acceptance of children with disabilities through reduction and removal of social stigma. Children learn to live in a world where not everyone is the same and to interact with others who have abilities that are different than their own. If the process is well-monitored and structured, inclusion can result in true understanding and friendships between children with different abilities. If not well structured and monitored, inclusion may result in children with disabilities being the victim of inattention, being over protected, or being stereotyped. Make the additional effort needed to go beyond the mere maintenance of students with exceptional needs in the nonspecialized setting, and all children benefit.

Now that we have discussed some of the contextual issues surrounding children who receive special education services, let's briefly discuss the different categories of special education. The following pie chart displays the current numbers of children served, in thousands, for these different categories, as well as the percentage of children receiving services that is represented by that category (the second, lighter colored percentage is the percentage in Hamilton County, Tennessee).

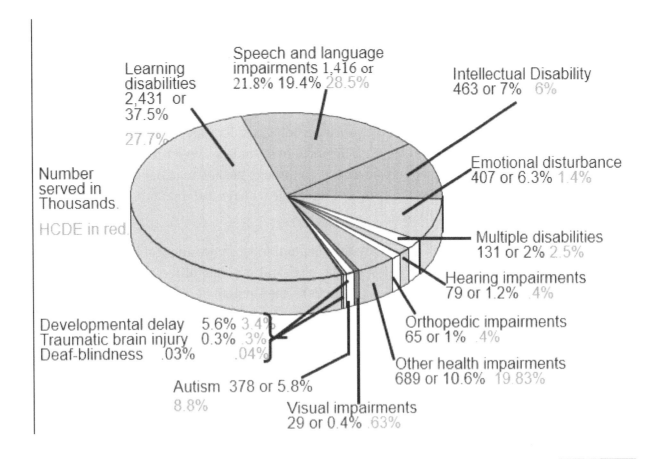

As you can see in this chart, the largest category nationally is specific learning disabilities, followed by speech and language disorders. In this section, I will give a brief overview of each category.

Learning Disabilities

The largest category, learning disabilities, includes a cluster of problems with learning. To be considered a learning disability, a child must present the following: a minimum IQ level, a significant difficulty in a school-related area, and the exclusion of other conditions. The main feature of learning disabilities is a discrepancy between ability and achievement, although not all discrepancies are a result of a disability. In other words, a child has the potential of performing academically at a certain level, but they are performing at a significantly lower level, and this gap between ability and performance is not due to another condition such as another disability or lack of motivation. Boys are classified with learning disabilities three times more than girls. This may in part be an actual reflection of sex difference, or it may be because boys who are struggling academically are more likely to engage in acting out behavior that "gets the noticed" whereas girls are taught by society to hide difficulties. Diagnosis of learning disabilities can be difficult because children may be embarrassed by their perceived difficulties and try to hide them.

The most common learning disability is dyslexia, a problem with learning to read. Dyslexia, sometimes called "reading disorder," is the most common learning disability; of all students with non-ADD/ADHD specific learning disabilities, 70%–80% have deficits in reading. The term "developmental dyslexia" is often used as a catchall term, but researchers assert that dyslexia is just one of several types of reading disabilities. A reading disability can affect any part of the reading process, including word recognition, word decoding, reading speed, prosody (oral reading with expression), and reading comprehension. Identical twin studies suggest that there is a genetic component. Subtle brain differences may be passed on through genetic material or through environmental influences. During reading, those with dyslexia have different brain wave patterns compared to those who do not have it.

The left side of the cerebral cortex, especially the temporal lobe, shows atypical functioning in children with dyslexia. Electrophysiological studies also confirm brain differences between these two groups. Studies of event-related potentials (ERPs) – the strength of the electrical impulses between neurons – reveals that above-average readers showed stronger ERPs, and the ERPs of strong readers were more concentrated in the left hemisphere. These finding indicate that left hemisphere dysfunction and reduced brain lateralization are related to reading problems.

Dyscalculia is a form of math-related disability that involves difficulties with learning math-related concepts (such as quantity, place value, and time), memorizing math-related facts, organizing numbers, and understanding how problems are organized on the page. Dyscalculics are often referred to as having poor "number sense."

Children who have motor skills substantially below what is expected for their age are diagnosed with **dyspraxia** – or developmental coordination disorder (DCD) as it is more formally known. They are not lazy, clumsy or unintelligent – in fact, their intellectual ability is in line with the general population – but they do struggle with everyday tasks that require coordination.

The term **dysgraphia** is often used as an overarching term for all disorders of written expression. Individuals with dysgraphia typically show multiple writing-related deficiencies, such as grammatical and punctuation errors within sentences, poor paragraph organization, multiple spelling errors, and excessively poor penmanship.[45]

Most children do not simply "outgrow" learning disabilities, but they may learn strategies to improve their academic achievement. Curriculum modifications may involve breaking tasks into smaller steps or allowing more time to finish schoolwork or exams.

ADD and AD/HD

The second large group in the learning disabilities category is children diagnosed with ADD or AD/HD. The terms "Attention Deficit Disorder" and "Attention Deficit / Hyperactivity Disorder" are often used interchangeably, but there is a distinction. In ADD, children consistently show "inattention" - difficulty in shifting and focusing attention on what they need to in order to succeed at a given task. In AD/HD, children consistently show inattention as well as hyperactivity and / or impulsivity. This involves ongoing inattention or hyperactivity-impulsivity in multiple settings. It is most commonly diagnosed after school entry.

The exact causes of ADD AD/HD are unknown; however, research has demonstrated that factors that many people associate with the development of ADD and AD/HD do not cause the disorder (including, minor head injuries, damage to the brain from complications during birth, food allergies, excess sugar intake, too much television, poor schools, or poor parenting). Research has found a number of significant risk factors affecting neurodevelopment and behavior expression. Events such as maternal alcohol and tobacco use that affect the development of the fetal brain can increase the risk for ADD and AD/HD. Injuries to the brain from environmental toxins such as lack of iron have also been implicated. There are many possible causes and heredity may play a role; there is evidence of a genetic linkage (runs in families). Neuroimaging studies show differences in the frontal lobe of the cerebral cortex. Other studies implicate subcortical brain structures such as the cerebellum.

For diagnosis, children undergo extensive evaluations. People with AD/HD show a persistent

---

pattern of inattention and/or hyperactivity–impulsivity that interferes with functioning or development:

Inattention: Six or more symptoms of inattention for children up to age 16, or five or more for adolescents 17 and older and adults; symptoms of inattention have been present for at least 6 months, and they are inappropriate for developmental level:
- Often fails to give close attention to details or makes careless mistakes in schoolwork, at work, or with other activities.
- Often has trouble holding attention on tasks or play activities.
- Often does not seem to listen when spoken to directly.
- Often does not follow through on instructions and fails to finish schoolwork, chores, or duties in the workplace (e.g., loses focus, side-tracked).
- Often has trouble organizing tasks and activities.
- Often avoids, dislikes, or is reluctant to do tasks that require mental effort over a long period of time (such as schoolwork or homework).
- Often loses things necessary for tasks and activities (e.g. school materials, pencils, books, tools, wallets, keys, paperwork, eyeglasses, mobile telephones).
- Is often easily distracted
- Is often forgetful in daily activities.

Hyperactivity and Impulsivity: Six or more symptoms of hyperactivity-impulsivity for children up to age 16, or five or more for adolescents 17 and older and adults; symptoms of hyperactivity-impulsivity have been present for at least 6 months to an extent that is disruptive and inappropriate for the person's developmental level:
- Often fidgets with or taps hands or feet, or squirms in seat.
- Often leaves seat in situations when remaining seated is expected.
- Often runs about or climbs in situations where it is not appropriate (adolescents or adults may be limited to feeling restless).
- Often unable to play or take part in leisure activities quietly.
- Is often "on the go" acting as if "driven by a motor".
- Often talks excessively.
- Often blurts out an answer before a question has been completed.
- Often has trouble waiting his/her turn.
- Often interrupts or intrudes on others (e.g., butts into conversations or games)

In addition, the following conditions must be met:
- Several inattentive or hyperactive-impulsive symptoms were present before age 12 years.

- Several symptoms are present in two or more settings, (such as at home, school or work; with friends or relatives; in other activities).

- There is clear evidence that the symptoms interfere with, or reduce the quality of, social, school, or work functioning.

- The symptoms are not better explained by another mental disorder (such as a mood disorder, anxiety disorder, dissociative disorder, or a personality disorder). The symptoms do not happen only during the course of schizophrenia or another psychotic disorder.

Based on the types of symptoms, three kinds (presentations) of ADD and AD/HD can occur:

- **Combined Presentation**: if enough symptoms of both criteria inattention and hyperactivity-impulsivity were present for the past 6 months

- **Predominantly Inattentive Presentation**: (ADD) if enough symptoms of inattention, but not hyperactivity-impulsivity, were present for the past six months

- **Predominantly Hyperactive-Impulsive Presentation**: if enough symptoms of hyperactivity-impulsivity, but not inattention, were present for the past six months.

Because symptoms can change over time, the presentation may change over time as well.[46]

The diagnosis of ADD and AD/HD can be made reliably using well-tested diagnostic interview methods. However, as of yet, there is no independent valid test for ADD or AD/HD. Among children, ADD and AD/HD frequently occurs along with other learning, behavior, or mood problems such as learning disabilities, oppositional defiant disorder, anxiety disorders, and depression.

A variety of medications and behavioral interventions are used to treat AD/HD. The most widely used medications are methylphenidate (Ritalin), D-amphetamine, and other amphetamines. These drugs are stimulants that affect the level of the neurotransmitter dopamine at the synapse. Nine out of 10 children improve while taking one of these drugs. It may sound strange that drugs that are stimulants are prescribed to children who have difficulty focusing their attention and have hyperactive behavior. The stimulant medications work because they stimulate the areas in the frontal lobe of the brain that are associated with self-control. The neurotransmitter dopamine is

---

[46] Symptoms and Diagnosis of ADHD by the CDC is in the public domain

vital in self-control functions of the frontal lobe. In this way, the stimulant allows the individual to have better self-control.

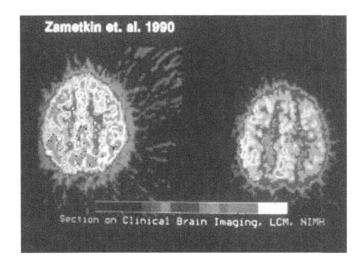

Figure: Brain scans of brains with (on the right side) and without (on the left side) AD/HD.[47]

The use of stimulant drugs, which may reduce symptoms by increasing inhibitory control of the frontal regions of the cerebral cortex, is controversial. Critics state a concern that the drugs are too widely prescribed. No "cure" exists; most individuals will continue to have symptoms all their lives. The most effective treatment appears to be a combination of stimulant medication, counseling or therapy, and a behavior management plan at school. In addition to the well-established treatments described above, some parents and therapists have tried a variety of nutritional interventions to treat ADD and AD/HD. A few studies have found that some children benefit from such treatments. Nevertheless, no well-established nutritional interventions have consistently been shown to be effective for treating ADD or AD/HD.[48]

<u>Sensory Disorders</u>
Sensory processing (sometimes called "sensory integration" or SI) is a term that refers to the way the nervous system receives messages from the senses and turns them into appropriate motor and behavioral responses. Whether you are biting into a hamburger, riding a bicycle, or reading a book, your successful completion of the activity requires processing sensation or "sensory integration." Sensory Processing Disorder (SPD, formerly known as "sensory integration dysfunction") is a condition that exists when sensory signals don't get organized into appropriate responses. A person with SPD finds it difficult to process and act upon information received through the senses,

---

[47] <u>Image</u> by the <u>National Institutes of Health</u> is in the public domain

[48] <u>Disease Prevention and Healthy Lifestyles</u> by Judy Baker, Ph.D. is licensed under <u>CC BY-SA</u>

which creates challenges in performing countless everyday tasks. Motor clumsiness, behavioral problems, anxiety, depression, school failure, and other impacts may result if the disorder is not treated effectively.

Speech and Language Disorders

In addition to learning disabilities, another large category of children who receive special education services is speech and language disorders. "Speech" disorders involve difficulties in producing spoken language; "Language" disorders are difficulties in understanding and processing the meaning of language. An early appearing speech disorder is alalia, a speech delay when child does not make typical attempts to verbally communicate.

Aphasia

A loss of the ability to produce spoken language is referred to as **aphasia**. Without the brain, there would be no language. The human brain has a few areas that are specific to language processing and production. When these areas are damaged or injured, capabilities for speaking can be lost, a disorder known as aphasia. These areas must function together in order for a person to develop, use, and understand language. For example, a stroke can result in Aphasia. In apraxia of speech an individual "knows" what they want to say, but can not due to disruption of neural pathways between speech centers in brain and speech muscles (e.g., following stroke or head injury).

Articulation disorder

An articulation disorder refers to the inability to correctly produce speech sounds (phonemes) because of imprecise placement, timing, pressure, speed, or flow of movement of the lips, tongue, or throat (NIDCD, 2016). These are problems problems pronouncing sounds correctly. Sounds can be substituted, left off, added or changed. These errors may make it hard for people to understand the speaker. They can range from problems with specific sounds, such as lisping to severe impairment in the phonological system. Most children have problems pronouncing words early on while their speech is developing. However, by age three, at least half of what a child says should be understood by a stranger. By age five, a child's speech should be mostly intelligible. Parents should seek help if by age six the child is still having trouble producing certain sounds. It should be noted that accents are not articulation disorders (Medline Plus, 2016a).

Fluency disorders

Fluency disorders affect the rate of speech. Speech may be labored and slow, or too fast for listeners to follow. The most common fluency disorder is stuttering.

Stuttering is a speech disorder in which sounds, syllables, or words are repeated or last longer than normal. These problems cause a break in the flow of speech, which is called dysfluency (Medline Plus, 2016b). About 5% of young children, aged two-five, will develop some stuttering that may last from several weeks to several years (Medline Plus, 2016c). Approximately 75% of children recover from stuttering. For the remaining 25%, stuttering can persist as a lifelong communication disorder (National Institute on Deafness and other Communication Disorders, NIDCD, 2016). This is called developmental stuttering and is the most common form of stuttering.

Brain injury, and in very rare instances, emotional trauma may be other triggers for developing problems with stuttering. In most cases of developmental stuttering, other family members share the same communication disorder. Researchers have recently identified variants in four genes that are more commonly found in those who stutter (NIDCD, 2016).

Voice disorders

Disorders of the voice involve problems with pitch, loudness, and quality of the voice (American Speech-Language and Hearing Association, 2016). For example, the child's voice may be too hoarse, too harsh, too loud, too high- or low-pitched for the speech to be understood by others. It only becomes a disorder when problems with the voice make the child unintelligible. In children, voice disorders are significantly more prevalent in males than in females. Between 1.4% and 6% of children experience problems with the quality of their voice. Causes can be due to structural abnormalities in the vocal cords and/or larynx, functional factors, such as vocal fatigue from overuse, and in rarer cases psychological factors, such as chronic stress and anxiety.[49]

Language integration disorder and language processing disorder

Language integration disorder is a receptive speech difficulty, meaning it is a problem with understanding language. The child has a typical level of hearing, but their brain struggles to decode words. Language processing refers to the ability to attach meaning to auditory information and formulate an expressive response. It is an extremely important skill that affects many areas of a child's life, so it is critical that it be correctly identified and effectively addressed.

Symptoms of a language processing disorder might include behaviors such as:
• Using generic language instead of a specific word (e.g. saying "the thing" instead of "the notebook")
• Taking a long time to respond to a question
• Experiencing difficulty following long or complicated directions
• Naming a general category instead of a specific word (e.g. saying "food" instead of "cake")
• Using descriptions instead of the intended word (e.g. saying "the yellow thing for writing" instead of "pencil")
• Being quick to say "I don't know" in response to a question
• Having difficulty understanding humor or idioms

---

[49] Lifespan Development: A Psychological Perspective by Martha Lally and Suzanne Valentine-French is licensed under CC BY-NC-SA 3.0

• Feeling lost when listening to stories with lots of events and characters

Auditory Processing Disorder

A processing deficit in the auditory modality that spans multiple processes is **auditory processing disorder** (APD). To date, APD diagnosis is mostly based on the utilization of speech material. Unfortunately, acceptable non-speech tests that allow differentiation between an actual central hearing disorder and related disorders such as specific language impairments are still not adequately available.

Audio Processing Disorder and Language Processing Disorder are similar. APD is an auditory disorder that is not the result of higher-order, more global deficit such as autism, intellectual disability, attention deficits, or similar impairments. Children with APD usually have at least some of the following symptoms:

.Find it hard to follow spoken directions, especially multi-step instructions

.Ask speakers to repeat what they've said, or saying, "huh?" or "what?"

.Be easily distracted, especially by background noise or loud and sudden noises

.Have trouble with reading and spelling, which require the ability to process and interpret sounds

.Struggle with oral (word) math problems

.Find it hard to follow conversations

.Have poor musical ability

.Find it hard to learn songs or nursery rhymes

.Have trouble remembering details of what was read or heard

Visual impairments

Another category of disabilities involves visual impairments. Low vision is visual acuity between 20/70 and 20/200. The term educationally blind means that one is unable to use one's vision in learning. The most common visual impairment is *myopia* (nearsightedness), and less common is *hyperopia* (farsightedness). *Strabismus,* eyes not properly aligned with each other, also occurs in children. Children born preterm are most at risk for visual problems

Hearing Impairments

Hearing impairments form another category of special education. Some hearing loss occurs in about 15% of children. A child is considered to have a hearing impairment in the educational sense when they can not use their hearing for learning. There is debate among experts in the best approach for children with hearing impairments. Some favor *oral approaches* that include lip reading, speech reading, and any hearing the child has. Others favor *manual approaches* based upon the use of sign language and finger spelling.

Orthopedic impairments

Orthopedic impairments result from restrictions in movement abilities due to muscle, bone, or joint problems. One type of orthopedic impairment is cerebral palsy. Cerebral palsy is characterized by a lack of muscular coordination, shaking, or unclear speech. There is a range in the severity of these symptoms and the impact of cerebral palsy. The most common type of cerebral palsy is called "spastic." The muscles of people with spastic cerebral palsy feel stiff and their movements may look stiff and jerky. Spasticity is a form of hypertonia, or increased muscle tone. This results in stiff muscles which can make movement difficult or even impossible. Spastic cerebral palsy is characterized by jerky movements, muscle tightness and joint stiffness. Cerebral palsy is Caused by a lack of oxygen before, during, or after birth (this is called Anoxia). This condition prevents the normal development of motor function.

Emotional Disorders

Emotional disorders are serious, persistent problems involving:

.Relationships

.Aggression

.Depression

.Fears related to personal or school matters

.Other inappropriate socioemotional issues

These are considered an Emotional Disorder when anxiety disrupts the child's ability to learn. The following sections will discuss some specific diagnosis that may be included in this category if they impact the child's school performance.

Anxiety

Many children have fears and worries, and will feel sad and hopeless from time to time. Strong fears will appear at different times during development. For example, toddlers are often very distressed about being away from their parents, even if they are safe and cared for. Although fears and worries are typical in children, persistent or extreme forms of fear and sadness feelings could be due to anxiety or depression. Because the symptoms primarily involve thoughts and feelings, they are called **internalizing disorders**.

When children do not outgrow the fears and worries that are typical in young children, or when there are so many fears and worries that interfere with school, home, or play activities, the child may be diagnosed with an anxiety disorder. Examples of different types of anxiety disorders include:

- Being very afraid when away from parents (separation anxiety)

- Having extreme fear about a specific thing or situation, such as dogs, insects, or going to the doctor (phobias)

- Being very afraid of school and other places where there are people (social anxiety)

- Being very worried about the future and about bad things happening (general anxiety)

- Having repeated episodes of sudden, unexpected, intense fear that come with symptoms like heart pounding, having trouble breathing, or feeling dizzy, shaky, or sweaty (panic disorder)

Anxiety may present as fear or worry, but can also make children irritable and angry. Anxiety symptoms can also include trouble sleeping, as well as physical symptoms like fatigue, headaches, or stomachaches. Some anxious children keep their worries to themselves and, thus, the symptoms can be missed.

Related conditions include Phobias, Obsessive-Compulsive Disorder and Post Traumatic Stress Disorder. Some other childhood anxiety related disorders include:

Generalized Anxiety Disorder – excessive worry
Panic Disorder – child suffers at least two panic or anxiety attacks, followed by at least one month of concern over having another
Social anxiety disorder – social phobia, intense fear of social interaction situations
Selective mutism (may also be classified as language disorder) child refuses to speak
PANDAS (Pediatric Autoimmune Neurological Disorder, Associated with Strep)– autoimmune response to certain types of Strep bacteria results in abrupt, dramatic onset of obsessive compulsive disorder, severely restricted food intake, anxiety, aggressive and / or oppositional behaviors, behavioral regression

Phobias
Specific Phobia is an intense irrational fear of a specific stimulus (including school phobia and agoraphobia, fear of leaving home). When a child who has a **phobia** (an extreme or irrational fear of or aversion to something) is exposed to the phobic stimulus (the stimuli varies), it almost invariably provokes an immediate anxiety response, which may take the form of a situational bound or situational predisposed panic attack. Children can show effects and characteristics when it comes to specific phobias. The effects of anxiety show up by crying, throwing tantrums, experiencing freezing, or clinging to the parent that they have the most connection with.

Post-Traumatic Stress Syndrome (PTSD)
Post-Traumatic Stress Disorder is an intense fear and anxiety after traumatic event. Exposure to traumatic events can have major developmental influences on children. While the majority of

children will not develop PTSD after a trauma, best estimates from the literature are that around a third of them will, higher than adult estimates. Some reasons for this could include more limited knowledge about the world, differential coping mechanisms employed, and the fact that children's reactions to trauma are often highly influenced by how their parents and caregivers react.

The impact of PTSD on children weeks after a trauma, show that up to 90% of children may experience heightened physiological arousal, diffuse anxiety, survivor guilt, and emotional liability. These are all normal reactions and should be understood as such (similar things are seen in adults. Those children still having these symptoms three or four months after a disaster, however, may be in need of further assessment, particularly if they show the following symptoms as well. For older children, warning signs of problematic adjustment include: repetitious play reenacting a part of the disaster; preoccupation with danger or expressed concerns about safety; sleep disturbances and irritability; anger outbursts or aggressiveness; excessive worry about family or friends; school avoidance, particularly involving somatic complaints; behaviors characteristic of younger children; and changes in personality, withdrawal, and loss of interest in activities.[50]

Obsessive Compulsive Disorder (OCD)

Although a diagnosis of OCD requires only that a person either has obsessions or compulsions, not both, approximately 96% of people experience both. For almost all people with OCD, being exposed to a certain stimuli (internal or external) will then trigger an upsetting or anxiety-causing obsession, which can only be relieved by doing a compulsion. For example, a person touches a doorknob in a public building, which causes an obsessive thought that they will get sick from the germs, which can only be relieved by compulsively washing their hands to an excessive degree. Some of the most common obsessions include unwanted thoughts of harming loved ones, persistent doubts that one has not locked doors or switched off electrical appliances, intrusive thoughts of being contaminated, and morally or sexually repugnant.[51]

Depression

Occasionally being sad or feeling hopeless is a part of every child's life. However, some children feel sad or uninterested in things that they used to enjoy, or feel helpless or hopeless in situations where they could do something to address the situations. When children feel persistent sadness and hopelessness, they may be diagnosed with depression.

We now know that youth who have depression may show signs that are slightly different from the typical adult symptoms of depression. Children who are depressed may complain of feeling sick, refuse to go to school, cling to a parent or caregiver, feel unloved, hopelessness about the future, or

---

[50] Abnormal Psychology by Lumen Learning references Abnormal Psychology: An e-text! by Dr. Caleb Lack, licensed under CC BY-NC-SA

[51] Disease Prevention and Healthy Lifestyles by Judy Baker, Ph.D. is licensed under CC BY-SA

worry excessively that a parent may die. Older children and teens may sulk, get into trouble at school, be negative or grouchy, are irritable, indecisive, have trouble concentrating, or feel misunderstood. Because normal behaviors vary from one childhood stage to another, it can be difficult to tell whether a child who shows changes in behavior is just going through a temporary "phase" or is suffering from depression.

With medication, psychotherapy, or combined treatment, most youth with depression can be effectively treated. Youth are more likely to respond to treatment if they receive it early in the course of their illness.

Autism Spectrum Disorder

Sometimes children's brains work differently. One form of this neurodiversity is **Autism spectrum disorder.** Individuals on the spectrum exhibit problems with:

- Personal interactions
- Verbal and nonverbal communication
- Repetitive behaviors
- May show atypical sensory responses

Autism spectrum disorder (ASD) is a developmental disorder that affects communication and behavior. Although autism can be diagnosed at any age, it is said to be a "developmental disorder" because symptoms generally appear in the first two years of life.

Autism spectrum disorder (ASD) describes a range of conditions classified as neuro-developmental disorders in the fifth revision of the American Psychiatric Association's Diagnostic and Statistical Manual of Mental Disorders (DSM-5). The DSM-5 revised the diagnosis of Autism Spectrum Disorder in May of 2013. The DSM-5 redefined the autism spectrum to encompass the previous (DSM-IV-TR) diagnoses of autism, Asperger syndrome, pervasive developmental disorder not otherwise specified (PDD-NOS), and childhood disintegrative disorder. Each of these disorders were characterized by social deficits and communication difficulties, repetitive behaviors and interests, sensory issues, and in some cases, cognitive delays. In the current definition of ASD, there are two domains where people with ASD must show persistent deficits. They include 1) persistent social communication and social interaction, and 2) restricted and repetitive patterns of behavior. If individual meets both criteria, then level of severity is indexed from 1-3.

Asperger syndrome was distinguished from autism in the earlier DSM-IV by the lack of delay or deviance in early language development. Additionally, individuals diagnosed with Asperger syndrome did not have significant cognitive delays. PDD-NOS was considered "subthreshold autism" and "atypical autism" because it was often characterized by milder symptoms of autism or symptoms in only one domain (such as social difficulties). In the DSM-5, both of these diagnoses have been subsumed into autism spectrum disorder.

Autism spectrum disorders are considered to be on a spectrum because each individual with ASD expresses the disorder uniquely and has varying degrees of functionality. Many have above-average intellectual abilities and excel in visual skills, music, math, and the arts, while others have significant disabilities and are unable to live independently. About 25 percent of individuals with ASD are nonverbal; however, they may learn to communicate using other means.

According to the *Diagnostic and Statistical Manual of Mental Disorders* (*DSM-5*), a guide created by the American Psychiatric Association used to diagnose mental disorders, people with ASD have:

- Difficulty with communication and interaction with other people

- Restricted interests and repetitive behaviors

- Symptoms that hurt the person's ability to function properly in school, work, and other areas of life

Autism is known as a "spectrum" disorder because there is wide variation in the type and severity of symptoms people experience. ASD occurs in all ethnic, racial, and economic groups. Although ASD can be a lifelong disorder, treatments and services can improve a person's symptoms and ability to function. The American Academy of Pediatrics recommends that all children be screened for autism.

As mentioned above, in 2013 a revised version of the *Diagnostic and Statistical Manual of Mental Disorders (DSM)* was released. This revision changed the way autism is classified and diagnosed. Using the previous version of the *DSM*, people could be diagnosed with one of several separate conditions:

- Autistic disorder

- Asperger's' syndrome

- Pervasive developmental disorder not otherwise specified (PDD-NOS)

In the current revised version of the *DSM* (the *DSM-5*), these separate conditions have been combined into one diagnosis called "autism spectrum disorder." Using the *DSM-5*, for example, people who were previously diagnosed as having Asperger's syndrome would now be diagnosed as having autism spectrum disorder. Although the "official" diagnosis of ASD has changed, there is nothing wrong with continuing to use terms such as Asperger's syndrome to describe oneself or to identify with a peer group. You will often still here individual's refer to themselves as "Aspies" or say that they "have" Asperger's syndrome. This may be because they were diagnosed before the change in the DSM, or it may be because they recognize that it is a way to communicate to others about their behavior.

Signs and Symptoms of ASD

People with ASD have difficulty with social communication and interaction, restricted interests, and repetitive behaviors. The list below gives some examples of the types of behaviors that are seen in people diagnosed with ASD. Not all people with ASD will show all behaviors, but most will show several.

Social Communication Symptoms

Social impairments in children with autism can be characterized by a distinctive lack of intuition about others. Unusual social development becomes apparent early in childhood. Infants with ASD show less attention to social stimuli, smile and look at others less often, and respond less to their own name. Toddlers with ASD differ more strikingly from social norms; for example, they may show less eye contact and turn-taking and may not have the ability to use simple movements to express themselves. Individuals with severe forms of ASD do not develop enough natural speech to meet their daily communication needs.

Social communication / interaction behaviors may include:

- Making little or inconsistent eye contact

- Tending not to look at or listen to people

- Rarely sharing enjoyment of objects or activities by pointing or showing things to others

- Failing to, or being slow to, respond to someone calling their name or to other verbal attempts to gain attention

- Having difficulties with the back and forth of conversation

- Often talking at length about a favorite subject without noticing that others are not interested or without giving others a chance to respond

- Having facial expressions, movements, and gestures that do not match what is being said

- Having an unusual tone of voice that may sound sing-song or flat and robot-like

- Having trouble understanding another person's point of view or being unable to predict or understand other people's actions

Restricted and Repetitive Behaviors

Children with ASD may exhibit repetitive or restricted behavior, including:

- Stereotypy—repetitive movement, such as hand flapping, head rolling, or body rocking.

- Compulsive behavior—exhibiting intention to follow rules, such as arranging objects in stacks or lines.

- Sameness—resistance to change; for example, insisting that the furniture not be moved or sticking to an unvarying pattern of daily activities.

- Restricted behavior—limits in focus, interest, or activity, such as preoccupation with a single television program, toy, or game.

- Self-injury—movements that injure or can injure the person, such as eye poking, skin picking, hand biting, and head banging.

- Restrictive / repetitive behaviors may include:

- Repeating certain behaviors or having unusual behaviors. For example, repeating words or phrases, a behavior called *echolalia*

- Having a lasting intense interest in certain topics, such as numbers, details, or facts

- Having overly focused interests, such as with moving objects or parts of objects

- Getting upset by slight changes in a routine

- Being more or less sensitive than other people to sensory input, such as light, noise, clothing, or temperature

People with ASD may also experience sleep problems and irritability. Although people with ASD experience many challenges, they may also have many strengths, including:

- Being able to learn things in detail and remember information for long periods of time

- Being strong visual and auditory learners

- Excelling in math, science, music, or art

Causes and Risk Factors of ASD

While scientists don't know the exact causes of ASD, research suggests that genes can act together with influences from the environment to affect development in ways that lead to ASD. Although scientists are still trying to understand why some people develop ASD and others don't, some risk factors include:

- Having a sibling with ASD

- Having older parents

- Having certain genetic conditions—people with conditions such as Down syndrome, fragile X syndrome, and Rett syndrome are more likely than others to have ASD

- Very low birth weight

While specific causes of ASD have yet to be found, many risk factors have been identified in the research literature that may contribute to its development. These risk factors include genetics, prenatal and perinatal factors, neuroanatomical abnormalities, and environmental factors. It is possible to identify general risk factors, but much more difficult to pinpoint specific factors.

ASD affects information processing in the brain by altering how nerve cells and their synapses connect and organize; thus, it is categorized as a neuro-developmental disorder. The results of family and twin studies suggest that genetic factors play a role in the etiology of ASD and other pervasive developmental disorders. Studies have consistently found that the prevalence of ASD in siblings of children with ASD is approximately 15 to 30 times greater than the rate in the general population. In addition, research suggests that there is a much higher concordance rate among monozygotic (identical) twins compared to dizygotic (fraternal) twins. It appears that there is no single gene that can account for ASD; instead, there seem to be multiple genes involved, each of which is a risk factor for part of the autism syndrome through various groups. It is unclear whether ASD is explained more by rare mutations or by combinations of common genetic variants.

A number of prenatal and perinatal complications have been reported as possible risk factors for ASD. These risk factors include maternal gestational diabetes, maternal and paternal age over 30, bleeding after first trimester, use of prescription medication (such as valproate) during pregnancy, and meconium (the earliest stool of an infant) in the amniotic fluid. While research is not conclusive on the relation of these factors to ASD, each of these factors has been identified more frequently in children with ASD than in developing youth without ASD.

Evidence for environmental causes is anecdotal and has not been confirmed by reliable studies. In the last few decades, controversy surrounded the idea that vaccinations may be the cause for many cases of autism; however, these theories lack scientific evidence and are biologically implausible. Even still, parental concern about a potential vaccine link with autism has led to lower rates of childhood immunizations, outbreaks of previously controlled childhood diseases in some countries, and the preventable deaths of several children.

There is no known cure for ASD, and treatment tends to focus on management of symptoms. The main goals when treating children with ASD are to lessen associated deficits and family distress and to increase quality of life and functional independence.[52] Treatment for ASD should begin as soon as possible after diagnosis. Early treatment for ASD is important as proper care can reduce individuals' difficulties while helping them learn new skills and make the most of their strengths.

Treatment for ASD should begin as soon as possible after diagnosis. Early treatment for ASD is important as proper care can reduce individuals' difficulties while helping them learn new skills and make the most of their strengths.

The wide range of issues facing people with ASD means that there is no single best treatment for ASD. So treatment is typically tailored to the individual person's needs. Working closely with a doctor or health care professional is an important part of finding the right treatment program. Intensive, sustained special-education programs and behavior therapy yearly in life can help children acquire self-care, social, and job skills. The most widely used therapy **is applied behavior analysis** (ABA); other available approaches include developmental models, structured teaching, speech and language therapy, social skills therapy, and occupational therapy.[53]

There has been increasing attention to the development of evidenced-based interventions for young children with ASD. Although evidence-based interventions for children with ASD vary in their methods, many adopt a psychoeducational approach to enhancing cognitive, communication, and social skills while minimizing behaviors that are thought to be problematic.

A doctor may use medication to treat some symptoms that are common with ASD. With medication, a person with ASD may have fewer problems with:

- Irritability
- Aggression
- Repetitive behavior
- Hyperactivity

[52] Children's Development by Ana R. Leon is licensed under CC BY 4.0

[53] Children's Development by Ana R. Leon is licensed under CC BY 4.0

- Attention problems

- Anxiety and depression

People with ASD may be referred to doctors who specialize in providing behavioral, psychological, educational, or skill-building interventions. These programs are typically highly structured and intensive and may involve parents, siblings, and other family members. Programs may help people with ASD:

- Learn life-skills necessary to live independently

- Reduce challenging behaviors

- Increase or build upon strengths

- Learn social, communication, and language skills[54]

Pervasive Developmental Disorder (PDD) or PPD (NOS) Not Otherwise Specified PDD –NOS
Pervasive developmental disorder (PDD) is a term used to refer to difficulties in socialization and delays in developing communicative skills. This is usually recognized before 3 years of age. A child with PDD may interact in unusual ways with toys, people, or situations, and may engage in repetitive movement. PDD is diagnosed and treatment is similar to ADHA and ASD. In 2013 the DSM- 5 discontinued using this as a diagnosis, however it is still used informally.[55]

Intellectual Disability
Intellectual Disability is a condition of limited mental ability in which an individual has a low IQ (usually below 70), AND difficulty in adaptive behavior (daily living skills). In addition to these two criteria, a diagnosis of intellectual disability must be made during childhood. About 5 million people in US fit this definition.

Down Syndrome
Sometimes called Trisomy 21, Down Syndrome occurs when extra chromosomal material on the 21st pair of chromosomes results in intellectual disability and physical differences. All children with the most typical form of Down Syndrome have intellectual disability, but the severity ranges from mild to profound. Children with Down Syndrome may or may not have other physical differences, including:
- Hypertonia - looser muscles and joints which may make the body seem "floppy"
- Lower muscle tone

---

[54] Autism Spectrum Disorder by the NIH is in the public domain

[55] Lifespan Development: A Psychological Perspective by Martha Lally and Suzanne Valentine-French is licensed under CC BY-NC-SA 3.0

- Heart difficulties
- Intestinal difficulties
- A rather flat face with a flattened bridge in the nose
- Eyes that tend to slant upwards and outwords
- Epicanthic folds - folds of skin between the lids in the corner of the eyes.

Socially and academically, children with Down Syndrome show the most progress when fully included in groups that contain "typically" developing peers, such as inclusive classrooms.

Down Syndrome Fact Sheet[56]

• Down syndrome occurs when an individual has a full or partial extra copy of chromosome 21. This additional genetic material alters the course of development and causes the characteristics associated with Down syndrome.

• There are three types of Down syndrome: trisomy 21 (nondisjunction) accounts for 95% of cases, translocation accounts for about 4%, and mosaicism accounts for about 1%.

• Down syndrome is the most commonly occurring chromosomal condition. Approximately one in every 700 babies in the United States is born with Down syndrome – about 6,000 each year.

• Down syndrome occurs in people of all races and economic levels.

• The incidence of births of children with Down syndrome increases with the age of the mother. But due to higher fertility rates in younger women, 80% of children with Down syndrome are born to women under 35 years of age.

• People with Down syndrome have an increased risk for certain medical conditions such as congenital heart defects, respiratory and hearing problems, Alzheimer's disease, childhood leukemia and thyroid conditions. Many of these conditions are now treatable, so most people with Down syndrome lead healthy lives.

• A few of the common physical traits of Down syndrome are: low muscle tone, small stature, an upward slant to the eyes, and a single deep crease across the center of the palm. Every person with Down syndrome is a unique individual and may possess these characteristics to different degrees or not at all.

• Life expectancy for people with Down syndrome has increased dramatically in recent decades – from 25 in 1983 to 60 today.

---

[56] Down Syndrome Fact Sheet by the National Down Syndrome Society is in the public domain.

• People with Down syndrome attend school, work, participate in decisions that affect them, have meaningful relationships, vote and contribute to society in many wonderful ways.

• All people with Down syndrome experience cognitive delays, but the effect is usually mild to moderate and is not indicative of the many strengths and talents that each individual possesses.

• Quality educational programs, a stimulating home environment, good health care and positive support from family, friends and the community enable people with Down syndrome to lead fulfilling and productive lives.

People with Down syndrome should always be referred to as people first.

• Instead of "a Down syndrome child," it should be "a child with Down syndrome." Also avoid "Down's child" and describing the condition as "Down's," as in, "He has Down's."

• Down syndrome is a condition or a syndrome, not a disease.

• People "have" Down syndrome, they do not "suffer from" it and are not "afflicted by" it.

• "Typically developing" or "typical" is preferred over "normal."

• "Intellectual disability" or "cognitive disability" has replaced "mental retardation" as the appropriate term

• NDSS strongly condemns the use of the word "retarded" in any derogatory context. Using this word is hurtful and suggests that people with disabilities are not competent.

Down vs. Down's

• NDSS uses the preferred spelling, Down syndrome, rather than Down's syndrome.

• Down syndrome is named for the English physician John Langdon Down, who characterized the condition, but did not have it. An "apostrophe s" connotes ownership or possession.

• While Down syndrome is listed in many dictionaries with both popular spellings (with or without an apostrophe s), the preferred usage in the United States is Down syndrome. The AP Stylebook recommends using "Down syndrome," as well.

Childhood Stress

Take a moment to think about how you deal with and how stress affects you. Now think about what the impact of stress may have on a child and their development?

Of course children experience stress and different types of stressors differently. Not all stress is bad. Normal, everyday stress can provide an opportunity for young children to build coping skills and poses little risk to development. Even more long-lasting stressful events such as changing schools or losing a loved one can be managed fairly well. But children who experience toxic stress or who live in extremely stressful situations of abuse over long periods of time can suffer long-lasting effects. The structures in the midbrain or limbic system such as the hippocampus and amygdala can be vulnerable to prolonged stress during early childhood (Middlebrooks and Audage, 2008). High levels of the stress hormone cortisol can reduce the size of the hippocampus and effect the child's memory abilities. Stress hormones can also reduce immunity to disease. If the brain is exposed to long periods of severe stress it can develop a low threshold making the child hypersensitive to stress in the future. Whatever the effects of stress, it can be minimized if a child learns to deal with stressors and develop coping strategies with the support of caring adults. It's easy to know when your child has a fever or other physical symptoms. However, a child's mental health problems may be harder to identify. [57]

Childhood Mental Health

Mental health problems can disrupt daily life at home, at school or in the community. Without help, mental health problems can lead to school failure, alcohol or other drug abuse, family discord, violence or even suicide. However, help is available. Talk to your health care provider if you have concerns about your child's behavior.

Mental health disorders are diagnosed by a qualified professional using the Diagnostic and Statistical Manual of Mental Disorders (DSM). This is a manual that is used as a standard across the profession for diagnosing and treating mental disorders.[58]

When You Have a Concern About a Child. What's in a Label?[59]

Children are continually evaluated as they enter and progress through school. If a child is showing a need, they should be assessed by a qualified professional who would make a recommendation or diagnosis of the child and give the type of instruction, resources, accommodations, and support that they should receive.

Ideally, a proper diagnosis or label is extremely beneficial for children who have educational,

---

[57] Lifespan Development - Module 5: Early Childhood by Lumen Learning references Psyc 200 Lifespan Psychology by Laura Overstreet, licensed under CC BY 4.0 (modified by Dawn Rymond)

[58] Disease Prevention and Healthy Lifestyles by Judy Baker, Ph.D. is licensed under CC BY-SA (modified by Dawn Rymond)

[59] Disease Prevention and Healthy Lifestyles by Judy Baker, Ph.D. is licensed under CC BY-SA (modified by Dawn Rymond)

When You Have a Concern About a Child. What's in a Label?

social, emotional, or developmental needs. Once their difficulty, disorder, or disability is labeled then the child will receive the help they need from parents, educators and any other professionals who will work as a team to meet the student's individual goals and needs.

However, it's important to consider that children that are labeled without proper support and accommodations or worse they may be misdiagnosed will have negative consequences. A label can also influence the child's self-concept, for example, if a child is misdiagnosed as having a learning disability; the child, teachers, and family member interpret their actions through the lens of that label. Labels are powerful and can be good for the child or they can go detrimental for their development all depending on the accuracy of the label and if they are accurately applied.

A team of people who include parents, teachers, and any other support staff will look at the child's evaluation assessment in a process called an Individual Education Plan (IEP). The team will discuss the diagnosis, recommendations, and the accommodations or help and a decisions will be made regarding what is the best for the child. This is time when parents or caregivers decide if they would like to follow this plan or they can dispute any part of the process. During an IEP, the team is able to voice concerns and questions. Most parents feel empowered when they leave these meetings. They feel as if they are a part of the team and that they know what, when, why, and how their child will be helped.

Children need time outdoors. Time outdoors is associated with lowered levels of the hormone cortisol, which is the biological indicator of stress. ,

6 PHYSICAL GROWTH AND HEALTH

Learning Objectives At the completion of this module, students will be able to:	Related Course Objective
6-1 Describe how the brain develops from infancy through early adolescence	1, 4
6-2 Describe physical growth from infancy to early adolescence.	1, 4
6-3 Describe three health challenges today's children face—sleep, obesity and other eating disorders, and substance use and exposure—and what you can do to address these challenges.	9
6-4 Describe health and safety issues that impact children.	1,4

Characteristics of Newborns

The average newborn in the United States weighs about 7.5 pounds and is about 20 inches in length. For the first few days of life, infants typically lose about 5 percent of their body weight as they eliminate waste and get used to feeding. This often goes unnoticed by most parents, but can be cause for concern for those who have a smaller infant. This weight loss is temporary, however, and is followed by a rapid period of growth.

By the time an infant is 4 months old, it usually doubles in weight and by one year has tripled its birth weight. By age 2, the weight has quadrupled. The average length at one year is about 26-32 inches.[60]

Two hormones are very important to this growth process. The first is Human Growth Hormone

---

[60] Lifespan Development - Module 4: Infancy by Lumen Learning references Psyc 200 Lifespan Psychology by Laura Overstreet, licensed under CC BY 4.0

(HGH) which influences all growth except that in the Central Nervous System (CNS). The hormone influencing growth in the CNS is called Thyroid Stimulating Hormone. Together these hormones influence the growth in early childhood.

Body Proportions

The head initially makes up about 50 percent of our entire length when we are developing in the womb. At birth, the head makes up about 25 percent of our length (think about how much of your length would be head if the proportions were still the same!).

By age 2.5 it comprises about 20 percent of our length. Imagine now how difficult it must be to raise one's head during the first year of life! And indeed, if you have ever seen a 2 to 4 month old infant lying on the stomach trying to raise the head, you know how much of a challenge this is.

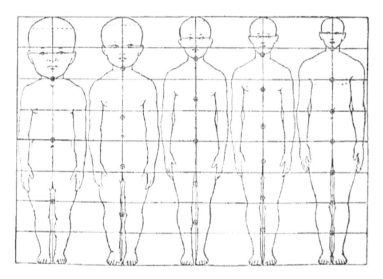

Body proportions from infancy to adulthood.[61]

Growth in Early Childhood

Children between the ages of 2 and 6 years tend to grow about 3 inches in height each year and gain about 4 to 5 pounds in weight each year. The 3 year old is very similar to a toddler with a large head, large stomach, short arms and legs. But by the time the child reaches age 6, the torso has lengthened and body proportions have become more like those of adults. The average 6 year old weighs approximately 46 pounds and is about 46 inches in height. This growth rate is slower than that of infancy.

Physical Growth in Middle Childhood

Middle childhood spans the years between early childhood and adolescence, children are approximately 6 to 11 or 12 years old. These children come in all shapes and sizes: height, weight,

---

[61]   Image is in the public domain

abilities, and disabilities. Physical growth rates are generally slow and steady during these years. However, growth spurts do occur during middle to late childhood (Spreen, Riser, & Edgell, 1995). Typically, a child will gain about 5-7 pounds a year and grow about 2 inches per year. They also tend to slim down and gain muscle strength. As bones lengthen and broaden and muscles strengthen, many children want to engage in strenuous physical activity and can participate for longer periods of time. In addition, the rate of growth for the extremities is faster than for the trunk, which results in more adult-like proportions. Long-bone growth stretches muscles and ligaments, which results in many children experiencing growing pains, at night, in particular

Brain Development

Some of the most dramatic physical change that occurs during infancy is in the brain. At birth, the brain is about 25 percent its adult weight and this is not true for any other part of the body. By age 2, it is at 75 percent its adult weight, at 95 percent by age 6 and at 100 percent by age 7 years. While most of the brain's 100 to 200 billion neurons are present at birth, they are not fully mature. During the next several years **dendrites** or connections between neurons will undergo a period of transient exuberance or temporary dramatic growth.[62]

There is a proliferation of these dendrites during the first two years so that by age 2, a single neuron might have thousands of dendrites. After this dramatic increase, the neural pathways that are not used will be eliminated thereby making those that are used much stronger.[63]. Because of this proliferation of dendrites, by age two a single neuron might have thousands of dendrites.

Synaptogenesis, or *the* formation of connections between neurons, continues from the prenatal period forming thousands of new connections during infancy and toddlerhood. This period of rapid neural growth is referred *to as* **Synaptic Blooming.**[64] This activity is occurring primarily in the cortex or the thin outer covering of the brain involved in voluntary activity and thinking.

---

[62] Lifespan Development - Chapter 4: Infancy - Physical Development by Lumen Learning references Psyc 200 Lifespan Psychology by Laura Overstreet, licensed under CC BY 4.0

[63] Lifespan Development - Module 4: Infancy by Lumen Learning references Psyc 200 Lifespan Psychology by Laura Overstreet, licensed under CC BY 4.0

[64] Lifespan Development: A Psychological Perspective by Martha Lally and Suzanne Valentine-French is licensed under CC BY-NC-SA 3.0

Components of the Neuron

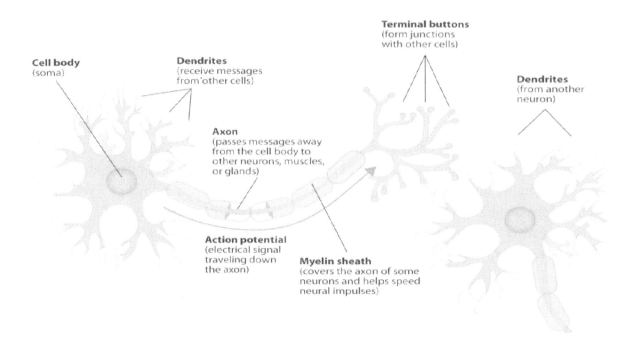

The neuron.[65]

The prefrontal cortex that is located behind our forehead continues to grow and mature throughout childhood and experiences an additional growth spurt during adolescence. It is the last part of the brain to mature and will eventually comprise 85 percent of the brain's weight. Experience will shape which of these connections are maintained and which of these are lost. Ultimately, about 40 percent of these connections will be lost (Webb, Monk, and Nelson, 2001). As the prefrontal cortex matures, the child is increasingly able to regulate or control emotions, to plan activity, strategize, and have better judgment. Of course, this is not fully accomplished in infancy and toddlerhood, but continues throughout childhood and adolescence.

Another major change occurring in the central nervous system is the development of **myelin**, a coating of fatty tissues around the axon of the neuron. Myelin helps insulate the nerve cell and speed the rate of transmission of impulses from one cell to another. This enhances the building of neural pathways and improves coordination and control of movement and thought processes. The development of myelin continues into adolescence but is most dramatic during the first several

---

[65]

years of life.[66]

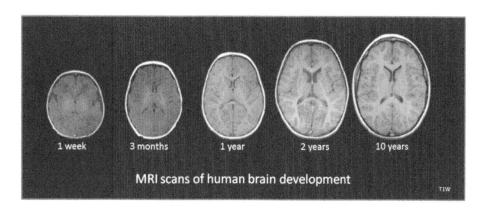

MRI scans of the human brain.[67]

Brain Maturation during Early Childhood

Brain Weight

The brain is about 75 percent its adult weight by two years of age. By age 6, it is approximately 95 percent its adult weight. Myelination and the development of dendrites continues to occur in the cortex and as it does, we see a corresponding change in the child's abilities. Significant development in the **prefrontal cortex** (the area of the brain behind the forehead that helps us to think, strategize, and control emotion) makes it increasingly possible to control emotional outbursts and to understand how to play games. Consider 4- or 5-year-old children and how they might approach a game of soccer. Chances are, every move would be a response to the commands of a coach standing nearby calling out, "Run this way! Now, stop. Look at the ball. Kick the ball!" And when the child is not being told what to do, he or she is likely to be looking at the clover on the ground or a dog on the other side of the fence! Understanding the game, thinking ahead, coordinating movement, and handling losing improve with practice and myelination.[68]

Brain Development during middle childhood

The brain reaches its adult size at about age 7. Then between 10 and 12 years of age, the frontal lobes become more developed and improvements in logic, planning, and memory are evident (van der Molen & Molenaar, 1994). The school-aged child is better able to plan and coordinate activity

---

[66] Lifespan Development - Module 4: Infancy by Lumen Learning references Psyc 200 Lifespan Psychology by Laura Overstreet, licensed under CC BY 4.0

[67] Image is in the public domain

[68] Lifespan Development - Module 5: Early Childhood by Lumen Learning references Psyc 200 Lifespan Psychology by Laura Overstreet, licensed under CC BY 4.0

using both the left and right hemispheres of the brain, which control the development of emotions, physical abilities, and intellectual capabilities. The attention span also improves as the prefrontal cortex matures. The myelin also continues to develop and the child's reaction time improves as well. Myelination improvement is one factor responsible for these growths.

From age 6 to 12, the nerve cells in the association areas of the brain, that is those areas where sensory, motor, and intellectual functioning connect, become almost completely myelinated (Johnson, 2005). This myelination contributes to increases in information processing speed and the child's reaction time. The **hippocampus**, which is responsible for transferring information from the short-term to long-term memory, also shows increases in myelination resulting in improvements in memory functioning (Rolls, 2000).

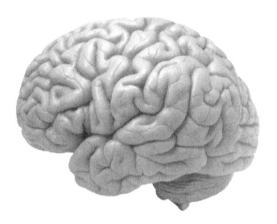

The human brain.[69]

Changes in the brain during this age enable not only physical development, but also allow children to understand what others think of them and dealing socially with the positive and negative consequences of that. Within this development period, children may struggle with mental health disorders or other health problems. As children are growing and becoming more capable, adults need to remember that children don't grow physically in isolation. The development of their bodies isn't separate from the changes that are occurring socially, emotionally, and cognitively. Awareness and understanding of their other developmental domains and needs will support the child during these changes.[70]

---

[69] Image by _DJ_ is licensed under CC BY-SA 2.0

[70] Children's Development by Ana R. Leon is licensed under CC BY 4.0 (modified by Dawn Rymond); Lifespan Development: A Psychological Perspective by Martha Lally and Suzanne Valentine-French is licensed under CC BY-NC-SA 3.0 (modified by Dawn Rymond)

Sleep

A newborn typically sleeps approximately 16.5 hours per 24-hour period. The infant sleeps in several periods throughout the day and night, which means they wake often throughout the day and night. (Salkind, 2005).[71]

Reflexes

Newborns are equipped with a number of **reflexes,** which are involuntary movements in response to stimulation. These include the sucking reflex (infants suck on objects that touch their lips automatically), the rooting reflex (which involves turning toward any object that touches the cheek), the palmar grasp (the infant will tightly grasp any object placed in its palm), and the dancing reflex (evident when the infant is held in a standing position and moves its feet up and down alternately as if dancing). These movements occur automatically and are signals that the infant is functioning well neurologically.

Some of the more common reflexes, such as the sucking reflex and rooting reflex, are important to feeding. The grasping and stepping reflexes are eventually replaced by more voluntary behaviors and motor skills. Within the first few months of life these reflexes disappear, while other reflexes, such as the eye-blink, swallowing, sneezing, gagging, and withdrawal reflex stay with us as they continue to serve important functions.[72]

---

[71] Lifespan Development: A Psychological Perspective (page 71) by Martha Lally and Suzanne Valentine-French is licensed under CC BY-NC-SA 3.0

[72] Lifespan Development: A Psychological Perspective (page 73) by Martha Lally and Suzanne Valentine-French is licensed under CC BY-NC-SA 3.0

Table: Some Common Infant Reflexes[73]

Reflex	Description	Image	Reflex	Description	Image
Sucking	Suck on anything that touches the lips	Figure [74]	**Moro**	A sudden noise or loss of support to the head and neck will cause infants to spread out their arms and legs then quickly contract the limbs inward	Figure [75]
Rooting	Turning the head when the cheek is touched	Figure [76]	**Tonic Neck**	When lying on the back with the head to one side infants will extend the arm and leg on that side while flexing the limbs on the opposite side (looks like a fencer pose).	Figure [77]

---

[73] Lifespan Development: A Psychological Perspective (page 74) by Martha Lally and Suzanne Valentine-French is licensed under CC BY-NC-SA 3.0 (modified by Antoinette Ricardo)

[74]   Image is in the public domain

[75]   Image is in the public domain

[76]   Image is in the public domain

[77]   Image by Samuel Finlayson is licensed under CC BY-SA 4.0

Reflex	Description	Image	Reflex	Description	Image
Grasp	Fingers automatically grip anything that touches the palm of the hand	Figure [78]	**Stepping**	Legs move in stepping like motion when feet touch a smooth surface	Figure [79]
Babinski	The toes will fan out and curl when the sole of the foot is stroked from heel to toe	Figure [80]			

Health

Infants and children depend on the adults that care for them to promote and protect their health. The following section addresses common physical conditions that can affect infants, the danger of shaking babies, and the importance of immunizations.

Common Physical Conditions and Issues during Infancy

Some physical conditions and issues are very common during infancy. Many are normal, and the infant's caregivers can deal with them if they occur. Mostly, it is a matter of the caregivers learning about what is normal for their infant and getting comfortable with the new routine in the household. New parents and caregivers often have questions about the following:

Bowel Movements

Infants' bowel movements go through many changes in color and consistency, even within the first few days after birth. While the color, consistency, and frequency of stool will vary, hard or dry stools may indicate dehydration and increased frequency of watery stools may indicate diarrhea.

---

[78]   Image by Raul Luna is licensed under CC BY 2.0

[79]   Image is in the public domain

[80]   Image by Medicus of Borg is licensed under CC BY-SA 3.0

Colic

Many infants are fussy in the evenings, but if the crying does not stop and gets worse throughout the day or night, it may be caused by colic. According to the American Academy of Pediatrics, about one-fifth of all infants develop colic, usually starting between 2 and 4 weeks of age. They may cry inconsolably or scream, extend or pull up their legs, and pass gas. Their stomachs may be enlarged. The crying spells can occur anytime, although they often get worse in the early evening.

The colic will likely improve or disappear by the age of 3 or 4 months. There is no definite explanation for why some infants get colic. Health care providers can help ensure there is no medical reason behind the crying.

Some infants seem to be soothed by being held, rocked, or wrapped snugly in a blanket. Some like a pacifier.

Shaken Baby Syndrome

Here is a PSA from the Center for Disease Control (CDC)

The crying.

The late-night feedings.

The diaper changes.

The exhaustion.

If you've ever been around a baby who won't stop crying, you know there's potential to get frustrated. Focus on calming yourself and understand that you may not be able to calm your baby. It's not your fault or your baby's.[81]

It's normal for healthy babies to cry and some babies cry much more than others. And they cannot always be consoled and caregivers can feel pushed to the limit. When caregivers lose control and shake a baby it can have devastating effects.

Shaken Baby Syndrome (SBS) is a severe form of physical child abuse. SBS may be caused from vigorously shaking an infant by the shoulders, arms, or legs. The "whiplash" effect can cause intracranial (within the brain) or intraocular (within the eyes) bleeding. Often there is no obvious external head trauma. Still, children with SBS may display some outward signs:

- Change in sleeping pattern or inability to be awakened

---

[81] Coping with Crying 3 PSA by the CDC is in the public domain

Shaken Baby Syndrome

- Confused, restless, or agitated state

- Convulsions or seizures

- Loss of energy or motivation

- Slurred speech

- Uncontrollable crying

- Inability to be consoled

- Inability to nurse or eat

SBS can result in death, mental retardation or developmental delays, paralysis, severe motor dysfunction, spasticity, blindness, and seizures.

Who's at Risk?

Small children are especially vulnerable to this type of abuse. Their heads are large in comparison to their bodies, and their neck muscles are weak. Children under one year of age are at highest risk, but SBS has been reported in children up to five years of age. Shaking often occurs in response to a baby crying or having a toilet-training accident. The perpetrator tends to be male and is primarily the biological father or the mother's boyfriend or partner. Caregivers are responsible for about 9%-21% of cases. The explanation typically provided by the caregiver—"I was playing with the baby"—does not begin to account for the severity of trauma. Many times there is also a history of child abuse.

Can It Be Prevented?

SBS is completely preventable. However, it is not known whether educational efforts will effectively prevent this type of abuse. Home visitation programs are shown to prevent child abuse in general. Because the child's father or the mother's partner often causes SBS, they should be included in home visitation programs. Home visits bring community resources to families in their homes. Health professionals provide information, healthcare, psychological support, and other services that can help people to be more effective parents and care-givers.

The Bottom Line

Shaking a baby can cause death or permanent brain damage. It can result in life-long

Shaken Baby Syndrome

disability.

Healthy strategies for dealing with a crying baby include:

- finding the reason for the crying
- checking for signs of illness or discomfort, such as diaper rash, teething, tight clothing;
- feeding or burping;
- soothing the baby by rubbing its back; gently rocking; offering a pacifier; singing or talking;
- taking a walk using a stroller or a drive in a properly-secured car seat;
- or calling the doctor if sickness is suspected

All babies cry. Caregivers often feel overwhelmed by a crying baby. Calling a friend, relative, or neighbor for support or assistance lets the caregiver take a break from the situation. If immediate support is not available, the caregiver could place the baby in a crib (making sure the baby is safe), close the door, and check on the baby every five minutes.[82]

Abusive Head Trauma

Shaken baby syndrome is part abusive head trauma (AHT), severe form of physical child abuse that results in an injury to the brain of a child. This is important to note because:

- Abusive head trauma is a leading cause of physical child abuse deaths in children under 5 in the United States.

- Abusive head trauma accounts for approximately one third of all child maltreatment deaths.

- The most common trigger for abusive head trauma is inconsolable crying.

- Babies less than one year old are at greatest risk of injury from abusive head trauma.[83]

Teething

Although newborns usually have no visible teeth, baby teeth begin to appear generally about 6 months after birth. During the first few years, all 20 baby teeth will push through the gums, and

---

[82] Shaken Baby Syndrome by the CDC is in the public domain

[83] Preventing Abusive Head Trauma in Children by the CDC is in the public domain

most children will have their full set of these teeth in place by age 3.

An infant's front four teeth usually appear first, at about 6 months of age, although some children don't get their first tooth until 12-14 months. As their teeth break through the gums, some infants become fussy, and irritable; lose their appetite; or drool more than usual.

The FDA does not recommend gum-numbing medications with an ingredient called benzocaine because they can cause a potentially fatal condition in young children. Safe forms of relief include a chilled teething ring or gently rubbing the child's gums with a clean finger.

Spitting Up/Vomiting
Spitting up is a common occurrence for young infants and is usually not a sign of a more serious problem. But if an infant is not gaining weight or shows other signs of illness, a health care provider should be consulted.

Urination
Infants urinate as often as every 1 to 3 hours or as infrequently as every 4 to 6 hours. In case of sickness or if the weather is very hot, urine output might drop by half and still be normal. If an infant shows any signs of distress while urinating or if any blood is found in a wet diaper medical care should be sought.

Diaper Rash
A rash on the skin covered by a diaper is quite common. It is usually caused by irritation of the skin from being in contact with stool and urine. It can get worse during bouts of diarrhea. Diaper rash usually can be prevented by frequent diaper changes.

Jaundice
Jaundice can cause an infant's skin, eyes, and mouth to turn a yellowish color. The yellow color is caused by a buildup of bilirubin, a substance that is produced in the body during the normal process of breaking down old red blood cells and forming new ones.

Normally the liver removes bilirubin from the body. But, for many infants, in the first few days after birth, the liver is not yet working at its full power. As a result, the level of bilirubin in the blood gets too high, causing the infant's color to become slightly yellow—this is jaundice. Although jaundice is common and usually not serious, in some cases, high levels of bilirubin could cause brain injury. All infants with jaundice need to be seen by a health care provider. Many infants need no treatment. Their livers start to catch up quickly and begin to remove bilirubin normally, usually within a few days after birth. For some infants, health care providers prescribe phototherapy—a treatment using a special lamp—to help break down the bilirubin in their bodies.

Protecting Health through Immunization

One way we can protect a child's health (and those around them) is through immunization. The vaccines (given through injection) may hurt a little…but the diseases they can prevent can hurt a lot more! Immunization shots, or vaccinations, are essential. They protect against things like measles, mumps, rubella, hepatitis B, polio, diphtheria, tetanus and pertussis (whooping cough). Immunizations are important for adults as well as for children. Here's why.

The immune system helps the human body fight germs by producing substances to combat them. Once it does, the immune system "remembers" the germ and can fight it again. Vaccines contain germs that have been killed or weakened. When given to a healthy person, the vaccine triggers the immune system to respond and thus build immunity.

Before vaccines, people became immune only by actually getting a disease and surviving it. Immunizations are an easier and less risky way to become immune. Vaccines are the best defense we have against serious, preventable, and sometimes deadly contagious diseases. Vaccines are some of the safest medical products available, but like any other medical product, there may be risks. Accurate information about the value of vaccines as well as their possible side effects helps people to make informed decisions about vaccination.

Potential Side Effects

Vaccines, like all medical products, may cause side effects in some people. Most of these side effects are minor, such as redness or swelling at the injection site. Read further to learn about possible side effects from vaccines.

Any vaccine can cause side effects. For the most part these are minor (for example, a sore arm or low-grade fever) and go away within a few days.[84] Serious side effects after vaccination, such as severe allergic reaction, are very rare.[85]

Remember, vaccines are continually monitored for safety, and like any medication, vaccines can cause side effects. However, a decision not to immunize a child also involves risk and could put the child and others who come into contact with him or her at risk of contracting a potentially deadly disease.

How Well Do Vaccines Work?

Vaccines work really well. No medicine is perfect, of course, but most childhood vaccines produce immunity about 90–100% of the time.

---

[84] Disease Prevention and Healthy Lifestyles references Contemporary Health Issues by Judy Baker, Ph.D., licensed under CC BY-SA 4.0

[85] Making the Vaccine Decision by the CDC is in the public domain

What about the argument made by some people that vaccines don't work that well . . . that diseases would be going away on their own because of better hygiene or sanitation, even if there were no vaccines?

That simply isn't true. Certainly better hygiene and sanitation can help prevent the spread of disease, but the germs that cause disease will still be around, and as long as they are they will continue to make people sick.

All vaccines must be licensed (approved) by the Food and Drug Administration (FDA) before being used in the United States, and a vaccine must go through extensive testing to show that it works and that it is safe before the FDA will approve it. Among these tests are clinical trials, which compare groups of people who get a vaccine with groups of people who get a control. A vaccine is approved only if FDA makes the determination that it is safe and effective for its intended use.

If you look at the history of any vaccine-preventable disease, you will virtually always see that the number of cases of disease starts to drop when a vaccine is licensed. Vaccines are the most effective tool we have to prevent infectious diseases.

Opposition to Vaccines

In 2010, a pertussis (whooping cough) outbreak in California sickened 9,143 people and resulted in 10 infant deaths: the worst outbreak in 63 years (Centers for Disease Control 2011b). Researchers, suspecting that the primary cause of the outbreak was the waning strength of pertussis vaccines in older children, recommended a booster vaccination for 11–12-year-olds and also for pregnant women (Zacharyczuk 2011). Pertussis is most serious for babies; one in five needs to be hospitalized, and since they are too young for the vaccine themselves, it is crucial that people around them be immunized (Centers for Disease Control 2011b). Several states, including California, have been requiring the pertussis booster for older children in recent years with the hope of staving off another outbreak.

But what about people who do not want their children to have this vaccine, or any other? That question is at the heart of a debate that has been simmering for years. Vaccines are biological preparations that improve immunity against a certain disease. Vaccines have contributed to the eradication and weakening of numerous infectious diseases, including smallpox, polio, mumps, chicken pox, and meningitis.

However, many people express concern about potential negative side effects from vaccines. These concerns range from fears about overloading the child's immune system to controversial reports about devastating side effects of the vaccines.[86]

---

[86] Disease Prevention and Healthy Lifestyles references Contemporary Health Issues by Judy Baker, Ph.D., licensed under CC BY-SA 4.0

Although children continue to get several vaccines up to their second birthday, these vaccines do not overload the immune system. Every day, an infant's healthy immune system successfully fights off thousands of antigens – the parts of germs that cause their immune system to respond. Even if your child receives several vaccines in one day, vaccines contain only a tiny amount of antigens compared to the antigens your baby encounters every day.

This is the case even if your child receives combination vaccines. Combination vaccines take two or more vaccines that could be given individually and put them into one shot. Children get the same protection as they do from individual vaccines given separately—but with fewer shots.[87]

One misapprehension is that the vaccine itself might cause the disease it is supposed to be immunizing against.[88] Vaccines help develop immunity by imitating an infection, but this "imitation" infection does not cause illness. Instead it causes the immune system to develop the same response as it does to a real infection so the body can recognize and fight the vaccine-preventable disease in the future. Sometimes, after getting a vaccine, the imitation infection can cause minor symptoms, such as fever. Such minor symptoms are normal and should be expected as the body builds immunity.[89]

Another commonly circulated concern is that vaccinations, specifically the MMR vaccine (MMR stands for measles, mumps, and rubella), are linked to autism. The autism connection has been particularly controversial. In 1998, a British physician named Andrew Wakefield published a study in Great Britain's Lancet magazine that linked the MMR vaccine to autism. The report received a lot of media attention, resulting in British immunization rates decreasing from 91 percent in 1997 to almost 80 percent by 2003, accompanied by a subsequent rise in measles cases (Devlin 2008). A prolonged investigation by the British Medical Journal proved that not only was the link in the study nonexistent, but that Dr. Wakefield had falsified data in order to support his claims (CNN 2011). Dr. Wakefield was discredited and stripped of his license, but the doubt still lingers in many parents' minds.

In the United States, many parents still believe in the now discredited MMR-autism link and refuse to vaccinate their children. Other parents choose not to vaccinate for various reasons like religious or health beliefs. In one instance, a boy whose parents opted not to vaccinate returned home to the U.S. after a trip abroad; no one yet knew he was infected with measles. The boy exposed 839 people to the disease and caused 11 additional cases of measles, all in other unvaccinated children,

---

[87] Making the Vaccine Decision by the CDC is in the public domain

[88] Disease Prevention and Healthy Lifestyles references Contemporary Health Issues by Judy Baker, Ph.D., licensed under CC BY-SA 4.0

[89] Making the Vaccine Decision by the CDC is in the public domain

including one infant who had to be hospitalized.

According to a study published in Pediatrics (2010), the outbreak cost the public sector $10,376 per diagnosed case. The study further showed that the intentional non-vaccination of those infected occurred in students from private schools, public charter schools, and public schools in upper-socioeconomic areas (Sugerman et al. 2010).[90]

The Immunization Schedule

On-time vaccination throughout childhood is essential because it helps provide immunity before children are exposed to potentially life-threatening diseases. Vaccines are tested to ensure that they are safe and effective for children to receive at the recommended ages.[91]

Fully vaccinated children in the U.S. are protected against sixteen potentially harmful diseases. Vaccine-preventable diseases can be very serious, may require hospitalization, or even be deadly — especially in infants and young children.[92]

Safety

There are different risks to infant safety. According to the CDC, nonfatal injury rates varied by age group.

- Nonfatal suffocation rates were highest for those less than 1 year of age.

- Rates for fires or burns, and drowning were highest for children 4 years and younger.

- Children 1 to 4 years of age had the highest rates of nonfatal falls and poisoning.

And the leading causes of injury death also differed by age group.

- For children less than 1 year of age, two–thirds of injury deaths were due to suffocation.

- Drowning was the leading cause of injury or death for those 1 to 4 years of age.[93]

---

[90]Disease Prevention and Healthy Lifestyles references Contemporary Health Issues by Judy Baker, Ph.D., licensed under CC BY-SA 4.0

[91] For Parents: Vaccines for Your Children by the CDC is in the public domain

[92] Vaccines for Your Children: Protect Your Child at Every Age by the CDC is in the public domain

[93] Protect the Ones You Love: Child Injuries are Preventable by the CDC is in the public domain

Car Seat Safety

Motor vehicle injuries are a leading cause of death among children in the United States. But many of these deaths can be prevented.

- In the United States, 723 children ages 12 years and younger died as occupants in motor vehicle crashes during 2016, and more than 128,000 were injured in 2016.

- One CDC study found that, in one year, more than 618,000 children ages 0-12 rode in vehicles without the use of a child safety seat or booster seat or a seat belt at least some of the time.

- Of the children ages 12 years and younger who died in a crash in 2016 (for which restraint use was known), 35% were not buckled up.[94]

Buckling children in age- and size-appropriate car seats, booster seats, and seat belts reduces the risk of serious and fatal injuries:

- Car seat use reduces the risk for injury in a crash by 71-82% for children when compared to seat belt use alone.

- Booster seat use reduces the risk for serious injury by 45% for children aged 4–8 years when compared with seat belt use alone.

- For older children and adults, seat belt use reduces the risk for death and serious injury by approximately half.[95]

Sudden Infant Death Syndrome and Safe Sleep

Sudden Infant Death Syndrome (SIDS) is identified when the death of a healthy infant occurs suddenly and unexpectedly, and medical and forensic investigation findings (including an autopsy) are inconclusive. SIDS is the leading cause of death in infants 1 to 12 months old, and approximately 1,500 infants died of SIDS in 2013 (CDC, 2015). Because SIDS is diagnosed when no other cause of death can be determined, possible causes of SIDS are regularly researched. One leading hypothesis suggests that infants who die from SIDS have

---

[94] Child Passenger Safety: Get the Facts by the CDC is in the public domain

[95] Child Passenger Safety: Get the Facts by the CDC is in the public domain

Sudden Infant Death Syndrome and Safe Sleep

abnormalities in the area of the brainstem responsible for regulating breathing (Weekes-Shackelford & Shackelford, 2005).[96]

Risk Factors

Babies are at higher risk for SIDS if they:

- Sleep on their stomachs

- Sleep on soft surfaces, such as an adult mattress, couch, or chair or under soft coverings

- Sleep on or under soft or loose bedding

- Get too hot during sleep

- Are exposed to cigarette smoke in the womb or in their environment, such as at home, in the car, in the bedroom, or other areas

- Sleep in an adult bed with parents, other children, or pets; this situation is especially dangerous if:

    o The adult smokes, has recently had alcohol, or is tired.

    o The baby is covered by a blanket or quilt.

    o The baby sleeps with more than one bed-sharer.

    o The baby is younger than 11 to 14 weeks of age.

Reducing the Risks

There have been dramatic improvements in reducing baby deaths during sleep since the 1990s, when recommendations were introduced to place babies on their back for sleep. However, since the late 1990s, declines have slowed.

In 2012, the Back to Sleep campaign became the Safe to Sleep campaign. Safe to Sleep aims to educate all caregivers about SIDS and safe sleep practices. Current recommendations to

Sudden Infant Death Syndrome and Safe Sleep

reduce the risk of SIDS and other sleep related causes of infant death:

- Always place baby on his or her back to sleep (for naps and at night).
- Use a firm and flat surface.
- Use only a tight fitting sheet on the sleep surface; no other bedding or soft items in the sleep area.
- Breastfeed.
- Share your room with a baby, but on a separate surface designed for infants (not your bed).
- Do not put soft objects, toys, crib bumpers, or loose bedding under, over, or anywhere near baby's sleep area.
- Do no smoke during pregnancy or allow smoking around baby.
- Consider giving baby a pacifier.
- Do not let baby get too hot during sleep.
- Get regular health care (including vaccines).
- Avoid products that go against safe sleep recommendations, especially those that claim to prevent or reduce the risk of SIDS.
- Do not use heart or breathing monitors to reduce the risk of SIDS.[97]

Toilet Training

Toilet training typically occurs after the second birthday. Some children show interest by age 2, but others may not be ready until months later. The average age for girls to be toilet trained is 29 months and for boys it is 31 months, and 98% of children are trained by 36 months (Boyse & Fitzgerald, 2010). The child's age is not as important as his/her physical and emotional readiness. If started too early, it might take longer to train a child.

According to The Mayo Clinic (2016b) the following questions can help parents determine if a child is ready for toilet training:

- Does your child seem interested in the potty chair or toilet, or in wearing underwear?

- Can your child understand and follow basic directions?

- Does your child tell you through words, facial expressions or posture when he or she needs to go?

---

[97] Ways to Reduce the Risk of SIDS and Other Sleep-Related Causes of Infant Death by the CDC is in the public domain

- Does your child stay dry for periods of two hours or longer during the day?

- Does your child complain about wet or dirty diapers?

- Can your child pull down his or her pants and pull them up again?

- Can your child sit on and rise from a potty chair?

If a child resists being trained or it is not successful after a few weeks, it is best to take a break and try again when they show more significant interest in the process. Most children master daytime bladder control first, typically within two to three months of consistent toilet training. However, nap and nighttime training might take months or even years.

Elimination Disorders

Some children experience elimination disorders including:

- **enuresis** - the repeated voiding of urine into bed or clothes (involuntary or intentional) after age 5

- **encopresis** - the repeated passage of feces into inappropriate places (involuntary or intentional).

The prevalence of enuresis is 5%-10% for 5 year-olds, 3%-5% for 10 year-olds and approximately 1% for those 15 years of age or older. Around 1% of 5 year- olds have encopresis, and it is more common in males than females. These are diagnosed by a medical professional and may require treatment.[98]

Sexual Development in Early Childhood

Self-stimulation is common in early childhood for both boys and girls. Curiosity about the body and about others' bodies is a natural part of early childhood as well. Caregivers should respond to this without undue alarm and without making the child feel guilty about their bodies. Instead, messages about what is going on and the appropriate time and place for such activities help the child learn what is appropriate.[99]

Health in Early Childhood

While preschoolers are becoming more and more independent, they depend on their caregivers to

---

[98] Lifespan Development: A Psychological Perspective by Martha Lally and Suzanne Valentine-French is licensed under CC BY-NC-SA 3.0

[99] Lifespan Development - Module 5: Early Childhood by Lumen references Psyc 200 Lifespan Psychology by Laura Overstreet, licensed under CC BY-SA 3.0

keep protecting and promoting their health. [100]

Vision and Hearing

Vision and hearing screening should begin during the preschool years and continue through middle chidhood. The most common vision problem in middle childhood is being nearsighted, otherwise known as Myopic. 25% of children will be diagnosed by the end of middle childhood. Being nearsighted can be corrected by wearing glasses with corrective lenses.

Children may have many ear infections in early childhood, but it's not as common within the 6-12 year age range. Otitis Media is an infection of rapid onset that usually presents with ear pain. In young children this may result in pulling at the ear, increased crying, and poor sleep. In early childhood, antibiotics are typically not needed and there are no associations between frequent ear aches in early childhood and language delays. Numerous ear infections during middle childhood may lead to headaches and migraines, which may result in hearing loss.[101]

Oral Health

Tooth decay (cavities) is one of the most common chronic conditions of childhood in the United States. Untreated tooth decay can cause pain and infections that may lead to problems with eating, speaking, playing, and learning. The good news is that tooth decay is preventable.

Fluoride varnish, a high concentration fluoride coating that is painted on teeth, can prevent about one-third (33%) of decay in the primary (baby) teeth. Children living in communities with fluoridated tap water have fewer decayed teeth than children who live in areas where their tap water is not fluoridated. Similarly, children who brush daily with fluoride toothpaste will have less tooth decay.

Applying dental sealants to the chewing surfaces of the back teeth is another way to prevent tooth decay. Studies in children show that sealants reduce decay in the permanent molars by 81% for 2 years after they are placed on the tooth and continue to be effective for 4 years after placement.[102]

The first visit to the dentist should happen after the first tooth erupts. After that, children should be seeing the dentist every six months.[103]

---

[100] Prevalence of Childhood Obesity in the United States by the CDC is in the public domain

[101] Rathus, Spencer A. (2011). Childhood & adolescence voyages in development. Belmont, CA: Wadsworth Cengage Learning.

[102] Children's Oral Health by the CDC is in the public domain

[103] Content by Jennifer Paris is licensed under CC BY 4.0

Dental Health during middle childhood

Children in middle childhood will start or continue to loose teeth. They experience the loss of deciduous, or "baby," teeth and the arrival of permanent teeth, which typically begins at age six or seven. It is important for children to continue seeing a dentist twice a year to be sure that these teeth are healthy.

The foods and nutrients that children consume are also important for dental health. Offer healthy foods and snacks to children and when children do eat sugary or sticky foods, they should brush their teeth afterward.

Children should floss daily and brush their teeth at least twice daily: in the morning, at bedtime, and preferably after meals. Younger children need help brushing their teeth properly. Try brushing their teeth first and letting them finish. You might try using a timer or a favorite song so that your child learns to brush for 2 minutes. Parents or caregivers are encouraged to supervise brushing until your child is 7 or 8 years old to avoid tooth decay.

The best defense against tooth decay is flossing, brushing and adding fluoride; a mineral found in most tap water. If your water doesn't have fluoride, ask a dentist about fluoride drops, gel or varnish. Also ask your child's dentist about sealants—a simple, pain-free way to prevent tooth decay. These thin plastic coatings are painted on the chewing surfaces of permanent back teeth. They quickly harden to form a protective shield against germs and food. If a small cavity is accidentally covered by a sealant, the decay won't spread because germs trapped inside are sealed off from their food supply.

Children's dental health needs continuous monitoring as children loose teeth and new teeth come in. Many children have some malocclusion (when the way upper teeth aren't correctly positioned slightly over the lower teeth, including under- and overbites) or malposition of their teeth, which can affect their ability to chew food, floss, and brush properly. Dentists may recommend that it's time to see an orthodontist to maintain proper dental health. Dental health is exceedingly important as children grow more independent by making food choices and as they start to take over flossing and brushing. Parents can ease this transition by promoting healthy eating and proper dental hygiene.[104]

Protection from Illness

Two important ways to help protect children from illness are immunization and handwashing.

---

[104] Chew on This - Healthy Teeth for Baby and Beyond by the National Institutes of Health is in the public domain (modified by Dawn Rymond)

Childhood by University of Hawai'i at Manoa Food Science and Human Nutrition Program is licensed under CC BY-NC-SA 4.0 (modified by Dawn Rymond)

Immunizations

While vaccines begin in infancy, it is important for children to receive additional doses of vaccines to keep them protected. These boosters, given between ages 4 and 6, are doses of the vaccines they received earlier in life to help them maintain the best protection against vaccine-preventable diseases.

Many states require children to be fully vaccinated (unless they have a medical reason to be exempt) before they can enroll in licensed child care or public school. If vaccinations were missed, a health care provider can help the child's caregivers to create a catch up schedule to ensure the child correctly "catches up" with the recommended childhood vaccination schedule.[105]

Handwashing

Handwashing is one of the best ways to prevent the spread of illness. It's important for children (and adults) to wash their hands often, especially when they are likely to get and spread germs, including:

- Before, during, and after preparing food.

- Before eating food.

- After blowing nose, coughing, or sneezing.

- After using the toilet.

- After touching an animal, animal feed, or animal waste.

- After touching garbage.

It's important for children to learn how to properly wash their hands. When washing hands children (and adults) should follow these five steps every time.

1. Wet your hands with clean, running water (warm or cold), turn off the tap, and apply soap.

2. Lather your hands by rubbing them together with the soap. Lather the backs of your hands, between your fingers, and under your nails.

3. Scrub your hands for at least 20 seconds. Need a timer? Hum or sing the *Happy Birthday* song or *ABCs* from beginning to end twice.

4. Rinse your hands well under clean, running water.

---

[105] Vaccines for Your Children: Protect Your Child at Every Age by the CDC is in the public domain

5. Dry your hands using a clean towel or air dry them.[106]

Caregivers can help keep children healthy by:

*   Teaching them good handwashing techniques.

*   Reminding their kids to wash their hands.

*   Washing their own hands with the children.[107]

Safety

Child injuries are preventable, yet more than 9,000 children (from 0-19 years) died from injuries in the US in 2009. Car crashes, suffocation, drowning, poisoning, fires, and falls are some of the most common ways children are hurt or killed. The number of children dying from injury dropped nearly 30% over the last decade. However, injury is still the number 1 cause of death among children.[108]

Children during early childhood are more at risk for certain injuries. Using data from 2000-2006, the CDC determined that:

*   Drowning was the leading cause of injury death between 1 and 4 years of age.

*   Falls were the leading cause of nonfatal injury for all age groups less than 15.

*   For children ages 0 to 9, the next two leading causes were being struck by or against an object and animal bites or insect stings.

*   Rates for fires or burns, and drowning were highest for children 4 years and younger.[109]

Here is a table summarizing some tips from the CDC to protect children from these injuries:

Preventing Injuries

---

[106] Wash Your Hands by the CDC is in the public domain

[107] Handwashing: A Family Activity by the CDC is in the public domain

[108] Child Injury by the CDC is in the public domain

[109] CDC Childhood Injury Report by the CDC is in the public domain

Type of Injury	Prevention Tips
Burns	<ul><li>Have smoke alarms on every floor and in all rooms people sleep in</li><li>Involve children in creating and practicing an escape plan</li><li>Never leave food cooking on the stove unattended; supervise any use of microwave</li><li>Make sure the water heater is set to 120 degrees or lower[110]</li></ul>
Drowning	<ul><li>Make sure caregivers are trained in CPR</li><li>Fence off pools; gates should be self-closing and self-latching</li><li>Have children wear life jackets in and around natural bodies of water</li><li>Supervise children in or near water (including the bathtub)[111]</li></ul>
Falls	<ul><li>Make sure playground surfaces are safe, soft, and made of impact absorbing material (such as wood chips or sand) at an appropriate depth and are well maintained</li><li>Use safety devices (such as window guards)</li><li>Make sure children are wearing protective gear during sports and recreation (such as bicycle helmets)</li><li>Supervise children around fall hazards at all times[112]</li></ul>
Poisoning	<ul><li>Lock up all medications and toxic products (such as cleaning solutions and detergents) in original packaging out of sight and reach of children</li><li>Know the number to poison control (1-800-222-1222)</li><li>Read and follow labels of all medications</li><li>Safely dispose of unused, unneeded, or expired prescription drugs and over the counter drugs, vitamins, and supplements[113]</li></ul>
Motor-accident, in vehicle	<ul><li>Children should still be safely restrained in a five point harnessed car seat</li><li>Children should be in back seat</li><li>Children should not be seated in front of an airbag</li></ul>
Motor-accident, pedestrian	<ul><li>Teach children about safety including:<ul><li>Walking on the sidewalk</li><li>Not assuming vehicles see you or will stop</li><li>Crossing only in crosswalks</li><li>Looking both ways before crossing</li><li>Never playing in the road</li><li>Not crossing a road without an adult</li></ul></li><li>Supervise children near all roadways and model safe behavior[114]</li></ul>

---

[110] Burn Prevention by the CDC is in the public domain

[111] Drowning Prevention by the CDC is in the public domain

[112] Poisoning Prevention by the CDC is in the public domain

[113] Road Traffic Safety by the CDC is in the public domain

[114] Safety Tips for Pedestrians by the Pedestrian and Bicycle Information Center is in the public domain

Diabetes in Childhood

Until recently diabetes in children and adolescents was thought of almost exclusively as type 1, but that thinking has evolved. Type 1 diabetes is the most common form of diabetes in children and is the result of a lack or production of insulin due to an overactive immune system. Type 2 diabetes is the most common form of diabetes in the U.S. It used to be referred to as adult-onset diabetes as it was not common during childhood. But with increasing rates of overweight and obesity in children and adolescents, more diagnoses are happening before adulthood. It is also important to note that Type 2 disproportionately affects minority youth.[115]

Asthma

Childhood asthma that is unmanaged may make it difficult for children to develop to their fullest potential. Asthma is a chronic lung disease that inflames and narrows the airways. Asthma causes recurring periods of wheezing (a whistling sound when you breathe), chest tightness, shortness of breath, and coughing. The coughing often occurs at night or early in the morning. Asthma affects people of all ages, but it most often starts during childhood. In the United States, more than 25 million people are known to have asthma. About 7 million of these people are children.

To understand asthma, it helps to know how the airways work. The airways are tubes that carry air into and out of your lungs. People who have asthma have inflamed airways. The inflammation makes the airways swollen and very sensitive. The airways tend to react strongly to certain inhaled substances. When the airways react, the muscles around them tighten. This narrows the airways, causing less air to flow into the lungs. The swelling also can worsen, making the airways even narrower. Cells in the airways might make more mucus than usual. Mucus is a sticky, thick liquid that can further narrow the airways. This chain reaction can result in asthma symptoms. Symptoms can happen each time the airways are inflamed.

Sometimes asthma symptoms are mild and go away on their own or after minimal treatment with asthma medicine. Other times, symptoms continue to get worse. When symptoms get more intense and/or more symptoms occur, you're having an asthma attack. Asthma attacks also are called flare-ups or exacerbations (eg-zas-er-BA-shuns).

Treating symptoms when you first notice them is important. This will help prevent the symptoms from worsening and causing a severe asthma attack. Severe asthma attacks may require emergency care, and they can be fatal. Asthma has no cure. Even when you feel fine, you still have the disease and it can flare up at any time.

---

[115] Diabetes by the National Institute of Diabetes and Digestive and Kidney Diseases is in the public domain

Preventing Type 2 Diabetes - Steps Toward a Healthier Life by the National Institutes of Health is in the public domain

However, with today's knowledge and treatments, most people who have asthma are able to manage the disease. They have few, if any, symptoms. They can live normal, active lives and sleep through the night without interruption from asthma. If you have asthma, you can take an active role in managing the disease. For successful, thorough, and ongoing treatment, build strong partnerships with your doctor and other health care providers.[116]

Nutrition

Nutritional needs change with age. Let's examine how caregivers should nourish children during the first years of life and some risks to nutrition that they should be aware of.

Breastfeeding

Breast milk is considered the ideal diet for newborns. Colostrum, the first breast milk produced during pregnancy and just after birth has been described as "liquid gold" (United States Department of Health and Human Services (USDHHS), 2011). It is very rich in nutrients and antibodies. Breast milk changes by the third to fifth day after birth, becoming much thinner, but containing just the right amount of fat, sugar, water and proteins to support overall physical and neurological development. For most babies, breast milk is also easier to digest than formula. Formula fed infants experience more diarrhea and upset stomachs. The absence of antibodies in formula often results in a higher rate of ear infections and respiratory infections. Children who are breastfed have lower rates of childhood leukemia, asthma, obesity, type 1 and 2 diabetes, and a lower risk of SIDS. The USDHHS recommends that mothers breastfeed their infants until at least 6 months of age and that breast milk be used in the diet throughout the first year or two.

Maternal Benefits of Breastfeeding

Several recent studies have reported that it is not just babies that benefit from breastfeeding. Breastfeeding stimulates contractions in the mother's uterus to help it regain its normal size, and women who breastfeed are more likely to space their pregnancies further apart. Mothers who breastfeed are at lower risk of developing breast cancer (Islami et al., 2015), especially among higher risk racial and ethnic groups (Islami et al., 2015; Redondo et al., 2012). Women who breastfeed have lower rates of ovarian cancer (Titus-Ernstoff, Rees, Terry, & Cramer, 2010), reduced risk for developing Type 2 diabetes (Schwarz et al., 2010; Gunderson, et al., 2015), and rheumatoid arthritis (Karlson, Mandl, Hankinson, & Grodstein, 2004). In most studies these benefits have been seen in women who breastfeed longer than 6 months.

Challenges to Breastfeeding

However, most mothers who breastfeed in the United States stop breastfeeding at about 6-8 weeks, often in order to return to work outside the home (USDHHS, 2011). Mothers can certainly continue to provide breast milk to their babies by expressing and freezing the milk to be bottle-fed

---

[116] Asthma by the National Heart, Lung, and Blood Institute is in the public domain

at a later time or by being available to their infants at feeding time. However, some mothers find that after the initial encouragement they receive in the hospital to breastfeed, the outside world is less supportive of such efforts. Some workplaces support breastfeeding mothers by providing flexible schedules and welcoming infants, but many do not. In addition, not all women may be able to breastfeed. Women with HIV are routinely discouraged from breastfeeding as the infection may pass to the infant. Similarly, women who are taking certain medications or undergoing radiation treatment may be told not to breastfeed (USDHHS, 2011).

Cost of Breastfeeding

In addition to the nutritional benefits of breastfeeding, breast milk does not have to be purchased. Anyone who has priced formula recently can appreciate this added incentive to breastfeeding. Prices for a year's worth of formula and feeding supplies can cost well over $1,500 (USDHHS, 2011).

But there are also those who challenge the belief that breast milk is free. For breastmilk to be completely beneficial for infants the mother's life choices will ultimately affect the quality of the nutrition an infant will receive. Let's consider the nutritional intake of the mother. Breastfeeding will both limit some food and drink choices as well as necessitate an increased intake of healthier options. A simple trip down the supermarket aisles will show you that nutritious and healthier options can be more expensive than some of the cheaper more processed options. A large variety of vegetable and fruits must be consumed, accompanied by the right proportions and amounts of the whole grains, dairy products, and fat food groups. Additionally, it is also encouraged for breastfeeding mothers to take vitamins regularly. That raises the question of how free breastfeeding truly is.

A Historic Look at Breastfeeding

The use of wet nurses, or lactating women hired to nurse others' infants, during the middle ages eventually declined and mothers increasingly breastfed their own infants in the late 1800s. In the early part of the 20th century, breastfeeding began to go through another decline. By the 1950s, it was practiced less frequently as formula began to be viewed as superior to breast milk.

In the late 1960s and 1970s, greater emphasis began to be placed on natural childbirth and breastfeeding and the benefits of breastfeeding were more widely publicized. Gradually rates of breastfeeding began to climb, particularly among middle-class educated mothers who received the strongest messages to breastfeed.

Today, women receive consultation from lactation specialists before being discharged from the hospital to ensure that they are informed of the benefits of breastfeeding and given support and

A Historic Look at Breastfeeding

encouragement to get their infants to get used to taking the breast. This does not always happen immediately and first time mothers, especially, can become upset or discouraged. In this case, lactation specialists and nursing staff can encourage the mother to keep trying until baby and mother are comfortable with the feeding.[117]

Alternatives to Breastfeeding

There are many reasons that mothers struggle to breastfeed or should not breastfeed, including: low milk supply, previous breast surgeries, illicit drug use, medications, infectious disease, and inverted nipples. Other mothers choose not to breastfeed. Some reasons for this include: lack of personal comfort with nursing, the time commitment of nursing, inadequate or unhealthy diet, and wanting more convenience and flexibility with who and when an infant can be fed. For these mothers and infants, formula is available. Besides breast milk, infant formula is the only other milk product that the medical community considers nutritionally acceptable for infants under the age of one year (as opposed to cow's milk, goat's milk, or follow-on formula). It can be used in addition to breastfeeding (supplementing) or as an alternative to breastmilk.

The most commonly used infant formulas contain purified cow's milk whey and casein as a protein source, a blend of vegetable oils as a fat source, lactose as a carbohydrate source, a vitamin-mineral mix, and other ingredients depending on the manufacturer. In addition, there are infant formulas which use soybeans as a protein source in place of cow's milk (mostly in the United States and Great Britain) and formulas which use protein hydrolysed into its component amino acids for infants who are allergic to other proteins[118].

One early argument given to promote the practice of breastfeeding was that it promoted bonding and healthy emotional development for infants. However, this does not seem to be the case. Breastfed and bottle-fed infants adjust equally well emotionally (Ferguson & Woodward, 1999). This is good news for mothers who may be unable to breastfeed for a variety of reasons and for fathers who might feel left out.

When, What, and How to Introduce Solid Foods

The American Academy of Pediatrics recommends children be introduced to foods other than breast milk or infant formula when they are about 6 months old. Every child is different. Here are some signs that show that an infant is ready for foods other than breast milk or infant formula:

---

[117] Children's Development by Ana R. Leon is licensed under CC BY 4.0

[118] Infant Formula by Wikipedia is licensed under CC BY-SA 3.0

- Child can sit with little or no support.

- Child has good head control.

- Child opens his or her mouth and leans forward when food is offered.

How Should Foods Be Introduced?

The American Academy of Pediatrics says that for most children, foods do not need to be given in a certain order. Children can begin eating solid foods at about 6 months old. By the time they are 7 or 8 months old, children can eat a variety of foods from different food groups. These foods include infant cereals, meat or other proteins, fruits, vegetables, grains, yogurts and cheeses, and more.

If feeding infant cereals, it is important to offer a variety of fortified infant cereals such as oat, barley, and multi-grain instead of only rice cereal. The Food and Drug Administration does not recommend only providing infant rice cereal because there is a risk for children to be exposed to arsenic.

Children should be allowed to try one food at a time at first and there should be 3 to 5 days before another food is introduced. This helps caregivers see if the child has any problems with that food, such as food allergies.

The eight most common allergenic foods are milk, eggs, fish, shellfish, tree nuts, peanuts, wheat, and soybeans. It is no longer recommended that caregivers delay introducing these foods to all children, but if there is a family history of food allergies, the child's doctor or nurse should be consulted.[119]

It may take numerous attempts before a child gains a taste for it. So caregivers should not give up if a food is refused on first offering.

USDA Infant Meal Patterns

The United States Department of Agriculture Food and Nutrition Service provides the following guidance for the day time feeding of infants and toddlers. It is important to remember that there are large individual differences from child to child. This is only a guideline, and it is important that parents feed their infant on demand – some days they may eat more and other days less.

---

[119] When, What, and How to Introduce Solid Foods by the CDC is in the public domain

Infant Meal Patterns[120]

Meal	0-5 months	6-11 months
Breakfast	4-6 fluid ounces breastmilk or formula	6-8 fluid ounces breastmilk or formula 0-4 tablespoons infant cereal, meat, fish, poultry, whole eggs, cooked dry beans or peas; or 0-2 ounces cheese; or 0-4 ounces (volume) cottage cheese; or 0-4 ounces yogurt; or a combination* 0-2 tablespoons vegetable, fruit, or both*
Lunch or Supper	4-6 fluid ounces breastmilk or formula	6-8 fluid ounces breastmilk or formula 0-4 tablespoons infant cereal, meat, fish, poultry, whole eggs, cooked dry beans or peas; or 0-2 ounces cheese; or 0-4 ounces (volume) cottage cheese; or 0-4 ounces yogurt; or a combination* 0-2 tablespoons vegetable, fruit, or both*
Snack	4-6 fluid ounces breastmilk or formula	2-4 fluid ounces breastmilk or formula 0-½ bread slice; or 0-2 crackers; or 0-4 tablespoons infant cereal or ready-to-eat cereal* 0-2 tablespoons vegetable, fruit, or both*

*Required when infant is developmentally ready. All serving sizes are minimum quantities of the food components that are required to be served.

The nutrition recommendations for toddlers are on the following page.

[120] Infant Meals by the USDA is in the public domain

Meal Patterns for Children (1-2 years)[121]

Meal	Ages 1-2
Breakfast	½ cup milk ¼ cup vegetables, fruit, or both ½ ounce equivalent grains
Lunch or Supper	½ cup milk 1 ounce meat or meat alternative 1/8 cup vegetables 1/8 cup fruits ½ ounce equivalent of grains
Snack	Select two of the following: ½ cup of milk ½ ounce meat or meat alternative ½ cup vegetables ½ cup fruit ½ ounce equivalent of grains

Note: All serving sizes are minimum quantities of the food components that are required to be served.

Child Malnutrition

There can be serious effects for children when there are deficiencies in their nutrition. Let's explore a few types of nutritional concerns.

Wasting

Children in developing countries and countries experiencing the harsh conditions of war are at risk for two major types of malnutrition, also referred to as wasting. Infantile **marasmus** refers to starvation due to a lack of calories and protein. Children who do not receive adequate nutrition lose fat and muscle until their bodies can no longer function. Babies who are breastfed are much less at

---

[121] Child and Adult Meals by the USDA is in the public domain

risk of malnutrition than those who are bottle-fed.

After weaning, children who have diets deficient in protein may experience **kwashiorkor** or the "disease of the displaced child," often occurring after another child has been born and taken over breastfeeding. This results in a loss of appetite and swelling of the abdomen as the body begins to break down the vital organs as a source of protein.

Around the world the rates of wasting have been dropping. However, according to the World Health Organization and UNICEF, in 2014 there were 50 million children under the age of five that experienced these forms of wasting, and 16 million were severely wasted (UNICEF, 2015). Worldwide, these figures indicate that nearly 1 child in every 13 suffers from some form of wasting. The majority of these children live in Asia (34.3 million) and Africa (13.9 million). Wasting can occur as a result of severe food shortages, regional diets that lack certain proteins and vitamins, or infectious diseases that inhibit appetite (Latham, 1997).

The consequences of wasting depend on how late in the progression of the disease parents and guardians seek medical treatment for their children. Unfortunately, in some cultures families do not seek treatment early, and as a result by the time a child is hospitalized the child often dies within the first three days after admission (Latham, 1997). Several studies have reported long- term cognitive effects of early malnutrition (Galler & Ramsey, 1989; Galler, Ramsey, Salt & Archer, 1987; Richardson, 1980), even when home environments were controlled (Galler, Ramsey, Morley, Archer & Salt, 1990). Lower IQ scores (Galler et al., 1987), poor attention (Galler & Ramsey, 1989), and behavioral issues in the classroom (Galler et al., 1990) have been reported in children with a history of serious malnutrition in the first few years of life.[122]

Milk Anemia
Milk Anemia in the United States: About 9 million children in the United States are malnourished (Children's Welfare, 1998). More still suffer from milk anemia, a condition in which milk consumption leads to a lack of iron in the diet. This can be due to the practice of giving toddlers milk as a pacifier-when resting, when riding, when waking, and so on. Appetite declines somewhat during toddlerhood and a small amount of milk (especially with added chocolate syrup) can easily satisfy a child's appetite for many hours. The calcium in milk interferes with the absorption of iron in the diet as well. Many preschools and daycare centers give toddlers a drink after they have finished their meal in order to prevent spoiling their appetites.[123]

---

[122] Lifespan Development: A Psychological Perspective by Martha Lally and Suzanne Valentine-French is licensed under CC BY-NC-SA 3.0

[123] Children's Development by Ana R. Leon is licensed under CC BY 4.0

Failure to Thrive

Failure to thrive (FTT) occurs in children whose nutritional intake is insufficient for supporting normal growth and weight gain. FTT typically presents before two years of age, when growth rates are highest. Parents may express concern about picky eating habits, poor weight gain, or smaller size compared relative to peers of similar age. Physicians often identify FTT during routine office visits, when a child's growth parameters are not tracking appropriately on growth curves.

FTT can be caused by physical or mental issues within the child (such as errors of metabolism, acid reflux, anemia, diarrhea, Cystic fibrosis, Crohn's disease, celiac disease, cleft palate, tongue tie, milk allergies, hyperthyroidism, congenital heart disease, etc.) It can also be caused by caregiver's actions (environmental), including inability to produce enough breastmilk, inadequate food supply, providing an insufficient number of feedings, and neglect. These causes may also co-exist. For instance, a child who is not getting sufficient nutrition may act content so that caregivers do not offer feedings of sufficient frequency or volume, and a child with severe acid reflux who appears to be in pain while eating may make a caregiver hesitant to offer sufficient feedings.[124]

Nutritional Concerns during Early Childhood

That slower rate of growth during early childhood is accompanied by a reduced appetite between the ages of 2 and 6. This change can sometimes be surprising to parents and lead to the development of poor eating habits. However, children between the ages of 2 and 3 need 1,000 to 1,400 calories, while children between the ages of 4 and 8 need 1,200 to 2,000 calories (Mayo Clinic, 2016a).[125]

Caregivers who have established a feeding routine with their child can find the reduction in appetite a bit frustrating and become concerned that the child is going to starve. However, by providing adequate, sound nutrition, and limiting sugary snacks and drinks, the caregiver can be assured that 1) the child will not starve; and 2) the child will receive adequate nutrition. Preschoolers can experience iron deficiencies if not given well-balanced nutrition or if they are given too much milk as calcium interferes with the absorption of iron in the diet as well.

Caregivers need to keep in mind that they are setting up taste preferences at this age. Young children who grow accustomed to high fat, very sweet and salty flavors may have trouble eating foods that have more subtle flavors such as fruits and vegetables. Consider the following advice about establishing eating patterns for years to come (Rice, F.P., 1997). Notice that keeping mealtime pleasant, providing sound nutrition and not engaging in power struggles over food are the

---

[124] Failure to Thrive by Wikipedia is licensed under CC BY-SA 3.0

[125] Children's Development by Ana R. Leon is licensed under CC BY 4.0

Lifespan Development: A Psychological Perspective by Martha Lally and Suzanne Valentine-French is licensed under CC BY-NC-SA 3.0

main goals.[126]

Tips for Establishing Healthy Eating Habits

- **Don't try to force your child to eat or fight over food.** Of course, it is impossible to force someone to eat. But the real advice here is to avoid turning food into a power struggle so that food doesn't become a way to gain favor with or express anger toward someone else.
- **Recognize that appetite varies.** Children may eat well at one meal and have no appetite at another. Rather than seeing this as a problem, it may help to realize that appetites do vary. Continue to provide good nutrition at each mealtime (even if children don't choose to eat the occasional meal).
- **Keep it pleasant.** This tip is designed to help caregivers create a positive atmosphere during mealtime. Mealtimes should not be the time for arguments or expressing tensions. You do not want the child to have painful memories of mealtimes together or have nervous stomachs and problems eating and digesting food due to stress.
- **No short order chefs.** While it is fine to prepare foods that children enjoy, preparing a different meal for each child or family member sets up an unrealistic expectation from others. Children probably do best when they are hungry and a meal is ready. Limiting snacks rather than allowing children to "graze" continuously can help create an appetite for whatever is being served.
- **Limit choices.** If you give your preschool aged child choices, make sure that you give them one or two specific choices rather than asking "What would you like for lunch?" If given an open choice, children may change their minds or choose whatever their sibling does not choose!
- **Serve balanced meals.** Meals prepared at home tend to have better nutritional value than fast food or frozen dinners. Prepared foods tend to be higher in fat and sugar content as these ingredients enhance taste and profit margin because fresh food is often more costly and less profitable. However, preparing fresh food at home is not costly. It does, however, require more activity. Including children in meal preparation can provide a fun and memorable experience.
- **Don't bribe.** Bribing a child to eat vegetables by promising dessert is not a good idea. First, the child will likely find a way to get the dessert without eating the vegetables (by whining or fidgeting, perhaps, until the caregiver gives in). Secondly, it teaches the child that some foods are better than others. Children tend to naturally enjoy a variety of foods until they are taught that some are considered less desirable than others. A child, for example, may learn the broccoli they have enjoyed is seen as yucky by others unless it's smothered in cheese sauce![127]

---

[126] Children's Development by Ana R. Leon is licensed under CC BY 4.0

[127] Children's Development by Ana R. Leon is licensed under CC BY 4.0

USDA Meal Patterns for Young Children

The United States Department of Agriculture Food and Nutrition Service provides the following guidance for the daytime feeding of children age 3 to 5.

Early Childhood Meal Patterns[128]

Meal	Ages 3-5
Breakfast	3/4 cup milk 1/2 cup vegetables, fruit, or both ½ ounce equivalent grains
Lunch or Supper	3/4 cup milk 1½ ounces meat or meat alternative 1/4 cup vegetables 1/4 cup fruits ½ ounce equivalent of grains
Snack	*Select two of the following:* ½ cup of milk ½ ounce meat or meat alternative ½ cup vegetables ½ cup fruit ½ ounce equivalent of grains

Nutritional Needs during middle childhood

A number of factors can influence children's eating habits and attitudes toward food. Family environment, societal trends, taste preferences, and messages in the media all impact the emotions that children develop in relation to their diet. Television commercials can entice children to consume sugary products, fatty fast foods, excess calories, refined ingredients, and sodium. Therefore, it is critical that parents and caregivers direct children toward healthy choices. [129]

Parents greatly impact their child's nutritional choices. This time in a child's life provides an opportunity for parents and other caregivers to reinforce good eating habits and to introduce new foods into the diet, while remaining mindful of a child's preferences. Parents should also serve as role models for their children, who will often mimic their behavior and eating habits. Parents must continue to help their school-aged child establish healthy eating habits and attitudes toward food. Their primary role is to bring a wide variety of health-promoting foods into the home, so that their

---

[128] https://fns-prod.azureedge.net/sites/default/files/cacfp/CACFP_MealBP.pdf

[129] Research on the Benefits of Family Meals. Dakota County, Minnesota. . Updated April 30, 2012. Accessed December 4, 2017.

children can make good choices.[130]

Let's think for a moment about what our parents and grandparents used to eat? What are some of the differences that you may have experienced as a child?

One hundred years ago, as families sat down to dinner, they might have eaten boiled potatoes or corn, leafy vegetables such as cabbage or collards, fresh-baked bread, and, if they were fortunate, a small amount of beef or chicken. Young and old alike benefitted from a sound diet that packed a real nutritional punch. Times have changed. Many families today fill their dinner plates with fatty foods, such as French Fries cooked in vegetable oil, a hamburger that contains several ounces of ground beef, and a white-bread bun, with a single piece of lettuce and a slice or two of tomato as the only vegetables served with the meal.

Our diet has changed drastically as processed foods, which did not exist a century ago, and animal-based foods now account for a large percentage of our calories. Not only has what we eat changed, but the amount of it that we consume has greatly increased as well, as plates and portion sizes have grown much larger. All of these choices impact our health, with short- and long-term consequences as we age. Possible effects in the short-term include excess weight gain and constipation. The possible long-term effects, primarily related to obesity, include the risk of cardiovascular disease, diabetes, hypertension, as well as other health and emotional problems for children. Centers for Disease Control and Prevention. "Overweight and Obesity: Health Consequences."[131]

During middle childhood, a healthy diet facilitates physical and mental development and helps to maintain health and wellness. School-aged children experience steady, consistent growth, but at a slower rate than they did in early childhood. This slowed growth rate can have lasting a lasting impact if nutritional, caloric, and activity levels aren't adjusted in middle childhood which can lead to excessive weight gain early in life and can lead to obesity into adolescence and adulthood.[132]

Making sure that children have proper nutrients will allow for optimal growth and development. Look at the figure below to familiarize yourself with food and the place setting for myplate guidelines for healthy meals.

---

[130] Childhood by University of Hawai'i at Mānoa Food Science and Human Nutrition Program is licensed under CC BY-NC-SA 4.0

[131] An Introduction to Nutrition by Maureen Zimmerman and Beth Snow is licensed under CC BY-NC-SA 3.0

[132] Childhood by University of Hawai'i at Mānoa Food Science and Human Nutrition Program is licensed under CC BY-NC-SA 4.0 (modified by Dawn Rymond)

Nutrition guidelines from the USDA.[133]

One way to encourage children to eat healthy foods is to make meal and snack time fun and interesting. Parents should include children in food planning and preparation, for example selecting items while grocery shopping or helping to prepare part of a meal, such as making a salad. At this time, parents can also educate children about kitchen safety. It might be helpful to cut sandwiches, meats, or pancakes into small or interesting shapes. In addition, parents should offer nutritious desserts, such as fresh fruits, instead of calorie-laden cookies, cakes, salty snacks, and ice cream. Studies show that children who eat family meals on a frequent basis consume more nutritious foods.[134]

Energy

Children's energy needs vary, depending on their growth and level of physical activity. Energy requirements also vary according to gender. Girls require 1,200 to 1,400 calories a day from age 2 to 8 and 1,400-1,800 for age 9 to 13. Boys also need 1,200 to 1.400 calories daily from age 4 to 8 but their daily caloric needs go up to 1,600-2,000 from age 9 to 13. This range represents individual differences, including how active the child is.[135]

Recommended intakes of **macronutrients** (protein, carbohydrates, and fats) and most **micronutrients** (vitamins and minerals) are higher relative to body size, compared with nutrient needs during adulthood. Therefore, children should be provided nutrient-dense food at meal- and snack-time. However, it is important not to overfeed children, as this can lead to childhood obesity, which is discussed in the next section.

---

[133] Image by the USDA is in the public domain

[134] Research on the Benefits of Family Meals. Dakota County, Minnesota. . Updated April 30, 2012. Accessed December 4, 2017.

[135] Parent Tips – Calories Needed Each Day by the NIH is in the public domain

Children and Vegetarianism

Another issue that some parents face with school-aged children is the decision to encourage a child to become a vegetarian or a vegan. Some parents and caregivers decide to raise their children as vegetarians for health, cultural, or other reasons. Preteens and teens may make the choice to pursue vegetarianism on their own, due to concerns about animals or the environment. No matter the reason, parents with vegetarian children must take care to ensure vegetarian children get healthy, nutritious foods that provide all the necessary nutrients.

Types of Vegetarian Diets

There are several types of vegetarians, each with certain restrictions in terms of diet:

- **Ovo-vegetarians.** Ovo-vegetarians eat eggs, but do not eat any other animal products.

- **Lacto-ovo-vegetarians.** Lacto-ovo-vegetarians eat eggs and dairy products, but do not eat any meat.

- **Lacto-vegetarians.** Lacto-vegetarians eat dairy products, but do not eat any other animal products.

- **Vegans.** Vegans eat food only from plant sources, no animal products at all.

Children who consume some animal products, such as eggs, cheese, or other forms of dairy, can meet their nutritional needs. For a child following a strict vegan diet, planning is needed to ensure adequate intake of protein, iron, calcium, vitamin B_{12}, and vitamin D. Legumes and nuts can be eaten in place of meat, soy or almond milk fortified with calcium and vitamins D and B_{12} can replace cow's milk. Parents must be informed and knowledgeable in order to support proper development for children with a vegetarian or vegan diet.[136]

Children and Malnutrition

Many may not know that malnutrition is a problem that many children face, in both developing nations and the developed world. Even with the wealth of food in North America, many children grow up malnourished, or even hungry. The US Census Bureau characterizes households into the following groups:

- food secure

- food insecure without hunger

- food insecure with moderate hunger

---

[136] An Introduction to Nutrition by Maureen Zimmerman and Beth Snow is licensed under CC BY-NC-SA 3.0

- food insecure with severe hunger

Millions of children grow up in food-insecure households with inadequate diets due to both the amount of available food and the quality of food. In the United States, about 20 percent of households with children are food insecure to some degree. In half of those, only adults experience food insecurity, while in the other half both adults and children are considered to be food insecure, which means that children did not have access to adequate, nutritious meals at times.[137]

Growing up in a food-insecure household can lead to a number of problems. Deficiencies in iron, zinc, protein, and vitamin A can result in stunted growth, illness, and limited development. Federal programs, such as the National School Lunch Program, the School Breakfast Program, and Summer Feeding Programs, work to address the risk of hunger and malnutrition in school-aged children. They help to fill the gaps and provide children living in food-insecure households with greater access to nutritious meals.[138]

School Lunch Programs[139]

Many school age children eat breakfast, snacks, and lunch at their schools. Therefore, it is important for schools to provide meals that are nutritionally sound. In the United States, more than thirty-one million children from low-income families are given meals provided by the National School Lunch Program. This federally funded program offers low-cost or free breakfast, snacks, and lunches to school facilities. School districts that take part receive subsidies from the US Department of Agriculture (USDA) for every meal they serve that must meet 2015 Dietary Guidelines for Americans.

Knowing that many children in the United States buy or receive free lunches in the school cafeteria, it might be worthwhile to look at the nutritional content of school lunches. You can obtain this information through your local school district's website. An example of a school menu from a school district in north central Texas is a meal consisting of pasta alfredo, bread stick, peach cup, tomato soup, a brownie, and 2% milk which is in compliance with Federal Nutritional Guidelines. Consider another menu from an elementary school in the state of Washington. This sample meal consists of chicken burger, tater tots, fruit, veggies, and 1% or nonfat milk. This meal is also in compliance with Federal Nutrition Guidelines but has about 300 fewer calories than the menu in Texas. This is a big difference in calories and nutritional value of these prepared lunches that are chosen and approved of by officials on behalf of children in these districts.

---

[137]Coleman-Jensen A, et al. Household Food Security in the United States in 2010. US Department of Agriculture, Economic Research Report, no. ERR-125; 2011.

[138] Lifespan Development - Module 6: Middle Childhood by Lumen Learning references Psyc 200 Lifespan Psychology by Laura Overstreet, licensed under CC BY 4.0 (modified by Dawn Rymond)

[139] Childhood by University of Hawai'i at Mānoa Food Science and Human Nutrition Program is licensed under CC BY-NC-SA 4.0 (modified by Dawn Rymond)

School Lunch Programs

Healthy School Lunch Campaigns helps to promote children's health. This is done by educating government officials, school officials, food-service workers, and parents and is sponsored by the Physicians Committee for Responsible Medicine. They educate and encourage schools to offer low-fat, cholesterol-free options in school cafeterias and in vending machines and work to improve the food served to children at school. Unfortunately, many school districts in the nation allow students to purchase chips, cookies, and ice cream along with their meals. These districts rely on the sale of these items in the lunchrooms to earn additional revenues. Not only are they making money off of children and families with junk food, they are also adding additional empty calories to their daily intake. These districts need to look at the menus and determine the rationale for offering additional snacks and desserts for children at their schools. Whether children receive free lunches, buy their own, or bring their lunch from home, quality nutrition is what is best for these growing bodies and minds.

Food Allergies

A **food allergy** occurs when the body has a specific and reproducible immune response to certain foods. The body's immune response can be severe and life threatening, such as anaphylaxis. Although the immune system normally protects people from germs, in people with food allergies, the immune system mistakenly responds to food as if it were harmful.

Eight foods or food groups account for 90% of serious allergic reactions in the United States: milk, eggs, fish, crustacean shellfish, wheat, soy, peanuts, and tree nuts.

The symptoms and severity of allergic reactions to food can be different between individuals, and can also be different for one person over time. Anaphylaxis is a sudden and severe allergic reaction that may cause death.[4] Not all allergic reactions will develop into anaphylaxis.

- Children with food allergies are two to four times more likely to have asthma or other allergic conditions than those without food allergies.

- The prevalence of food allergies among children increased 18% during 1997-2007, and allergic reactions to foods have become the most common cause of anaphylaxis in community health settings.

- Although difficult to measure, research suggests that approximately 4% of children and adolescents are affected by food allergies.

The CDC recommends that as part of maintaining a healthy and safe environment for children, caregivers should:

- Be aware of any food allergies.

- Educate other children and all adults that care for a child with food allergies.

- Ensure the daily management of food allergies.

- Prepare for food allergy emergencies.[140]

Food Allergies and Food Intolerance

Food intolerance and food allergies are an issue for some school-aged children. Recent studies show that three million children under age eighteen are allergic to at least one type of food.

Some of the most common **food allergies** come from foods that include peanuts, milk, eggs, soy, wheat, and shellfish. An allergy occurs when a protein in food triggers an immune response, which results in the release of antibodies, histamine, and other defenders that attack foreign bodies. Possible symptoms include itchy skin, hives, abdominal pain, vomiting, diarrhea, and nausea. Symptoms usually develop within minutes to hours after consuming a food allergen. Children can outgrow a food allergy, especially allergies to wheat, milk, eggs, or soy.[141]

Anaphylaxis is a life-threatening reaction that results in difficulty breathing, swelling in the mouth and throat, decreased blood pressure, shock, or even death. Milk, eggs, wheat, soybeans, fish, shellfish, peanuts, and tree nuts are the most likely to trigger this type of response. A dose of the drug epinephrine is often administered via a "pen" to treat a person who goes into anaphylactic shock.[142]

---

[140] Food Allergies in Schools by the CDC is in the public domain

[141] Childhood by University of Hawai'i at Mānoa Food Science and Human Nutrition Program is licensed under CC BY-NC-SA 4.0

[142] Food Allergy Quick Facts. National Institutes of Health, US Department of Health and Human Services. Updated March 27, 2017. Accessed December 10, 2017.

An EpiPen.[143]

Some children experience a **food intolerance**, which does not involve an immune response. A food intolerance is marked by unpleasant symptoms that occur after consuming certain foods. Lactose intolerance, though rare in very young children, is one example. Children who suffer from this condition experience an adverse reaction to the lactose in milk products. It is a result of the small intestine's inability to produce enough of the enzyme lactase. Symptoms of lactose intolerance usually affect the gastro-intestinal tract and can include bloating, abdominal pain, gas, nausea, and diarrhea. An intolerance is best managed by making dietary changes and avoiding any foods that trigger the reaction.[144]

Childhood Obesity

Childhood obesity is a complex health issue. It occurs when a child is well above the normal or healthy weight for his or her age and height. Childhood obesity is a serious problem in the United States putting children at risk for poor health. In 2015-2016, 13.9% of 2- to 5-year-olds were obese.

Where people live can affect their ability to make healthy choices. Obesity disproportionally affects children from low-income families.

Causes of Obesity

The causes of excess weight gain in young people are similar to those in adults, including factors such as a person's behavior and genetics. Behaviors that influence excess weight gain include:

- eating high calorie, low-nutrient foods
- not getting enough physical exercise
- sedentary activities (such as watching television or other screen devices)
- medication use
- sleep routines

Consequences of Obesity

The consequences of childhood obesity are both immediate and long term. It can affect physical as well as social and emotional well-being.

More Immediate Health Risks
  ○ High blood pressure and high cholesterol, which are risk factors for cardiovascular

---

[143] Image by Sean William is licensed under CC BY-SA 3.0

[144] Lactose Intolerance. National Institute of Diabetes and Digestive and Kidney Diseases. Updated June 2014. Accessed December 4, 2017.; Childhood by University of Hawai'i at Mānoa Food Science and Human Nutrition Program is licensed under CC BY-NC-SA 4.0

disease (CVD).

- ○ Increased risk of impaired glucose tolerance, insulin resistance, and type 2 diabetes.
- ○ Breathing problems, such as asthma and sleep apnea.
- ○ Joint problems and musculoskeletal discomfort.
- ○ Fatty liver disease, gallstones, and gastro-esophageal reflux (i.e., heartburn).

Childhood obesity is also related to

- ○ Psychological problems such as anxiety and depression.
- ○ Low self-esteem and lower self-reported quality of life.
- ○ Social problems such as bullying and stigma.

Future Health Risks

- ○ Children who have obesity are more likely to become adults with obesity.[11] Adult obesity is associated with increased risk of a number of serious health conditions including heart disease, type 2 diabetes, and cancer.
- ○ If children have obesity, their obesity and disease risk factors in adulthood are likely to be more severe.[145]

Being Overweight and Obesity in Children

Excess weight and obesity in children is associated with a variety of medical conditions including high blood pressure, insulin resistance, inflammation, depression, and lower academic achievement (Lu, 2016). Being overweight has also been linked to impaired brain functioning, which includes deficits in executive functioning, working memory, mental flexibility, and decision making (Liang, Matheson, Kaye, & Boutelle, 2014). Children who ate more saturated fats performed worse on relational memory tasks, while eating a diet high in omega-3 fatty acids promoted relational memory skills (Davidson, 2014). Using animal studies, Davidson et al. (2013) found that large amounts of processed sugars and saturated fat weakened the blood-brain barrier, especially in the hippocampus. This can make the brain more vulnerable to harmful substances that can impair its functioning. Another important executive functioning skill is controlling impulses and delaying gratification. Children who are overweight show less inhibitory control than normal weight children, which may make it more difficult for them to avoid unhealthy foods (Lu, 2016). Overall, being overweight as a child increases the risk for cognitive decline as one ages.

The current measurement for determining excess weight is the **Body Mass Index (BMI)** which expresses the relationship of height to weight. According to the Centers for Disease Control and Prevention (CDC), childrens whose BMI is at or above the 85th percentile for their age are considered **overweight**, while children who are at or above the 95th percentile are considered **obese** (Lu, 2016). In 2011-2012 approximately 8.4% of 2-5 year-olds were considered overweight or obese, and 17.7% of 6-11 year-olds were overweight or obese (CDC, 2014b).[146]

---

[145] Childhood Obesity Causes & Consequences by the CDC is in the public domain

Obesity Rates for Children: About 16 to 33 percent of American children are obese (U. S. Department of Health and Human Services, 2005). This is defined as being at least 20 percent over their ideal weight. The percentage of obesity in school-aged children has increased substantially since the 1960s and has in fact doubled since the 1980s. This is true in part because of the introduction of a steady diet of television and other sedentary activities. In addition, we have come to emphasize high fat, fast foods as a culture. Pizza, hamburgers, chicken nuggets and "lunchables" with soda have replaced more nutritious foods as staples. The decreased participation in school physical education and youth sports is just one of many factors that has led to an increase in children being overweight or obese.

Being Overweight Can Be a Lifelong Struggle

A growing concern is the lack of recognition from parents that children are overweight or obese. Katz (2015) referred to this as "**oblivobesity**". Black et al. (2015) found that parents in the United Kingdom (UK) only recognized their children as obese when they were above the 99.7th percentile while the official cut-off for obesity is at the 85th percentile. Oude Luttikhuis, Stolk, and Sauer (2010) surveyed 439 parents and found that 75% of parents of overweight children said the child had a normal weight and 50% of parents of obese children said the child had a normal weight. For these parents, overweight was considered normal and obesity was considered normal or a little heavy. Doolen, Alpert, and Miller (2009) reported on several studies from the United Kingdom, Australia, Italy, and the United States, and in all locations parents were more likely to misperceive their children's weight. Black, Park, and Gregson (2015) concluded that as the average weight of children rises, what parents consider normal also rises. If parents cannot identify if their children are overweight they will not be able to intervene and assist their children with proper weight management.

An added concern is that the children themselves are not accurately identifying if they are overweight. In a United States sample of 8-15 year-olds, more than 80% of overweight boys and 70% of overweight girls misperceived their weight as normal (Sarafrazi, Hughes, & Borrud, 2014). Also noted was that as the socioeconomic status of the children rose, the frequency of these misconceptions decreased. It appeared that families with more resources were more conscious of what defines a healthy weight.

Results of Childhood Obesity

Children who are overweight tend to be rejected, ridiculed, teased and bullied by others (Stopbullying.gov, 2016). This can certainly be damaging to their self-image and popularity. In addition, obese children run the risk of suffering orthopedic problems such as knee injuries, and they have an increased risk of heart disease and stroke in adulthood (Lu, 2016). It is hard for a

---

[146] Lifespan Development: A Psychological Perspective by Martha Lally and Suzanne Valentine-French is licensed under CC BY-NC-SA 3.0

child who is obese to become a non-obese adult. In addition, the number of cases of pediatric diabetes has risen dramatically in recent years.

Behavioral interventions, including training children to overcome impulsive behavior, are being researched to help overweight children (Lu, 2016). Practicing inhibition has been shown to strengthen the ability to resist unhealthy foods. Parents can help their overweight children the best when they are warm and supportive without using shame or guilt. They can also act like the child's frontal lobe until it is developed by helping them make correct food choices and praising their efforts (Liang, et al., 2014). Research also shows that exercise, especially aerobic exercise, can help improve cognitive functioning in overweight children (Lu, 2016). Parents should take caution against emphasizing diet alone to avoid the development of any obsession about dieting that can lead to eating disorders. Instead, increasing a child's activity level is most helpful.

Dieting is not really the answer. If you diet, your basal metabolic rate tends to decrease thereby making the body burn even fewer calories in order to maintain the weight. Increased activity is much more effective in lowering the weight and improving the child's health and psychological well-being. Exercise reduces stress and being an overweight child, subjected to the ridicule of others can certainly be stressful. Parents should take caution against emphasizing diet alone to avoid the development of any obsession about dieting that can lead to eating disorders as teens. Again, helping children to make healthy food choices and increasing physical activity will help prevent childhood obesity.[147]

Exercise, Physical Fitness, and Sports
Recess and Physical Education: Recess is a time for free play and Physical Education (PE) is a structured program that teaches skills, rules, and games. They're a big part of physical fitness for school age children. For many children, PE and recess are the key component in introducing children to sports. After years of schools cutting back on recess and PE programs, there has been a turn around, prompted by concerns over childhood obesity and the related health issues. Despite these changes, currently only the state of Oregon and the District of Columbia meet PE guidelines of a minimum of 150 minutes per week of physical activity in elementary school and 225 minutes in middle school (SPARC, 2016).

Organized Sports: Pros and Cons
Middle childhood seems to be a great time to introduce children to organized sports, and in fact, many parents do. Nearly 3 million children play soccer in the United States (United States Youth Soccer, 2012). This activity promises to help children build social skills, improve athletically and

---

[147] Lifespan Development: A Psychological Perspective by Martha Lally and Suzanne Valentine-French is licensed under CC BY-NC-SA 3.0 (modified by Dawn Rymond); Lifespan Development - Module 6: Middle Childhood by Lumen Learning references Psyc 200 Lifespan Psychology by Laura Overstreet, licensed under CC BY 4.0 (modified by Dawn Rymond)

learn a sense of competition. However, the emphasis on competition and athletic skill can be counterproductive and lead children to grow tired of the game and want to quit. In many respects, it appears that children's activities are no longer children's activities once adults become involved and approach the games as adults rather than children. The U. S. Soccer Federation recently advised coaches to reduce the amount of drilling engaged in during practice and to allow children to play more freely and to choose their own positions. The hope is that this will build on their love of the game and foster their natural talents.

Sports are important for children. Children's participation in sports has been linked to:

- Higher levels of satisfaction with family and overall quality of life in children

- Improved physical and emotional development

- Better academic performance

Yet, a study on children's sports in the United States (Sabo & Veliz, 2008) has found that gender, poverty, location, ethnicity, and disability can limit opportunities to engage in sports. Girls were more likely to have never participated in any type of sport.

This study also found that fathers may not be providing their daughters as much support as they do their sons. While boys rated their fathers as their biggest mentor who taught them the most about sports, girls rated coaches and physical education teachers as their key mentors. Sabo and Veliz also found that children in suburban neighborhoods had a much higher participation in sports than boys and girls living in rural or urban centers. In addition, Caucasian girls and boys participated in organized sports at higher rates than minority children. With a renewed focus, males and females can benefit from all sports and physical activity.[148]

---

7 MOTOR DEVELOPMENT

Learning Objectives At the completion of this chapter, students will be able to:	Related Course Objective
7-1 Describe the development of Large Motor skills from infancy to late childhood.	1, 4
7-2 Describe the development of small motor skills from infancy to late childhood.	1,4
7-3 Describe how contextual factors, such as access to materials, child sex, and culture can impact the development of motor skills.	1, 2, 4

Sensation and Perception

Defining Sensation and Perception: it is important to distinguish between how the terms "sensation" and "perception are used. Sensation occurs when information from the environment makes contact with one or more of the sensory receptors—eyes, ears, tongue, nostrils, and skin. Perception is the interpretation of the sensation when the message from the sensory register reaches the brain.

Throughout much of history, the newborn was considered a passive, disorganized being who possessed minimal abilities. William James, an early psychologist, had described the newborn's world as "a blooming, buzzing confusion," (Shaffer, 1985). However, current research techniques have demonstrated just how developed the newborn is with especially organized sensory and perceptual abilities. Considerable sensory and perceptual development takes place in the first 2 years of life.

Vision

The womb is a dark environment void of visual stimulation. Consequently, vision is the most poorly developed sense at birth and time is needed to build those neural pathways between the eye and the brain. Newborns typically cannot see further than 8 to 16 inches away from their faces (which is about the distance from the newborn's face to the mother/caregiver when an infant is breastfeeding/bottle-feeding). At birth their visual acuity is about 20/500 which means that an infant can see something at 20 feet that an adult with normal vision could see at 500 feet. Thus, the world probably looks blurry to young infants (newborns are very "near sighted"). Because of their poor visual acuity, they look longer at checkerboards with fewer large squares than with many small squares. Infants' thresholds for seeing a visual pattern are higher than adults'. Thus, toys for infants are sometimes manufactured with black and white patterns rather than pastel colors because the higher contrast between black and white makes the pattern more visible to the immature visual system. By about 6 months, infants' visual acuity improves and approximates adult 20/25 acuity. An infant's color perception is limited at birth because there are fewer "cones" in the eyes; by about 3-months of age an infant's color vision is similar to an adult's. Depth perception is present at birth.

Very young infants prefer looking at:

- Stripes rather than plain colors

- Three-dimensional objects rather than two-dimensional objects

- Human faces rather than picture of scrambled human facial features

- Patterns over solid colors

When viewing a person's face, newborns do not look at the eyes the way adults do; rather, they tend to look at the chin—a less detailed part of the face. However, by 2 or 3 months, they will seek more detail when exploring an object visually and begin showing preferences for unusual images over familiar ones, for patterns over solids, for faces over patterns, and for three-dimensional objects over flat images. Newborns have difficulty distinguishing between colors, but within a few months they are able to discriminate between colors as well as adults do. Sensitivity to binocular depth cues, which require inputs from both eyes, is evident by about 3 months and continues to develop during the first 6 months. By 6 months, the infant can perceive depth perception in pictures as well (Sen, Yonas, & Knill, 2001). Infants who have experience crawling and exploring will pay greater attention to visual cues of depth and modify their actions accordingly (Berk, 2007).

As children grow through the early childhood years and then middle childhood, it is important that they receive regular vision screening. This regular vision screening should begin before age 3. Annual screening can help to detect problems early. In addition to problems such as *myopia* (or near-sightedness; near objects are clear but far are blurry) *hyperopia* (or far-sightedness; near objects are blurry but far objects are clear), children can experience a number of visual problems. One example is *strabismus*, sometimes called "cross eye," in which a child can not simultaneously align both eyes. Early surgery can often correct severe cases, and more mild cases may be corrected through exercise and therapy. Another example is *amblyopia*, the medical term used when the vision in one of the eyes is reduced because the eye and the brain are not working together properly. The eye itself looks normal, but it is not being used normally because the brain is favoring the other eye. This condition is also sometimes called lazy eye.

Hearing

The infant's sense of hearing is very keen at birth, and the ability to hear is evident as soon as the 7th month of prenatal development. In fact, an infant can distinguish between very similar sounds as early as one month after birth (for example, between the sounds "puh" and "buh")and can distinguish between a familiar and unfamiliar voice even earlier. Infants prefer human voices over other sounds, and they prefer the pitch and loudness of a female voice over a male voice. Newborns also prefer their mother's voices over another female when speaking the same material (DeCasper & Fifer, 1980).

Infants are especially sensitive to the frequencies of sounds in human speech and prefer the exaggeration of infant-directed speech, which will be discussed later. Additionally, infants are innately ready to respond to the sounds of any language, but some of this ability will be lost by 7 or 8 months as the infant becomes familiar with the sounds of a particular language and less sensitive to sounds that are part of an unfamiliar language. Additionally, they will register in utero specific information heard from their mother's voice. The "Cat in the Hat study" illustrates this.

Early Hearing

DeCasper and Spence (1986) tested 16 infants whose mothers had previously read to them prenatally. The mothers read several passages to their fetuses, including the first 28 paragraphs of *The Cat in the Hat*, beginning when they were 7 months pregnant. The fetuses

Early Hearing

had been exposed to the stories on average of 67 times or 3.5 hours.

During the testing, the infants were able to choose between recordings of two stories, one of which was a story their mothers read to them while in the womb, based on how fast they sucked on their pacifiers. They showed a preference for the stories that their mothers read to them while in the womb.[149]

Hearing only gets worse across the lifespan – we are born with the greatest natural level of hearing that we will have. It is important that children have regular hearing screenings as they grow in the preschool and elementary school years.

Touch and Pain

Immediately after birth, a newborn is sensitive to touch and temperature, and is also highly sensitive to pain, responding with crying and cardiovascular responses (Balaban & Reisenauer, 2013). Infants are capable of *haptic discrimination,* which means that they discriminate between objects by feel. For example, when an infant is shown a typical smooth pacifier, then with some slight of hand has a "bumpy" pacifier placed in their mouth, they will show surprise. Infants can also discriminate between two objects by weight.

Taste and Smell

Taste and smell are well developed at birth. Studies of taste and smell demonstrate that babies respond with different facial expressions, suggesting that certain preferences are innate. Newborns can distinguish between sour, bitter, sweet, and salty flavors and show a preference for sweet flavors. Newborns also prefer the smell of their mothers. An infant only 6 days old is significantly more likely to turn toward its own mother's breast pad than to the breast pad of another baby's mother (Porter, Makin, Davis, & Christensen, 1992), and within hours of birth an infant also shows a preference for the face of its own mother (Bushnell, 2001; Bushnell, Sai, & Mullin, 1989).

Infants seem to be born with the ability to perceive the world in an intermodal way; that is, through stimulation from more than one sensory modality. For example, infants who sucked on a pacifier with a smooth surface preferred looking at visual models of a pacifier with a smooth surface. But those that were given a pacifier with a textured surface preferred to look at a visual model of a pacifier with a textured surface.[150]

---

[149] Lifespan Development: A Psychological Perspective (page 76) by Martha Lally and Suzanne Valentine-French is licensed under CC BY-NC-SA 3.0

[150] Lifespan Development: A Psychological Perspective (pages 76-77) by Martha Lally and Suzanne Valentine-French

GROSS (or, LARGE) MOTOR SKILLS

Voluntary movements involve the use of large muscle groups and are typically large movements of the arms, legs, head, and torso. They are referred to as gross motor skills (or large motor skills). (note: "Gross motor" and "Large motor" mean exactly the same thing; you may see either term used when referring to children's development and they may be used interchangeably). These skills begin to develop first. Examples include moving to bring the chin up when lying on the stomach, moving the chest up, rocking back and forth on hands and knees, and then crawling. But it also includes exploring an object with one's feet as many babies do as early as 8 weeks of age if seated in a carrier or other device that frees the hips. This may be easier than reaching for an object with the hands, which requires much more practice (Berk, 2007). And sometimes an infant will try to move toward an object while crawling and surprisingly move backward because of the greater amount of strength in the arms than in the legs! This also tends to lead infants to pulling up on furniture, usually with the goal of reaching a desired object. Usually this will also lead to taking steps and eventually walking.

Large motor (or Gross motor) skills involve the large muscles of the body. After crawling, all typically developing children will eventually learn to walk. This locomotion requires new learning in balance and posture – what the infant learned while crawling about their position in space and balance will have to be re-learned and adjusted through practice as they walk. Development in the second year includes things like pulling toys while walking, walking quickly and running stiffly, and climbing stairs.

The first large motor skills in infancy involve gaining head control (remember the cepholocaudal principle of development), for example learning to sit up requires the strength the lift and to balance the head. In addition to first gaining control over the head, sitting requires control of many different muscles – head and neck, shoulders and back and hips. Sitting also requires balance in space – many infants first sit in a sort of tripod position with one or both hands on the floor between their legs and their legs outstretched.

As an infant masters (mastering a motor skill means being able to perform the skill without conscious, deliberate effort), infants begin to learn to reach for objects while sitting. The motor skills that the child has learned involving reaching while prone – for example, reaching with their hands and feet for a mobile while on their back in a crib (infants were able to make contact with objects by 3-4 months) – must be relearned now that they are sitting up. Reaching while sitting requires arm control, visual coordination to know where the object is located in space, and the ability to maintain balance while reaching.

Eventually the infant may learn to crawl. Babies start to cra#d3d3d3wl when their body has developed enough upper body strength to pull themselves forward, typically about 7- to 9-months of age. Learning to crawl begins gradually and often by mistake. It is often a response to reaching for something that is just out of reach and the frustration pushes the infant to nudge themselves further toward the desired object. It is important to understand that there is no single "path" through which all infants progress. "Crawling" on the belly is usually followed by "creeping" (just the hands and feet on floor). Some infants crawl on the belly and never creep with just their hands and feet on the floor. Some crawl like a bear. Some like Mowgli in the jungle book with their legs straight. Some just scoot from one place to another on their bottoms. Some only crawl backwards. The important thing is that they are getting to where they want to go, and they are exercising their muscles to strengthen their hands, arms, feet and legs for walking. No matter what sequence of crawling an infant progresses through, or even if they crawl at all, all typically developing infants learn to walk. As infants crawl, what they learned about reaching and balance while sitting up doesn't completely help them. They must learn new information about reaching and balance now that they are crawling. After a few weeks of crawling a fear of heights becomes apparent and infants become more realistic in their crawling attempts.

Learning to walk typically starts with "cruising" - walking while holding on to furniture. First steps are often supported by adults holding on the infant's hands or body. Beginning walking is typified by the feet being wide apart (the bottoms of infant and toddler feet are very flat as a fatty pad fills the space that will later be arched), small steps, and a toddle back and forth as the infant steps (this is the source of the term "toddler"). What infants learned about reaching and balance while they were creeping and crawling doesn't completely help them as they begin to walk – again, they must learn new information about reaching and balancing as they walk. As the infant experiences changes in terrain, they must learn to adjust their balance and posture. For example, a child who has learned to walk outside my revert back to crawling when they first go outside and are in the grass or on a slope.

A note about age-related milestones:

Remember the discussion of DAP earlier in this book. I proposed that for a developmentally appropriate practices understanding of a given child, three viewpoints were necessary. First, age-related expectations for the child. Second, how culture and environment have impacted the child. And third, the center of the model was individual aspects of that unique child. No two children develop in the exact same way. For example, I know how a "typical" 3-year-old will hold a pair of scissors. However, there are some 3-year-olds who have had a lot of experience with using scissors and who have been in an environment that encourages children to use scissors. I wouldn't be surprised if such a child looked more like a "typical" 4-year-old using the scissors. On the other hand, there are some 3-year-olds who have no interest in scissors and have never used them

---

before. They might look more like "typical" 2-year-olds.

The purpose of presenting age-related milestones here is not to say that such milestones represent "correct" or even "best" development. The goal is to share age-related expectations so that professionals who will work with young children possess the knowledge necessary for making good developmentally appropriate practice judgments. It is my expectation that readers understand that there is a RANGE in the timing of behaviors that are "typical." Moreover, remember that culture as well as individual factors impact the timing of behaviors.

There are a great deal of individual and cultural variations in the emergence of motor skills. These differences in timing may be related to cultural practices. Recall the example with culture and learning to walk that was introduced earlier in the book as an example. When surveyed, mothers in Jamaica say that infants should walk at an earlier age than do mothers in the US. In turn, when they are observed, infants in Jamaica actually do walk a little sooner on average than infants in the US. The mothers in Jamaica are more likely to exercise the legs of their infants and the infants do walk a little earlier. However, even though the Jamaican infants walk earlier on average, there are some US infants who will walk earlier than some Jamaican infants. In contrast, in modern China it is considered "dirty" to allow an infant on the ground or floor and so infants are discouraged from crawling. Infants in China do walk a little later than do infants in the US. However, even though the US infants walk earlier on average than the Chinese infants, there are some infants in China that will walk earlier that some infants in the US. In fact, even though Jamaican infants walk a little earlier and Chinese infants walk a little later, the age that infants begin to walk in Jamaica, the US and China all fall within the "typical" range of infant walking (about ~11- to 14-months).

Gross Motor Milestones

As stated above, children grow very quickly and meet physical milestones rapidly in the first few years of life. The following is a table of the major milestones (behaviors or physical skills seen in infants and children as they grow and develop that typically occur within normal range) that occur in children during those first formative years. [151]

Gross Motor Milestones[152]

[151]Children's Development by Ana R. Leon is licensed under CC BY 4.0

[152]Developmental milestones record by the U.S. National Library of Medicine is in the public domain

Typical Age	What Most Children Do by This Age
2 months	• Can hold head up and begins to push up when lying on tummy • Makes smoother movements with arms and legs
4 months	• Holds head steady, unsupported • Pushes down on legs when feet are on a hard surface • May be able to roll over from tummy to back • Brings hands to mouth • When lying on stomach, pushes up to elbows
6 months	• Rolls over in both directions (front to back, back to front) • Begins to sit without support • When standing, supports weight on legs and might bounce • Rocks back and forth, sometimes crawling backward before moving forward
9 months	• Stands, holding on • Can get into sitting position • Sits without support • Pulls to stand • Crawls
1 year	• Gets to a sitting position without help • Pulls up to stand, walks holding on to furniture ("cruising") • May take a few steps without holding on

Typical Age	What Most Children Do by This Age
	• May stand alone
18 months	• Walks alone • May walk up steps and run • Pulls toys while walking • Can help undress self
2 years	• Stands on tiptoe • Kicks a ball • Begins to run • Climbs onto and down from furniture without help • Walks up and down stairs holding on • Throws ball overhand

One way to think about milestones during infancy, as in the table above, is to specify an age where the majority of children demonstrate the skill. For example, in the table above, the majority of children at four months of age demonstrate the ability to roll over. Another way to present this sort of milestone is through a range of time in which the majority of children will display the trait. For example, in the table below, the milestone of rolling over is met by most children in the range of 2-5 months. Both tables are correct – most children will roll over by 4-months, and most will display the behavior first at some time between 2-5 months. The presentation of a range of months has the benefit of recognizing that there is a range of time in which emergence of a behavior is "typical."

Infancy milestones:

Roll over = 2-5 months

Sit without support = 4.5 – 7.5 months

Stand with support = 5-10 months

Pull self to stand = 6-10 months

Walk using furniture for support = 7-13 month

Stand alone easily = 10-14 months

Toddler milestones:

13-18 months = walk flat footed and stiffly. Can pull a toy attached to a string. Use hands and legs to climb up steps, ride on four-wheeled toys.

18-24 months: walk quickly or run stiffly for short distances, balance on feet in a squat position while playing on the floor, walk backward without falling, stand and kick a ball without falling, stand and throw a ball, jump in place.

Gross Motor Skills in Early Childhood Years

Children continue to improve their gross motor skills as they run and jump. They frequently ask their caregivers to "look at me" while they hop or roll down a hill. Children's songs are often accompanied by arm and leg movements or cues to turn around or move from left to right. Here is a table showing the progression of gross motor skills that children will typically develop during early childhood:

Gross Motor Milestones

Typical Age	What Most Children Do by This Age
3 years	<ul><li>Climbs well</li><li>Runs easily</li><li>Pedals a tricycle (3-wheel bike)</li><li>Walks up and down stairs, one foot on each step</li></ul>
4 years	<ul><li>Hops and stands on one foot up to 2 seconds</li></ul>

Typical Age	What Most Children Do by This Age
	• Catches a bounced ball most of the time
5 years	• Stands on one foot for 10 seconds or longer • Hops; may be able to skip • Can do a somersault • Can use the toilet on own • Swings and climbs

Activities to Support Gross Motor Skills

Here are some activities focused on play that young children enjoy and that support their gross motor skill development.

- Tricycle
- Slides
- Swings
- Sit-n-Spin
- Mini trampoline
- Bowling pins (can use plastic soda bottles also)
- Tent (try throwing blankets over chairs and other furniture to make a fort)
- Playground ladders
- Suspension bridge on playground
- Tunnels (try throwing a bean bag chair underneath for greater challenge)
- Ball play (kick, throw, catch)
- Simon Says
- Target games with bean bags, ball, etc.
- Dancing/moving to music
- Pushing self on scooter or skateboard while on stomach

Locomotor Skill	Three-year-old	Four-year-old	Five-year-old
Running	Run with lack of control in stops and starts Overall pattern more fluid than 2-year-old Run with flat foot action Inability to turn quickly	Run with control over starts, stops, and turns Speed is increasing Longer stride than 3-year-old Non-support period lengthening Can run 35 yards in 20-29 seconds	Run well established and used in play activities Control of run in distance, speed, and direction improving Speed is increasing Stride width increasing Non-support period lengthening
Galloping	Most children cannot gallop Early attempts are some variation of the run pattern	43% of children are attempting to learn to gallop During this year most children learn to gallop Early gallop pattern somewhat of a run and leap step	78% can gallop Can gallop with a right lead foot Can gallop with a left lead foot Can start and stop at will
Hopping	Can hop 10 times consecutively on both feet Can hop 1-3 times on one foot Great difficulty experienced with hop	33% are proficient at hopping Can hop 7-9 hops on one foot Hop pattern somewhat stiff and not fluid	79% become proficient during this year Can hop 10 or more hops on one foot Hop characterized by more spring-like action in

Locomotor Skill	Three-year-old	Four-year-old	Five-year-old
	pattern Attempts characterized by gross overall movement and a lot of arm movement		ankles, knees, and hips Can hop equally well on either leg
Climbing	Ascends stairs using mark time foot pattern During this year, ascending stairs is achieved with alternate foot pattern Descending stairs mostly with mark time foot pattern Climbing onto and off of low items continues to improve with higher heights being conquered	Ascends stairs using alternate foot pattern Descends stairs with alternate foot pattern Can climb a large ladder with alternate food pattern Can descend large ladder slowly with alternate foot pattern	Climbing skill increasing 70% can climb a rope ladder with bottom free 37% can climb a pole 32% can climb a rope with bottom free 14% can climb an overhead ladder with 15 degree incline Climbing includes more challenging objects such as trees, jungle gyms, large beans, etc.

Locomotor Skill	Three-year-old	Four-year-old	Five-year-old
Skipping	Skip is characterized by a shuffle step Can skip on one foot and walk on the other Actual true skip pattern seldom performed	14% can skip One footed skip still prevalent Overall movement stiff and undifferentiated Excessive arm action frequently occurring Skip mostly flat-footed	72% are proficient Can skip with alternate foot pattern Overall movement more smooth and fluid More efficient use of arms Skip mostly on the balls of feet
Jumping	42% are proficient Jumping pattern lacks differentiation Lands without knee bend to absorb force Minimal crouch for take-off Arms used ineffectively Can jump down from 28" height 68% can hurdle jump 3½"	72% are proficient Jumping pattern characterized by more preliminary crouch Can do standing broad jump 8-10" Can do running broad jump 23-33" 90% can hurdle jump 5" 51% can hurdle jump 9½"	81% are skillful Overall jumping pattern more smooth and rhythmical Use of arm thrust at take-off evident More proficient landing Can do standing broad jump 15-18" Can do running broad jump 28-35", vertical Can jump and reach 2½'

Locomotor Skill	Three-year-old	Four-year-old	Five-year-old
			90% can hurdle jump 8" 68% can hurdle jump 21½"
Balance Beam	Balance beam walking pattern characterized by mark time sequences Can traverse 25' walking path that is one inch wide in 31.5 seconds with 18 step-offs Can walk 3" wide beam forward 7.4', backward 3.9' 44% can touch knee down and regain standing position on 3" wide beam	Balance beam walking pattern characterized by alternate shuffle step Can traverse 25' walking path that is 1" wide in 27.7 seconds with 6 step-offs Can walk 3" wide beam forward 8.8', backward 5.8' 68% can touch knee down and regain standing position on 3' wide beam	beam walking characterized by alternate step pattern Can traverse 25' walking path that is 1" wide in 24.1 seconds with 3 step-offs Can walk 3" wide beam forward 11', backward 8.1' 84% can touch knee down and regain standing position on 3' wide beam

Preschoolers are in almost constant motion. In terms of the amount of movement, the preschool years are the time of the highest activity level of any age in the life span (the larger bodies of elementary school-age-children means that middle childhood is the time of highest activity if we measure it by the number of calories consumed and used). Preschoolers need daily large motor activities and exercise – this increases their physical as well as visual awareness. An example of an important large motor skill in the toddler and preschool years is climbing stairs, presented in the following table:

Climbing and Descending stairs:

Two-year-olds

Ascend stairs using marked-time climbing. May require assistance from an adult.

Descend stairs using marked-time climbing. Often require assistance from an adult.

Three-year-olds

Can ascend stairway unaided, alternating feet.

Because balance is a greater problem when walking down stairs than when walking up, children usually maintain marked-time climbing until they are about 4 years-old.

Can climb to top of a jungle gym, but may have difficulty coming down without instruction or assistance.

50% rated as proficient in climbing on jungle gyms.

Four-year-olds

Descends long stairway by alternating feet, if supported; with no support, marks time.

Ascending skills mastered.

Five-year-olds

Ascending skills mastered.

Descends long stairway, alternating feet, unaided.

In addition to descriptions of age-related expectations of large motor development, some aspects of motor development are described using stages. The following table presents an example of this type of description, stages in catching a ball.

Stages of Catching a Ball

Stage 1 : Delayed arm reaction

Arms straight in front until ball contact, then scooping action to chest

Feet stationary

Stage 2: Arms encircle as ball approaches;

Ball is "hugged" to chest

Feet are stationary or may take one step

Stage 3: To chest catch

Arms "scoop" under ball

Single step may be used to approach ball

Stage 4: Catch with hands only

Feet stationary or limited to one step

Stage 5: Catch with hands only while body moves through space

Children do not jump abruptly from one stage to the next, but there are periods where the performance is changing, improving, and displaying some of the characteristics of a subsequent stage.

Fine (or, Small) Motor Skills

More exact movements of the feet, toes, hands, and fingers are referred to as **fine motor skills** (or small motor skills; the terms are interchangeable). These include the ability to reach and grasp an object in coordination with vision. Newborns cannot grasp objects voluntarily but do wave their arms toward objects of interest. At about 4 months of age, the infant is able to reach for an object, first with both arms and within a few weeks, with only one arm. At this age, grasping an object involves the use of the fingers and palm, but no thumbs. Reaching and grasping requires coupling perceptual skills with motor skills.

Use of the thumb comes at about 9 months of age when the infant is able to grasp an object using the forefinger and thumb. This is known as the **pincer grip**. This ability greatly enhances the ability to control and manipulate an object and infants take great delight in this newfound ability. They may spend hours picking up small objects from the floor and placing them in containers. And as those objects will often next go into the mouth, caregivers must be vigilant about keeping items small enough to be choking hazards out of reach of little fingers. By 9 months, an infant can also watch a moving object, reach for it as it approaches and grab it. This is quite a complicated set of actions if we remember how difficult this would have been just a few months earlier.[153] The development of motor skills typically involves a progression from large motor to small motor. This is consistent with the proximodistal course of physical development. For example, for infants reaching initially involves movement of the whole shoulders and elbows crudely, and later to movements of the wrists and rotation of the hands, and then to coordination of the fingers and thumb. Experience affects reaching and grasping, and the skill becomes more refined during the first 2 years. At age 3 skill is still emerging from the infant ability to place and handle things. At age 4 coordination is improved and movements and placements of objects are more precise. At age 5 the hand, arm and body move together under better eye command.

Physical Fine Motor Milestones

While fine motor skills are slower to develop (in accordance with proximodistal development), pretty remarkable progress is made in fine motor development during the first two years. As stated above, in the first few years of life children go from having no intentional fine motor control to being able to manipulate objects to play and learn, as well as beginning to care of themselves. The following is a table of the major milestones in fine motor development; remember the discussion in the large motor section of the importance of remembering cultural and environmental influences on age-related expectations.

---

[153] Children's Development by Ana R. Leon is licensed under CC BY 4.0

Infant and Toddler Fine Motor Development:

2 – 2.5 months = hold rattle briefly, glance from one object to another

3-4 months play with rattle, inspect fingers, reach for dangling toys, visually track moving objects, mouthing objects

4-5 months = pick up object from chest, hold two objects, transfer object from one hand to another

5-6 months = bang objects in play, look for object while sitting

6-7 months = reach out to grasp small objects, manipulate objects

7-8 months = grasps with thumb and finger, pulls string to obtain object

8-9 months = persists in reaching for out of reach objects, searches for dropped object

10-11 months = crude release of objects, pincer grasp, pushes rolling toy along, hits cup with spoon

12-18 months = places block on top of another block, scribbles with large crayons, turns pages in large books, places objects in cups, etc.

18-24 months = scribbles and imitates arcs in drawing, turns doorknob with both hands, uscrews a lid, places large pegs in pegboard, connects and takes apart strings of pop-beads, zips and unzips large zippers, attempts at Velcro.

Fine Motor Milestones[154]

Typical Age	What Most Children Do by This Age
2 months	• Grasps reflexively • Does not reach for objects • Holds hands in fist

---

[154] Developmental Milestones by the CDC is in the public domain

Typical Age	What Most Children Do by This Age
4 months	• Brings hands to mouth • Uses hands and eyes together, such as seeing a toy and reaching for it • Follows moving things with eyes from side to side • Can hold a toy with whole hand (**palmar grasp**) and shake it and swing at dangling toys
6 months	• Reaches with both arms • Brings things to mouth • Begins to pass things from one hand to the other
9 months	• Puts things in mouth • Moves things smoothly from one hand to the other • Picks up things between thumb and index finger (pincer grip**)**
1 year	• Reaches with one hand • Bangs two things together • Puts things in a container, takes things out of a container • Lets things go without help • Pokes with index (pointer) finger
18 months	• Scribbles on own • Can help undress herself • Drinks from a cup • Eats with a spoon with some accuracy • Stacks 2-4 objects

Typical Age	What Most Children Do by This Age
2 years	• Builds towers of 4 or more blocks • Might use one hand more than the other • Makes copies of straight lines and circles • Enjoys pouring and filling • Unbuttons large buttons • Unzips large zippers • Drinks and feeds self with more accuracy

Here is a table showing how fine motor skills progress during early childhood for children that are typically developing.

Fine Motor Milestones[155]

Typical Age	What Most Children Do by This Age
3 years	• Copies a circle with pencil or crayon • Turns book pages one at a time • Builds towers of more than 6 blocks • Screws and unscrews jar lids or turns door handle
4 years	• Pours, cuts with supervision, and mashes own food • Draws a person with 2 to 4 body parts • Uses scissors • Starts to copy some capital letters
5 years	• Can draw a person with at least 6 body parts • Can print some letters or numbers • Copies a triangle and other geometric shapes • Uses a fork and spoon and sometimes a table knife

The following table displays fine motor skills typically developed during early childhood. The skills are listed in approximate order of difficulty in each period (for example, in the 3-year-old period, "pastes using pointer finger" is considered more difficult than "approximates a circle in

---

[155] Developmental Milestones by the CDC is in the public domain

drawing.")

37 to 48 months	49 to 60 months	61 to 72 months
.Approximates a circle in drawing .Cuts paper .Pastes using pointer finger .Turns book pages one at a time .Builds 3-block bridge .Builds 8-block tower .Draws 0 and + .Dresses and undresses doll .Unscrews jar lids .Pours from pitcher without spilling	.Strings and laces shoelace .Cuts following a line .Strings 10 beads .Copies figure X .Draws person with 2- 4 body parts .Opens and places clothespins (one- handed) .Builds a 5-block bridge .Pours from various containers .Prints first name	.Folds paper in halves and quarters .Traces around hand .Draws rectangle, circle, square, triangle .Cuts interior piece from paper .Uses crayons appropriately .Makes clay object with 2 small parts .Reproduces letters .Copies 2 short words

Manipulation/Manipulatives

By 2-3 years: Most children place simple geometric shapes in puzzle; string large beads; turn pages of book; work four-piece puzzle; use pegboard with large pegs; stack small wooden blocks; do a fingerplay (fingers not independent); roll, squeeze and pound play dough.

By 4-5 years: Most children can string small wooden beads; work a five-piece puzzle; use pegboard with small pegs; use fingers more independently; make balls and use tools with play dough (use cookie cutter).

By 5-6 years: Most children can work a twelve-piece puzzle; build complex structures with small blocks; braid; use fingers independently in fingerplays; attempt a pinch pot, coil pot, or "sculpture."

By 6-7 years: Most children can build complex structures with small interlocking blocks; make a pinch, coil port, or sculpture of clay or play dough.

By 7-8 years: Most children can swing a hammer accurately; sew and knit.

Scissors, Paste and Glue

By 2-3 years: Most children snip paper easily (cuts at edge of paper); scissors and paper held incorrectly; use large globs of paste or glue with little control.

By 3-4 years: Most children make one full cut with scissors (cuts one length of scissors); hand position may be incorrect; makes two full cuts (two lengths of scissors) have trouble cutting on straight line; use globs of paste or glue but have more control; use index finger to apply paste.

By 4-5 years: Most children cut on a straight line and a corner (90-degree angle) moving paper hand forward; use correct hand position; keep paste and glue in right spot and use reasonable amount.

By 5-6 years:Most children can cut on a curve; cut out geometric figure; cut interior angle (inside angle less than 90 degrees); cut out obtuse and acute angles; cut out a complex figure from a magazine; use scissors

Self-Help Skills

By 2-3 years: Most children can eat with spoon; hold cup in one hand; put on a coat (unassisted); unbutton clothes. Zip and unzip *Large* zippers, open door by turning knob, string large beads

By 4-5 years: Most children can eat correctly with fork; button and unbutton clothes; dress and undress without assistance, zip zippers haltingly; put coat on hanger; cut with scissors, following line, copy triangles, crosses, some letters.

By 5-6 years: Most children can button/unbutton clothes; zip zippers; eat with knife and fork; use knife to cut soft food; dress/undress; comb and brush hair; tie single overhand knot, tie shoelaces around age 6; draw person with six parts, copy some numerals and simple words.

Use of writing instrument

By 2-3 years:	Most children grasp writing implement with whole hand or fist; jab at paper; make scribbles with movement of the whole arm; copy vertical and horizontal lines.
By 3-4 years:	Most children try a three-point grasp but position on instrument is inconsistent; copy a cross and a circle; scribble with spots of intense color; use horizontal and vertical lines, crosses, and circles in pictures.
By 4-5 years:	Most children use correct hand grasp but position on instrument still inconsistent; copy a square and some letters (from first and last name); draw suns; draw human figures, a head with facial features (placement of eye, nose, mouth may not be correct); draw human figures with stick arms and legs and facial parts in correct place; scribble with repeated features and on a horizontal line (looks like writing); scribble leaving space between "words."
By 5-6 years:	Most children can form written letters (many inverted or mirror images); color between lines; draw buildings, cars, and boats (proportions incorrect — people are larger than buildings); trees and flowers; draw with correct proportions; incorporate letters into scribbling; write letters of first name (may not write letters in a line); write letters of last name (may not write letters in a line); draw rectangle, circle, and square.

Visual Pathways

Children's drawings are representative of the development of visual pathways; as children's brains mature the images in their drawings change. Early scribbles and dots illustrate the use of simple motor skills. No real connection is made between an image being visualized and what is created on paper. Early drawings emphasize flatness of drawing and painting. For toddlers, art activities are centered on the sensation of the activity itself, such as the feel of the brush on the paper or the sight of the color blue mixing with the color yellow to make green. As toddlers emerge in to the preschool years, their art activities continue to be focused on the process in the here-and-now, not the product of the final outcome. Three and four-year-olds often engage in art activities with no clear goal or outcome in mind. They are in the present, as if telling a story with their drawing that they are making up as they go. For this reason, it is best for adults not to ask a preschooler "what is it?" concerning their art – often the child has no end goal in mind. Instead, adults say "tell me about your picture" or "you are working so hard mixing those colors, tell me all about it." Open-ended art activities provide a hands-on approach to problem solving skills and reinforce ideas of scale, space, motion and distance.

There are a series of stages that young children go through in artistic drawings. Piaget described three basic stages of drawing: scribbling, shape and design, and pictorial. In 1970 Rhoda Kellog examined more than one million drawings by children and twenty basic scribbles; she differentiated Piaget's second stage of "shape and design" to three stages: placement, shape, and design. The first of these is the placement stage, typical of ages 2 and 3. Here the child emerges from scribbles to purposefully placing patterns on the page. The next stage is the shape stage at about age 3. Here the child begins to draw six different basic shapes: squares, circles, rectangles, triangles, crosses, and x's. The first shape that most children master is the circle. The children quickly enter the design stage (which is why Piaget considered shape and design a single stage), in which they begin to mix two of the basic shapes in to more complex designs. An example is a radial, which are lines emerging from a point, and mandalas, which are circles or squares combined with crosses or x's. It is not until about age 4 or 5 that children progress to the pictorial stage in which they produce objects that adults recognize. They begin to draw pictures that represent reality and their surroundings, as they now understand that one thing can symbolize another.

Stage	Age	Progress
Scribbles	1-2	Scribbles on paper
Placement Stage	2-3	Placement of patterns
Shape Stage	3	Diagrams of 6 basic shapes
Design Stage	3-4	Mix 2 basic shapes into more complex designs
Pictorial Stage	4-5	Objects that adults recognize

At age 3, the child begins to draw wispy creatures with heads and not much other detail. For many children, a basic shape of a circle will be combined with radials and this will become the child's first named drawing – a sun. Often this comes after an adult or peer names the drawing as the sun, and the child agrees and sets out to make more suns. For many children, the sun shape becomes the first drawing of a person – a "sun person" - as a face is drawn in the sun and two radials are expanded out to become arms and two are extended down to become legs. The "sun person" becomes a "tadpole person." Eventually, a child may draw a line across the two legs to form a closed separate body – arms typically still radiate from the head at first. By age 5 or 6 drawings become more realistic. Gradually pictures begin to have more detail and incorporate more parts of the body. Arm buds become arms and faces take on noses, lips and eventually eyelashes.

Basic Scribbles Age 1-2

Placement Stage age 2-3

Shape Stage Age 3[156]

Six typical shapes

[156]   All of these Images are public domain, "artwork" by Mary Hadley Meece

Design Stage age 3-4

mandalas and radials

Pictorial Stage age 5

Children's first representational drawings are often of a "sun." The sun gives rise to the "sun face" which in turn becomes the "tad pole person" as the rays of the sun are adapted in to arms and legs of the tadpole person.

Fine Motor Skills and Physical Development

Fine motor skill development in art and writing reflects brain development. Between ages 3 and 6, the left hemisphere of the brain grows dramatically. This side of the brain or hemisphere is typically involved in language skills. The right hemisphere continues to grow throughout early childhood and is involved in tasks that require spatial skills such as recognizing shapes and patterns. The **corpus callosum** which connects the two hemispheres of the brain undergoes a growth spurt between ages 3 and 6 and results in improved coordination between right and left hemisphere tasks. Fine motor skills in art and writing also reflect increasing hand-eye coordination, strength and dexterity.

The development of art and writing reflect the proximodistal characteristic of development – early writing attempts use whole arm movements, then more refined movements of the wrist and hand, then movements of the fingers. Consider this list of the three stages of writing. Toddlers, in stage 1, use whole movements when holding a writing instrument. Usually only the pencil or marker is touching the paper. We even see this sometimes in 3-year-old children. In stage 2, the hand and little finger rest on the desk or paper but not the forearm and wrist. The hand tends to move as one unit, rather than the fingers controlling the writing instrument. In stage 3, the forearm is on the paper or desk, and there is more wrist rotation. The hand is the anchor and the writing movement is done with the fingers. There is less whole arm movement. The following table shows age related changes in the use of writing instruments:

Use of Writing Instrument
By 2-3 years: Most children grasp writing implement with whole hand or fist; jab at paper; make scribbles with movement of the whole arm; copy vertical and horizontal lines.
By 3-4 years: Most children try a three-point grasp but position on instrument is inconsistent; copy a cross and a circle; scribble with spots of intense color; use horizontal and vertical lines, crosses, and circles in pictures.
By 4-5 years: Most children use correct hand grasp but position on instrument still inconsistent; copy a square and some letters (from first and last name); draw suns; draw human figures, a head with facial features (placement of eye, nose, mouth may not be correct); draw human figures with stick arms and legs and facial parts in correct place; scribble with repeated features and on a horizontal line (looks like writing); scribble leaving space between "words."

Children progress through a series of grasps in holding writing instruments. Many different grasps can be used by children, but there are three major types of grasps that most children will progress through: Supinate grasp, pronate grasp, and tripod grasp.

Supinate grasp the first stage in holding a writing or drawing implement; used by young preschoolers on drawing and writing tools; all four fingers and thumb wrap around writing instrument to form a fist, palm facing up. Writing is done with the entire hand. Implement is often grasped in the middle of the instrument rather than near the tip. This does not give them much control over the marks because the entire hand, wrist, and arm are involved in the movements rather than the fingers. Writing is done with entire hand. (Sometimes called a power grip or a fisted grip or "cylindrical grip").

Pronate grasp the second stage in holding a writing or drawing implement (happens between the supinate and tripod grasp); similar to supinate in that entire hand grips implement, but palm is down rather than up. Thumb and forefinger play an increasing role in writing and drawing (also called "digital grip.")

Tripod grip - as preschoolers get older, they switch to a tripod grip, holding the instrument between the fingers and thumb. This is a mature grip on a writing instrument, between 3 fingers - thumb, index finger, and middle finger; the third and last stage of writing grips. (sometimes referred to as a precision grip.

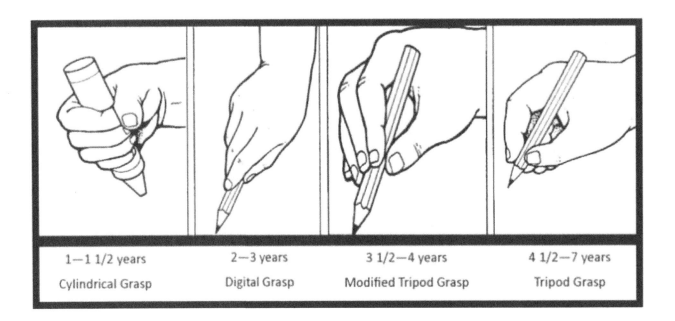

1—1 1/2 years	2—3 years	3 1/2—4 years	4 1/2—7 years
Cylindrical Grasp	Digital Grasp	Modified Tripod Grasp	Tripod Grasp

Activities to Support Fine Motor Skills
Children's fine motor skills improve with practice. Cultural experience affects drawings. Children's fine motor skills flourish in sociocultural contexts where tools are available and adults value fine motor and art activitie. Here are some fun activities that will help children continue to refine their fine motor abilities. Girls often exceed boys in fine motor skills. This may be because cultures emphasize fine motor skill activities for girls more than boys. It is important that all children have opportunities to engage in and practice fine motor skills. Fine motor skills are slower to develop than gross motor skills, so it is important to have age appropriate expectations and play-based activities for children.

- Pouring water into a container
- Drawing and coloring
- Using scissors
- Finger painting
- Fingerplays and songs (such as the Itsy, Bitsy Spider)
- Play dough
- Lacing and beading
- Practicing with large tweezers, tongs, and eye droppers

Children between ages 6 and 9, show significant improvement in their abilities to perform motor skills. This development growth allows children to gain greater control over the movement of their bodies, mastering many gross and fine motor skills that were beyond that of the younger child. Eye-hand coordination and fine motor skills allow for children to become better at writing and cutting. Children's drawings become increasingly detailed. Sports and extracurricular activities may become a part of the lives of children during middle childhood due to their physical growth and capabilities.

8 Classic Theories of Learning and Cognition

Learning Objectives At the completion of this chapter, students will be able to:	Related Course Objective
8-1 Describe major concepts of behaviorism and how these apply in the classroom.	1 3 5
8-2 Describe major concepts of Piaget's theory of cognitive development, describe how they are foundational to constructivism, and how these apply in the classroom.	1 3 5
8-3 Describe major concepts of Vygotsky's sociocultural theory and how these apply in the classroom.	1 3 5
8-4 Explain similarities and differences among the theories discussed in this unit.	1 3 5

Behaviorism and Learning Theory

Pavlov

Ivan Pavlov (1880-1937) was a Russian physiologist interested in studying digestion. As he recorded the amount of salivation his laboratory dogs produced as they ate, he noticed that they actually began to salivate before the food arrived as the researcher walked down the hall and toward the cage. The dogs knew that the food was coming because they had learned to associate the footsteps with the food. The key word here is "learned". A learned response is called a "conditioned" response.

Pavlov began to experiment with this "psychic" reflex. He began to ring a bell, for instance, prior to introducing the food. Sure enough, after making this connection several times, the dogs could be made to salivate to the sound of a bell. Once the bell had become an event to which the dogs had learned to salivate, it was called a conditioned stimulus. The act of salivating to a bell was a response that had also been learned, now termed in Pavlov's jargon, a conditioned response.

Notice that the response, salivation, is the same whether it is conditioned or unconditioned (unlearned or natural). What changed is the stimulus to which the dog salivates. One is natural (unconditioned) and one is learned (conditioned).

Classical Conditioning

Classical conditioning is a form of learning whereby a **conditioned stimulus** (CS) becomes associated with an unrelated **unconditioned stimulus** (US), in order to produce a behavioral response known as a **conditioned response** (CR). The conditioned response is the learned response to the previously neutral stimulus. The unconditioned stimulus is usually a biologically significant stimulus such as food or pain that elicits an **unconditioned response** (UR) from the start. The conditioned stimulus is usually neutral and produces no particular response at first, but after conditioning it elicits the conditioned response.

If we look at Pavlov's experiment, we can identify these four factors at work:

- The unconditioned response was the salivation of dogs in response to seeing or smelling their food.
- The unconditioned stimulus was the sight or smell of the food itself.
- The conditioned stimulus was the ringing of the bell. During conditioning, every time the animal was given food, the bell was rung. This was repeated during several trials. After some time, the dog learned to associate the ringing of the bell with food and to respond by salivating. After the conditioning period was finished, the dog would respond by salivating

when the bell was rung, even when the unconditioned stimulus (the food) was absent.
- The conditioned response, therefore, was the salivation of the dogs in response to the conditioned stimulus (the ringing of the bell)[157].

Neurological Response to Conditioning
Consider how the conditioned response occurs in the brain. When a dog sees food, the visual and olfactory stimuli send information to the brain through their respective neural pathways, ultimately activating the salivary glands to secrete saliva. This reaction is a natural biological process as saliva aids in the digestion of food. When a dog hears a buzzer and at the same time sees food, the auditory stimuli activates the associated neural pathways. However, since these pathways are being activated at the same time as the other neural pathways, there are weak synapse reactions that occur between the auditory stimuli and the behavioral response. Over time, these synapses are strengthened so that it only takes the sound of a buzzer to activate the pathway leading to salivation.

Operant Conditioning
Operant conditioning is a theory of behaviorism, a learning perspective that focuses on changes in an individual's observable behaviors. In **operant conditioning** theory, new or continued behaviors are impacted by new or continued consequences. Research regarding this principle of learning was first studied by Edward L. Thorndike in the late 1800's, then brought to popularity by B.F. Skinner in the mid-1900's. Much of this research informs current practices in human behavior and interaction.

Skinner's Research
Thorndike's initial research was highly influential on another psychologist, B.F. Skinner. Almost half a century after Thorndike's first publication of the principles of operant conditioning, Skinner attempted to prove an extension to this theory—that all behaviors were in some way a result of operant conditioning. Skinner theorized that if a behavior is followed by reinforcement, that behavior is *more* likely to be repeated, but if it is followed by punishment, it is *less* likely to be repeated. He also believed that this learned association could end, or become extinct, if the reinforcement or punishment was removed.

To prove this, he placed rats in a box with a lever that when tapped would release a pellet of food. Over time, the amount of time it took for the rat to find the lever and press it became shorter and shorter, until finally the rat would spend most of its time near the lever eating. This behavior

---
[157] Children's Development by Ana R. Leon is licensed under CC BY 4.0

became less consistent when the relationship between the lever and the food was compromised. This basic theory of operant conditioning is still used by psychologists, scientists, and educators today.

Shaping, Reinforcement Principles, and Schedules of Reinforcement

Operant conditioning can be viewed as a process of action and consequence. Skinner used this basic principle to study the possible scope and scale of the influence of operant conditioning on animal behavior. His experiments used shaping, reinforcement, and reinforcement schedules in order to prove the importance of the relationship that animals form between behaviors and results.

All of these practices concern the setup of an experiment. **Shaping** is the conditioning paradigm of an experiment. The form of the experiment in successive trials is gradually changed to elicit a desired target behavior. This is accomplished through reinforcement, or reward, of the segments of the target behavior, and can be tested using a large variety of actions and rewards.

The experiments were taken a step further to include different schedules of reinforcement that become more complicated as the trials continued. By testing different reinforcement schedules, Skinner learned valuable information about the best ways to encourage a specific behavior, or the most effective ways to create a long-lasting behavior. Much of this research has been replicated on humans, and now informs practices in various environments of human behavior[158].

Positive and Negative Reinforcement

Sometimes, adding something to the situation is reinforcing as in the cases we described above with cookies, praise and money. **Positive reinforcement** involves adding something to the situation in order to encourage a behavior. Other times, taking something away from a situation can be reinforcing. For example, the loud, annoying buzzer on your alarm clock encourages you to get up so that you can turn it off and get rid of the noise. Children whine in order to get their parents to do something and often, parents give in just to stop the whining. In these instances, negative reinforcement has been used.

---

[158] Children's Development by Ana R. Leon is licensed under CC BY 4.0

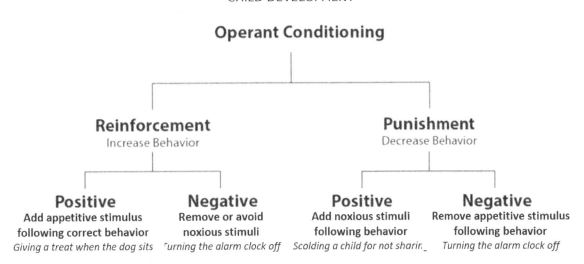

Reinforcement in operant conditioning.[159]

Operant conditioning tends to work best if you focus on trying to encourage a behavior or move a person into the direction you want them to go rather than telling them what not to do. **Reinforcers** are used to encourage a behavior; punishers are used to stop behavior. A **punisher** is anything that follows an act and decreases the chance it will reoccur. But often a punished behavior doesn't really go away. It is just suppressed and may reoccur whenever the threat of punishment is removed. For example, a child may not cuss around you because you've washed his mouth out with soap, but he may cuss around his friends. Or a motorist may only slow down when the trooper is on the side of the freeway. Another problem with punishment is that when a person focuses on punishment, they may find it hard to see what the other does right or well. And punishment is stigmatizing; when punished, some start to see themselves as bad and give up trying to change.

Reinforcement can occur in a predictable way, such as after every desired action is performed, or intermittently, after the behavior is performed a number of times or the first time it is performed after a certain amount of time. The schedule of reinforcement has an impact on how long a behavior continues after reinforcement is discontinued. So a parent who has rewarded a child's actions each time may find that the child gives up very quickly if a reward is not immediately forthcoming. Think about the kinds of behaviors that may be learned through classical and operant conditioning. But sometimes very complex behaviors are learned quickly and without direct

---

[159] Image by Curtis Neveu is licensed under CC BY-SA 3.0 (Modified from source image)

reinforcement. Bandura's Social Learning covered later in the chapter explains how[160].

Watson and Behaviorism

Another theorist who added to the spectrum of the behavioral movement was John B. Watson. Watson believed that most of our fears and other emotional responses are classically conditioned. He had gained a good deal of popularity in the 1920s with his expert advice on parenting offered to the public. He believed that parents could be taught to help shape their children's behavior and tried to demonstrate the power of classical conditioning with his famous experiment with an 18 month old boy named "Little Albert." Watson sat Albert down and introduced a variety of seemingly scary objects to him: a burning piece of newspaper, a white rat, etc. But Albert remained curious and reached for all of these things. Watson knew that one of our only inborn fears is the fear of loud noises so he proceeded to make a loud noise each time he introduced one of Albert's favorites, a white rat. After hearing the loud noise several times paired with the rat, Albert soon came to fear the rat and began to cry when it was introduced.

Watson filmed this experiment for posterity and used it to demonstrate that he could help parents achieve any outcomes they desired, if they would only follow his advice. Watson wrote columns in newspapers and in magazines and gained a lot of popularity among parents eager to apply science to household order. Parenting advice was not the legacy Watson left us, however. Where he really made his impact was in advertising. After Watson left academia, he went into the world of business and showed companies how to tie something that brings about a natural positive feeling to their products to enhance sales. Thus the union of sex and advertising![161].

Sometimes we do things because we've seen it pay off for someone else. They were operantly conditioned, but we engage in the behavior because we hope it will pay off for us as well. This is referred to as vicarious reinforcement (Bandura, Ross and Ross, 1963).

Do parents socialize children or do children socialize parents?

Bandura (1986) suggests that there is interplay between the environment and the individual. We are not just the product of our surroundings, rather we influence our surroundings. There is interplay between our personality and the way we interpret events and how they influence us. This concept is called reciprocal determinism. An example of this might be the interplay between

---

[160] Lifespan Development - Module 4: Infancy by Lumen Learning references Psyc 200 Lifespan Psychology by Laura Overstreet, licensed under CC BY 4.0

[161] Lifespan Development - Module 4: Infancy by Lumen Learning references Psyc 200 Lifespan Psychology by Laura Overstreet, licensed under CC BY 4.0

parents and children. Parents not only influence their child's environment, perhaps intentionally through the use of reinforcement, etc., but children influence parents as well. Parents may respond differently with their first child than with their fourth. Perhaps they try to be the perfect parents with their firstborn, but by the time their last child comes along they have very different expectations both of themselves and their child. Our environment creates us and we create our environment.

Social Learning Theory
Albert Bandura is a leading contributor to **social learning theory**. He calls our attention to the ways in which many of our actions are not learned through conditioning; rather, they are learned by watching others (1977). Young children frequently learn behaviors through imitation. Sometimes, particularly when we do not know what else to do, we learn by modeling or copying the behavior of others. A new employee, on his or her first day of a new job might eagerly look at how others are acting and try to act the same way to fit in more quickly. Adolescents struggling with their identity rely heavily on their peers to act as role-models. Newly married couples often rely on roles they may have learned from their parents and begin to act in ways they did not while dating and then wonder why their relationship has changed.

Constructivism: changes in how students think

Behaviorist models of learning may be helpful in understanding and influencing what students do, but teachers usually also want to know what students are thinking, and how to enrich what students are thinking. For this goal of teaching, some of the best help comes from **constructivism,** which is a perspective on learning focused on how students actively create (or "construct") knowledge out of experiences. Constructivist models of learning differ about how much a learner constructs knowledge independently, compared to how much he or she takes cues from people who may be more of an expert and who help the learner's efforts (Fosnot, 2005; Rockmore, 2005). For convenience these are called **psychological constructivism** and **social constructivism,** even though both versions are in a sense explanations about thinking within individuals.

Psychological constructivism: the independent investigator

The main idea of psychological constructivism is that a person learns by mentally organizing and reorganizing new information or experiences. The organization happens partly by relating new experiences to prior knowledge that is already meaningful and well understood. Stated in this general form, individual constructivism is sometimes associated with a well-known educational philosopher of the early twentieth century, **John Dewey** (1938-1998). Although Dewey himself did not use the term constructivism in most of his writing, his point of view amounted to a type of constructivism, and he discussed in detail its implications for educators. He argued, for example, that if students indeed learn primarily by building their own knowledge, then teachers should adjust the curriculum to fit students' prior knowledge and interests as fully as possible. He also argued that a curriculum could only be justified if it related as fully as possible to the activities and responsibilities that students will probably have later, after leaving school. To many educators these days, his ideas may seem merely like good common sense, but they were indeed innovative and progressive at the beginning of the twentieth century.

Piaget

Jean Piaget is the most noted theorist when it comes to children's cognitive development. He believed that children's cognition develops in stages. He explained this growth in the following stages:

- Sensory Motor Stage (Birth through 2 years old)
- Preoperational Stage (2-7 years old)
- Concrete Operational Stage (7-11 years old)
- Formal Operational Stage (12 years old- adulthood)

Piaget and Sensorimotor Intelligence

The sensorimotor Stage is the first of Piaget's stages. It lasts from birth to about 2 years of age. Piaget believed that infants construct an understanding of the world by coordinating sensory experiences with physical, motoric actions. It is only at the end of the sensorimotor stage that toddlers begin the use of symbols. Piaget describes intelligence in infancy as sensorimotor or based on direct, physical contact. Infants taste, feel, pound, push, hear, and move in order to experience the world. Let's explore the transition infants make from responding to the external world reflexively as newborns to solving problems using mental strategies as two years old.

Table Substages of Piaget's Sensorimotor Stage[162]

Substage	Age	Description
Substage One: Simple Reflexes	Birth to 1 month	This active learning begins with automatic movements or reflexes. A ball comes into contact with an infant's cheek and is automatically sucked on and licked.
Substage Two: Primary	1 to 4 months	The infant begins to discriminate between objects and adjust responses accordingly as reflexes are replaced with voluntary

---

[162] Children's Development by Ana R. Leon is licensed under CC BY 4.0

Substage	Age	Description
Circular Reactions		movements. An infant may accidentally engage in a behavior and find it interesting such as making a vocalization. This interest motivates trying to do it again and helps the infant learn a new behavior that originally occurred by chance. At first, most actions have to do with the body, but in months to come, will be directed more toward objects.
Substage Three: Secondary Circular Reactions	4 to 8 months	The infant becomes more and more actively engaged in the outside world and takes delight in being able to make things happen. Repeated motion brings particular interest as the infant is able to bang two lids together from the cupboard when seated on the kitchen floor.
Substage Four: Coordination of circular reactions	8 to 12 months	The infant can engage in behaviors that others perform and anticipate upcoming events. Perhaps because of continued maturation of the prefrontal cortex, the infant becomes capable of having a thought and carrying out a planned, goal-directed activity such as seeking a toy that has rolled under the couch. The object continues to exist in the infant's mind even when out of sight and the infant now is capable of making attempts to retrieve it.
Substage Five: Tertiary Circular Reactions	12 to 18 months	The infant more actively engages in experimentation to learn about the physical world. Gravity is learned by pouring water from a cup or pushing bowls from high chairs. The caregiver tries to help the child by picking it up again and placing it on the tray. And what happens? Another experiment! The child pushes it off the tray again causing it to fall and the caregiver to pick it up again!
Substage Six: Internalization of Schemes and Early Representational thought	18 months to 2 years	The child is now able to solve problems using mental strategies, to remember something heard days before and repeat it, to engage in pretend play, and to find objects that have been moved even when out of sight. Take for instance, the child who is upstairs in a room with the door closed, supposedly taking a nap. The doorknob has a safety device on it that makes it impossible for the child to turn the knob. After trying several times in vain to push the door or turn the doorknob, the child carries out a mental strategy learned from prior experience to get the door opened-he knocks on the door! The child is now better equipped with mental strategies for problem-solving.

Sensorimotor Substages

Substage 1: Simple Reflexes (Birth to 1 Month)

In the first month of life, infants' behaviors reflect innate reflexes—automatic responses to particular stimuli. For instance, if you put a nipple or pacifier in or near a newborn's mouth, she will automatically suck on it. If you put something against the palm of a newborn's hand, his fingers will automatically close around it. Many of these inborn reflexes are designed to keep he infant alive. The infant soon begins to modify some reflexes to better accommodate to the environment—for instance, by learning to distinguish between a nipple and the surrounding areas of a breast or bottle. And other reflexes, such as the tendency to grab onto something placed in the hand, fade away over time.

Substage 2: Primary Circular Reactions (1–4 Months)

In the first few months of life, infants' behaviors are focused almost exclusively on their own bodies (in Piaget's terminology, the behaviors are primary) and are repeated over and over again (i.e., they are circular). Infants also begin to refine their reflexes and combine them into more complex actions. For example, an infant might now open and close her hand and then put it in her mouth.

Substage 3: Secondary Circular Reactions (4–8 Months)

Sometime around 4 months, infants become more aware of and more responsive to the outside world (their behaviors become secondary), and they begin to notice that their behaviors can have interesting effects on the objects around them. For instance, an infant may pick up and then drop a favorite stuffed animal; each time his caregiver gives the animal back to him, he may drop it again and yet fret that he no longer has it. Infants in this substage seem fascinated by the effects of their actions, although at this point they are not necessarily making a conscious connection between the particular things they do and the resulting consequences.

Substage 4: Coordination of Secondary Circular Reactions (8–12 Months)

After repeatedly observing that certain actions lead to certain consequences, infants gradually acquire knowledge of cause-effect relationships. Accordingly, they begin to engage in goal-directed behavior: They behave in ways that they know will bring about desired results. They also begin to combine behaviors in new ways to accomplish their goals. For example, when an infant sees the string of a pull-toy near her, rather than crawling over to the toy she might instead reach out and grab the string and then purposely pull the string in order to acquire the toy. Yet another acquisition at this substage is *object permanence*, the realization that physical objects continue to exist even when they are removed from view. Object permanence is nderstanding that objects and events continue to exist even when they cannot be seen, heard, or touched. For example, when a caregiver hides an attractive toy beneath a pillow, the infant knows that the toy still exists, also knows where it exists, and will attempt to retrieve it.

Substage 5: Tertiary Circular Reactions (12–18 Months)

Beginning sometime around their first birthday, infants show increasing flexibility and creativity in their behaviors, and their experimentation with objects often leads to new outcomes (the term tertiary reflects this new versatility in previously acquired responses).

Piaget illustrated tertiary circular reactions with a description of his daughter Jacqueline, then 14 months old:

"Jacqueline holds in her hands an object which is new to her; a round, flat box which she turns all over, shakes, rubs against the bassinet, etc. She lets it go and tries to pick it up. But she only succeeds in touching it with her index finger, without grasping it. She nevertheless makes an attempt and presses on the edge. The box then tilts up and falls again. Jacqueline, very much interested in this fortuitous result, immediately applies herself to studying it....

Jacqueline immediately rests the box on the ground and pushes it as far as possible (it is noteworthy that care is taken to push the box far away in order to reproduce the same conditions as the first attempt, as though this were a necessary condition for obtaining the result). Afterward Jacqueline puts her finger on the box and presses it. But as she places her finger on the center of the box she simply displaces it and makes it slide instead of tilting it up. She amuses herself with this game and keeps it up (resumes it after intervals, etc.) for several minutes. Then, changing the point of contact, she finally again places her finger on the edge of the box, which tilts it up. She repeats this many times, varying the conditions, but keeping track of her discovery: now she only presses on the edge!(Piaget, 1952, p. 272).

Substage 6: Internalization of Schemes (18–24 Months)

Piaget proposed that in the latter half of the second year, young children develop symbolic thought, the ability to represent and think about objects and events in terms of internal, mental entities, or symbols. They may "experiment" with objects in their minds, first predicting what will happen if they do something to an object, then transforming their plans into action. To some degree, mental prediction and planning replace overt trial-and-error as growing toddlers experiment and attempt to solve problems. The capacity for mental representation is seen in the emergence of deferred imitation, the ability to recall and copy another person's behaviors hours or days after their behaviors have been observed. Although infants show some ability to imitate others' actions quite early in life, up until now, Piaget suggested, they have imitated only the behaviors they see someone else demonstrating on the spot. Their newly acquired ability to recall and imitate other people's past actions enables them to engage in make-believe and pretend play—for instance, by "talking" on a toy telephone or "driving" with the toy steering wheel attached to their car seats.

Evaluating Piaget's Sensorimotor Stage

Piaget opened up a new way of looking at infants with his view that their main task is to coordinate their sensory impressions with their motor activity. However, the infant's cognitive world is not as neatly packaged as Piaget portrayed it, and some of Piaget's explanations for the cause of change are debated. In the past several decades, sophisticated experimental techniques have been devised to study infants, and there have been a large number of research studies on infant development. Much of the new research suggests that Piaget's view of sensorimotor development needs to be modified (Baillargeon, 2014; Brooks & Meltzoff, 2014; Johnson & Hannon, 2015).

Object Permanence

One necessary modification would be to when children develop object permanence. Infants seem to be able to recognize that objects have permanence at much younger ages than Piaget proposed (even as young as 3.5 months of age).

The A-not-B Error

The data does not always support Piaget's claim that certain processes are crucial in transitions from one stage to the next. For example, in Piaget's theory, an important feature in the progression into substage 4, *coordination of secondary circular reactions,* is an infant's inclination to search for a hidden object in a familiar location rather than to look for the object in a new location. Thus, if a toy is hidden twice, initially at location A and subsequently at location B, 8- to 12-month-old infants search correctly at location A initially. But when the toy is subsequently hidden at location B, they make the mistake of continuing to search for it at location A. **A-not-B error** is the term used to describe this common mistake. Older infants are less likely to make the A-not-B error because their concept of object permanence is more complete.

Researchers have found, however, that the A-not-B error does not show up consistently (Sophian, 1985). The evidence indicates that A-not-B errors are sensitive to the delay between hiding the object at B and the infant's attempt to find it (Diamond, 1985). Thus, the A-not-B error might be due to a failure in memory. Another explanation is that infants tend to repeat a previous motor behavior (Clearfield & others, 2006; Smith, 1999).

Early childhood is a time of pretending, blending fact and fiction, and learning to think of the world using language. As young children move away from needing to touch, feel, and hear about the world toward learning some basic principles about how the world works, they hold some pretty interesting initial ideas. For example, while adults have no concerns with taking a bath, a child of three might genuinely worry about being sucked down the drain.

A child might protest if told that something will happen "tomorrow" but be willing to accept an explanation that an event will occur "today after we sleep." Or the young child may ask, "How long are we staying? From here to here?" while pointing to two points on a table. Concepts such as tomorrow, time, size and distance are not easy to grasp at this young age. Understanding size, time, distance, fact and fiction are all tasks that are part of cognitive development in the preschool years.[163]

Piaget's Preoperational Intelligence

Piaget's stage that coincides with early childhood, ages 2 to 7, is the **preoperational stage.** By "*operations*" Piaget meant an internalized set of actions: mental actions or thoughts. During this stage children become capable of representational thought and stable concepts are formed. Mental reasoning improves but magical beliefs emerge. Egocentrism strengthens, then weakens. Because thought is still flawed and not well organized, young children's reasoning ability still limited. The word operational implies "logical", so these children were thought to be illogical. However, they were learning to use language or to think of the world symbolically. Let's examine some of Piaget's assertions about children's cognitive abilities at this age.

Pretend Play

Pretending is a favorite activity at this time. A toy has qualities beyond the way it was designed to function and can now be used to stand for a character or object unlike anything originally intended. A teddy bear, for example, can be a baby or the queen of a faraway land! Some children at this age have imaginary friends. The term "sociodramatic play" is sometimes used to describe pretend play in which children act out stories as they play. Sociodratic play may exercise and expand children's memory and ad linguistic skills.

According to Piaget, children's pretend play helps them solidify new schemes they were developing cognitively. This play, then, reflects changes in their conceptions or thoughts. However, children also learn as they pretend and experiment. Their play does not simply represent

---

[163] Lifespan Development - Module 5: Early Childhood by Lumen Learning references Psyc 200 Lifespan Psychology by Laura Overstreet, licensed under CC BY 4.0

what they have learned (Berk, 2007).

There are two substages of the preoperational stage. The *Symbolic Function stage* is the first substage of the preoperational stage. The symbolic function substage occurs about ages 2 to 4. During this substage a child gains the ability to mentally represent an object not present. Their drawings are imaginative. There are two primary limitations on preoperational thought during the symbolic function substage. First, *Egocentrism*, the inability to distinguish between one's own perspective and someone else's. The second is *Animism* the belief that inanimate objects have lifelike qualities and are capable of action.

Egocentrism

Egocentrism in early childhood refers to the tendency of young children to think that everyone sees things in the same way as the child. Piaget assessed egocentrism with the Three Mountains Task. Piaget's classic experiment on egocentrism involved showing children a 3-dimensional model of a mountain and asking them to describe what a doll that is looking at the mountain from a different angle might see. Children tend to choose a picture that represents their own view, rather than that of the doll. However, children tend to use different sentence structures and vocabulary when addressing a younger child or an older adult. This indicates some awareness of the views of others.

Figure – Piaget's egocentrism experiment.[164]

Syncretism

Syncretism refers to a tendency to think that if two events occur simultaneously, one caused the other. An example of this is a child putting on their bathing suit to turn it to summertime.

Animism

Attributing lifelike qualities to objects is referred to as **animism**. The cup is alive, the chair that falls down and hits the child's ankle is mean, and the toys need to stay home because they are tired. Cartoons frequently show objects that appear alive and take on lifelike qualities. Young children do seem to think that objects that move may be alive but after age 3, they seldom refer to objects as being alive (Berk, 2007).

The second substage of the preoperation stage is the *Intuitive Thought Substage*. During this substage, Children begin to use primitive reasoning and seek answers to all sorts of questions. This substage occurs at about 4 to 7 years of age.

Classification Errors

Preoperational children have difficulty understanding that an object can be classified in more than one way. For example, if shown three white buttons and four black buttons and asked whether there are more black buttons or buttons, the child is likely to respond that there are more black buttons. As the child's vocabulary improves and more schemes are developed, the ability to classify objects improves.[165]

Conservation Errors

Conservation refers to the ability to recognize that moving or rearranging matter does not change the quantity. Let's look at an example. A father gave a slice of pizza to 10-year-old Keiko and another slice to 3-year-old Kenny. Kenny's pizza slice was cut into five pieces, so Kenny told his sister that he got more pizza than she did. Kenny did not understand that cutting the pizza into smaller pieces did not increase the overall amount. This was because Kenny exhibited **Centration,** or focused on only one characteristic of an object to the exclusion of others.

Kenny focused on the five pieces of pizza to his sister's one piece even though the total amount was the same. Keiko was able to consider several characteristics of an object than just one. Because children have not developed this understanding of conservation, they cannot perform mental operations.

---

[165] Lifespan Development - Module 5: Early Childhood by Lumen Learning references Psyc 200 Lifespan Psychology by Laura Overstreet, licensed under CC BY 4.0

The classic Piagetian experiment associated with conservation involves liquid (Crain, 2005). As seen below, the child is shown two glasses (as shown in a) which are filled to the same level and asked if they have the same amount. Usually the child agrees they have the same amount. The researcher then pours the liquid from one glass to a taller and thinner glass (as shown in b). The child is again asked if the two glasses have the same amount of liquid. The preoperational child will typically say the taller glass now has more liquid because it is taller. The child has concentrated on the height of the glass and fails to conserve.[166]

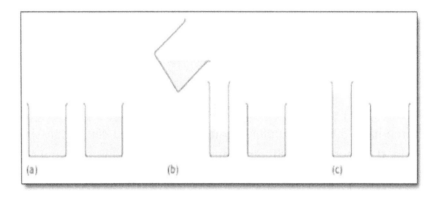

Figure – Piagetian liquid conservation experiments.[167]

Cognitive Schemas

As introduced in the first chapter, Piaget believed that in a quest for cognitive equilibrium, we use schemas (categories of knowledge) to make sense of the world. And when new experiences fit into existing schemas, we use assimilation to add that new knowledge to the schema. But when new experiences do not match an existing schema, we use accommodation to add a new schema. During early childhood, children use accommodation often as they build their understanding of the world around them.

Piaget's Theory of Cognitive Development

Concrete Operational Thought

As children continue into elementary school, they develop the ability to represent ideas and events more flexibly and logically. Their rules of thinking still seem very basic by adult standards and usually operate unconsciously, but they allow children to solve problems more systematically than before, and therefore to be successful with many academic tasks. In the concrete operational stage, for example, a child may unconsciously follow the rule: "If nothing is added or taken away, then the amount of something stays the same." This simple principle helps children to understand certain arithmetic tasks, such as in adding or subtracting zero from a number, as well as to do certain classroom science experiments, such as ones involving judgments of the amounts of liquids when mixed. Piaget called this period the concrete operational stage because children mentally "operate" on concrete objects and events.[168]

The concrete operational stage is defined as the third in Piaget's theory of cognitive development. This stage takes place around 7 years old to 11 years of age, and is characterized by the development of organized and rational thinking. Piaget (1954a) considered the concrete stage a major turning point in the child's cognitive development, because it marks the beginning of logical or operational thought. The child is now mature enough to use logical thought or operations (i.e. rules) but can only apply logic to physical objects (hence concrete operational). Children gain the abilities of conservation (number, area, volume, orientation) and reversibility.[169]

During the concrete operational stage children can think in a more logical fashion. They gain the ability to classify or divide things into different sets or subsets and to consider their interrelationships. Children also gain the ability to do reversible mental actions on real, concrete objects. During this stage children work in a mentally more flexible manner due to the ability to focus on more than single property of an object. They also are able to assume others' viewpoints, for example they can pick out appropriate gifts for others. However, thinking during the operational stage is still limited in that children cannot reason abstractly. Operational stage children need to have concrete objects in sight to reason about them.

Let's look at the following cognitive skills that children typically master during Piaget's concrete

---

[168]

[169]

operational stage.[170] :

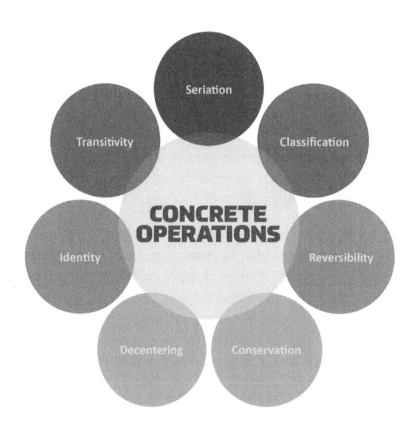

Figure – The cognitive skills developed during the concrete operational stage.[171]

Seriation: Arranging items along a quantitative dimension, such as length or weight, in a methodical way is now demonstrated by the concrete operational child. For example, they can methodically arrange a series of different-sized sticks in order by length, while younger children approach a similar task in a haphazard way.[172]

---

[170] Concrete Operational Stage Image by Simply Psychology is licensed under CC BY-NC-ND 3.0; Lifespan Development: A Psychological Perspective by Martha Lally and Suzanne Valentine-French is licensed under CC BY-NC-SA 3.0

[171] Image by Ian Joslin is licensed under CC BY 4.0

[172] Lifespan Development: A Psychological Perspective by Martha Lally and Suzanne Valentine-French is licensed under CC BY-NC-SA 3.0

Figure - Caption: Putting these rectangles from smallest to largest is seriation.[173]

Classification: As children's experiences and vocabularies grow, they build **schema** and are able to organize objects in many different ways. They also understand classification hierarchies and can arrange objects into a variety of classes and subclasses.

Reversibility: The child learns that some things that have been changed can be returned to their original state. Water can be frozen and then thawed to become liquid again. But eggs cannot be unscrambled. Arithmetic operations are reversible as well: $2 + 3 = 5$ and $5 - 3 = 2$. Many of these cognitive skills are incorporated into the school's curriculum through mathematical problems and in worksheets about which situations are reversible or irreversible.

Conservation: An example of the preoperational child's thinking; if you were to fill a tall beaker with 8 ounces of water this child would think that it was "more" than a short, wide bowl filled with 8 ounces of water? Concrete operational children can understand the concept of conservation, which means that changing one quality (in this example, height or water level) can be compensated for by changes in another quality (width). Consequently, there is the same amount of water in each container, although one is taller and narrower and the other is shorter and wider.

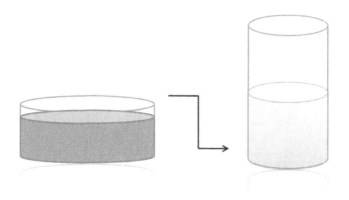

Figure – Beakers displaying the idea of conservation.[174]

Decentration: Concrete operational children no longer focus on only one dimension of any object (such as the height of the glass) and instead consider the changes in other dimensions too (such as the width of the glass). This allows for conservation to occur.

Figure – Children looking at these glasses demonstrate decentration when looking at more than one attribute i.e. tall, short, and wide narrow.[175]

Identity: One feature of concrete operational thought is the understanding that objects have qualities that do not change even if the object is altered in some way. For instance, mass of an object does not change by rearranging it. A piece of chalk is still chalk even when the piece is broken in two.[176]

Transitivity: Being able to understand how objects are related to one another is referred to as transitivity, or transitive inference. This means that if one understands that a dog is a mammal, and that a boxer is a dog, then a boxer must be a mammal.[177]

Looking at Piaget's Theory

Take a constructivist approach:

Facilitate rather than direct learning

Consider child's knowledge and level of thinking

Use ongoing assessment

Promote student's intellectual health

Turn classroom into setting of exploration and discovery

Today most researchers conclude that Piaget's descriptions of thought were accurate, and would still be obtained today, but that Piaget's may have misinterpreted his observations. Disagreement with Piaget is over Piaget's interpretation, not the results he observed. For example, Piaget's stages may not be as pure as he thought, in that children can be thought to perform mental actions at earlier ages than he thought possible. For example, infants can demonstrate an understanding of object permanence at earlier ages than Piaget thought. Researchers have obtained findings indicating that cognitive development is considerably more continuous than Piaget claimed. Thus, the debate between those who emphasize discontinuous, stage-like changes in cognitive development and those who emphasize gradual continuous changes remains a lively one.[178]

---

[176] Lifespan Development: A Psychological Perspective by Martha Lally and Suzanne Valentine-French is licensed under CC BY-NC-SA 3.0

[177] Transitivity by Boundless is licensed under CC BY-SA 4.0

[178] Lifespan Development: A Psychological Perspective by Martha Lally and Suzanne Valentine-French is licensed

Today, "Neo-Piagetians" re-interpret Piaget's findings through the lens of information processing models. These researchers suggest that what Piaget viewed as qualitative changes in children's thought was actually reflections of limits to memory capacity, speed of processing, and processing effectiveness.

Vygotsky's sociocultural cognitive development theory

Development Is Determined By Environmental Factors

Piaget set the tone for much of current-day research but his theory has also received a great deal of criticism. Many believe that Piaget ignored the huge influence that society and culture have in shaping a child's development. At a similar time, another researcher named Lev Vygotsky (1896–1934) had come to similar conclusions as Piaget about children's development, in thinking that children learned about the world through physical interaction with it. However, where Piaget felt that children moved naturally through different stages of development, based on biological predispositions and their own individual interactions with the world, Vygotsky claimed that adult or peer intervention was a much more important part of the developmental process.

Like Piaget, Vygotsky was a constructivist who believed that children actively construct their knowledge and understanding. He did not think that adults simply transferred knowledge to children like pouring water from a pitcher. He believed that learning took place through social relationships; ways of thinking and understanding develop primarily through social interaction. Vygotsky concentrated on the child's immediate social and cultural environment and his or her interactions with adults and peers. He argued that development occurred first through children's immediate social interactions, and then moved to the individual level as they began to internalize their learning. While Piaget saw the child as actively discovering the world through individual interactions with it, Vygotsky saw the child as more of an apprentice, learning through a social environment of others who had more experience and were sensitive to the child's needs and abilities.[179]

Vygotsky's Sociocultural Theory of Cognitive Development

Lev Vygotsky was a Russian psychologist who argued that culture has a major impact on a child's cognitive development. He believed that the social interactions with adults and more

[179] Children's Development by Ana R. Leon is licensed under CC BY 4.0

knowledgeable peers can facilitate a child's potential for learning. Vygotsky viewed the mind as shaped by culture, and that cognitive development depended on tools provided by society, such as language. Without this interpersonal instruction, he believed children's minds would not advance very far as their knowledge would be based only on their own discoveries. Let's review some of Vygotsky's key concepts.

Zone of Proximal Development and Scaffolding

Vygotsky's best known concept is the zone of proximal development (ZPD). The lower limit is what a child can achieve independently. The upper limit is what can be achieved with guidance and assistance of adults and more skilled children. Vygotsky stated that children should be taught in the ZPD, which occurs when they can perform a task with assistance, but not quite yet on their own. With the right kind of teaching, however, they can accomplish it successfully. A good teacher identifies a child's ZPD and helps the child stretch beyond it. Then the adult (teacher) gradually withdraws support until the child can then perform the task unaided. Researchers have applied the metaphor of scaffolds (the temporary platforms on which construction workers stand) to this way of teaching. Scaffolding is the temporary support that parents or teachers give a child to do a task. Through scaffolding the adult or older peer changes their level of support over the course of the teaching session to fit the child's current performance level. This can be through guided participation, in which the adult or older peer participates in the activity with the child while stretching and supporting the child's understanding of skills through dialogue. For example, a preschooler might be able to work a 10-piece puzzle on their own with no support, but they might be able to work a 25-piece puzzle along with an adult who points on the straight edge on the border pieces or asks questions about matching colors.

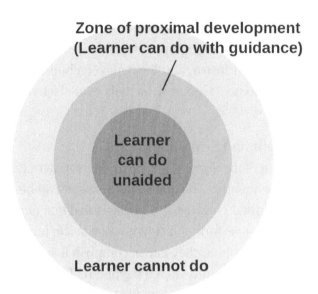

Figure – Zone of proximal development.[180]

Private Speech

Do you ever talk to yourself? Why? Chances are, this occurs when you are struggling with a problem, trying to remember something, or feel very emotional about a situation. Children talk to themselves too. Piaget interpreted this as **egocentric speech** or a practice engaged in because of a child's inability to see things from another's point of view. Vygotsky, however, believed that children talk to themselves in order to solve problems or clarify thoughts. As children learn to think in words, they do so aloud before eventually closing their lips and engaging in **private speech** or inner speech. In this way, Vygotsky thought that children use language to plan, guide and monitor their behavior.

Thinking out loud eventually becomes thought accompanied by internal speech, and talking to oneself becomes a practice only engaged in when we are trying to learn something or remember something. As egocentric speech is replaced by private speech, it declines as children grow older. As private speech becomes more internalized, it only "comes out" when tasks are difficult, novel or challenging. This inner speech is not as elaborate as the speech we use when communicating with others (Vygotsky, 1962).[181]

Teaching Strategies based on Vygotsky

- Impact on education: cooperative learning

- Use child's ZPD

- Use more-skilled peers as teachers

- Monitor and encourage private speech

- Effectively assess the child's ZPD

- Place instruction in meaningful context

- Transform classroom to allow cooperative activities

Contrast with Piaget

Both Piaget and Vygotsky were constructivists who believe that children were active in constructing knowledge. Whereas Piage believed that children construct knowledge by transforming, organizing and reorganizing mental operations through interacting with the environment, Vygotsky was a social constructivist whose approach emphasized the social opportunities for learning that Piaget ignored.

Piaget was highly critical of teacher-directed instruction, believing that teachers who take control of the child's learning place the child into a passive role (Crain, 2005). Further, teachers may present abstract ideas without the child's true understanding, and instead they just repeat back what they heard. Piaget believed children must be given opportunities to discover concepts on their own. Both theories view teachers as facilitators. However, as previously stated, Vygotsky did not believe children could reach a higher cognitive level without instruction from more learned individuals. Who is correct? Both theories certainly contribute to our understanding of how children learn.

---

[181] Lifespan Development - Module 5: Early Childhood by Lumen Learning references Psyc 200 Lifespan Psychology by Laura Overstreet, licensed under CC BY 4.0

9 INFORMATION PROCESSING AND INTELLIGENCE

Learning Objectives At the completion of this module, students will be able to:	Related Course Objective
9-1 Discuss how information processing develops with age and varies across individuals.	1 3 5
9-2 Identify age trends in memory, and effective memory strategies.	1 5
9-3 Describe intelligence, including single- and multiple-factor models of intelligence.	4
9-4 Recognize how motivation contributes to student performance	4

In this chapter there are separate, but related, topics.

First, this chapter contains information describing children's theory of mind. This is an important aspect of development as children begin to understand how the minds of other people that they interact with work.

Second, is the information processing view on cognitive development. There is no single "information processing theory," but instead this is a collection of mini-theories that use modern computer science as a metaphor for how human beings take in, process, and use information.

These models focus on aspects of cognition such as attention, short- and long-term memory, and problem solving. It is thought that biological maturation of the brain, along with increased experience, results in increases in problem solving. For example, just as the RAM and hard drive of a computer can be upgraded, physical brain development and increased use of strategies results in increased space and speed in memory. Information processing theorists believe that cognitive development that appeared to be the result of qualitative change to Piaget is actually the result of quantitative changes in capacity and speed of processing.

Third, this chapter focuses on individual differences in intelligence. Piaget, Vygotsky and information processing theories describe typical aspects of cognitive development that every child is thought to progress through. However, these views do not explain why some children always do well on, for example, spelling tests whereas other struggle. Why do we view some children as "smart?" To answer this, we need to focus on how we define "intelligence" in the first place. What do we mean by "intelligence?"

Children's Understanding of the World
Both Piaget and Vygotsky believed that children actively try to understand the world around them. More recently developmentalists have added to this understanding by examining how children organize information and develop their own theories about the world.

Theory-Theory
The tendency of children to generate theories to explain everything they encounter is called **theory-theory**. This concept implies that humans are naturally inclined to find reasons and generate explanations for why things occur. Children frequently ask question about what they see or hear around them. When the answers provided do not satisfy their curiosity or are too complicated for them to understand, they generate their own theories. In much the same way that scientists construct and revise their theories, children do the same with their intuitions about the world as they encounter new experiences (Gopnik & Wellman, 2012). One of the theories they start to generate in early childhood centers on the mental states; both their own and those of others.

Theory of Mind
Theory of mind refers to the ability to think about other people's thoughts. This mental mind reading helps humans to understand and predict the reactions of others, thus playing a crucial role in social development. The ability to infer mental states in others, such as beliefs, desires, knowledge, and intentions. This is sometimes called "people reading." One common method for determining if a child has reached this mental milestone is the false belief task, described below.

The research began with a clever experiment by Wimmer and Perner (1983), who tested whether children can pass a false-belief test (see Figure 4.17). The child is shown a picture story of Sally, who puts her ball in a basket and leaves the room. While Sally is out of the room, Anne comes along and takes the ball from the basket and puts it inside a box. The child is then asked *where* Sally thinks the ball is located when she comes back to the room. Is she going to look first in the box or in the basket? The right answer is that she will look in the basket, because that's where she put it and thinks it is; but we have to infer this **false belief** against our own better knowledge that the ball is in the box.

This is very difficult for children before the age of four because of the cognitive effort it takes. Three-year-olds have difficulty distinguishing between what they once thought was true and what they now know to be true. They feel confident that what they know now is what they have always known (Birch & Bloom, 2003). Even adults need to think through this task (Epley, Morewedge, & Keysar, 2004).

Sample False-Belief Test (Example 1)

George leaves an object in a drawer

While George is gone, someone moves the object to a cupboard

The child is asked "Where will George look for the object?"

Children younger than about four believe George will look in the cupboard

Sample False-Belief Test (Example 2)

Children are shown a labeled box, such as a crayon box

Children are shown that something unexpected is inside, like buttons

Children are asked "What will George think is in the box?"

Children younger than about age four believe George will expect to find buttons in the box

To be successful at solving this type of task the child must separate what he or she "knows" to be true from what someone else might "think" is true. In Piagetian terms, they must give up a tendency toward egocentrism. The child must also understand that what guides people's actions and responses are what they "believe" rather than what is reality. In other words, people can mistakenly believe things that are false and will act based on this false knowledge. Consequently, prior to age four children are rarely successful at solving such a task (Wellman, Cross & Watson, 2001).

Appearance vs. Reality Test

Children are shown a deceptive object, like a sponge that looks like a rock

They are asked what the object looks like (rock) and what it really is (sponge)

They are asked "What will George think it is?"

Children younger than about four believe George will think it is a sponge

Researchers examining the development of theory of mind have been concerned by the overemphasis on the mastery of false belief as the primary measure of whether a child has attained theory of mind. Wellman and his colleagues (Wellman, Fang, Liu, Zhu & Liu, 2006) suggest that theory of mind is comprised of a number of components, each with its own developmental timeline (see Table 4.2).

Two-year-olds understand the diversity of desires, yet as noted earlier it is not until age four or five that children grasp false belief, and often not until middle childhood do they understand that people may hide how they really feel. In part, because children in early childhood have difficulty hiding how they really feel.

Cultural Differences in Theory of Mind

Those in early childhood in the US, Australia, and Germany develop theory of mind in the sequence outlined above. Yet, Chinese and Iranian preschoolers acquire knowledge access before diverse beliefs (Shahaeian, Peterson, Slaughter & Wellman, 2011). Shahaeian and colleagues suggested that cultural differences in childrearing may account for this reversal. Parents in collectivistic cultures, such as China and Iran, emphasize conformity to the family and cultural values, greater respect for elders, and the acquisition of knowledge and academic skills more than they do autonomy and social skills (Frank, Plunkett & Otten, 2010). This could reduce the degree of familial conflict of opinions expressed in the family. In contrast, individualistic cultures encourage children to think for themselves and assert their own opinion, and this could increase the risk of conflict in beliefs being expressed by family members.

As a result, children in individualistic cultures would acquire insight into the question of diversity of belief earlier, while children in collectivistic cultures would acquire knowledge access earlier in the sequence. The role of conflict in aiding the development of theory of mind may account for the earlier age of onset of an understanding of false belief in children with siblings, especially older siblings (McAlister & Petersen, 2007; Perner, Ruffman & Leekman, 1994).

This awareness of the existence of theory of mind is part of social intelligence, such as recognizing that others can think differently about situations. It helps us to be self-conscious or aware that others can think of us in different ways and it helps us to be able to be understanding or be empathetic toward others. Moreover, this mind reading ability helps us to anticipate and predict people's actions. The awareness of the mental states of others is important for communication and social skills.[182]

During middle and late childhood children make strides in several areas of cognitive function including the capacity of working memory, their ability to pay attention, and their use of memory strategies. Both changes in the brain and experience foster these abilities.

In this section, we will look at how children process information, think and learn, allowing them to increase their ability to learn and remember due to an improvement in the ways they attend to, store information, and problem solve.[183]

What Predicts Theory of Mind Ability?

Information processing (inhibitory control, working memory)

Verbal ability

Parent's mind-mindedness (comments about child's desires and thoughts) and attachment

Parents' talking about others' mental states

Peers and siblings

Humor

Humor involves social-cognitive play that produces smiling, laughing, feelings of amusement. Humor may be intentional or accidental, and humor may be verbal (such as jokes) or nonverbal (such as exaggerated movements). Laughter is not necessarily a response to humor. Humor is triggered by cognitive insight and serves many social functions. Humor can express satisfaction and enjoyment of play or social interaction. It serves to establish and continue relationships. Humor can provide social cohesion and establish group membership as children share humor with each other. It can also serve to relieve stress and anxiety.

---

[182] Lifespan Development: A Psychological Perspective by Martha Lally and Suzanne Valentine-French is licensed under CC BY-NC-SA 3.0

[183] Lifespan Development: A Psychological Perspective by Martha Lally and Suzanne Valentine-French is licensed under CC BY-NC-SA 3.0

Age Trends in Humor

What children find funny provides a window into cognitive development:

Infants: physical stimulation

Toddlers: word distortions, rhymes

Preschoolers: distortions of the physical world

1st graders: knock, knock jokes

3rd graders: play on words, homonyms

5th graders: sarcasm

Teens: witticisms and put-downs

Information Processing

Memory and Attention

Information processing theories are a different subject than Theory of Mind (don't get confused, this section starts a new topic). There is not one single "information processing theory" but instead there are several information processing "mini theories." Information processing theories use the vocabulary of computer science to describe human thinking. The mind is viewed through a computer metaphor: it takes in information, stores it, transforms it and acts on it. Information processing theorists do not propose that the mind actually works like a computer, they use the computer as a metaphor for thinking how the mind works. They emphasize how individuals manipulate information, monitor information, and strategize about information. In this view, the child's processing of information is seen as analogous to how a computer processes information, with an emphasis on attention, memory, and processing speed.

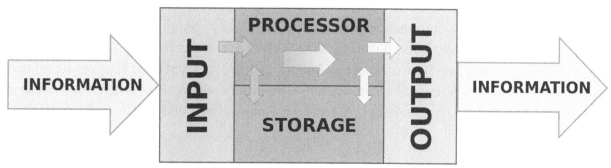

Figure – How information is processed.[184]

---

[184] Image by Gradient drift is in the public domain

Attention

Changes in attention have been described by many as the key to changes in human memory (Nelson & Fivush, 2004; Posner & Rothbart, 2007). However, attention is not a unified function; it is comprised of sub-processes. The ability to switch our focus between tasks or external stimuli is called **divided attention** or **multitasking.** This is separate from our ability to focus on a single task or stimulus, while ignoring distracting information, called **selective attention**. Different from these is **sustained attention**, or the ability to stay on task for long periods of time. Moreover, we also have attention processes that influence our behavior and enable us to inhibit a habitual or dominant response, and others that enable us to distract ourselves when upset or frustrated.

Divided Attention

Young children (age 3-4) have considerable difficulties in dividing their attention between two tasks, and often perform at levels equivalent to our closest relative, the chimpanzee, but by age five they have surpassed the chimp (Hermann, Misch, Hernandez-Lloreda & Tomasello, 2015; Hermann & Tomasello, 2015). Despite these improvements, 5-year-olds continue to perform below the level of school-age children, adolescents, and adults. With age, children are more likely to plan and organize their attentional behavior. At older ages, attentional skills help guide actions.

Selective Attention

Cognitive flexibility (also called attention shifting) is the ability to change how you think about something, switch perspectives, and adjust to changing demands. Inhibitory control is the ability to keep from processing irrelevant information, or to repress a response. Selective attention is the ability to focus on specific stimuli, while ignoring others. Selective attention requires both the ability to attend to a stimuli as well as inhibitory control necessary to ignore other stimuli. Children's ability with selective attention tasks improve as they age – there is dramatic improvement between the preschool years and age 8. However, this ability is also greatly influenced by the child's temperament (Rothbart & Rueda, 2005), the complexity of the stimulus or task (Porporino, Shore, Iarocci & Burack, 2004), and along with whether the stimuli are visual or auditory (Guy, Rogers & Cornish, 2013). Guy et al. (2013) found that children's ability to selectively attend to visual information outpaced that of auditory stimuli. This may explain why young children are not able to hear the voice of the teacher over the cacophony of sounds in the typical preschool classroom (Jones, Moore & Amitay, 2015). Jones and his colleagues found that 4 to 7 year-olds could not filter out background noise, especially when its frequencies were close in sound to the target sound. In comparison, 8- to 11-year-old children often performed similar to adults.

Sustained Attention

Most measures of sustained attention typically ask children to spend several minutes focusing on one task, while waiting for an infrequent event, while there are multiple distractors for several minutes. Berwid, Curko-Kera, Marks & Halperin (2005) asked children between the ages of 3 and 7 to push a button whenever a "target" image was displayed, but they had to refrain from pushing the button when a non-target image was shown. The younger the child, the more difficulty he or she had maintaining their attention.

Attention: Infants begin to pay attention and resist distractions; for example, infants prefer to look at increasingly complex things. Cognitive development in early childhood is related to attention in infancy. In early childhood, preschoolers have difficulty focusing on relevant information needed to solve a given problem versus more salient information that may be more appealing. The ability to inhibit irrelevant information improves during middle childhood, with there being a sharp improvement in selective attention from age six into adolescence (Vakil, Blachstein, Sheinman, & Greenstein, 2009). Children also improve in their ability to shift their attention between tasks or different features of a task (Carlson, Zelazo, & Faja, 2013). A younger child who is asked to sort objects into piles based on type of object, car versus animal, or color of object, red versus blue, would likely have no trouble doing so. But if you ask them to switch from sorting based on type to now having them sort based on color, they would struggle because this requires them to suppress the prior sorting rule. An older child has less difficulty making the switch, meaning there is greater flexibility in their intentional skills. These changes in attention and working memory contribute to children having more strategic approaches to challenging tasks.

Neo-Piagetians

As previously discussed, Piaget's theory has been criticized on many fronts, and updates to reflect more current research have been provided by the **Neo-Piagetians**, *or* those theorists who provide "new" interpretations of Piaget's theory. Morra, Gobbo, Marini and Sheese (2008) reviewed Neo-Piagetian theories, which were first presented in the 1970s, and identified how these "new" theories combined Piagetian concepts with those found in Information Processing. Similar to Piaget's theory, Neo-Piagetian theories believe in constructivism, assume cognitive development can be separated into different stages with qualitatively different characteristics, and advocate that children's thinking becomes more complex in advanced stages. Unlike Piaget, Neo-Piagetians believe that aspects of information processing change the complexity of each stage, not logic as determined by Piaget.

One important distinction is that Piaget's stages describe cognitive development as a series of qualitative changes. The Neo-Piagetian perspective is that the cognitive skills that Piaget observed and thought reflected qualitiative change were actually the result of quantitative changes in attention, memory, speed and capacity of processing, and problem solving that only appeared to be qualitiative change. Thus, the information processing perspective views cognitive development as quantitative change.

Neo-Piagetians propose that working memory capacity is affected by biological maturation, and therefore restricts young children's ability to acquire complex thinking and reasoning skills. Increases in working memory performance and cognitive skills development coincide with the timing of several neurodevelopmental processes. These include myelination, axonal and synaptic pruning, changes in cerebral metabolism, and changes in brain activity (Morra et al., 2008).

Myelination especially occurs in waves between birth and adolescence, and the degree of myelination in particular areas explains the increasing efficiency of certain skills. Therefore, brain maturation, which occurs in spurts, affects how and when cognitive skills develop. Additionally, all Neo-Piagetian theories support that experience and learning interact with biological maturation in shaping cognitive development.[185]

Memory

Memory is a central feature of cognitive development. Memory involves how an individual retains information over time. Based on studies of adults, people with amnesia, and neurological research on memory, researchers have proposed several "types" of memory (see Figure 4.14). **Sensory memory** (also called the sensory register) is the first stage of the memory system, and it stores sensory input in its raw form for a very brief duration; essentially long enough for the brain to register and start processing the information. Studies of auditory sensory memory show that it lasts about one second in 2 year-olds, two seconds in 3-year-olds, more than two seconds in 4-year-olds, and three to five seconds in 6-year-olds (Glass, Sachse, & von Suchodoletz, 2008). Other researchers have also found that young children hold sounds for a shorter duration than do older children and adults, and that this deficit is not due to attentional differences between these age groups, but reflects differences in the performance of the sensory memory system (Gomes et al., 1999). The second stage of the memory system is called short-term or **working memory**. Working memory is the component of memory in which current conscious mental activity occurs.

Working memory often requires conscious effort and adequate use of attention to function effectively. As you read earlier, children in this age group struggle with many aspects of attention and this greatly diminishes their ability to consciously juggle several pieces of information in memory. The capacity of working memory, that is the amount of information someone can hold in consciousness, is smaller in young children than in older children and adults. The typical adult and teenager can hold a 7 digit number active in their short-term memory. The typical 5-year-old can hold only a 4 digit number active. This means that the more complex a mental task is, the less efficient a younger child will be in paying attention to, and actively processing, information in order to complete the task.

Short-Term Memory Storage

Short-term memory (or working memory) is the ability to hold information for a short duration of

---

[185]

time (on the order of seconds). In the process of encoding, information enters the brain and can be quickly forgotten if it is not stored further in the short-term memory. Information can be held in short-term memory for 15 to 30 seconds without rehearsal. The capacity of short term memory increases during early childhood. Short term memory capacity averages at two digits or items at ages 2 to 3. At age 5 it is about four items. This increases to a span of 5 digits at age 7 and about six items at age 9. In one study: memory span increased from 3 digits at age 2 to 5 digits at age 7. George A. Miller suggested that the capacity of short-term memory storage for adults is approximately seven items plus or minus two, but modern researchers are showing that this can vary depending on variables like the stored items' phonological properties. When several elements (such as digits, words, or pictures) are held in short-term memory simultaneously, their representations compete with each other for recall, or degrade each other. Thereby, new content gradually pushes out older content, unless the older content is actively protected against interference by rehearsal or by directing attention to it. The use of memory strategies such as rehearsal, organization, and elaboration can expand short term memory effectiveness.

Information in the short-term memory is readily accessible, but for only a short time. It continuously decays, so in the absence of rehearsal (keeping information in short-term memory by mentally repeating it) it can be forgotten.

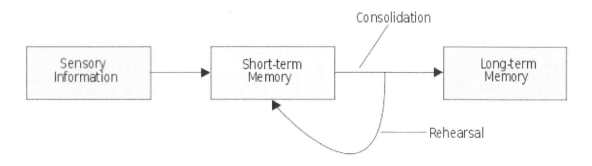

Figure – Diagram of the memory storage process.[186]

The capacity of short term memory (or working memory) expands during middle and late childhood, research has suggested that both an increase in processing speed and the ability to inhibit irrelevant information from entering memory are contributing to the greater efficiency of working memory during this age (de Ribaupierre, 2002). Changes in **myelination** and **synaptic pruning** in the **cortex** are likely behind the increase in processing speed and ability to filter out irrelevant stimuli (Kail, McBride-Chang, Ferrer, Cho, & Shu, 2013).

---

[186] Image by Wikipedia is licensed under CC BY-SA 3.0

Changes in attention and the working memory system also involve changes in executive function. **Executive function (EF)** refers to self-regulatory processes, such as the ability to inhibit a behavior or cognitive flexibility, that enable adaptive responses to new situations or to reach a specific goal. *Executive functions* refers to the brain's control of its own information processing. The brain must control attention and focus on a task, hold information during reasoning, retrieve information from long-term storage, monitor sequences of behavior, detect errors and make corrections, and shift ongoing functions to more urgent functions. Executive functions are essential for self-control and for high-level cognition, that is, any activity that requires effortful, complex thought. Executive function skills gradually emerge during early childhood and continue to develop throughout childhood and adolescence. Like many cognitive changes, brain maturation, especially the prefrontal cortex, along with experience influence the development of executive function skills.

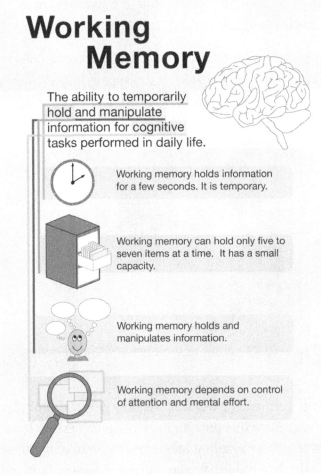

Figure – Working memory expands during middle and late childhood.[187]

A child shows higher executive functioning skills when the parents are more warm and responsive, use scaffolding when the child is trying to solve a problem, and provide cognitively stimulating environments for the child (Fay-Stammbach, Hawes & Meredith, 2014). For instance, scaffolding was positively correlated with greater cognitive flexibility at age two and inhibitory control at age four (Bibok, Carpendale & Müller, 2009). In Schneider, Kron-Sperl and Hunnerkopf's (2009) longitudinal study of 102 kindergarten children, the majority of children used no strategy to remember information, a finding that was consistent with previous research. As a result, their memory performance was poor when compared to their abilities as they aged and started to use more effective memory strategies.

The third component in memory is **long-term memory**, which is also known as permanent memory. A basic division of long-term memory is between declarative and non-declarative memory.

- **Declarative memories**, sometimes referred to as **explicit memories**, are memories for facts or events that we can consciously recollect. Declarative memory is further divided into semantic and episodic memory.

  .**Semantic memories** are memories for facts and knowledge that are not tied to a timeline,

  .**Episodic memories** are tied to specific events in time.

- **Non- declarative memories**, sometimes referred to as **implicit memories**, are typically automated skills that do not require conscious recollection.

Autobiographical memory is our personal narrative. Adults rarely remember events from the first few years of life. In other words, we lack autobiographical memories from our experiences as an infant, toddler and very young preschooler. This is called infantile amnesia, and most adults remember little from the first three years of life. Several factors contribute to the emergence of autobiographical memory including brain maturation,, particularly immaturity of the prefrontal lobe, improvements in language, opportunities to talk about experiences with parents and others, the development of theory of mind, and a representation of "self" (Nelson & Fivush, 2004). Two-year-olds do remember fragments of personal experiences, but these are rarely coherent accounts of past events (Nelson & Ross, 1980). Between 2 and 2 1⁄2 years of age children can provide more information about past experiences. However, these recollections require considerable prodding by adults (Nelson & Fivush, 2004). Over the next few years children will form more detailed autobiographical memories and engage in more reflection of the past.

If we want to remember something tomorrow, we have to consolidate it into long-term memory today. **Long-term memory** is the final, semi-permanent stage of memory. Unlike sensory and short-term memory, long-term memory has a theoretically infinite capacity, and information can remain there indefinitely. Long-term memory has also been called reference memory, because an individual must refer to the information in long-term memory when performing almost any task. Long-term memory can be broken down into two categories: explicit and implicit memory.

Explicit Memory
Explicit memory, also known as conscious or **declarative memory**, involves memory of facts, concepts, and events that require conscious recall of the information. In other words, the individual must actively think about retrieving the information from memory. This type of information is *explicitly* stored and retrieved—hence its name. Explicit memory can be further subdivided into **semantic memory**, which concerns facts, and episodic memory, which concerns primarily personal or autobiographical information. Recognition memory is usually better than recall memory. Recognition memory is the type of memory used on a multiple choice test – one must recognize the information when it is presented. Recall memory is the type of memory used on a fill in the blank test – one must recall the information rather than identifying it. Recognition involves encoding and retention. Recall involves use of strategies for retrieval, and knowledge about materials at hand and about about memory itself (metamemory).

Episodic Memory
Episodic memory is used for more contextualized memories. They are generally memories of specific moments, or episodes, in one's life. As such, they include sensations and emotions associated with the event, in addition to the who, what, where, and when of what happened. An example of an episodic memory would be recalling your family's trip to the beach. Autobiographical memory (memory for particular events in one's own life) is generally viewed as either equivalent to, or a subset of, episodic memory. One specific type of autobiographical memory is a flashbulb memory, which is a highly detailed, exceptionally vivid "snapshot" of the moment and circumstances in which a piece of surprising and consequential (or emotionally arousing) news was heard. For example, many people remember exactly where they were and what they were doing when they heard of the terrorist attacks on September 11, 2001. This is because it is a flashbulb memory.

Semantic and episodic memory are closely related; memory for facts can be enhanced with episodic memories associated with the fact, and vice versa. For example, the answer to the factual question "Are all apples red?" might be recalled by remembering the time you saw someone eating a green apple. Likewise, semantic memories about certain topics, such as football, can contribute to more detailed episodic memories of a particular personal event, like watching a football game. A person that barely knows the rules of football will remember the various plays and outcomes of the game in much less detail than a football expert. In 1978, Chi carried out a classic study on chess expertise. In the study, children who were experts in chess had better recall memory of the position of chess pieces than did adults who were not experts in chess. However, the adults had better memory spans than did the children who were chess experts when memory was assessed with other tasks that did not include chess positions. These findings do not suggest that there is something about Chess that aids in memory development. Instead, these findings suggest that expertise in a subject is associated with better memory about that subject. Further research supports this finding, for example, children who play soccer are better at recalling events in a story about soccer than are others.

Implicit Memory

In contrast to explicit (conscious) memory, **implicit** (also called "unconscious" or "procedural") **memory** involves procedures for completing actions. These actions develop with practice over time. Athletic skills are one example of implicit memory. You learn the fundamentals of a sport, practice them over and over, and then they flow naturally during a game. Rehearsing for a dance or musical performance is another example of implicit memory. Everyday examples include remembering how to tie your shoes, drive a car, or ride a bicycle. These memories are accessed without conscious awareness—they are automatically translated into actions without us even realizing it. As such, they can often be difficult to teach or explain to other people. Implicit memories differ from the semantic scripts described above in that they are usually actions that involve movement and motor coordination, whereas scripts tend to emphasize social norms or behaviors.

Long-Term Memory Storage

In contrast to short-term memory, **long-term memory** is the ability to hold semantic information for a prolonged period of time. Items stored in short-term memory move to long-term memory through rehearsal, processing, and use. The capacity of long-term memory storage is much greater than that of short-term memory, and perhaps unlimited. Long term-memory is relatively permanent. However, the duration of long-term memories is not entirely permanent; unless a memory is occasionally recalled, it may fail to be recalled on later occasions. This is known as forgetting. We can forget things we knew due to decay, retrieval failure, or interference. Young children are able to remember a large amount of information when aided with appropriate cues and prompts. However, young children are particularly vulnerable to having their recollections influenced by intentional or unintentional misleading prompts. Susceptibility to misleading prompts is influenced by children's age and individual differences. For this reason, care must be used when children are eyewitnesses in court: although their memories can be very accurate, the accuracy can be affected by a number of factors.

Long-term memory storage can be affected by traumatic brain injury or lesions. Amnesia, a deficit in memory, can be caused by brain damage. Anterograde amnesia is the inability to store new memories; retrograde amnesia is the inability to retrieve old memories. These types of amnesia indicate that memory does have a storage process[188].

Children's memories are influenced by their experience. We form scripts of familiar experiences and events that give us frameworks that assist in recall. Scripts are cognitive frameworks or schemas for events, a general outline of events that typically happen in a given situation. These become more elaborate during early childhood and can help children remember. However, preschoolers may incorporate fictitious elements into their accounts of real events. Differences in recall are due to cultural and maternal factors, as well as to the type of event being remembered.

Memory Strategies: The term metamemory means understanding or thinking about how memory works. Children's skill at metamemory increases with age, and this is associated with increased memory efficiency through the use of strategies. Children as young as age two can learn to use a memory strategy, however, young children are not very skilled in using memory strategies and there may be some cognitive inflexibility in children as old as 3 to 4 due to lack of understanding. In early childhood memory strategies, memory accuracy, and autobiographical memory emerge. Early childhood is seen by many researchers as a crucial time period in memory development (Posner & Rothbart, 2007). Bjorklund (2005) describes a developmental progression in the acquisition and use of memory strategies. Such strategies are often lacking in younger children, but increase in frequency as children progress through elementary school. Examples of memory strategies include rehearsing information you wish to recall, visualizing and organizing information, creating rhymes, such as "i" before "e" except after "c", or inventing acronyms, such as "roygbiv" to remember the colors of the rainbow. Schneider, Kron-Sperl, and Hünnerkopf (2009) reported a steady increase in the use of memory strategies from ages six to ten in their longitudinal study. Moreover, by age ten many children were using two or more memory strategies to help them recall information. Schneider and colleagues found that there were considerable individual differences at each age in the use of strategies, and that children who utilized more strategies had better memory performance than their same aged peers.

"Fuzzy trace theory" helps to explain one aspect of the improvement in memory as we grow older. When asked to recall information, preschoolers will attempt to repeat all of the information verbatim with precise details. As metamememory increases, children in middle childhood realize that it is more important to remember the gist, or central idea, of the information than to repeat all of the information word-for-word. In this way, older children will relate the main or central ideas and are more successful on memory tasks.

Cognitive Processes

As children enter school and learn more about the world, they develop more categories for concepts and learn more efficient strategies for storing and retrieving information. One significant

---

[188] <u>Children's Development</u> by Ana R. Leon is licensed under <u>CC BY 4.0</u>

reason is that they continue to have more experiences on which to tie new information. In other words, their **knowledge base**, knowledge in particular areas that makes learning new information easier, expands (Berger, 2014).

Metacognition: refers to the knowledge we have about our own thinking and our ability to use this awareness to regulate our own cognitive processes (Bruning, Schraw, Norby, & Ronning, 2004). Children in this developmental stage also have a better understanding of how well they are performing a task, and the level of difficulty of a task. As they become more realistic about their abilities, they can adapt studying strategies to meet those needs. Young children spend as much time on an unimportant aspect of a problem as they do on the main point, while older children start to learn to prioritize and gauge what is significant and what is not. As a result, they develop metacognition.

Critical thinking, *or* a detailed examination of beliefs, courses of action, and evidence, involves teaching children how to think. The purpose of critical thinking is to evaluate information in ways that help us make informed decisions. Critical thinking involves better understanding a problem through gathering, evaluating, and selecting information, and also by considering many possible solutions. Ennis (1987) identified several skills useful in critical thinking. These include: Analyzing arguments, clarifying information, judging the credibility of a source, making value judgments, and deciding on an action. Metacognition is essential to critical thinking because it allows us to reflect on the information as we make decisions.

As children grow older, they are better able to strategize about multiple aspects of a problem. Across all children, there are improvements in their ability in problem solving as they grow older. However, children differ in their cognitive process and these differences predict both their readiness for school, academic performance, and testing in school. (Prebler, Krajewski, & Hasselhorn, 2013).[189]

Classroom Implications of Information Processing:

Reduce working memory and executive load

Focus attention

Strengthen executive functions

Reduce Working Memory and Executive Load

---

[189] Lifespan Development: A Psychological Perspective by Martha Lally and Suzanne Valentine-French is licensed under CC BY-NC-SA 3.0

Limit your talking. Present information at appropriate speed.

Reduce distractions in your classroom.

Increase your student's expertise. Make thinking automatic where possible.

Provide external storage. Write on board, provide partial notes.

Carve problems into smaller subtasks that can be performed sequentially.

Cognitive Milestones

Children are actively learning about the world as they perceive it from the time they are in the womb. Here is a table of some of the cognitive milestones infants and toddlers typically develop.

Cognitive Milestones[190]

Typical Age	What Most Children Do by This Age
2 months	<ul><li>Pays attention to faces</li><li>Begins to follow things with eyes and recognize people at a distance</li><li>Begins to act bored (cries, fussy) if activity doesn't change</li></ul>
4 months	<ul><li>Lets you know if she is happy or sad</li><li>Responds to affection</li><li>Reaches for toy with one hand</li><li>Uses hands and eyes together, such as seeing a toy and reaching for it</li><li>Follows moving things with eyes from side to side</li><li>Watches faces closely</li><li>Recognizes familiar people and things at a distance</li></ul>
6 months	<ul><li>Looks around at things nearby</li><li>Brings things to mouth</li><li>Shows curiosity about things and tries to get things that are out of reach</li><li>Begins to pass things from one hand to the other</li></ul>
9 months	<ul><li>Watches the path of something as it falls</li><li>Looks for things he sees you hide</li><li>Plays peek-a-boo</li><li>Puts things in mouth</li><li>Moves things smoothly from one hand to the other</li><li>Picks up things like cereal o's between thumb and index finger</li></ul>

---

[190] Developmental Milestones by the CDC is in the public domain

Typical Age	What Most Children Do by This Age
1 year	• Explores things in different ways, like shaking, banging, throwing • Finds hidden things easily • Looks at the right picture or thing when it's named • Copies gestures • Starts to use things correctly; for example, drinks from a cup, brushes hair • Bangs two things together • Puts things in a container, takes things out of a container • Lets things go without help • Pokes with index (pointer) finger • Follows simple directions like "pick up the toy"
18 months	• Knows what ordinary things are for; for example, telephone, brush, spoon • Points to get the attention of others • Shows interest in a doll or stuffed animal by pretending to feed • Points to one body part • Scribbles on own • Can follow 1-step verbal commands without any gestures; for example, sits when you say "sit down"
2 years	• Finds things even when hidden under two or three covers • Begins to sort shapes and colors • Completes sentences and rhymes in familiar books • Plays simple make-believe games • Builds towers of 4 or more blocks • Might use one hand more than the other • Follows two-step instructions such as "Pick up your shoes and put them in the closet." • Names items in a picture book such as a cat, bird, or dog

Milestones of Cognitive Development

The many theories of cognitive development and the different research that has been done about how children understand the world, has allowed researchers to study the milestones that children who are typically developing experience in early childhood. Here is a table that summarizes those.

Cognitive Milestones[191]

Typical Age	What Most Children Do by This Age
3 years	• Can work toys with buttons, levers, and moving parts • Plays make-believe with dolls, animals, and people • Does puzzles with 3 or 4 pieces • Understands what "two" means
4 years	• Names some colors and some numbers • Understands the idea of counting • Starts to understand time • Remembers parts of a story • Understands the idea of "same" and "different" • Plays board or card games • Tells you what he thinks is going to happen next in a book
5 years	• Counts 10 or more things • Knows about things used every day, like money and food

Numeracy

Based upon his experiments with conservation, Piaget believed that children did not develop a true concept of natural numbers until the age of six or so. Gelman and Gallistel argued in 1978 that any child who could count following three cardinal principles possessed a concept of number. The first was *ordinality,* recognizing that counting always follows the same order (1, 2, 3, and so on). The second is the principle of *cardinality* the understanding that the last number that one says in the list is the total number in the set (e.g., a child counts "one, two, three" and recognizes that there are three objects in total), the third is *one-to-one correspondence*, the understanding that there is one number for each object. These three principles are "how to count" principles, and Gelman and Gallistel state that there are two additional principles concerning "what to count": *abstraction* – the three counting principles can be applied to any set, whether tangible or not, and *order-irrelevance* – it doesn't matter if the objects are counted from left-to-right or right-to-left, for example, as long as all are included the order does not matter. We see evidence of these five counting principles by two to three years old, although preschoolers do not always use them consistently. Preschoolers can show mastery of one principle without the others (for example, by counting objects in correct order but without one-to-one correspondence).

---

[191] Developmental Milestones by the CDC is in the public domain

Intelligence

One question that has puzzled scientists and philosophers is "What is intelligence?" Intelligence is difficult to define in ways that we can all agree on, and so measuring intelligence becomes difficult. Common definitions of intelligence include things like problem solving skills and verbal ability. Is intelligence determined by the extent of knowledge that one posses? How man "facts" a person knows? How quickly someone can think? How many items on a list a person can remember? How cleverly a person can solve a puzzle? Or is there something else that makes up "intelligence?" One way to think about intelligence might be "what function does it serve?" or what is an individual's ability to learn from and adapt to experiences of everyday life? How would you define intelligence? Is there a single thing that is "intelligence" or a set of different things? If it is different things, do they overlap or are they completely separate?

However we define it, it is clear that "intelligence" is something that we can only measure indirectly. We can not simply put someone's brain on a scale and claim that the resulting weight is a measure of intelligence. Likewise, there is no scan that we can do of a brain to measure intelligence. Instead, we must devise assessments that measure things that we think are related to intelligence or that indicate intelligence.

One important point about the word "intelligence" is that it suggests that there are individual differences between children in their cognitive performance. When we discussed Learning Theory, Piaget, Vygotsky, and Information Processing, the different perspectives described processes that all children were thought to go through in their cognitive development. But why is one child considered very intelligent and another child considered less so? Why does one child always do well on tests in spelling but struggle in math, while another struggles on spelling tests? What is the source of these individual differences?

Intelligence Testing: The What, the Why, and the Who

Measuring Intelligence: Standardization and the Intelligence Quotient

The desire to assess individual differences in children's cognitive development gave rise to the development of intelligence tests. The goal of most intelligence tests is to measure "g," the general intelligence factor. Think of "g" as "overall" intelligence. Good intelligence tests are **reliable,** meaning that they are consistent over time, and also demonstrate **validity,** meaning that they actually measure intelligence rather than something *else*. Because intelligence is such an important part of individual differences, psychologists have invested substantial effort in creating and improving measures of intelligence, and these tests are now considered the most accurate of all psychological tests.

Intelligence changes with age. A 3-year-old who could accurately multiply 183 by 39 would certainly be intelligent, but a 25-year-old who could not do so would be seen as unintelligent. Thus understanding intelligence requires that we know the norms or standards in a given population of people at a given age. The **standardization** of a test involves giving it to a large number of people at different ages and computing the average score on the test at each age level.

Once the standardization has been accomplished, we have a picture of the average abilities of people at different ages and can calculate a person's **mental age**, which is the age at which a person is performing intellectually. If we compare the mental age of a person to the person's chronological age, the result is the **Intelligence Quotient (IQ),** a measure of intelligence that is adjusted for age. A simple way to calculate IQ is by using the following formula:

IQ = mental age ÷ chronological age × 100.

Thus a 10-year-old child who does as well as the average 10-year-old child has an IQ of 100 (10 ÷ 10 × 100), whereas an 8-year-old child who does as well as the average 10-year-old child would have an IQ of 125 (10 ÷ 8 × 100). Most modern intelligence tests are based on the relative position of a person's score among people of the same age, rather than on the basis of this formula, but the idea of intelligence "ratio" or "quotient" provides a good description of the score's meaning. For most measures of IQ, a score of 100 represents the average score at that age. Scores above 100 reflect above average scores, and those below 100 reflect below average scores.

The Flynn Effect

It is important that intelligence tests be standardized on a regular basis, because the overall level of intelligence in a population may change over time. The Flynn effect refers to the observation that scores on intelligence tests worldwide have increased substantially over the past decades (Flynn, 1999). Although the increase varies somewhat from country to country, the average increase is about 3 IQ points every 10 years. There are many explanations for the Flynn effect, including better nutrition, increased access to information, and more familiarity with multiple-choice tests (Neisser, 1998). But whether people are actually getting smarter is debatable (Neisser,1997). [192]

[192] Introduction to Psychology - Measures of Intelligence references Psychology by OpenStax CNX, licensed under

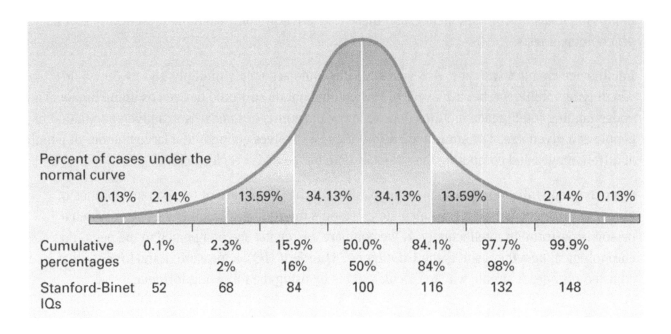

Percent of cases under the normal curve								
0.13%	2.14%	13.59%	34.13%	34.13%	13.59%		2.14%	0.13%

Cumulative percentages	0.1%		2.3%		15.9%		50.0%		84.1%		97.7%		99.9%	
			2%		16%		50%		84%		98%			

Stanford-Binet IQs	52	68	84	100	116	132	148

The Value of IQ TestingThe value of IQ testing is most evident in educational or clinical settings. Children who seem to be experiencing learning difficulties or severe behavioral problems can be tested to ascertain whether the child's difficulties can be partly attributed to an IQ score that is significantly different from the mean for her age group. Without IQ testing—or another measure of intelligence—children and adults needing extra support might not be identified effectively. People also use IQ testing results to seek disability benefits from the Social Security Administration.

IQ tests have sometimes been used as arguments in support of insidious purposes, such as the **eugenics movement,** which was the science of improving a human population by controlled breeding to increase desirable heritable characteristics. However, the value of this test is important to help those in need.[193]

Intelligence Tests and Those Who Created Them

Alfred Binet & Théodore Simon - Stanford- Binet Intelligence Test

From 1904- 1905 the French psychologist Alfred Binet (1857–1914) and his colleague Théodore

Simon (1872–1961) began working on behalf of the French government to develop a measure that would identify children who would not be successful with the regular school curriculum. The goal was to help teachers better educate these students (Aiken, 1994).

Binet and Simon developed what most psychologists today regard as the first intelligence test, which consisted of a wide variety of questions that included the ability to name objects, define words, draw pictures, complete sentences, compare items, and construct sentences. Binet and Simon (Binet, Simon, & Town, 1915; Siegler, 1992) believed that the questions they asked the children all assessed the basic abilities to understand, reason, and make judgments.

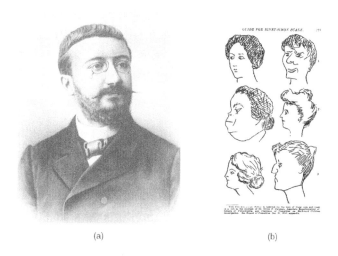

(a)   (b)

Figure (a) Alfred Binet (b) This page is from a 1908 version of the Binet-Simon

Intelligence Scale. Children being tested were asked which face, of each pair, was prettier.[194]

Soon after Binet and Simon introduced their test, the American psychologist Lewis Terman at Stanford University (1877–1956) developed an American version of Binet's test that became known as the *Stanford- Binet Intelligence Test.* The Stanford-Binet is a measure of general intelligence made up of a wide variety of tasks including vocabulary, memory for pictures, naming of familiar objects, repeating sentences, and following commands.[195]

---

[194] Images are in the public domain

[195] Introduction to Psychology - Measures of Intelligence references Psychology by OpenStax CNX, licensed under CC BY 4.0

David Wechsler- Wechsler-Bellevue Intelligence Scale

In 1939, David Wechsler, a psychologist who spent part of his career working with World War I veterans, developed a new IQ test in the United States. Wechsler combined several subtests from other intelligence tests used between 1880 and World War I. These subtests tapped into a variety of verbal and nonverbal skills, because Wechsler believed that intelligence encompassed "the global capacity of a person to act purposefully, to think rationally, and to deal effectively with his environment" (Wechsler, 1958, p. 7). He named the test the **Wechsler-Bellevue Intelligence Scale** (Wechsler, 1981). This combination of subtests became one of the most extensively used intelligence tests in the history of psychology.

Today, there are three intelligence tests credited to Wechsler, the Wechsler Adult Intelligence Scale-fourth edition (WAIS-IV), the Wechsler Intelligence Scale for Children (WISC-V), and the Wechsler Preschool and Primary Scale of Intelligence—Revised (WPPSI-III) (Wechsler, 2002). These tests are used widely in schools and communities throughout the United States, and they are periodically normed and standardized as a means of recalibration.

Bias of IQ Testing

Intelligence tests and psychological definitions of intelligence have been heavily criticized since the 1970s for being biased in favor of Anglo-American, middle-class respondents and for being inadequate tools for measuring non-academic types of intelligence or talent. Intelligence changes with experience, and intelligence quotients or scores do not reflect that ability to change. What is considered smart varies culturally as well, and most intelligence tests do not take this variation into account. For example, in the West, being smart is associated with being quick. A person who answers a question the fastest is seen as the smartest, but in some cultures being smart is associated with considering an idea thoroughly before giving an answer. A well- thought out, contemplative answer is the best answer.[196]

Group differences and cultural bias

There are differences in average scores on IQ tests among subgroups in the US. On average, white children score higher on IQ tests than African American children (of course, "average" means the

---

[196] Sociology: Brief Edition – Agents of Socialization by Steven E. Barkan is licensed under CC BY-NC-SA 3.0

Introduction to Psychology - Measures of Intelligence references Psychology by OpenStax CNX, licensed under CC BY 4.0

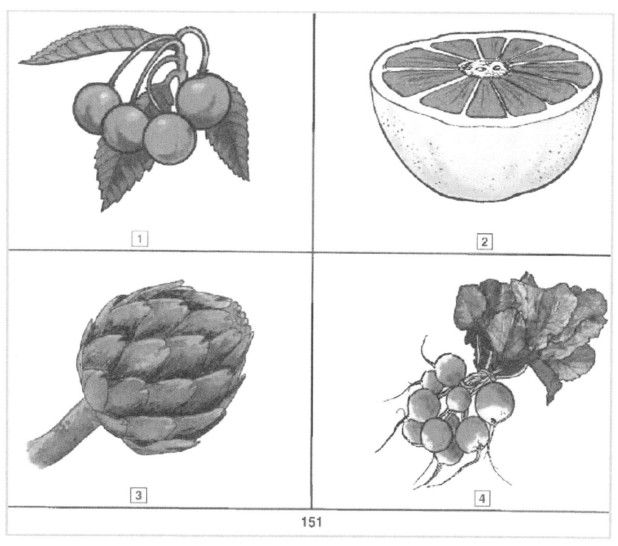

151

Figure – items from a standardized test of receptive vocabulary[197]

total average, and many black children score higher than many white children). Average scores for Hispanic children fall between black and white children, whereas scores for average scores Asian-American children fall above those of white children. To some degree, this may reflect differences in parenting practices in these different cultural groups – e.g., parents in some groups may focus on activities that are more related to those that are being assessed by the tests. These differences also may reflect biases of tests themselves, for example the vocabulary words used may be more likely to be used by a given group. For example, one measure of children's receptive vocabulary showed children four line drawings – a playground swing, a house, a truck with a camper, and an airplane. Children are asked to "put their finger on the house." Children in migrant farm working families often put their finger on the camper. Is this an incorrect answer based upon the child's experience? Such an answer was counted as incorrect in the calculation of IQ scores. Consider this question

[197] Pichette, François & Béland, Sébastien & Leśniewska, Justyna. (2019). Detection of Gender-Biased Items in the Peabody Picture Vocabulary Test. Languages. 4. 10.3390/languages4020027.

that asks children to "point to citrus" - are there potential sources of bias?

More importantly, group differences in IQ scores diminish when children reach college age. This suggests that the difference that were obtained as children reflect either bias in how the tests assess children living in different cultures. For this reason, there have been attempts to develop "culture-fair tests." These are intelligence tests intended to not be culturally biased. There are two main approaches. The first type attempts to design questions that will be familiar to children of all social and ethnic backgrounds. The second involves designing tests that have no verbal questions (but even this can be culturally biased; consider if one culture promotes puzzle working and another does not, then a measure that relies on puzzles would likely have a bias towards the culture that promotes puzzles).

Children's surroundings have an effect on their IQ scores. When the environment supports intellectual skills development, higher IQ scores are obtained. Parental educational level is correlated with children's IQ scores. Most researchers endorse the idea that some combination of genetic and environmental factors interact in predicting individual differences in IQ scores.

The term *Heritability* refers to the fraction of variance in a given trait in a population that is attributed to genetics. For example, if a trait was completely due to genetics, the heritability index for the trait would be 100%. If there was absolutely no genetic component to the trait, the heritability index would be 0%. Heritability refers to a specific population or group, not to individuals. Researchers have been intrigued with examining the heritability of IQ scores for years. Twin studies, in which identical twins raised in the same environment are compared to those raised in separate environments, adoption studies, where adopted children's IQ scores are compared to their biological parents and their adopted parents, and other designs. Across all studies, the consensus is that the heritability index for intelligence is a little over 50%. However, this value changes for different measures of intelligence, different aspects of intelligence, and different groups. For example, the heritability index for IQ scores is lower for African-American children than for white American children. Why would that be so? Differences such as this suggest that the influence of culture on IQ scores may be more complex than heritability indices are capable of detecting. Computing a heritability index treats genetic and environmental influences as factors that can be separated. In reality, the interaction between the two is so complex and multifaceted that this is not possible. For example, even twins separated at birth and raised in separate adoptive homes are likely to share some level of environmental similarity, such as socio-economic status, geographic location, access to schools and so on. It is impossible to remove all of the potential confounding factors. Also, remember from the Flynn effect that nothing is guaranteed in the measurement of IQ. Another consideration in defining intelligence is the question of whether measures of intelligence should reflect a single, central "intelligence" or if the construct of "intelligence" would be more appropriately conceptualized as having multiple aspects. Earlier in this section the term "g" was introduced as representing "general intelligence." The idea of "g" reflects the idea that measures of different aspects of intelligence tend to correlate with each other to some degree. This shared variance between the measures is the general intelligence that is thought to overlap the different measures. Today most researchers accept a hierarchical model of intelligence in which different skills are considered as separate aspects of general intelligence. A different way to think about intelligence is to conceptualize different aspects of intelligence that do not overlap with each other, such as "g," but instead or relatively independent. Two of these sorts of models come from Sternberg and Gardner.

Triarchic Theory of Intelligence

An alternative view of intelligence is presented by Sternberg (1997; 1999). Sternberg offers three types of intelligences. Sternberg provided background information about his view of intelligence in a conference, where he described his frustration as a committee member charged with selecting graduate students for a program in psychology. He was concerned that there was too much emphasis placed on aptitude test scores (we will discuss this later in the chapter) and believed that there were other, less easily measured, qualities necessary for success in life.

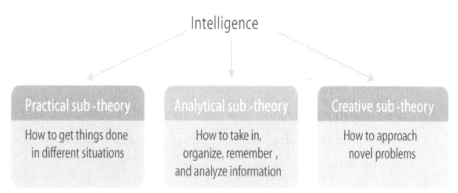

- **Analytical** (componential) sometimes described as academic: includes the ability to solve problems of logic, verbal comprehension, vocabulary, and spatial abilities.

- **Creative** (experiential): the ability to apply newly found skills to novel situations

- **Practical** (contextual): the ability to use common sense and to know what is called for in a situation. [198]

[198] Lifespan Development – Module 6: Middle Childhood by Lumen Learning references Psyc 200 Lifespan

Howard Gardner's Theory of Multiple Intelligences

Another champion of the idea of specific types of intelligences rather than one overall intelligence is the psychologist Howard Gardner (1983, 1999). Gardner argued that it would be evolutionarily functional for different people to have different talents and skills, and proposed that there are nine intelligences that can be differentiated from each other. Gardner contends that these are also forms of intelligence. A high IQ does not always ensure success in life or necessarily indicate that a person has common sense, good interpersonal skills, or other abilities important for success. Gardner investigated intelligences by focusing on children who were talented in one or more areas. He identified these 9 intelligences based on other criteria including a set developmental history and psychometric findings.[199] Howard Gardner (1983, 1998, 1999) suggests that there are not one, but nine domains of intelligence. The first three are skills that are measured by IQ tests:

Table - Howard Gardner's Multiple Intelligences[200]

Intelligence	Description
Linguistic	The ability to speak and write well
Logical-mathematical	The ability to use logic and mathematical skills to solve problems
Spatial	The ability to think and reason about objects in three dimensions
Musical	The ability to perform and enjoy music
Kinesthetic (body)	The ability to move the body in sports, dance, or other physical activities
Interpersonal	The ability to understand and interact effectively with others
Intrapersonal	The ability to have insight into the self
Naturalistic	The ability to recognize, identify, and understand animals, plants, and other living things
Existential	The ability to understand and have concern from life's larger questions, the

Psychology by Laura Overstreet, which is licensed under CC BY 3.0 (modified by Dawn Rymond)

[199] Lifespan Development: A Psychological Perspective by Martha Lally and Suzanne Valentine-French is licensed under CC BY-NC-SA 3.0

[200] Lifespan Development: A Psychological Perspective by Martha Lally and Suzanne Valentine-French is licensed under CC BY-NC-SA 3.0; Table adapted from Gardner, H. (1999). *Intelligence reframed: Multiple intelligences for the 21st century*. New York, NY: Basic Books.

Intelligence	Description
	meaning of life, and other spiritual matters

The concept of multiple intelligences has been influential in the field of education, and teachers have used these ideas to try to teach differently for individual students. For instance, to teach math problems to students who have particularly good kinesthetic intelligence, a teacher might encourage the students to move their bodies or hands according to the numbers. On the other hand, some have argued that these "intelligences" sometimes seem more like "abilities" or "talents" rather than real intelligence. There is no clear conclusion about how many intelligences there are. Are a sense of humor, artistic skills, dramatic skills, and so forth also separate intelligences?[201]

A Spectrum of Intellectual Development

The results of studies assessing the measurement of intelligence show that IQ is distributed in the population in the form of a **Normal Distribution (or bell curve),** which is the pattern of scores usually observed in a variable that clusters around its average. In a normal distribution, the bulk of the scores fall toward the middle, with many fewer scores falling at the extremes. The normal distribution of intelligence shows that on IQ tests, as well as on most other measures, the majority of people cluster around the average (in this case, where IQ = 100), and fewer are either very smart or very dull (see below). The normal distribution of IQ scores in the general population shows that most people have about average intelligence, while very few have extremely high or extremely low intelligence.[202]

---

[201] Lifespan Development: A Psychological Perspective by Martha Lally and Suzanne Valentine-French is licensed under CC BY-NC-SA 3.0

[202] Introduction to Psychology - Measures of Intelligence references Psychology by OpenStax CNX, licensed under CC BY 4.0

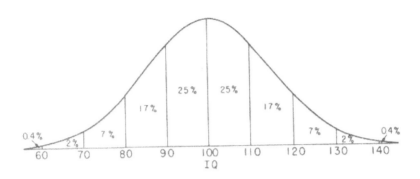

Figure – 84% of people have an IQ score between 80 and 120.[203]

Distribution of IQ Scores in the General Population

This means that about 2% of people score above an IQ of 130, often considered the threshold for giftedness, and about the same percentage score below an IQ of 70, often being considered the threshold for an intellectual disability.

Intellectual Disabilities

One end of the distribution of intelligence scores is defined by people with very low IQ. **Intellectual disability** (or **intellectual developmental disorder**) is assessed based on cognitive capacity (IQ) and adaptive functioning. In other words, IQ scores alone do not substantiate the diagnosis of an intellectual disability, it is only when the individual is also unable to meet their daily goals independently. For example, an individual who has an IQ of 65, takes the bus to their work, and lives in an apartment where they are able to meet their needs would not be considered intellectually disabled. The severity of the disability is based on adaptive functioning, or how well the person handles everyday life tasks. About 1% of the United States population, most of them males, fulfill the criteria for intellectual developmental disorder, but some children who are given this diagnosis lose the classification as they get older and better learn to function in society. A particular vulnerability of people with low IQ is that they may be taken advantage of by others, and this is an important aspect of the definition of intellectual developmental disorder (Greenspan, Loughlin, & Black, 2001).

One example of an intellectual developmental disorder is **Down syndrome**, a chromosomal disorder caused by the presence of all or part of an extra 21st chromosome. The incidence of Down syndrome is estimated at approximately 1 per 700 births, and the prevalence increases as the

---

mother's age increases (CDC, 2014a). People with Down syndrome typically exhibit a distinctive pattern of physical features, including a flat nose, upwardly slanted eye, a protruding tongue, and a short neck. Fortunately, societal attitudes toward individuals with intellectual disabilities have changed over the past decades. We no longer use terms such as "retarded," "moron," "idiot," or "imbecile" to describe people with intellectual differences, although these were the official psychological terms used to describe degrees of what was referred to as "mental retardation" in the past. Laws such as the Americans with Disabilities Act (ADA) have made it illegal to discriminate on the basis of mental and physical disability.

Giftedness

Being **gifted** refers to children who have an IQ of 130 or higher (Lally & Valentine-French, 2015). In addition to above-average IQ, definitions of "giftedness" usually include having a superior talent for something. Children labeled as gifted have been described as precocious, "marching to their own drummer," and having a passion to master their talent. Having an extremely high IQ is clearly less of a problem than having an extremely low IQ but there may also be challenges to being particularly smart. It is often assumed that school children who are labeled as "gifted" may have adjustment problems that make it more difficult for them to create and maintain social relationships. However, this does not seem to be the case. On the contrary, gifted children have fewer problems than their peers and are described as acting more mature. No relationships have been found between giftedness and mental disorders.

As you might expect based on our discussion of intelligence, there are also different types and areas of intelligence and giftedness. Some children are particularly good at math or science, some at automobile repair or carpentry, some at music or art, some at sports or leadership, and so on. There is a lively debate among scholars about whether it is appropriate or beneficial to label some children as "gifted and talented" in school and to provide them with accelerated special classes and other programs that are not available to everyone. Although doing so may help the gifted kids (Colangelo & Assouline, 2009), it also may isolate them from their peers and make such provisions unavailable to those who are not classified as "gifted." Testing for high IQ or for disabilities needs to be critically looked at so that the good that these tests were created for are not used for undesirable purposes.[204]

Testing in Schools

How do we know so much about what children learn in schools? In the next section we'll look at

---

[204] Lifespan Development: A Psychological Perspective by Martha Lally and Suzanne Valentine-French is licensed under CC BY-NC-SA 3.0

the different types of tests and what the schools are testing. Children's academic performance is often measured with the use of standardized tests. Those tests include, but are not limited to Achievement and Aptitude tests.

Achievement tests are used to measure what a child has already learned. Achievement tests are often used as measures of teaching effectiveness within a school setting and as a method to make schools that receive tax dollars (such as public schools, charter schools, and private schools that receive vouchers) accountable to the government for their performance.

Aptitude tests are designed to measure a student's ability to learn or to determine if a person has potential in a particular program. These are often used at the beginning of a course of study or as part of college entrance requirements. The Scholastic Aptitude Test (SAT) and Preliminary Scholastic Aptitude Test (PSAT) are perhaps the most familiar aptitude tests to students in grades 6 and above. Learning test taking skills and preparing for SATs has become part of the training that some students in these grades receive as part of their pre-college preparation. Other aptitude tests include the MCAT (Medical College Admission Test), the LSAT (Law School Admission Test), and the GRE (Graduate Record Examination). Intelligence tests are also a form of aptitude test, which designed to measure a person's ability to learn.[205]

Are achievement tests and aptitude tests the same as IQ tests? How do they differ? Differences in performance in achievement tests are not necessarily due to differences in IQ or intelligence. For example, a discrepancy between the potential to perform at an academic level above that actually performed may be due to specific learning disabilities such as dyslexia or ADD/ADHD. Another factor that can account for a difference between ability and performance is motivation. Achievement motivation is an individual's desire for achievement, to accomplish something, to reach a standard of excellence, and willingness to expend the effort necessary to excel. There are many theories of motivation that have conceptualized motivation in variety of ways. For convenience here, we will examine some of the main concepts and findings about student motivation and achievement.

One factor that can impact achievement is *stereotype threat*. This occurs when a child is afraid of being judged on the basis of a negative stereotype about the child's sex, race or culture. The fear can result in anxiety that interferes with the child's performance. By middle childhood, children are very aware of ethnic stereotypes, and children of groups that are stigmatized are particularly aware of negative stereotypes. Children can be confronted with a stereotype threat that increases

---

[205] Sociology: Brief Edition – Agents of Socialization by Steven E. Barkan is licensed under CC BY-NC-SA 3.0

264

their anxiety, for example, in response to taking a test, which reduces their mental capacity to process the information necessary for performing well. By the transition to early adolescence, many children minority children in low-SES homes begin to devalue school performance and state that it is not important to them. They disengage from academics as a way to protect themselves, resulting in lowered motivation to participate in academic activities and lower school performance. In fact, self-discipline – measured in effort and delay of gratification – is a better predictor of report grades than is IQ (Duckworth, Quinn & Tskayama, 2012).

Another important distinction is between extrinsic and intrinsic motivation. Extrinsic motivation is based upon achieving external incentives, such as receiving awards or avoiding punishment. Intrinsic motivation is driven by internal factors, such as self-determination, curiosity, challenge and effort. The extrinsically motivated child wants to perform well on a test to get the rewards associated with good grades. The outcome of the grade itself is what is important. The intrinsically motivated child wishes to learn more about the material. The grade itself is not as important as is the desire to grow in knowledge and satisfy curiosity.

Orientation towards mastery can also impact school achievement. Ten- to twelve-year-olds who are high in academic self-esteem and motivation make mastery-oriented attributions about their achievement. This means that the attribute their successes to their own ability. If they do well, they believe it is because of their own ability. Ability is viewed as something that can change and can be increased. Children with mastery orientation believe that they can improve their ability by trying harder and taking on new challenges. They believe that ability can be improved through effort. They attribute failure to factors that can be changed or controlled. For example, perhaps they did not try hard enough and can try harder, or perhaps the test was too hard and could be modified. This means that children with the mastery orientation are persistent whether they succeed or fail. They are task oriented and concerned with learning strategies and the process of achievement.

On the other hand, some children develop a hapless orientation. This is a sort of learned helplessness in which the child attributes their failures to their own ability. If they do poorly on an assignment, they interpret that as confirmation of their belief that they are not capable. Children with a hapless orientation attribute their successes to external sources – if they do well, they infer that the assignment must have been easy. These children may focus on performance goals – they are extrinsically motivated to obtain positive evaluations and avoid negative evaluations. Children with high levels of performance orientation focus only on the outcome, on the desire to win or to avoid confirmation of negative thoughts about themselves.

Parents and teachers can influence student's motivation and attributions through self-fulfilling prophecies. If they suggest to the child that they are not capable, the child is more likely to develop a hapless orientation. When parents hold a fixed view of ability – that ability is an innate trait that can not be improved through practice – they may transfer that view to the child. Parents with this view may believe that little can be done to improve performance and so they more ignore information that suggests the child can do better than the parent expects. Children with a hapless orientation often have parents who do not believe that their child is very capable.

Self-Efficacy is the belief that one can master situations and produce favorable outcomes. It is a child's belief of whether or not they will succeed if they try something. Self-efficacy is a critical factor in achievement and motivation. Self-efficacy is linked with intrinsic motivation. Self-efficacy and achievement improve when individuals set goals that are specific, proximal, and

challenging.

There is also an achievement gap in the US. Children who are in middle or upper SES homes tend to score higher on markers of achievement - such as grades, achievement test scores, and graduation rates – than do children in lower SES homes. Because African-American and Hispanic / Latino children disproportionately live in poverty, they also are disproportionately impacted by the achievement gap. There have been several policy attempts to close this gap, often by focusing on improving scores in high-stakes achievement testing. Cultural factors – such as the value that a given culture places on educational achievement – can have an impact on the achievement gap. It is true that children in our society do not have equal access to quality in schools. Children in middle class homes are more likely to attend schools that are better funded and have more resources. A "pedagogy of poverty" can also exacerbate the achievement gap. This occurs when we show lower expectations to children in poverty. Because we expect less of them, they pick up the lowered expectation from adults and internalize it. High quality teaching and warm and supportive teacher-student relationships have been shown to be effective in closing the achievement gap.

There are cultural differences in achievement. Inside the US, Asian-American parents tend to view ability as trait that can be improved with training and practice. Asian-American students tend to outperform other children in measures of school achievement. Internationally, US students lag behind other industrialized nations in achievement test scores for math and science. This gap widens as children grow older. There are cultural differences that may play into this. For example, teachers in Asia tend to spend more time on math than teachers in the US, and US parents have lower expectations in math for their children than do parents in Asia. On the other hand, the US also does not compare well with Scandinavian countries who do not share the math practices of the teachers in Asia. Compared to other industrialized countries, the US has a greater percentage of children living in poverty. Middle-class students in the US perform more like students in other countries in international comparisons. The achievement gap within the US may account for the achievement gap between the US and other nations.

In this photo, two students work together on Google Classroom using a chromebook. Technology has become widely used throughout education.

10 Language and Literacy

Learning Objectives	Related Course Objective
At the completion of this module, students will be able to:	
10-1 Describe how language develops with age, and how to promote language development.	1 6
10-2 Describe how literacy skills develop with age, and how to promote good reading and writing skills.	1 6
10-3 Apply the major theories of learning and cognition to literacy.	1 6

The word *Language* means a form of communication (verbal, written, gestures) based on system of symbols. Human languages are highly organized and based upon rules. Languages is characterized by *Infinite generativity*. This is the ability to produce an endless number of meaningful sentences using a finite set of words and rules. This is because you can use the rules of language to generate an infinite number of communications.

What Is The Nature of Language and How Does It Develop?

Types of language

There are two broad types of language. First is *Nonverbal language.* Nonverbal language is "body language," and includes things communication through hand signs, eye contact, nonlexical sounds, voice tone and other means that are not the content of words. The second type of language is *Verbal language.* Verbal language involves using words to communicate. There are two aspects of verbal language:

Receptive - the words one understands

Expressive – the words one says or produces

Receptive Vocabulary is always greater than expressive. This means that at any given age, a child understand a greater number of words than the number of words that the child produces through speech.

Introduction to Linguistics

Language is such a special topic that there is an entire field, linguistics, devoted to its study. Linguistics views language in an objective way, using the **scientific method** and rigorous research to form **theories** about how humans acquire, use, and sometimes abuse language. There are a few major branches of linguistics, which are useful to understand in order to learn about language development.

Language's Rule Systems:

Phonetics and Phonology
Phonology involves the sound system of language and forms the basis and sequences for sets of words. A **phoneme** is the smallest unit of sound that makes a meaningful difference in a given language. The word "bit" has three phonemes, /b/, /i/, and /t/ (in transcription, phonemes are placed between slashes), and the word "pit" also has three: /p/, /i/, and /t/. The word "chat" has three phonemes, /ch/ /a/ and /t/. A phoneme is not synonymous with "letter." For example, the letter "c" has two phonemes: /s/ as in "cider" and /k/ as in "cat." The phoneme /ch/ is a phoneme because you can't break that sound down anymore, but it is two letters. The sound "fff" as in "fish" can be made with the letters "f" or "ph" as in "photo," but it is one phoneme. In spoken languages, phonemes are produced by the positions and movements of the vocal tract, including our lips, teeth, tongue, vocal cords, and throat, whereas in sign languages phonemes are defined by the shapes and movement of the hands. English contains about 45 phonemes.

Phonological Awareness is the bility to identify phonemes or the sound structure of language. For example, say plig without the l, or think about which word does not rhyme out of "bat, pad, had"? Infants are able to distinguish between phonemes in the languages that they here, and phonological awareness is important later in learning to read.

Whereas phonemes are the smallest units of sound in language, **phonetics** is the study of individual speech sounds; **phonology** is the study of phonemes, which are the speech sounds of an individual language. These two heavily overlapping subfields cover all the sounds that humans can make, as well as which sounds make up different languages.

Morpheme and Morphology

A **morpheme** is a string of one or more phonemes *that* makes up the smallest units of meaning in a language. Some morphemes, such as one-letter words like "I" and "a," are also phonemes, but most morphemes are made up of combinations of phonemes. Some morphemes are prefixes and suffixes used to modify other words. For example, the syllable "re-" as in "rewrite" or "repay" means "to do again," and the suffix "-est" as in "happiest" or "coolest" means "to the maximum." the word "girl" is a morpheme; you can have "girlscouts" and "girlfriends" but you can't break down the meaning of "girl" any further.

Morphology is the study of words and other meaningful units of language like suffixes and prefixes. A morphologist would be interested in the relationship between words like "dog" and "dogs" or "walk" and "walking," and how people figure out the differences between those words.

Syntax

Syntax is the set of rules of a language by which we construct sentences. Syntax involves the ways words combine to form acceptable phrases and sentencesEach language has a different syntax. The syntax of the English language requires that each sentence have a noun and a verb, each of which may be modified by adjectives and adverbs. Some syntaxes make use of the order in which words appear, while others do not.

Syntax is the study of sentences and phrases, or how people put words into the right order so that they can communicate meaningfully. All languages have underlying rules of syntax, which, along with morphological rules, make up every language's grammar. An example of syntax coming into play in language is "Eugene walked the dog" versus "The dog walked Eugene." Word order is important in conveying meaning. The order of words is not arbitrary—in order for the sentence to convey the intended meaning, the words must be in a certain order.[206] Syntactical rules vary across

---

[206] Beginning Psychology – Intelligence and Language by Charles Stangor is licensed under CC BY-NC-SA 3.0

languages. For example, in Spanish one might say "la escuela roja," but in English one would say "the red school." Every language is different. In English, an adjective comes before a noun ("red school"), whereas in Spanish, the adjective comes after ("escuela [school] roja [red]."

Semantics

Semantics, generally, is about the meaning of words and sentences. This involves the vocabulary of a given language. Someone who studies semantics is interested in words and what real-world object or concept those words denote, or point to.

Pragmatics

Pragmatics is an even broader field that studies how the context of a sentence contributes to meaning. Pragmatics involves appropriate use of language in context - using language according to sociocultural rules. Examples include saying "please" and "thank you;" or taking turns in a conversation. Some languages have different forms of use in formal situations than in informal. Pragmatics also involves how the situational context effects meaning. For example, someone shouting "Fire!" has a very different meaning if they are in charge of a seven-gun salute than it does if they are sitting in a crowded movie theater.) Languages have different rules that can impact pragmatics. In German, you can put noun after noun together to form giant compound words; in Chinese, the pitch of your voice determines the meaning of your words. in American Sign Language, you can convey full, grammatical sentences with tense and aspect by moving your hands and face. But all languages have structural underpinnings that make them logical for the people who speak and understand them.[207]

Cognitive Language and Communication

When learning one or more languages in middle childhood, children are able to understand that there are many complex parts including comprehension, fluency, and meaning when communicating. The following are areas of cognitive language and communication. We can use the term *metalinguistics* to refer to thinking about language and its use.

Lexicon

Every language has its rules, which act as a framework for meaningful communication. But what do people fill that framework up with? The answer is, of course, words. Every human language has a **lexicon**—the sum total of all of the words in that language. By using grammatical rules to combine words into logical sentences, humans can convey an infinite number of concepts.

---

[207] Child Development – Unit 6: Language Development references Psychology.by Boundless, licensed under CC BY-SA 4.0

Grammar

Because all language obeys a set of combinatory rules, we can communicate an infinite number of concepts. While every language has a different set of rules, all languages do obey rules. These rules are known as grammar. Speakers of a language have internalized the rules and exceptions for that language's grammar. There are rules for every level of language—word formation (for example, native speakers of English have internalized the general rule that -ed is the ending for past-tense verbs, so even when they encounter a brand-new verb, they automatically know how to put it into past tense); phrase formation (for example, knowing that when you use the verb "buy," it needs a subject and an object; "She buys" is wrong, but "She buys a gift" is okay); and sentence formation.

Older children are also able to learn new rules of grammar with more flexibility. While younger children are likely to be reluctant to give up saying "I goed there", older children will learn this rather quickly along with other rules of grammar.

Vocabulary

One of the reasons that children can classify objects in so many ways is that they have acquired a vocabulary to do so. By fifth grade, a child's vocabulary has grown to 40,000 words. It grows at a rate that exceeds that of those in early childhood. This language explosion, however, differs from that of younger children because it is facilitated by being able to associate new words with those already known, and because it is accompanied by a more sophisticated understanding of the meanings of a word.

Context

Words do not possess fixed meanings but change their interpretation as a function of the context in which they are spoken. We use **contextual information**—the information surrounding language—to help us interpret it. Context is how everything within language works together to convey a particular meaning. Context includes tone of voice, body language, and the words being used. Depending on how a person says something, holds his or her body, or emphasizes certain points of a sentence, a variety of different messages can be conveyed. For example, the word "awesome," when said with a big smile, means the person is excited about a situation. "Awesome," said with crossed arms, rolled eyes, and a sarcastic tone, means the person is not thrilled with the situation.[208]

New Understanding

Those in middle and late childhood are also able to think of objects in less literal ways. For

---

[208] Beginning Psychology – Intelligence and Language by Charles Stangor is licensed under CC BY-NC-SA 3.0

example, if asked for the first word that comes to mind when one hears the word "pizza", the younger child is likely to say "eat" or some word that describes what is done with a pizza. However, the older child is more likely to place pizza in the appropriate category and say "food". This sophistication of vocabulary is also evidenced by the fact that older children tell jokes and delight in doing so. They may use jokes that involve plays on words such as "knock- knock" jokes or jokes with punch lines. Young children do not understand play on words and tell "jokes" that are literal or slapstick, such as "A man fell down in the mud! Isn't that funny?"[209]

Language Milestones

Do newborns communicate? Absolutely! However, they do not communicate with the use of language. Instead, they communicate their thoughts and needs with body posture (being relaxed or still), gestures, cries, and facial expressions. A person who spends adequate time with an infant can learn which cries indicate pain and which ones indicate hunger, discomfort, or frustration as well as translate their vocalizations, movements, gestures and facial expressions. Cries have different sound properties, conveying different meanings. At birth, infants prefer human voices to other complex sounds, and they prefer female voices over male voices, and they prefer their own mother's voice over other females' voices.

How Language Develops in Infancy

Babbling and other vocalizations

Crying: present at birth, signals distress

Cooing: begins about 1 to 4 months

Babbling: occurs in middle of first year, strings of consonant-vowel combinations begins about 3-8 months

Gestures: begins about 8 to 12 months; about same for hearing and deaf children

---

[209] Lifespan Development - Module 6: Middle Childhood by Lumen Learning references Psyc 200 Lifespan Psychology by Laura Overstreet, licensed under CC BY 4.0

Beginning Psychology – Intelligence and Language by Charles Stangor is licensed under CC BY-NC-SA 3.0

Stages of Language Development

•Intentional Vocalizations: Cooing and taking turns: Infants begin to vocalize and repeat vocalizations within the first couple of months of life. That gurgling, musical vocalization called cooing can serve as a source of entertainment to an infant who has been laid down for a nap or seated in a carrier on a car ride. Cooing serves as practice for vocalization as well as the infant hears the sound of his or her own voice and tries to repeat sounds that are entertaining. Infants also begin to learn the pace and pause of conversation as they alternate their vocalization with that of someone else and then take their turn again when the other person's vocalization has stopped. Cooing initially involves making vowel sounds like "oooo." Later, consonants are added to vocalizations such as "nananananana," called babbling.

•Babbling and gesturing: At about three to eight months of age, infants begin making even more elaborate vocalizations that include the sounds required for any language. Guttural sounds, clicks, consonants, and vowel sounds stand ready to equip the child with the ability to repeat whatever sounds are characteristic of the language heard. Eventually, these sounds will no longer be used as the infant grows more accustomed to a particular language. Deaf babies also use gestures to communicate wants, reactions, and feelings. Because gesturing seems to be easier than vocalization for some toddlers, sign language is sometimes taught to enhance one's ability to communicate by making use of the ease of gesturing. The rhythm and pattern of language is used when deaf babies sign just as it is when hearing babies babble.

•Infants can discriminate most sounds in world languages. From birth to 6 months infants are *Universal Linguists.* These "Citizens of the Word" can recognize most sound changes in any language. This ability declines after about 6 months, as infants learn their own language(s) that they have been exposed to in their environment. They gradually lose the ability to recognize sound changes in other languages. Around 7–8 months, infants begin to segment individual words from stream of fluent speech in the language(s) they are exposed to in their environment. At about 8-9 months, infants are able to detect word boundaries in their home language(s).

•Understanding: Receptive language for family names begins. By 9-10 months receptive language for objects begins. At around ten months of age, the infant can understand more than he or she can say. You may have experienced this phenomenon as well if you have ever tried to learn a second language. You may have been able to follow a conversation more easily than to contribute to it.

- First words and cultural influences: First words are typically spoken between 10 to 15 months. First words if the child is using English tend to be nouns (there is a *noun bias* in English). In the US, first words often name important people, familiar animals and objects, body parts, and greetings. The child labels objects such as cup or ball. Names of common objects are prominent among children's first words in English, perhaps because their meaning is easier to encode. In a verb-friendly language such as Chinese, however, children may learn more verbs. This may also be due to the different emphasis given to objects based on culture. Chinese children may be taught to notice action and relationship between objects while children from the United States may be taught to name an object and its qualities (color, texture, size, etc.). These differences can be seen when comparing interpretations of art by older students from China and the United States.

- Holophrastic speech: Children begin using their first words at about 12 or 13 months of age and may use partial words to convey thoughts at even younger ages. These one word expressions are referred to as **holophrastic speech**. For example, the child may say "ju" for the word "juice" and use this sound when referring to a bottle. The listener must interpret the meaning of the holophrase and when this is someone who has spent time with the child, interpretation is not too difficult. They know that "ju" means "juice" which means the baby wants some milk! But, someone who has not been around the child will have trouble knowing what is meant. Imagine the parent who to a friend exclaims, "Ezra's talking all the time now!" The friend hears only "ju da ga" which, the parent explains, means "I want some milk when I go with Daddy."

- Underextension: A child who learns that a word stands for an object may initially think that the word can be used for only that particular object. Only the family's Irish Setter is a "doggie". This is referred to as **underextension.** More often, however, a child may think that a label applies to all objects that are similar to the original object. In **overextension** all animals become "doggies", for example.

- Vocabulary growth spurt: Receptive language grows dramatically between 10-15 months. One year olds to 13-month olds typically have a receptive vocabulary of about 50 words, but their expressive vocabulary does not reach 50 words until about 18-months. But by the time they become toddlers, they have an expressive vocabulary of about 200 words and begin putting those words together in telegraphic speech (I think of it now as 'text message' speech because texting is more common and is similar in that text messages typically only include the minimal amount of words to convey the message). At 15-18 months, toddlers can follow simple commands. Toddlers this age may produce sentence-long utterances with nonsense words that are expressed in meaningful tones. Word learning begins slowly at ~2 words per week, with a vocabulary spurt beginning when ~9 words per day are learned.

- Two word sentences and **telegraphic speech**: Words are soon combined and 18 month old toddlers can express themselves further by using expressions such as "baby bye-bye" or "doggie pretty". Words needed to convey messages are used, but the articles and other parts of speech necessary for grammatical correctness are not yet used. These expressions sound like a telegraph (or perhaps a better analogy today would be that they read like a text message) where unnecessary words are not used. "Give baby ball" is used rather than "Give the baby the ball." Or a text message of "Send money now!" rather than "Dear Mother. I really need some money to take care of my expenses."[210]

In the first two years of life, children go from communicating by crying to being able to express themselves with words. Here is a table of common language milestones for infants and toddlers.

Table - Language Milestones[211]

Typical Age	What Most Children Do By This Age
2 months	.Coos, makes gurgling sounds .Turns head toward sounds
4 months	.Begins to babble .Babbles with expression and copies sounds he hears .Cries in different ways to show hunger, pain, or being tired
6 months	.Responds to sounds by making sounds .Strings vowels together when babbling ("ah," "eh," "oh") and likes taking turns with parent while making sounds .Responds to own name .Makes sounds to show joy and displeasure .Begins to say consonant sounds (jabbering with "m," "b")

---

[210] Children's Development by Ana R. Leon is licensed under CC BY 4.0

[211] Developmental Milestones by the CDC is in the public domain

Typical Age	What Most Children Do By This Age
9 months	.Understands "no" .Makes a lot of different sounds like "mamamama" and "babababa" .Copies sounds and gestures of others .Uses fingers to point at things
9-10 months	.Receptive language for objects begins .Deaf children stop babbling .First gestures emerge and are used to communicate
1 year	.Responds to simple spoken requests .Uses simple gestures, like shaking head "no" or waving "bye-bye" .Makes sounds with changes in tone (sounds more like speech) .Says "mama" and "dada" and exclamations like "uh-oh!" .Tries to say words you say
18 months	.Says several single words .Says and shakes head now .Points to show others what is wanted
2 years	.Points to things or pictures when they are named .Knows names of familiar people and body parts .Says sentences with 2 to 4 words .Follows simple instructions .Repeats words overheard in conversation .Points to things in a book

Child-Directed Speech

Why is a horse a "horsie"? Have you ever wondered why adults tend to use "baby talk" or that sing-song type of intonation and exaggeration used when talking to children? This represents a universal tendency and is known as **child-directed speech** or parentheses (historically referred to as motherese). It involves exaggerating the vowel and consonant sounds, using a high-pitched voice, and delivering the phrase with great facial expression. Why is this done? It may be in order to clearly articulate the sounds of a word so that the child can hear the sounds involved. Or it may be because when this type of speech is used, the infant pays more attention to the speaker and this sets up a pattern of interaction in which the speaker and listener are in tuned with one another.[212]

Language Growth

---

[212] Children's Development by Ana R. Leon is licensed under CC BY 4.0

There are two styles of early word acquisition that are seen in English speaking US children. The first is the *Referential pattern* in which children learn more nouns than any other type of word. The second is the *Expressive pattern* in which children learn more types of other words. The speed of acquisition of vocabulary is the same for children in both groups. In main stream US cultures, the referential pattern is more common.

During the ages of 18–24 months first sentences emerge. The average length of utterances is only 2 words. This is the beginning of syntax and telegraphic speech. At this age common phrases (e.g., "thank you" or "stop it") are treated as one big word. Fast mapping (figuring out the meaning of a word by how it is used in context) is evident, but children may need multiple exposures for learning to "stick."

There is a vocabulary spurt between 18 months to 2 years. On average, children go from an expressive vocabulary of 50 words at 18 months to an expressive vocabulary of 200 words at 2 years. Overextensions and underextensions are common.

Overextension: applying words too broadly "The use of a word beyond its customary semantic boundary"

Underextension: applying word too narrowly

Vocabulary Growth

Growth of vocabulary is very rapid during a child's second and third year. A child's vocabulary expands from an average of about 200 words at age 2 to to an average vocabulary of 500-600 words at 30 months, to over 10,000 words at age 6. Grammatical words (e.g., "of," "the") are used by ages 2 to 3 years, as children begin to speak in full sentences. This rapid growth in vocabulary may be dependent on brain maturation, especially increases in myelination and development in Wernicke's area and Broca's area. The rapid increase in vocabulary is facilitated through a process called *fast-mapping.* New words are learned on the basis of very little input. Words are easily learned by making connections between new words and concepts already known. Fast-mapping may be facilitated by three assumptions: the whole-object assumption (if someone says "table" then the name for the whole thing must be "table"), the taxonomic assumption (if this thing is a "table" then things like it must also be "tables"), and the mutual exclusivity assumption (if that thing is a "table" then this different thing must be something else). The parts of speech that are learned depend on the language and what is emphasized. Children speaking verb-friendly languages such as Chinese and Japanese, tend to learn nouns more readily. But, those learning less verb-friendly languages such as English, seem to need assistance in grammar to master the use of verbs (Imai, et al, 2008).

Literal Meanings

Children can repeat words and phrases after having heard them only once or twice. But they do not always understand the meaning of the words or phrases. This is especially true of expressions or figures of speech which are taken literally. For example, two preschool-aged girls began to laugh loudly while listening to a audio-recording of Disney's "Sleeping Beauty" when the narrator reports, "Prince Phillip lost his head!" They imagine his head popping off and rolling down the hill as he runs and searches for it. Or a classroom full of preschoolers hears the teacher say, "Wow! That was a piece of cake!" The children began asking "Cake? Where is my cake? I want cake!"

Overregularization

Children learn rules of grammar as they learn language but may apply these rules inappropriately at first. For instance, a child learns to add "ed" to the end of a word to indicate past tense. Then form a sentence such as "I goed there. I doed that." This is typical at ages 2 and 3. They will soon learn new words such as "went" and "did" to be used in those situations.

The Impact of Training

Remember Vygotsky and the zone of proximal development? Children can be assisted in learning language by others who listen attentively, model more accurate pronunciations and encourage elaboration. The child exclaims, "I goed there!" and the adult responds, "You went there? Say, 'I went there.' Where did you go?" Children may be ripe for language as Chomsky suggests, but active participation in helping them learn is important for language development as well. The process of scaffolding is one in which the adult (or more skilled peer) provides needed assistance to the child as a new skill is learned.

Early Childhood Language Milestones

The prior aspects of language development in early childhood can also be summarized into the progression of milestones children typically experience from ages 3 to 5. Here is a table of those.

Table - Language Milestones[213]

---

[213] Developmental Milestones by the CDC is in the public domain

Typical Age	What Most Children Do By This Age
3 years	.Follows instructions with 2 or 3 steps .Can name most familiar things .Understands words like "in," "on," and "under" .Says first name, age, and sex .Names a friend .Says words like "I," "me," "we," and "you" and some plurals (cars, dogs, cats) .Talks well enough for strangers to understand most of the time .Carries on a conversation using 2 to 3 sentences
4 years	.Knows some basic rules of grammar, such as correctly using "he" and "she" .Sings a song or says a poem from memory such as the "Itsy Bitsy Spider" or the "Wheels on the Bus" .Tells stories .Can say first and last name
5 years	.Speaks very clearly .Tells a simple story using full sentences .Uses future tense; for example, "Grandma will be here." .Says name and address

Age Trends in Language

<u>Early Childhood</u>

Preschoolers are almost fluent in speech

Adults use child-directed speech (motherese)

<u>Development of language and vocabulary</u>

Growth of vocabulary

Children are acquiring words at a rapid pace

During preschool years, average of five words/day

Built-in biases that facilitate language:

Mutual exclusivity bias: if this word means "this" thing, then it can not mean "that" thing

Fast mapping: figuring out the meaning of a word in the course of conversation

Syntactic bootstrapping: understanding the meaning of a word based on how it used, based upon a child's knowledge of other words used in the sentence

<u>Understanding Phonology and Morphology</u>

Most preschoolers gradually become sensitive to sounds of speech

Children know morphological rules

Learn morphemes, the smallest grammatical units, in a fixed sequence

Children abstract rules and apply them to novel situations

Overregularize, inappropriate use of grammatical rules

<u>Understanding Syntax</u>

Preschoolers show growing mastery of complex rules for how words should be ordered

Elementary school children become skilled at using syntactical rules to construct lengthy, complex sentences

<u>Advances in Semantics</u>

Speaking vocabulary for 6-year-olds ranges from 8,000 to 14,000 words

Word learning rate between ages 1 and 6 is 5 to 8 words per day

Average 6-year-old learns 22 words a day

<u>Advances in Pragmatics</u>

3-year-olds use displacement, ability to talk about things physically absent

4-year-olds: develop sensitivity to needs of others in conversation

4- to 5-year-olds learn to change speech style to suit the situation

Language impairments

Late talkers

Fewer than 50 words by age 2, no combinations

By age 5, 75% will have outgrown this deficit

Predictors of persistent difficulties:

- Trouble with using third person singular

- Trouble using past tense

- Adult relatives who experienced language delays

Language Development in the School-Age Child

Human language is the most complex behavior on the planet and, at least as far as we know, in the universe. Language involves both the ability to comprehend (receptive) spoken and written (expressive) words and to create communication in real time when we speak or write. Most languages are oral, generated through speaking. Speaking involves a variety of complex cognitive, social, and biological processes including operation of the vocal cords, and the coordination of breath with movements of the throat and mouth, and tongue. Other languages are sign languages, in which the communication is expressed by movements of the hands. The most common sign language is American Sign Language (ASL), currently spoken by more than 500,000 people in the United States alone.

Although language is often used for the transmission of information ("turn right at the next light and then go straight," "Place tab A into slot B"), this is only its most mundane function. Language also allows us to access existing knowledge, to draw conclusions, to set and accomplish goals, and to understand and communicate complex social relationships. Language is fundamental to our ability to think, and without it we would be nowhere near as intelligent as we are.

Language can be conceptualized in terms of sounds, meaning, and the environmental factors that help us understand it. Phonemes are the elementary sounds of our language, morphemes are the smallest units of meaning in a language, syntax is the set of grammatical rules that control how words are put together, and contextual information is the elements of communication that are not part of the content of language but that help us understand its meaning. Understanding how language works means reaching across many branches of psychology—everything from basic **neurological** functioning to high-level **cognitive** processing. Language shapes our social interactions and brings order to our lives. Complex language is one of the defining factors that make us human.[214]

Age Trends in Language

Middle Childhood

Begin to play with language; use it in humor

Vocabulary explosion; about 20 words per day

Most words are figured out by reasoning, not taught

At age 6: 10,000 words; age 11: 40,000

Children learn words that they hear or that matters to them

They also learn the remaining rules of grammar not previously mastered

Reading and writing have prominent role in language

Learn to use in more complex ways

Metalinguistic awareness

Allows children to think about their language

Use language in culturally appropriate ways

Start to appreciate ambiguity in language

This contributes to an appreciation of jokes

Middle Childhood

Development of pragmatic and communication skills

---

[214] Beginning Psychology – Intelligence and Language by Charles Stangor is licensed under CC BY-NC-SA 3.0

Pragmatic skills, the ability to use language to achieve varied aims in different circumstances

Become more adept at monitoring listeners' levels of knowledge and status, and adjusting

Persuasive skills develop rapidly

E.g., better understanding of how to sway parental objections

 Adolescence

Vocabulary continues to grow

Syntax continues to develop

Sentences become longer and more complex

Improved pragmatics as students adapt language to the audience

Humor includes sophisticated wordplay

Theories of Language Development

Humans, especially children, have an amazing ability to learn language. Within the first year of life, children will have learned many of the necessary concepts to have functional language, although it will still take years for their capabilities to develop fully. As we just explained, some people learn two or more languages fluently and are bilingual or multilingual. Here is a recap of the theorists and theories that have been proposed to explain the development of language, and related brain structures, in children.

Skinner: Operant Conditioning

The behaviorists posit that language is acquired via various types of learning. B. F. Skinner believed that children learn language through **operant conditioning**; in other words, children receive "rewards" for using language in a functional manner. For example, a child learns to say the word "drink" when she is thirsty; she receives something to drink, which reinforces her use of the word for getting a drink, and thus she will continue to do so. This follows the four-term contingency that Skinner believed was the basis of language development—motivating operations, discriminative stimuli, response, and reinforcing stimuli. Skinner also suggested that children learn language through imitation of others, prompting, and shaping. It may be that some aspects of language are acquired this way. However, this theory does not do a very good job of explaining many of the facets of language development – most of children's utterances are never reinforced.

Social Pragmatics

Another view emphasizes the child's active engagement in learning language out of a need to communicate. The child seeks information, memorizes terms, imitates the speech heard from others and learns to conceptualize using words as language is acquired. Many would argue that all three of these dynamics foster the acquisition of language (Berger, 2004)[215].

Chomsky: Language Acquisition Device

The view known as **nativism** advocated by Noam Chomsky suggests that infants are equipped with a neurological construct referred to as the **language acquisition device** or LAD that makes infants ready for language. Language develops as long as the infant is exposed to it. No teaching, training, or reinforcement is required for language to develop. Noam Chomsky's work discusses the biological basis for language and claims that children have innate abilities to learn language. Chomsky terms this innate ability the "language acquisition device" (LAD). Chomsky's focus is on the innate capacity for language— the idea that we are born with an understanding of language and that humans biologically prewired for language. He believes children instinctively learn

---

[215] Children's Development by Ana R. Leon is licensed under CC BY 4.0

language without any formal instruction. In his view, the infant is born with the Mental ability to impose structure on the infant's linguistic environment and an inborn understanding of basic rules of language. He also believes children have a natural need to use language, and that in the absence of formal language children will develop a system of communication to meet their needs. He has observed that all children make the same type of language errors, regardless of the language they are taught. Chomsky also believes in the existence of a "universal grammar," which posits that there are certain grammatical rules all human languages share. Some evidence exists to support this view, for example, the universality of some aspects of language, and the presence of brain structures that are related to language. However, his research does not identify areas of the brain or a genetic basis that enables humans' innate ability for language.

Piaget: Assimilation and Accommodation

Jean Piaget's theory of language development suggests that children use both assimilation and accommodation to learn language. **Assimilation** is the process of changing one's environment to place information into an already-existing schema (or idea). **Accommodation** is the process of changing one's schema to adapt to the new environment. Piaget believed children need to first develop mentally before language acquisition can occur. According to him, children first create mental structures within the mind (schemas) and from these schemas, language development happens.

Vygotsky: Zone of Proximal Development

Lev Vygotsky's theory of language development focused on social learning and **the zone of proximal development (ZPD).** The ZPD is a level of development obtained when children engage in social interactions with others; it is the distance between a child's *potential* to learn and the *actual learning* that takes place. Vygotsky's theory also demonstrated that Piaget underestimated the importance of social interactions in the development of language. In the social interactionist view, linguistic skill is viewed as a form of social skill development. This is supported by the evidence that cultural context affects language development. Critics note that it cannot account as well for grammatical as for semantic development.

Contemporary View of Language

Vocabulary depends on practice and modeling

Children actively figure out language

Reason by analogy

Reason using statistics

Supports a more environmentalist than nativist view, but does not rule out the possibility of some core knowledge

Biological and Environmental Influences

Interactionist View of Language Development

Biology and sociocultural experiences contribute to language development

Parents and teachers construct LASS— language acquisition support system

Children acquire native language without explicit teaching

Brain's Role in Language

We know that some areas of the brain are especially linked to language. For example, individuals who have a stroke or other damage to the brain may experience *aphasia*. Aphasia is brain damage that involves a loss of ability to use words. Two areas of the brain that are known to be important for language are Broca's area and Wernicke's area. Broca's area os a structure in the brain's left frontal lobe that directs the muscle movements involved in speech production. Wernicke's area is a structure in the brain's left hemisphere that is involved in language comprehension.

Is There a Critical Period for Learning Language?

Critical period advocates cite Isolation and abuse cases like "Genie," brain development studies that show the timing of blooming and pruning, and the example of preschoolers' rapid language learning to suggest that there is a critical period for language development. However, behaviorists and other critical period opponents point out that learning about language continues beyond preschool.

Dialects

Children may speak *dialects* that are different from standard English. The word "dialect" is defined as "a particular form of a language which is peculiar to a specific region or social group." It is important that educators and other adults respect students' right to maintain their heritage dialects. Adults should not directly or indirectly suggest to a child that the dialect that they speak is inferior to Standard American English. However, in addition to the dialect children should also learn standard English. This is because standard English is the language of education and commerce. The ability to converse in standard English is an important element of success in education and careers. The term *code switching* refers to using different language varieties for different situations. Code switching is the ability to shift between two languages or two dialects to meet the demands of a conversation of social context. Children who speak a dialect other than standard English can be taught to code switch and use stand English as well as maintaining their heritage dialect.

African American English Vernacular

Some children may speak an African-American English vernacular. This is a style of speech that has some slightly different rules than Standard American English. For example, a child may say "ax," "bidness," and "posed to" for ask, business, and supposed to. Additional qualities of the African American English Vernacular include:

- Stress the first syllable in words like PO-lice and DE-troit.
- Omit possessive /s/ as in That man hat is on the table.
- Omit final /ed/ as in They talk yesterday.
- Omit contractions as in She done well.
- Omit final consonants as in las for last.
- Unique use of done as in I done did her hair or I done her hair.
- Unique use of be as in He be happy.
- Use f for th as in toof for tooth.

Source: Suárez-Orozco, Gaytán, Pakes, O'Connor, and Rhodes (2010).

It is important that adults recognize that vernaculars, such as the African-American vernacular or the Appalachian vernacular are different speaking styles. This does not mean that they are inferior to standard English, just different. It can help a child in long term to intentionally teach "code switching." This means that the child retains their vernacular but also grows in competence in Standard English, and recognizes situations in which each is relevant.

Classroom Implications of Language Development

To help students develop better language ability:

- Be responsive; encourage infants to make sounds, elaborate on what children say
- Encourage use of Standard English
- Read to students, encourage them to read to themselves
- Explicitly teach vocabulary
- Help students use new words in multiple ways
- Use academic language

Bilingual language acquisition

Bilingualism around the world is common and diverse. Although **monolingual** speakers (those that only speak one language) often do not realize it, the majority of children around the world are **bilingual**, (they understand and use two languages). (Meyers- Sutton, 2005). Even in the United States, which is a relatively monolingual society, more than 47 million people speak a language other than English at home, and about 10 million of these people are children or youth in public schools (United States Department of Commerce, 2003). The large majority of bilingual students (75%) are Hispanic, but the rest represent more than a hundred different language groups from around the world. In larger communities throughout the United States, it is therefore common for a single classroom to contain students from several language backgrounds at once. In classrooms, as in other social settings, bilingualism exists in different forms and degrees.

The student who speaks both languages fluently has a definite cognitive advantage. As you might suspect and research confirmed, a fully fluent bilingual student is in a better position to express concepts or ideas in more than one way, and to be aware of doing so (Jimenez, Garcia, & Pearson, 1995; Francis, 2006). Having a large vocabulary in a first language has been shown to save time in learning vocabulary in a second language (Hansen, Umeda & McKinney, 2002).[216]

In the US there are two common approaches to second language instruction. The first is called

---

[216] Lifespan Development: A Psychological Perspective by Martha Lally and Suzanne Valentine-French is licensed under CC BY-NC-SA 3.0

"English as a second language (ESL)" in which the school day is taught entirely in English to encourage use of the English language. The second is a Bilingual approach that is additive (add English to the home language) rather than subtractive (English replaces home language). In this approach, children receive Instruction in academic areas in both English and in their native language. Through these methods, additive bilingualism encouraged and fluency in a second language is added to competence in native language. This is beneficial because children with limited English proficiency may take 2–5 years to speak English well enough to meet practical challenges of daily life and may take 4–7 years to be able to do academic work in English.

Bilingualism

There are differences in how the Brain processes native languages (languages that a child has been exposed to since soon after birth) and languages that are learned later. Broca's area is involved in processing first and second languages. Neuroimaging studies show activation of Broca's area and frontal cortex of left hemisphere when native English speakers read English.

Native signers also show activation in the left hemisphere and right hemisphere. as well as Broca's area. The timing of exposure to the second language affects brain organization.

Bilingual Education Guidelines

- Devote time to teaching English
- Integrate oral and written English language instruction into content-area teaching
- Directly teach vocabulary
- Teach Standard English grammar and syntax explicitly
- Teach language skills as early as possible
- Build strong skills in the heritage language (preschoolers)
- Encourage English use in informal settings at school
- Remember Standard English lags behind conversational English
- Support additive bilingualism (not subtractive)

The following pages are handouts from the power point presentation of the ESL module that corresponds to ECHD 2435. At UTC, each class has an ESL module. This is the module for the Child Development class.

Teachers HELP
(Helping English Language Proficiency)
Module 3
Development

Student Learning Outcomes

Student learning outcomes for this module are consistent with what teachers need to know and be able to do in designing/implementing/evaluating students' academic achievement based on the TESOL/CAEP Professional Teaching Standards and identified in the next two slides. The entire Standards document may be found at http://www.tesol.org/advance-the-field/standards/tesol-caep-standards-for-p-12-teacher-education-programs

---

Student Learning Outcomes (cont.)

Domain 1. Language

Standard 1.b. Language Acquisition and Development   Candidates understand and apply theories and research in language acquisition and development to support their ELLs' English language and literacy learning and content-area achievement.

Domain 2. Culture

Candidates know, understand, and use major concepts, principles, theories, and research related to the nature and role of culture   and cultural groups to construct supportive learning environments   for ELLs.

Student Learning Outcomes (cont.)

Domain 3. Planning, Implementing, and Managing Instruction

Standard 3.a. Planning for Standards-Based ESL and Content Instruction   Candidates know, understand, and apply concepts, research, and best practices to plan classroom instruction in a supportive learning environment for ELLs. They plan for multilevel classrooms with learners from diverse backgrounds using standards-based ESL and content curriculum.

Standard 3.b. Implementing and Managing Standards-Based ESL and Content Instruction Candidates know, manage, and implement a variety of standards-based teaching strategies and techniques for developing and integrating English listening, speaking, reading, and writing. Candidates support ELLs' access to the core curriculum by teaching language through academic content.

Standard 3.c. Using Resources and Technology Effectively in ESL and Content Instruction
Candidates are familiar with a wide range of standards-based materials, resources, and technologies, and choose, adapt, and use them in effective ESL and content teaching.

Student Learning Outcomes (cont.)

Domain 4. Assessment

Standard 4.a. Issues of Assessment for English Language Learners   Candidates demonstrate understanding of various assessment issues as they affect ELLs, such as accountability, bias, special education testing, language proficiency, and accommodations in formal testing situations.

Domain 5. Professionalism

Standard 5.a. ESL Research and History   Candidates demonstrate knowledge of history, research, educational public policy, and current practice in the field of ESL teaching and apply this knowledge to inform teaching and learning.

Standard 5.b. Professional Development, Partnerships, and Advocacy Candidates take advantage of professional growth opportunities and demonstrate the ability to build partnerships with colleagues and students' families, serve as community resources, and advocate for ELLs.

Why Do I Need to Know About English Learners?

This question is best answered by information on the next three slides from WIDA.

WIDA is an organization that advances academic language development and academic achievement for children and youth who are culturally and linguistically diverse.

WIDA provides high quality standards, assessments, research, and professional learning for educators.

Tennessee is a member of WIDA.

Let's take a look at the Cornerstone of the WIDA Standards, Guiding Principles of Language Development.

1. Students' languages and cultures are valuable resources to be tapped and incorporated into schooling.

2. Students' home, school, and community experiences influence their language development.

3. Students draw on their metacognitive, metalinguistic, and metacultural awareness to develop proficiency in additional languages.

---

4. Students' academic language development in their native language facilitates their academic language development in English. Conversely, students' academic language development in English informs their academic language development in their native language.

5. Students learn language and culture through meaningful use and interaction.

6. Students use language in functional and communicative ways that vary according to context.

---

7. Students develop language proficiency in listening, speaking, reading, and writing interdependently, but at different rates and in different ways.

8. Students' development of academic language and academic content knowledge are inter-related processes.

9. Students' development of social, instructional, and academic language, a complex and long-term process, is the foundation for their success in school.

10. Students' access to instructional tasks requiring complex thinking is enhanced when linguistic complexity and instructional support match their levels of language proficiency.

Module 3 Summary

- English Learners (ELs) – Who are they?
- How ELs develop a second (or additional) language
  - Receptive language and Productive language
  - Language Environment is important - Quantity and Quality Matter
  - Interaction is essential
  - Learner characteristics are important
- Becoming proficient in English
  - Conversational English
  - Academic English
- WIDA
  - 'Can Do'
- Supporting ELs oral language development

Module 3 Summary (cont.)

- Unique needs of adolescent ELs - still learning English and academic content
- Cultural diversity and culturally-responsive teaching
- Ways to help families and the community support ELs
  - Learn and use student's language
  - Educate parents on U.S. schools and on their rights
  - Recruit volunteers and provide information on educational opportunities
- "Accelerators" to language learning

Who IS an English Learner** (EL)?

- English Learners (ELs) are "students 3-21 years old who are enrolled in elementary or secondary school but who do not speak, read, write, or understand English well enough to
  - 1) read at a proficient level on state achievement tests,
  - 2) be successful in a classroom in which English is the language of instruction, or
  - 3) fully participate in society." (No Child Left Behind (NCLB) Act of 2001)

  **NOTE: 60% of English Learners were born in the United States.

Percentage of ELs born in versus outside U.S.

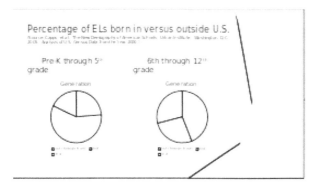

Pre-K through 5th grade

Generation

6th through 12th grade

Generation

"English Learner" or "EL" should be used in reference to students meeting these criteria. The Federal government uses the term, "LEP" (Limited English Proficient), but teachers in the field avoid this outdated term.

"EL" refers to the learner. "ESL" or "ESOL" refers to the language supports provided to students. (Student - English Learner or EL; Teacher - ESL or ESOL teacher.)

What is the Growth of ELs in the US?

- Over the last decade, the number of ELs has increased by more than 51-60% while the overall school population has grown by 3-7%.(Center for Public Education, 2012)

- By the 2030s, the US Census Bureau projects that ELs will increase from roughly 22% to 40% of the school-age population. (Center for Public Education, 2012)

- The Southeast region is the most rapidly growing EL population. (https://www.newamerica.org/education-policy/edcentral/s outheast-els/)

What is the Growth of ELs in Tennessee and Hamilton County?

- The number of K-12 ELs increased from 8,000 to 30,537 students from 1997 to 2010.
- As of 2017, 5,000 Hamilton County students speak a language other than English as their primary language.
- HCDE students come from 38 countries and speak over 40 different languages.
- Spanish, Kanjobal, and Mam are the most frequently spoken native languages used by local children.
- Many students students from Central or South America do not speak Spanish.
- Kanjobal and Mam are Mayan-based dialects spoken in Guatemala.

How do EL students develop English as their second/additional language?

ELs typically develop their second language (L2) through multiple stages of language acquisition similar to the way they developed their native language (L1).

General principles:

- Receptive language precedes productive language
- Language environment (quantity & quality) is important
- Interaction is critical
- Child/student characteristics play a role
- Translanguaging will occur & should not be discouraged
  - Fluid shift from one language to another to communicate with different people for different purposes
  - Sometimes called "codeswitching"
  - (See WIDA Standards at https://www.wida.us/standards/eld.aspx)

Receptive versus productive language

Receptive language competencies: comprehension/understanding
  listening
  reading

Productive language competencies: output
  speaking
  writing

ELs may understand what they hear for several weeks or months before they begin to use words, phrases, and sentences to express what they think and know.

Language environment is Important

Quantity Matters:
- Need frequent opportunities to hear the language spoken

Quality Matters:
- Rich language
- Spoken by a more fluent speaker
- Tailored to current level of language and cognitive development (Scaffolding)
- "Comprehensible Input" - strategies designed to make content understandable to an English Learner (ex. slower speech, modeling, visuals, etc.)

Interaction is essential!

Mere exposure to language is not enough, no matter how much or how high quality

- How much foreign language would you learn from watching a TV show?
- How much do you remember from your high school foreign language class?
- How much MORE would you learn from traveling or living abroad and conversing frequently with native speakers?

Language learners need practice in real-life social contexts

Language learners need real-time, individualized, responsive feedback

Language learners need interaction with peers as well as adults/teachers

Learner characteristics are important

Age and L1 fluency
- Younger learners may have an advantage in learning speech sounds and grammar
  - "sensitive" period for language development
- Older learners more fluent in L1 may be better able to "transfer" their knowledge of L1 to English, and may actually have a faster rate of English learning as a result
- Older learners may have greater social concerns about identity, fitting in

L1 and L2 similarity
- Students who speak a native language with a similar structure, sound system, and vocabulary to English may learn it more quickly

Learner characteristics are important (cont.)

Background
- Students with stable home lives, better educated parents, higher socioeconomic status may have an easier time learning English than those coming from backgrounds with frequent moves, separation from family, trauma from war or violence, poverty, etc.

Personality and Motivation
- Anxious, cautious or shy students may be less willing to express themselves and more concerned about making mistakes or being embarrassed
- Students who see English as more desirable to learn (use it as more useful, have more positive attitudes toward English speakers, more contact with English speakers, etc.) may learn English more quickly

How long will it take ELs to become proficient in English?

- Hakuta, Butler, & Witt (2000) write:

"Even in districts that are considered the most successful in teaching English to [English learner] students, oral proficiency takes three to five years to develop and academic English proficiency can take four to seven years."

- English language acquisition will be a unique journey for each EL dependent upon many factors: students' age, their parents' educational levels, prior experience with schooling, country of origin, whether they are immigrants by choice or refugees from war torn nations, etc.

How long will it take ELs to become proficient in English? (cont.)

Conversational English - develops in three to five years

Conversational English is also called social English, "playground" English, or BICS ("Basic Interpersonal Communication Skills")

Academic English - develops in four to seven years

The language of books/school in math, science, social studies, and language arts is more complicated and abstract than social language, and it uses vocabulary and sentence structure not typically used in oral language

Academic English is also known as academic language, academic dialect, or CALP ("Cognitive Academic Language Proficiency")

Teachers who say: "Well, Emilia talks to her friends like she was born speaking English, but she's just not trying hard enough in school," simply don't understand the challenge that ELs face when learning the complexities of academic language.

ELs will learn to read more quickly if they can already read/write in their native language, and they will use academic language more quickly if they already use it in their native language.

For more information on English language acquisition, see https://econ.wida.us.

What is WIDA?

- WIDA exists to advance academic language development and achievement for culturally and linguistically diverse children and youth.
- It has developed high quality standards, assessments, research, and professional development for teachers.
- WIDA's vision is to be the most trusted and valued resource available to support English language learners.
- Its CAN DO philosophy rejects a "deficit model" and recognizes/builds upon the assets, contributions, and potential of ELs.
- WIDA facilitates communication among teachers, state agencies, policy-makers, and experts.
- It fights language discrimination, cultural biases, and racism in education.

WIDA Stages of Language Acquisition

- The stages are based on the broad WIDA "Can Do" descriptors for the levels of English Language Proficiency, PreK-12.
- WIDA is a consortium of more than 30 states in the U.S.
- WIDA members have developed and adopted common standards and assessments for English language proficiency.
- For specific grade level clusters (PreK-K, 1-2, 3-5, etc.) download detailed descriptive charts at http://www.wida.us/standards/CAN_DOs/

The WIDA Levels of English Language Development in "CAN DO" descriptors

Level of Language	Name of Level
Level 1	Entering
Level 2	Beginning
Level 3	Developing
Level 4	Expanding
Level 5	Bridging
Level 6	Reaching

Level of Language	"CAN DO" Characteristics of the Learner
Level 1: Entering	• LISTENING: point to stated pictures, words, phrases; follow one-step oral directions; match oral statements to objects, figures, or illustrations • SPEAKING: name objects, people, pictures; answer WH- questions (who, what, when, where, which) • READING: match icons and symbols to words, phrases, or environmental print; identify concepts about print and text • WRITING: label objects, pictures, diagrams; draw in response to a prompt; produce icons, symbols, words, phrases to convey messages

Level of Language	"CAN DO" Characteristics of the Learner
Level 2: Beginning	• LISTENING: sort pictures, objects according to oral instructions; follow two-step oral directions; match information from oral descriptions to objects, illustrations • SPEAKING: ask WH- questions; describe pictures, events, objects, people; restate facts • READING: locate and classify information; identify facts and explicit messages; select language patterns associated with facts • WRITING: make lists; produce drawings, phrases, short sentences, notes; give information requested from oral or written directions

Level of Language	"CAN DO" Characteristics of the Learner
Level 3: Developing	• LISTENING: locate, select, order information from oral descriptions; follow multi-step oral directions; categorize or sequence oral information using pictures, objects • SPEAKING: formulate hypotheses, make predictions; describe processes, procedures; retell stories or events • READING: sequence pictures, events, processes; identify main ideas; use context clues to determine meaning of words • WRITING: produce bare-bones expository or narrative texts; compare/contrast information; describe events, people, processes, procedures

Level of Language	"CAN DO" Characteristics of the Learner
Level 4: Expanding	• LISTENING: compare/contrast functions, relationships from oral information; analyze and apply oral information; identify cause and effect from oral discourse • SPEAKING: discuss stories, issues, concepts; give speeches, oral reports; offer creative solutions to issues, problems • READING: interpret information or data; find details that support main ideas; identify word families, figures of speech • WRITING: summarize information from graphics or notes; edit and revise writing; create original ideas or detailed responses

Level of Language	"CAN DO" Characteristics of the Learner
Level 5: Bridging	• LISTENING: draw conclusions from oral information; construct models based on oral discourse; make connections from oral discourse • SPEAKING: engage in debates; explain phenomena, give examples, and justify responses; express and defend points of view • READING: conduct research to glean information from multiple sources; draw conclusions from explicit and implicit text • WRITING: apply information to new contexts; react to multiple genres and discourses; author multiple forms/genres of writing

Level of Language	"CAN DO" Characteristics of the Learner
Level 6: Reaching	At this level, the EL uses social/academic language with native competency in reading, writing, speaking, and listening in all content areas and at grade level. The EL at this level is indistinguishable from the native English speaker.

What can I do to support ELs' oral language development?

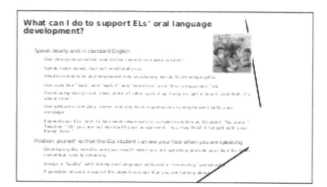

Speak clearly and in standard English
- Use clear pronunciation and diction (avoid increased volume)
- Speak more slowly (but not unnaturally so)
- Shorten sentences and emphasize key vocabulary words for developing ELs
- Use cues like "look" and "watch" and "write this" and "this is important" etc.
- Avoid using slang/idioms/jargon of other words (it may be hard to get in touch with that; it's about time)
- Use gestures, role play, mime, and any facial expressions to emphasize/clarify your message
- Expand your ELs' ideas to increase responses to complete sentences (Student: "No share." Teacher: "Oh, you are not sharing? Physics assignment. You may finish it tonight with your friend Ana.")

Position yourself so that the EL student can see your face when you are speaking
- Developing ELs need to see your mouth when you are speaking and see your face for additional nonverbal cues to meaning
- Assign a "buddy" with strong oral language skills and a "mentoring" personality
- If possible, show a visual of the object/concept that you are talking about

What can I do to support ELs' oral language development? (cont)

- Offer ELs the opportunity to repeat what you have said
- Accept gestures, pantomime and/or drawings with entering/beginning ELs
- Make your classroom a safe space where your ELs will never be embarrassed or ashamed of their errors
- Do not correct grammatical or pronunciation errors; focus on the EL's meaning. Simply model the correct form in your response
- Reinforce your ELs' progress; be enthusiastic about their development from point A to point B
- Provide ELs abundant oral practice with peers and with the teacher
- Create certain predictable routines in your class (e.g. taking attendance, reading lunch options, making announcements, reading homework assignments, etc.)
- SMILE (often!) and be encouraging about every effort made by the EL (acknowledge "approximations" for the target knowledge or skill)

Adolescent ELs have unique needs as compared to their elementary-age counterparts . . .

"It should be understood that adolescent ELLs are second language learners who are still developing their proficiency in academic English. Moreover, they are learning English at the same time they are studying core content areas through English. **Thus, English language learners must perform double the work of native English speakers in the country's middle and high schools.** And, at the same time, they are being held to the same accountability standards as their native English-speaking peers."

Adolescent ELs have unique needs as compared to their elementary-age counterparts . . .

These students:
- may not yet have social language for informal communication
- may not know how U.S. schools operate
- may not know U.S. culture and the "hidden rules" about social interactions, physical proximity, clothing, food/dining, idioms/slang, etc.
- have fewer years to master the English language before they need to graduate
- are beyond the ages/grades when literacy instruction is usually provided to students
- may have below-grade-level literacy in their native language

---

Adolescent ELs have unique needs as compared to their elementary-age counterparts . . .

"We know that English language learners need 4-7 years of targeted English language development in order to reach average performance levels on state or national exams (Thomas & Collier, 2002), but many schools do not provide programs for that length of time. However, if these learners are provided with consistent, effective programs and appropriate materials, they can be successful in school."

Adolescent ELs have unique needs as compared to their elementary-age counterparts . . .

Teachers need to incorporate both language and content objectives into their lessons to promote academic literacy and use instructional interventions that can reduce the achievement gap between English language learners and native English-speaking students. Research-based strategies that have shown positive student outcomes include:
- Integrating listening, speaking, reading, and writing skills in all lessons for all proficiencies
- Teaching the components and processes of reading and writing
- Focusing on vocabulary development
- Building and activating prior knowledge
- Teaching language through content and themes
- Using native language strategically
- Pairing technology with instruction
- Motivating adolescent ELLs through choice

Cultural diversity and culturally-responsive teaching

- Research suggests that knowing about and integrating children's culture in the classroom can improve a teacher's effectiveness.
- "Student diversity challenges us to explore ways to bridge cultural differences and develop culturally sensitive teaching practices that recognize and accept these differences."
- Some cultural differences are obvious
  - foods, holidays, arts, clothing
- Other cultural influences are less visible, but impact how we view the world and interact with others
  - concepts of family, responsibility, education, and success

(See www.colorincolorado.org/article/culturally-responsive-instruction holiday and religious celebrations.)

Cultural diversity and culturally-responsive teaching

Consider your responses to the following statements. To what extent do you agree, disagree, or neither?

1. I don't think of my students in terms of their race or ethnicity. I am color blind when it comes to my teaching.
2. The gap in the achievement among students of different socioeconomic levels is about poverty, not race.
3. Teachers should adapt their teaching to the distinctive cultures of African-American, Latino, Asian, and Native American students.
4. When students come from homes where education is not a high priority, they don't do their homework and their parents don't come to school events. This lack of parental support undermines my efforts to help these students.
5. It is not fair to ask students who are struggling with English to take on challenging academic assignments.
6. Students of different ethnic/racial cultures often have different learning styles, and good teachers try to match their instruction to these learning styles.
7. Grouping students of different levels of achievement for instruction may benefit some students but it can undermine the progress that could otherwise be made by higher-achieving students.

Cultural diversity and culturally-responsive teaching

1. "Appreciating the potential influence of [culture, language, beliefs, values,] can enhance the effectiveness of instruction."
2. The income achievement gap is nearly twice that of the black-white racial achievement gap.
3. "Within broad racial and ethnic groupings (e.g. Latino and Asian) there are very big average differences related to subgroups (e.g. Chinese Americans and Cambodian Americans) and social class differences within groups." There is no substitute for developing relationships with individual students and differentiating where possible.
4. "Parents often cannot get to the school, feel that that they lack the knowledge of resources to help, or feel that they do not know what their role should be. This is especially true, of course, for families from some cultures, for those who do not feel comfortable with English, and for single parents who may work more than one job and have responsibilities for caring for other children."

Cultural diversity and culturally-responsive teaching (cont)

1. "Difficulty with English is often perceived by educators as limited academic ability. Teachers need to guard against having low expectations for ELs and using biased assessments that reinforce those low expectations. This challenge is to engage all students in learning content at relatively high levels."
2. Students may have learning preferences, "but this does not mean that [their] brains function differently when [they] learn. And if our preferences are reinforced we may fail to learn how to learn in other ways." Again, know your individual students and differentiate when it supports student learning.
3. "The success of heterogeneous groups depends a great deal on the extent to which teachers carefully structure group work and prepare all students to participate, taking into account the needs and dispositions of each student. There are also times when students need instruction targeted on particular skills and should be grouped with students who have similar needs."

"Teachers should be expected to accept, explore, and understand different perspectives and to be prepared as citizens of a multicultural and global society."

- Look for ways to integrate cultural traditions of your EL families throughout your school.
- Add classroom visuals reflecting the racial and ethnic diversity of the classroom. (No sombreros or Asians working in the rice fields.)
- Incorporate books with multicultural themes and different perspectives into classroom readings.
- Explore themes that are common to all cultures.
- Take interest in students' lives outside of school and ask questions about community events and traditions.
- Ensure major assignments do not fall on religious or cultural holidays.
- Integrate ethnic art, music, and games into classroom activities.
- Support ELs and their families with materials in their native language (if possible).
- Use current world events to teach students to read, think, and discuss from multiple perspectives.

What are some meaningful ways that I can work with families, school personnel, community members to support ELs in my classroom?

The following are modified from
http://www.colorincolorado.org/article/14314/

See also "Tools and Resources for Ensuring Meaningful Communication with LEP Parents" at http://www2.ed.gov/about/offices/list/ocr/ela/english-learner-toolkit/index.html

Use their preferred language

- Identify family strengths. Some teachers "may need to shift from a deficit model—focusing on what families aren't doing—to a strengths-based model that acknowledges that families want to help their students succeed" (Moore, 2011, in http://www2.ed.gov/about/list/oela/english-learner-toolkit/index.html). Ask parents how they want to be involved and how the school and community can create opportunities for that involvement.
- Find a fully bilingual interpreter. Whether a school employee, parent liaison, family member, friend or community member, this person can translate for parent-teacher conferences, back-to-school nights, PTA meetings, and regular communication. It is best to find an adult and not rely on the student as the translator, as this practice can disempower the parent.
- Encourage families of ELs to support native language maintenance in the home. (For more information on fostering parent involvement, see http://www.ed.gov/about/offices/list/oelp/dpg/reports.html)

Translate the written communications that you send home.

Find a way to send home personal notes and materials in the home language, if possible. This will keep parents in the loop on issues such as report cards, school events, and homework. Try to offer complete translations in a straightforward way that parents can understand.

Learn some of your student's home language yourself.

Even if it is just some common words and greetings, using a family's language will make them feel welcome. Put parents in touch with bilingual staff. Give parents a list of names and phone numbers of bilingual staff in the school and district who they can contact to deal with educational concerns. Also encourage them to reach out to other parents who are bilingual or monolingual so they can share experiences and help one another.

Educate Parents on the U.S. School System

To support their children's education, the parents of your EL students need to understand how the U.S. school system and culture work. Listen to parents' concerns, answer their questions, and provide them with written materials in their language, if possible. Make sure that they understand things like how your school works. If necessary, review school hours, school holidays, school rules, school trajectory from pre-kindergarten through high school, and the school's administrative hierarchy. Explain your school curriculum, standards, benchmarks, and materials. Explain that teachers hope and expect that parents will help with homework, find tutors, read books, tell stories, take their children to the library, visit the classroom, and become involved in the school.

Parent Rights

Make certain that your EL parents know about their rights regarding access to interpreters and translated materials from your school, free lunch programs, your school's EL curriculum, supplementary school services that may be available to their children, and anything else that parents at your school have a right to know.

Recruit Volunteers

If parents are willing to volunteer their time, find out what their interests and skills are. EL parents may be able to help with a variety of activities, such as cooking food for school-wide holidays, telling stories, teaching a dance, teaching a skill, or making presentations.

Adult Learning Opportunities

Immigrant families may be unaware of the opportunities available to them. Another way to reach out to parents is to make them aware of learning opportunities for themselves. Somewhere in your community there are likely to be English and/or native language literacy classes for adults, family literacy projects, and parenting classes. Be sure to verify that families are eligible to receive the services offered regardless of immigration status. To be most effective, this list should be made available in families' languages and English and updated regularly.

Additional Resource

See also
https://www.newamerica.org/education-policy/edcentr
al/engaging-parents-english-learners/
for a brief article that addresses challenges and ways
to succeed in meaningfully involving parents of ELs.

Final thoughts on "accelerators" to language learning (Law & Eckes, 2010)

Accelerators

Language learning is easier for ELs when...
- the purpose of using language—reading, writing, speaking, listening—is real and natural
- the focus is on communication
- there are lots of opportunities to talk and interact with native English speakers
- talk is about interesting topics
- mistakes are a part of learning
- language is always used in students' without context, not as isolated letters, words, or sentences
- language has a purpose for the learner
- students speak only when they're ready
- sufficient time is provided for learning
- students can talk to each other in their own language
- the first language is viewed as a valuable resource

Module 3 Recap

- English Learners (ELs) – Who are they?
- How ELs develop a second (or additional) language
  - Receptive language and Productive language
  - Language Environment is important - Quantity and Quality Matter
  - Interaction is essential
  - Learner characteristics are important
- Becoming proficient in English
  - Conversational English
  - Academic English
- WIDA
  - "Can Do"
- Supporting ELs oral language development

Module 3 Recap (cont.)

- Unique needs of adolescent ELs - still learning English and academic content
- Cultural diversity and culturally-responsive teaching
- Ways to help families and the community support ELs
  - Learn and use student's language
  - Educate parents on U.S. schools and on their rights
  - Recruit volunteers and provide information on educational opportunities
- "Accelerators" to language learning.

Teachers HELP (Helping English Language Proficiency)

- This module was created by UT-Chattanooga faculty (Anne Gamble, M.Ed., Sarah Sandefur, Ph.D., and Amye Warren, Ph.D.) with funding from National Professional Development Grant #T3657120172-15 from the U.S. Department of Education, 2012-2017

Literacy

<u>Five stages of learning to read (Chall)</u>
Stage 0 (0–6 years): letter recognition and prereading skills
Stage 1 (7–8 years): translate letters and sounds into words
Stage 2 (9–14 years): fluency gained
Stage 3 (also 9–14): learn how to acquire information from print
Stage 4 (14–18 years): learn to coordinate multiple perspectives

A huge milestone in early and middle childhood is learning to read and write. While the foundations of this were laid in infancy and early childhood, formal instruction on this process usually happens during the school-age years. There isn't always complete agreement on how children are best taught to read. The following approaches to teaching reading are separated by their methodology, but today, models of reading strive for a balance between the two types of reading methods because they are both recognized as essential for learning to read.

Whole language approach
    Teaches reading of entire words from the outset
Basic skills approach
    Emphasizes awareness of the sound patterns of language
Unified approach: combines both

Whole-language approach	Instruction should parallel children's natural language learning; reading materials should be whole and meaningful
Basic-skills-and-phonetics approach	Stresses phonetics and basic rules for translating symbols into sounds; early reading instruction should involve simplified materials

- A **phonics-based approach** teaches reading by making sure children can understand letter-sound correspondences (how letters sound), automatically recognize familiar words, and decode unfamiliar words. This ability to break the code of reading allows children to read words they have never heard spoken before.

- The **whole-language approach** attempts to teach reading as naturally as possible. As the sounds of words don't have meaning, the focus is on reading words and sentences in context (such as real books), rather than learning the sounds and phonemes that make up words.[217]

When done correctly, a "whole-language" approach includes phonetic instruction. A combination of the two approaches seems to be best.

Reading Skill Components

Phonological awareness: sounds

Vocabulary: words you know

Decoding: identify new words

Fluency: speed of decoding

Comprehension: understand text

Preliteracy (Emergent Literacy)

Children's emergent literacy and early mathematical skills are affected by culture and context. Many U.S. children know the alphabet before they enter kindergarten. Emergent literacy skills depend on other skills, for example, phonemic awareness, the ability to hear and manipulate the sounds of spoken language. It is important that parents and adults read along to children beginning in infancy and toddlerhood. Children should experience feelings of success and pride in early reading and writing exercises. Their early efforts should be encouraged. Young children need models who use and value written language to communicate to emulate.

Promoting Print Concepts

Draw preliterate children's attention to:

- letters on the page or in the environment
- words on the page or in the environment
- where to begin reading
- reading from left-to-right and top-to-bottom

---

[217] Cognition and Instruction/Learning to Read by Wikibooks is licensed under CC BY-SA 3.0

- ask questions about all of the above (e.g., Do you know this word? Do you see a letter that is in your name?)

Age Trends in Literacy

Infancy & Toddlerhood

Emergent literacy: develop skills that are precursors to reading and writing

Say the alphabet, name a letter & its sound, repeat a story, recognize familiar words

Print concepts (e.g., books are read from left to right, top to bottom)

Write with scribbles at first

Early Childhood

Typically not yet reading to themselves

First real written word is usually their own name

In kindergarten learn to form letters correctly and to pair them with sounds

Begin to write with real letters

Letters may be backwards, upside down, etc.

Use "invented spelling" - phonetically spelling words, using their phonetic knowledge to approximate spelling sounds

Middle Childhood

Children begin to read independently

Learn to write

Around 4th grade, use reading and writing to learn other things

Become better spellers

Specific Reading Disability

Dyslexia is a learning disability in which a child with typical range intelligence and exposure to print has difficulty learning to read. Dyslexia is characterized by difficulty decoding and recognizing words accurately and/or fluently. The successful intervention is high-quality reading instruction (focusing on letter knowledge, phonological awareness, decoding, word-recognition strategies).

Promoting Phonological Awareness and Decoding Skills:

- Directly teach names of letters and their sounds
- Use games and rhymes to teach phonemes
- Give spelling lists
- Read to students
- Talk about the book
- Read familiar and unfamiliar books
- Read information books

Promoting Fluency:

- Provide guided oral reading
- Provide frequent practice reading

Promoting Vocabulary and Comprehension:

- Teach decoding skills through phonological awareness and knowledge of letters and their sounds
- Teach vocabulary
- Teach comprehension strategies
- Discuss texts; have students critique and question texts in group discussion

Promoting Writing Skills

- Provide handwriting instruction
- Provide instruction in writing strategies
- Teach specific steps of writing, give feedback, and guide revision
- Provide opportunity to write, especially using authentic activities

Emergent Literacy skills, such as understanding that text is read from left to right, from top to bottom, that one side of the book is up and the other is down, that pages turn from front to back, that printed letters in groups symbolize words, and so on, form the basis of learning to read. These

toddlers are exploring books, and with adults reading to the regularly they will opportunities to tell stories from memory and to to tell stories based upon the pictures. These are important steps in getting ready to read on their own.

11 Temperament and Attachment

Learning Objectives At the completion of this module, students will be able to:	Related Course Objective
11-1 Apply knowledge of the different classifications of attachments and what they mean for learners' well-being to promote secure attachment and school bonding in the classroom.	1 7
11-2 Analyze how temperament and personality influence learners' success at school and provide a good fit for the personalities in the classroom.	1 7
11-3 Define attachment and temperament.	1 7
11-4 Describe the stages and development of Attachment.	1 7
11-5 Identify dimensions of Temperament.	1 7

To a new born infant, crying is a way to communicate needs to the world around them. Young infants cry to signal that they are hungry, or cold, or wet. The purpose of these cries is to elicit a response from the environment. As infants grow, how should parents best respond to a crying child? Over the years, this has been a controversy among experts. Two different views can be summarized as follows.

Attachment view: In this view, a quick response to crying is viewed as an important ingredient in the development of a strong caregiver-infant relationship. Responsiveness is thought to encourage the development of a sense of trust and security in the infant. Advocates of the attachment view stress that parents should respond to a baby when it cries to provide a predictable, warm and comforting environment.

Behaviorist view: In this view, a quick response is viewed as rewarding the crying. As a reward, responsiveness is hypothesized to increase the frequency and intensity of crying. Responsiveness is scenes as something that reinforces crying and spoils the child. Advocates of this view suggest that parents should ignore an infant when she cries, and let her "cry it out"

The preponderance of research supports the attachment view. A quick parental response to comfort crying infants is associated with LOWER rates of crying later, not higher. Today, most experts would support the attachment view, but you can still hear behaviorist views from time to time.

In this unit, two views of infant self and emotional development – the temperament view and the attachment theory view, will be examined. First, it is helpful to recognize a couple of emotional milestones that most infants express. The first is *stranger anxiety*: the fear and wariness of strangers that becomes most Intense from 9 to 12 months. Infants this age show a less intense reaction when the strangers are children, or to smiling strangers. The second is *separation protest*: when the infant displays distress at being separated from a caregiver. This behavior peaks at about 15 months for infants in the U.S. Separation protest Is present in all cultures, but the timing at which the behavior is displayed and the rates at which children display separation protest can be different in different cultures. Why do infants demonstrate behaviors such as stranger anxiety and separation protest? Two theoretical views – temperament and attachment theory – offer different explanations. Let us turn first to the study of temperament.

Temperament

Perhaps you have spent time with a number of infants. How were they alike? How did they differ? How do you compare with your siblings or other children you have known well? You may have noticed that some seemed to be in a better mood than others and that some were more sensitive to noise or more easily distracted than others. These differences may be attributed to temperament. **Temperamen**t is the innate characteristics of the infant, including mood, activity level, and emotional reactivity, noticeable soon after birth. Temperament is one's behavioral style and characteristic emotional response. Temperament refers to stable individual differences in a variety of characteristics. These temperamental individual differences are though to be In-born, the result of genes and biology.

In a 1956 landmark study, Chess and Thomas (1996) evaluated 141 children's temperament based on parental interviews. Referred to as the New York Longitudinal Study, infants were assessed on 10 dimensions of temperament including:

- activity level

- rhythmicity (regularity of biological functions)

- approach/withdrawal (how children deal with new things)

- adaptability to situations

- intensity of reactions

- threshold of responsiveness (how intense a stimulus has to be for the child to react)

- quality of mood

- distractibility

- attention span

- persistence

Dimensions of Temperament:

1) activity level -- the tendency to be in physical motion;

2) rhythmicity -- regularity of biological function, for example, eating and sleeping at regular times;

3) approach or withdrawal -- the child's initial reaction to any new stimulation;

4) adaptability -- flexibility of behavior following the initial reaction.

5) intensity of reaction -- energy level of responses;

6) threshold of responsiveness -- intensity of stimulus required to produce a reaction. What does it take to get the child to react?

7) quality of mood -- this refers to the proportion of happy, friendly moods to unhappy, unfriendly or negative moods.

---

8) distractibility -- degree to which extraneous stimulation disrupts ongoing behavior;

9-10) attention span and persistence -- refers to the length of time activities are maintained and the child's tolerance for difficulty. How long can they stay at a task if the task is difficult?

Based on the infants' behavioral profiles using these ten dimensions, the infants were categorized into three general types of temperament:

Table - Types of Temperament

Type	Percentage	Description
Easy	40%	• Able to quickly adapt to routine and new situations • Remains calm • Easy to soothe • Usually in positive mood
Difficult	10%	• Reacts negatively to new situations • Has trouble adapting to routine • Usually negative in mood • Cries frequently
Slow-to-warm-up	15%	• Low activity level • Adjusts slowly to new situations • As well as adaptability, intensity of mood is low • Often negative in mood

As can be seen the percentages do not equal 100% as some children were not able to be placed neatly into one of the categories. About 35% did not fit in any one category. Think about how each type of child should be approached to improve interactions with them. An easy child requires less intervention, but still has needs that must not be overlooked. A slow-to-warm-up child may need to be given advance warning if new people or situations are going to be introduced. A child with a difficult temperament may need to be given extra time to burn off their energy.

Other researchers have expanded upon Thomas and Chess's work. Kagan focused on shy, subdued, timid children. Kagan viewed this shyness as an inborn trait, inhibition to new and unfamiliar objects and events. Kagan found that the amount of inhibition that children display shows considerable stability from infant through early childhood (both inhibition and the lack of inhibition). Bates and Rothbart were interested in differences in children's skill at self-regulation. They classified dimensions of temperament such as "extraversion/surgency," consisting of positive affect, impulsivity, and sensation seeking, "negative affectivity" the degree to which an infant was easily distressed, and "effortful control," the degree of effort required for the infant to control affect and maintain self-control.

Researchers have measured infant and young children's temperament in a variety of ways, including behavioral measures reported on by parents, behavioral measures observed by researchers in a laboratory setting, and physiological measures such as electrophysiological measurements and electroencephalogram (EEG) and fMRI activity. Temperament is thought to have biological roots, with at least some aspects being inherited in our genes. The importance of environmental influences comes through the degree to which caregiving practices fit the needs of an individual child's temperamental dispotions. A caregiver who is ability accurately read and respond to the child's individual temperament will enjoy a **goodness-of-fit**, meaning their styles match and communication and interaction can flow. Parents who recognize each child's temperament and accept it, will nurture more effective interactions with the child and encourage more adaptive functioning.[218] Accommodation of caregiving to the environment to the child's temperament results in the degree of "match" between the child's temperament and environmental demands. In this view, the impact of biology comes first (temperament), and the importance of the environment is in how it "fits" with the biology.

Parenting Is Bidirectional

Not only do parents affect their children, children influence their parents. A child's characteristics, such as temperament, affect parenting behaviors and roles. For example, an infant with an easy temperament may enable parents to feel more effective, as they are easily able to soothe the child and elicit smiling and cooing. On the other hand, a cranky or fussy infant elicits fewer positive reactions from his or her parents and may result in parents feeling less effective in the parenting role (Eisenberg et al., 2008). Over time, parents of more difficult children may become more punitive and less patient with their children (Clark, Kochanska, & Ready, 2000; Eisenberg et al., 1999; Kiff, Lengua, & Zalewski, 2011). Parents who have a fussy, difficult child are less satisfied with their marriages and have greater challenges in balancing work and family roles (Hyde, Else-Quest, & Goldsmith, 2004). Thus, child temperament is one of the child characteristics that influences how parents behave with their children.

---

[218] Lifespan Development: A Psychological Perspective by Martha Lally and Suzanne Valentine-French is licensed under CC BY-NC-SA 3.0

Temperament theory points out the importance of attention to and respect for individuality in children. It this view, it is important for parents to structure the child's environment to support the child's individual temperament. This means there is no "one size fits all" approach to what is the "best" parenting practice. What works best for one child may not be best for another, because of in-born temperamental differences. The "difficult child" may not fit well with packaged parenting programs or general advice. Instead, it is important that caregivers be flexible in their responses. Additionally, parents should be careful to avoid labeling a child in a way that may result in a self-fulfilling prophecy (for example, "she is my shy child...")

Personality

Temperament does not change dramatically as we grow up, but we may learn how to work around and manage our temperamental qualities. Temperament may be one of the things about us that stays the same throughout development. In contrast, **personality**, defined as an individual's consistent pattern of feeling, thinking, and behaving, is the result of the continuous interplay between biological disposition and experience.

Personality also develops from temperament in other ways (Thompson, Winer, & Goodvin, 2010). As children mature biologically, temperamental characteristics emerge and change over time. A newborn is not capable of much self-control, but as brain-based capacities for self- control advance, temperamental changes in self-regulation become more apparent. For example, a newborn who cries frequently doesn't necessarily have a grumpy personality; over time, with sufficient parental support and increased sense of security, the child might be less likely to cry.

In addition, personality is made up of many other features besides temperament. Children's developing self-concept, their motivations to achieve or to socialize, their values and goals, their coping styles, their sense of responsibility and conscientiousness, as well as many other qualities are encompassed into personality. These qualities are influenced by biological dispositions, but even more by the child's experiences with others, particularly in close relationships, that guide the growth of individual characteristics. Indeed, personality development begins with the biological foundations of temperament but becomes increasingly elaborated, extended, and refined over time. The newborn that parents gazed upon thus becomes an adult with a personality of depth and nuance.[219]

---

[219] Lifespan Development: A Psychological Perspective by Martha Lally and Suzanne Valentine-French is licensed under CC BY-NC-SA 3.0

Culture and Personality

The term **culture** refers to all of the beliefs, customs, ideas, behaviors, and traditions of a particular society that are passed through generations. Culture is transmitted to people through language as well as through the modeling of behavior, and it defines which traits and behaviors are considered important, desirable, or undesirable.

Within a culture there are norms and behavioral expectations. These cultural norms can dictate which personality traits are considered important. The researcher Gordon Allport considered culture to be an important influence on traits and defined common traits as those that are recognized within a culture. These traits may vary from culture to culture based on differing values, needs, and beliefs. Positive and negative traits can be determined by cultural expectations: what is considered a positive trait in one culture may be considered negative in another, thus resulting in different expressions of personality across cultures.

Considering cultural influences on personality is important because Western ideas and theories are not necessarily applicable to other cultures (Benet-Martinez & Oishi, 2008). There is a great deal of evidence that the strength of personality traits varies across cultures, and this is especially true when comparing individualist cultures (such as European, North American, and Australian cultures) and collectivist cultures (such as Asian, African, and South American cultures). People who live in **individualist cultures** tend to believe that independence, competition, and personal achievement are important. In contrast, people who live in **collectivist cultures** tend to value social harmony, respectfulness, and group needs over individual needs. These values influence personality in different but substantial ways; for example, Yang (2006) found that people in individualist cultures displayed more personally-oriented personality traits, whereas people in collectivist cultures displayed more socially-oriented personality traits.[220]

Gender and Personality

In much the same manner that cultural norms can influence personality and behavior, gender norms (the behaviors that males and females are expected to conform to in a given society) can also influence personality by emphasizing different traits between different genders.

Ideas of appropriate behavior for each gender (masculine and feminine) vary among cultures and tend to change over time. For example, aggression and assertiveness have historically been emphasized as positive masculine personality traits in the United States. Meanwhile,

---

[220] Lifespan Development - Module 4: Infancy by Lumen Learning references Psyc 200 Lifespan Psychology by Laura Overstreet, licensed under CC BY 4.0

submissiveness and caretaking have historically been held as ideal feminine traits. While many gender roles remain the same, others change over time. In 1938, for example, only 1 out of 5 Americans agreed that a married woman should earn money in industry and business. By 1996, however, 4 out of 5 Americans approved of women working in these fields. This type of attitude change has been accompanied by behavioral shifts that coincide with changes in trait expectations and shifts in personal identity for men and women.[221]

Attachment Theory

Attachment is the close bond with a caregiver from which the infant derives a sense of security. Attachment is not the same as "bonding." The term bonding usually refers to feelings of closeness that originate from the parents to the infant. The term attachment refers to a bidirectional relationship between the infant and the parent. It moves from parent to infant as well as from infant to parent. The formation of attachments in infancy has been the subject of considerable research as attachments have been viewed as foundations for future relationships. Additionally, attachments form the basis for confidence and curiosity as toddlers, and as important influences on self-concept. Let us first look at some of the theoretical views that influenced the development of attachment theory.

Freud's Psychoanalytic Theory
Freud was one of the first theorists to note the central importance of parent-child emotional bonds. Freud that that infants were in the oral stage, and that infants become attached to person or object giving oral satisfaction. According to Freud (1938), infants are oral creatures who obtain pleasure from sucking and mouthing objects. Freud believed the infant will become attached to a person or object that provides this pleasure. Consequently, infants were believed to become attached to their mother because she was the one who satisfied their oral needs and provided oral pleasure. Freud further believed that the infants will become attached to their mothers "if the mother is relaxed and generous in her feeding practices, thereby allowing the child a lot of oral pleasure," (Shaffer, 1985, p. 435).

Erikson: Trust vs. Mistrust
As previously discussed, Erikson formulated an eight-stage theory of psychosocial development.

[221] Lifespan Development - Module 4: Infancy by Lumen Learning references Psyc 200 Lifespan Psychology

Erikson was in agreement on the importance of a secure base, arguing that the most important goal of infancy was the development of a basic sense of trust in one's caregivers. Consequently, the first stage, trust vs. mistrust, highlights the importance of attachment. Erikson maintained that the first year to year and a half of life involves the establishment of a sense of trust (Erikson, 1982) and is therefore key to forming a positive attachment relationship. Infants are dependent and must rely on others to meet their basic physical needs as well as their needs for stimulation and comfort. A caregiver who consistently meets these needs instills a sense of trust or the belief that the world is a trustworthy place. In Erikson's view, the caregiver should not worry about overly indulging a child's need for comfort, contact or stimulation. Infants experience the world as either secure and comfortable or insecure and uncomfortable However, as infants age and experience the challenges of subsequent stages, continuity is not guaranteed.

Problems Establishing Trust

Erikson (1982) believed that mistrust could contaminate all aspects of one's life and deprive the individual of love and fellowship with others. Consider the implications for establishing trust if a caregiver is unavailable or is upset and ill-prepared to care for a child. Or if a child is born prematurely, is unwanted, or has physical problems that make him or her more challenging to parent. Under these circumstances, we cannot assume that the parent is going to provide the child with a feeling of trust.

Harlow's Research

In one classic study, Wisconsin University psychologists Harry and Margaret Harlow investigated the responses of young rhesus monkeys to explore if breastfeeding was the most important factor to the development of attachment.

The infant monkeys were separated from their biological mothers, and two surrogate mothers were introduced to their cages. The first mother (the wire mother) consisted of a round wooden head, a mesh of cold metal wires, and a bottle of milk from which the baby monkey could drink. The second mother was a foam-rubber form wrapped in a heated terry-cloth blanket. The infant monkeys went to the wire mother for food, but they overwhelmingly preferred and spent significantly more time with the warm terry-cloth mother. The warm terry-cloth mother provided no food but did provide comfort (Harlow, 1958) and the infant monkeys showed a strong preference for the terry cloth mother. They showed this preferences even when the bottle for feeding was attached to the wire mesh mother. The infant's need for physical closeness and touching is referred to as **contact comfort**. Contact comfort is believed to be the foundation for attachment. The Harlows' studies confirmed that babies have social as well as physical needs. Both monkeys and human babies need a secure base that allows them to feel safe. From this base, they can gain the confidence they need to venture out and explore their worlds. Harlow's results counter Freud's view of the importance of oral satisfaction. If Freud was correct, the monkeys would seek comfort through oral satisfaction of the surrogate with the milk bottle. Instead the need for "Contact comfort" was demonstrated by the primates.

Ethological Theory

In the ethological vie, behavior is thought to be strongly influenced by biology and evolution. For example, Lorenz found that baby geese have an inborn trait to imprint on the first mother that is seen. This imprinting is characterized by a critical or sensitive period. The imprinting studies by Lorenz demonstrated that imprinting involves rapid, innate learning within a critical period of time. Lorenz believed that imprinting existed because it helped the baby geese to survive, and so those that imprinted were more likely to live to adulthood and pass the trait to their offspring.

Bowlby's Theory

Building on the psychoanalytic perspective as well as ethology and the work of Harlow and others, John Bowlby developed the concept of attachment theory. He defined attachment as the affectional bond or tie that an infant forms with the mother (Bowlby, 1969). An infant must form this bond with a primary caregiver in order to have normal social and emotional development. In addition, Bowlby proposed that this attachment bond is very powerful and continues throughout life. He used the concept of secure base to define a healthy attachment between parent and child (Bowlby, 1982). A **secure base** is a parental presence that gives the child a sense of safety as the child explores the surroundings.

Bowlby said that two things are needed for a healthy attachment: The caregiver must be responsive to the child's physical, social, and emotional needs; and the caregiver and child must engage in mutually enjoyable interactions (Bowlby, 1969). Additionally, Bowlby observed that infants would go to extraordinary lengths to prevent separation from their parents, such as crying, refusing to be comforted, and waiting for the caregiver to return.

Bowlby also observed that these same expressions were common to many other mammals, and consequently argued that these negative responses to separation serve an evolutionary function. Because mammalian infants cannot feed or protect themselves, they are dependent upon the care and protection of adults for survival. Thus, those infants who were able to maintain proximity to an attachment figure were more likely to survive and reproduce.

Bowlby did not think that attachment relationships developed instantly. Instead, he believed that attachment relationships develop over time. To Bowlby, these are BIDIRECTIONAL relationships: both from infant to caregiver and from caregiver to infant. Bowlby believed that inborn signaling abilities, for example, crying, led to the development of emotional bonds needed for survival. Attachment is a deep and enduring specific bond. Bowlby proposed that the development of attachment occurs in four phases, increasing the child's chances of survival.

Bowlby's view of attachment: a biological drive for the infant to develop a relationship with the caregiver.

Phase 1: preattachment phase = birth to 2 mos.

Phase 2: attachment-in-making phase from 2 to 7 mos.

Phase 3: clear-cut attachment phase from 7 to 24 mos.

Phase 4: formation of reciprocal relationships from 24 mos. on

---

Attachment Phase 1

In the preattachment phase, which spans from birth to about age 6-8 weeks, babies' automatic reflexes, and activities such as grasping, crying, and rooting, will cause caregivers to want to attach to babies. Caregivers will feel needed and want to meet all their babies' needs. However, at this time, babies are not yet attached to any one caregiver, and they do not care if they're held or cared for by strangers. However, some research suggests that babies know their mothers' voice and unique scent from birth and recognize their mother that way. During this phase, babies may sometimes respond to social interaction from caregivers; at other times, babies may not readily respond at all. Babies can smile automatically in response to voice and touch from birth to about age 2 months, which encourages caregivers to interact with them. This interaction will increase their mental, emotional, and social growth and learning.

Attachment Phase 2

During the attachment-in-making phase, which spans from about age 6-8 weeks to about 6 to 8 months, babies begin to react differently and more quickly to primary caregivers than strangers, and they start building trust in caregivers to fulfill needs. They are slowly starting to count on their caregivers to take care of them. However, infants at this stage are still not distressed at being separated from particular caregivers. During this stage, they continue to make gestures and actions that help encourage caregivers to bond with them. Babies begin making eye contact around age 2 months, and can smile intentionally between ages 3 to 5 months. They start reaching for familiar people and caregivers, as well.

Attachment Phase 3

During the clear-cut attachment phase from about age 6 to 8 months to age 18 to 24 months, babies become solidly attached to their caregivers and separation anxiety emerges. Babies want to maintain contact with main caregivers and they will express their displeasure in ways such as clinging to Mom, following Grandma around to the door, or crying when Dad leaves. During this phase, babies are also beginning to develop social skills and interactions beyond just attachment. Babies can start playing simple social games like "Pat-a-Cake" around 9 to 11 months. They also like to participate in social rituals like saying hello and goodbye, and chiming in at social functions such as family dinnertime. Babies will also begin social referencing, looking for social cues from other peoples' emotional and physical reactions to new stimuli in order to know how they should respond. For example, they will watch how their caregivers react to hugs from friends or a knock on the door.

Attachment Phase 4

The final phase of attachment, the formation of reciprocal relationships, spans from about age 18 months to 24 months and beyond, is a time when babies start negotiating with caregivers to meet their needs and to keep them feeling safe and attached. They'll express their needs and desires in order to keep feeling satisfied. Also during this time, babies start to understand "no" and other boundaries that make certain objects and activities off-limits. They may try to "cover up" when caught doing something wrong in order not to get in trouble. Social interactions continue to mature as they observe family routines and start to participate in them. They also begin "to and fro" play with caregivers and other peers. While this isn't quite interactive play yet, they start realizing they can include other people in their fun and play.

Internal working model of relationships

Bowlby believed that an infant who experienced a relationship with a caregiver that was predictable and safe developed an internal working model of relationships that was predictable and safe. On the other hand, if the attachment relationship was unpredictable or scary the infant developed a working model of relationships as negative. This model was carried forward to become the lens that future relationships were viewed from. These models are "working" in that information from future relationships can update the original models. In other words, a child with a negative internal working model of relationships can come to view relationships as more positive through later positive experiences. However, because these internal working models are the original model that relationships are applied to, information from future relationships are interpreted through the lens of the model and so the models are difficult to change. Because these are models of relationships, Bowlby thought that these internal working models formed the basis of both children's view of themselves as well as their view of others. Thus, the attachment relationship is viewed as formative for a chld's self-perceptions and social perceptions.

Mary Ainsworth and the Strange Situation

Developmental psychologist Mary Ainsworth, a student of John Bowlby, continued studying the development of attachment in infants. Ainsworth and her colleagues created a laboratory test that measured an infant's attachment to his or her parent. The test is called **The Strange Situation** because it is conducted in a context that is unfamiliar to the child and therefore likely to heighten the child's need for his or her parent (Ainsworth, 1979).

Ainsworth's strange situation: assesses infant's attachment to caregiver

Requires infant to move through a series of introductions, separations, and reunions

1. The child's caregiver is told to sit in the corner and encourage the child to play with the toys and to minimize their interactions with the child besides encouraging them to play. They are left alone for 3 minutes.

2. A stranger enters & stays for 3 minutes - then caregiver leaves the child alone with the stranger for 3 minutes or until the infant gets too upset.

3. The caregiver returns & stranger leaves till the child resumes play.

4. The caregiver leaves the child alone for 3 minutes.

5. A stranger enters & attempts to comfort child for 3 minutes.

6. The stranger leaves as caregiver returns & comforts child.

During the procedure, which lasts about 20 minutes, the parent and the infant are first left alone, while the infant explores the room full of toys. Then a strange adult enters the room and talks for a minute to the parent, after which the parent leaves the room. The stranger stays with the infant for a few minutes, and then the parent again enters and the stranger leaves the room. During the entire session, a video camera records the child's behaviors, which are later coded by the research team. The investigators were especially interested in how the child responded to the caregiver leaving and returning to the room, referred to as the "reunion." On the basis of their behaviors, the children are categorized into one of four groups where each group reflects a different kind of attachment relationship with the caregiver. One style is secure and the other three styles are referred to as insecure.

- Securely attached: ("Type B") – a pattern of relationship between child and caregiver which follows the expected pattern including the secure base phenomenon. A child with a **secure attachment style** usually explores freely while the caregiver is present and may engage with the stranger. The child will typically play with the toys and bring one to the caregiver to show and describe from time to time. The child may be upset when the caregiver departs, but is also happy to see the caregiver return.

- Insecure resistant (ambivalent): ("Type C")– a pattern of relationship between child and caregiver characterized by the absence of the secure base phenomenon, high levels of anxiety and an ambivalent or resistive pattern of actions toward the caregiver. A child with an **ambivalent** (sometimes called resistant) **attachment style** is wary about the situation in general, particularly the stranger, and stays close or even clings to the caregiver rather than exploring the toys. When the caregiver leaves, the child is extremely distressed and is ambivalent when the caregiver returns. The child may rush to the caregiver, but then fails to be comforted when picked up. The child may still be angry and even resist attempts to be soothed.

- Insecure avoidant: ("Type A")– an attachment pattern characterized by hostility toward and avoidance of the caregiver. A child with an **avoidant attachment style** will avoid or ignore the mother, showing little emotion when the mother departs or returns. The child may run away from the mother when she approaches. The child will not explore very much, regardless of who is there, and the stranger will not be treated much differently from the mother.

- Insecure disorganized: ("Type D")– a pattern of relationship between an infant and a caregiver characterized by instability and wide swings of emotional reactions. A child with a **disorganized/disoriented attachment style** seems to have an inconsistent way of coping with the stress of the strange situation. The child may cry during the separation, but avoid the mother when she returns, or the child may approach the mother but then freeze or fall to the floor.

How common are the attachment styles among children in the United States? It is estimated that about 65 percent of children in the United States are securely attached. Twenty percent exhibit avoidant styles and 10 to 15 percent are ambivalent. Another 5 to 10 percent may be characterized as disorganized.

In all cultures, secure attachment is the normative pattern. However, variations also occur across cultures in the percentage of children who fall in the insecure categories. Some cultural differences in attachment styles have been found (Rothbaum, Weisz, Pott, Miyake, & Morelli, 2010). For example, German parents value independence and Japanese mothers are typically by their children's sides. As a result, the rate of insecure-avoidant attachments is higher in Germany and insecure-resistant attachments are higher in Japan. These differences reflect cultural variation rather than true insecurity, however (van Ijzendoorn and Sagi, 1999).

Keep in mind that methods for measuring attachment styles have been based on a model that reflects middle-class, U. S. values and interpretation. Methods for assessing attachment styles among children from 12 months to 5 years involve using a **Q-sort technique** in which a large number of behaviors are recorded on cards and the observer sorts the cards in a way that reflects the type of behavior that occurs within the situation (Waters, 1987). There are 90 items in the third version of the Q-sort technique, and examples of the behaviors assessed include:

- When child returns to mother after playing, the child is sometimes fussy for no clear reason.
- When the child is upset or injured, the child will accept comforting from adults other than mother.
- Child often hugs or cuddles against mother, without her asking or inviting the child to do so.
- When the child is upset by mother's leaving, the child continues to cry or even gets angry after she is gone.

At least two researchers observe the child and parent in the home for 1.5-2 hours per visit. Usually two visits are sufficient to gather adequate information. The parent is asked if the behaviors observed are typical for the child. This information is used to test the validity of the Strange Situation classifications across age, cultures, and with clinical populations.

Caregiver Consistency

Results of studies focusing on the stability of attachment as children grow older vary. Stability declines when the family is disorganized or has certain types of problems such as hostility and stress. Most infants are attached to many people. Infants form multiple attachment figures in addition to mothers, such as father, grandparents, caregivers, and so on. Qualities of infants, of parents, and of the child's environment may affect the security of attachment.

Having a consistent caregiver may be jeopardized if the infant is cared for in a child care setting with a high turnover of staff or if institutionalized and given little more than basic physical care. Infants who, perhaps because of being in orphanages with inadequate care, have not had the opportunity to attach in infancy may still form initial secure attachments several years later. However, they may have more emotional problems of depression, anger, or be overly friendly as they interact with others (O'Connor et. al., 2003).

Attachment relationship is impacted by:

Qualities of infants

Infant temperament

Parental qualities

caregiving sensitivity

caregiver responsiveness

Environmental qualities

Family economic circumstances

Amount of nonmaternal caregiving

Amount of separation

Social Deprivation

Severe deprivation of parental attachment can lead to serious problems. According to studies of children who have not been given warm, nurturing care, they may show developmental delays, failure to thrive, and attachment disorders (Bowlby, 1982). **Non-organic failure to thrive** is the diagnosis for an infant who does not grow, develop, or gain weight on schedule. In addition, postpartum depression can cause even a well-intentioned mother to neglect her infant.

Reactive Attachment Disorder

Children who experience social neglect or deprivation, repeatedly change primary caregivers that limit opportunities to form stable attachments, or are reared in unusual settings (such as institutions) that limit opportunities to form stable attachments can certainly have difficulty forming attachments. According to the Diagnostic and Manual of Mental Disorders, 5th edition (American Psychiatric Association, 2013), those children experiencing neglectful situations and also displaying markedly disturbed and developmentally inappropriate attachment behavior, such as being inhibited and withdrawn, minimal social and emotional responsiveness to others, and limited positive affect, may be diagnosed with **Reactive Attachment Disorder.** This disorder often occurs with developmental delays, especially in cognitive and language areas. Fortunately, the majority of severely neglected children do not develop Reactive Attachment Disorder, which occurs in less than 10% of such children. The quality of the caregiving environment after serious neglect affects the development of this disorder.

The significance of Attachment

Qualities of infants' attachment relationships predict much about later development. Securely attached infants are more competent at older ages. These infants show advanced patterns of play and demonstrate cognitive advantages. Why is this so? There are multiple views Some developmentalists believe secure attachment in the first year provides the important foundation for psychological development. Others believe that too much emphasis placed on the attachment bond in infancy ignores diversity of socializing agents and contexts. For example, maybe children who are simply more verbal or outgoing develop more positive relationships with caregivers and also show more competence as they grow. Thus, these researchers view associations between attachment and later development as a child effect that causes both.

Attachment vs Temperament

Attachment Theory and Temperament Theory are contrary to each other. *Temperament Theory* suggests that in-born traits and dispositions form "who we are" – the environment is important only in how it fits the child's temperament. *Attachment Theory* proposes that relationships with caregivers form "who we are" - biology is important only in how it impacts what the child first brings to the relationships, and the biological drive to form the relationship.

Resiliency

Being able to overcome challenges and successfully adapt is **resiliency.** Even young children can exhibit strong resilience to harsh circumstances. Resiliency can be attributed to certain personality factors, such as an easy-going temperament. Some children are warm, friendly, and responsive, whereas others tend to be more irritable, less manageable, and difficult to console, and these differences play a role in attachment (Gillath, Shaver, Baek, & Chun, 2008; Seifer, Schiller, Sameroff, Resnick, & Riordan, 1996). It seems safe to say that attachment, like most other developmental processes, is affected by an inter play of genetic and socialization influences.

Receiving support from others also leads to resiliency. A positive and strong support group can help a parent and child build a strong foundation by offering assistance and positive attitudes toward the newborn and parent. In a direct test of this idea, Dutch researcher van den Boom (1994) randomly assigned some babies' mothers to a training session in which they learned to better respond to their children's needs. The research found that these mothers' babies were more likely to show a secure attachment style in comparison to the mothers in a control group that did not receive training.[222]

---

[222] Lifespan Development: A Psychological Perspective by Martha Lally and Suzanne Valentine-French is licensed under CC BY-NC-SA 3.0

12 SELF AND EMOTIONAL DEVELOPMENT

Learning Objectives At the completion of this module, students will be able to:	Related Course Objective
11-1 Explain the importance of emotions for learners' success in the classroom, and how to create an emotionally healthy classroom.	1 7
11-2 Recognize age-appropriate ability to regulate emotion, and describe how to coach students to more effectively regulate their emotions.	1 7
11-3 Describe the importance of reading others' emotions, and describe strategies for improving students' empathy.	1 7
11-4 Describe how the self-system functions and how to promote positive self-esteem.	1 7
11-5 Describe how gender and ethnic identity develop.	1 7

Emergence of self

The development of a sense of self is an important task in childhood. There are many terms that are important to understand in the study of children's "self system":

Self-esteem: one's feelings of worth; positive or negative evaluation

Self-concept: the differentiated conception of self that includes categories like academic self concept, social self-concept, and athletic self-concept

Global self-concept is sometimes used synonymously with the term self-esteem, but really the terms are different. Self-esteem is a judgment of positive or negative, whereas self-concept is descriptive and not positive or negative. Self-esteem is an evaluation, self-concept is a description. Both are related to, but different from, the term "self-efficacy."

Self-efficacy: confidence that one can accomplish a specific behavior, and it is future-oriented. Self-efficacy is the belief that "I try it, will I succeed or not?"

Development of sense of self: Psychologists describe infants as seeing themselves as an extension of their caregiver; "individuation" is the process through which infants begin to see themselves as a unique individual. During the second year of life, children begin to recognize themselves as they gain a sense of self as separate from their primary caregiver. In a classic experiment by Lewis and Brooks (1978) children 9 to 24 months of age were placed in front of a mirror after a spot of rouge was placed on their nose as their mothers pretended to wipe something off the child's face. If the child reacted by touching his or her own nose rather than that of the "baby" in the mirror, it was taken to suggest that the child recognized the reflection as him or herself. Lewis and Brooks found that somewhere between 15 and 24 months most infants developed a sense of self-awareness. **Self-awareness** is the realization that you are separate from others (Kopp, 2011). Once a child has achieved self-awareness, the child is moving toward understanding social emotions such as guilt, shame or embarrassment, as well as, sympathy or empathy.[223]

Interactionism and Views of Self
Early childhood is a time of forming an initial sense of self. A **self-concept** or idea of who we are, what we are capable of doing, and how we think and feel is a social process that involves taking into consideration how others view us. So, in order to develop a sense of self, you must have interaction with others. Interactionist theorists, Cooley and Mead offer two interesting explanations of how a sense of self develops.

[223] Lifespan Development: A Psychological Perspective by Martha Lally and Suzanne Valentine-French is licensed under CC BY-NC-SA 3.0

Cooley

Charles Horton Cooley (1964) suggests that our self-concept comes from looking at how others respond to us. This process, known as the **looking-glass self** involves looking at how others seem to view us and interpreting this as we make judgments about whether we are good or bad, strong or weak, beautiful or ugly, and so on. Of course, we do not always interpret their responses accurately so our self-concept is not simply a mirror reflection of the views of others. After forming an initial self-concept, we may use it as a mental filter screening out those responses that do not seem to fit our ideas of who we are. Some compliments may be negated, for example. The process of the looking-glass self is pronounced when we are preschoolers, or perhaps when we are in a new school or job or are taking on a new role in our personal lives and are trying to gauge our own performances. When we feel more sure of who we are, we focus less on how we appear to others.[224]

Mead

Herbert Mead (1967) offers an explanation of how we develop a social sense of self by being able to see ourselves through the eyes of others. There are two parts of the self: the "I" which is the part of the self that is spontaneous, creative, innate, and is not concerned with how others view us and the "me" or the social definition of who we are.

When we are born, we are all "I" and act without concern about how others view us. But the socialized self begins when we are able to consider how one important person views us. This initial stage is called "taking the role of the significant other". For example, a child may pull a cat's tail and be told by his mother, "No! Don't do that, that's bad" while receiving a slight slap on the hand. Later, the child may mimic the same behavior toward the self and say aloud, "No, that's bad" while patting his own hand. What has happened? The child is able to see himself through the eyes of the mother. As the child grows and is exposed to many situations and rules of culture, he begins to view the self in the eyes of many others through these cultural norms or rules. This is referred to as "taking the role of the generalized other" and results in a sense of self with many dimensions. The child comes to have a sense of self as student, as friend, as son, and so on.

Exaggerated Sense of Self

One of the ways to gain a clearer sense of self is to exaggerate those qualities that are to be incorporated into the self. Preschoolers often like to exaggerate their own qualities or to seek validation as the biggest, smartest, or child who can jump the highest. This exaggeration tends to be replaced by a more realistic sense of self in middle childhood.

Self-Esteem

Early childhood is a time of forming an initial sense of self. **Self-concept** is our self-description according to various categories, such as our external and internal qualities. In contrast, **self- esteem** is an evaluative judgment about who we are. The emergence of cognitive skills in this age group results in improved perceptions of the self, but they tend to focus on external qualities, which are referred to as the **categorical self**. When researchers ask young children to describe themselves, their descriptions tend to include physical descriptors, preferred activities, and favorite possessions. Thus, the **self-description** of a 3-year-old might be a 3-year-old girl with red hair, who likes to play with blocks. However, even children as young as three know there is more to themselves than these external characteristics.

Harter and Pike (1984) challenged the method of measuring personality with an open-ended question as they felt that language limitations were hindering the ability of young children to express their self-knowledge. They suggested a change to the method of measuring self-concept in young children, whereby researchers provide statements that ask whether something is true of the child (e.g., "I like to boss people around", "I am grumpy most of the time"). They discovered that in early childhood, children answer these statements in an internally consistent manner, especially after the age of four (Goodvin, Meyer, Thompson & Hayes, 2008) and often give similar responses to what others (parents and teachers) say about the child (Brown, Mangelsdorf, Agathen, & Ho, 2008; Colwell & Lindsey, 2003).

Young children tend to have a generally positive self-image. This optimism is often the result of a lack of social comparison when making self-evaluations (Ruble, Boggiano, Feldman, & Loeble, 1980), and with comparison between what the child once could do to what they can do now (Kemple, 1995). However, this does not mean that preschool children are exempt from negative self-evaluations. Preschool children with insecure attachments to their caregivers tend to have lower self-esteem at age four (Goodvin et al., 2008). Maternal negative affect (emotional state) was also found by Goodwin and her colleagues to produce more negative self-evaluations in preschool children.

Self-Control

Self-control is not a single phenomenon, but is multi-facetted. It includes **response initiation,** the ability to not initiate a behavior before you have evaluated all of the information, **response inhibition,** the ability to stop a behavior that has already begun, and **delayed gratification**, the ability to hold out for a larger reward by forgoing a smaller immediate reward (Dougherty, Marsh, Mathias, & Swann, 2005). It is in early childhood that we see the start of self-control, a process that takes many years to fully develop. In the now classic "Marshmallow Test" (Mischel, Ebbesen, & Zeiss, 1972) children are confronted with the choice of a small immediate reward (a marshmallow) and a larger delayed reward (more marshmallows). Walter Mischel and his colleagues over the years have found that the ability to delay gratification at the age of four predicted better academic performance and health later in life (Mischel, et al., 2011). Self- control is related to executive function, discussed earlier in the chapter. As executive function improves, children become less impulsive (Traverso, Viterbori, & Usai, 2015).[225]

Self-Control and Play

Thanks to the new Centre for Research on Play in Education, Development and Learning (PEDaL), Whitebread, Baker, Gibson and a team of researchers hope to provide evidence on the role played by play in how a child develops.

"A strong possibility is that play supports the early development of children's self-control," explains Baker. "These are our abilities to develop awareness of our own thinking processes – they influence how effectively we go about undertaking challenging activities."

In a study carried out by Baker with toddlers and young preschoolers, she found that children with greater self-control solved problems quicker when exploring an unfamiliar set-up requiring scientific reasoning, regardless of their IQ. "This sort of evidence makes us think that giving children the chance to play will make them more successful and creative problem-solvers in the long run."

If playful experiences do facilitate this aspect of development, say the researchers, it could be extremely significant for educational practices because the ability to self-regulate has been shown to be a key predictor of academic performance.

Gibson adds: "Playful behavior is also an important indicator of healthy social and emotional development. In my previous research, I investigated how observing children at play can give us important clues about their well being and can even be useful in the diagnosis of neurodevelopmental disorders like autism."[226]

---

[225] Lifespan Development: A Psychological Perspective by Martha Lally and Suzanne Valentine-French is licensed under CC BY-NC-SA 3.0

[226] Play's the Thing by the University of Cambridge is licensed under CC BY 4.0

Self-Understanding

Children in middle childhood have a more realistic sense of self than do those in early childhood. That exaggerated sense of self as "biggest" or "smartest" or "tallest" gives way to an understanding of one's strengths and weaknesses. This can be attributed to greater experience in comparing one's own performance with that of others and to greater cognitive flexibility. A child's self-concept can be influenced by peers and family and the messages they send about a child's worth. Contemporary children also receive messages from the media about how they should look and act. Movies, music videos, the internet, and advertisers can all create cultural images of what is desirable or undesirable and this too can influence a child's self-concept.

Remarkably, young children begin developing social understanding very early in life and are also able to include other peoples' appraisals of them into their self-concept, including parents, teachers, peers, culture, and media. Internalizing others' appraisals and creating social comparison affect children's **self-esteem,** which is defined as an evaluation of one's identity. Children can have individual assessments of how well they perform a variety of activities and also develop an overall, global self-assessment. If there is a discrepancy between how children view themselves and what they consider to be their ideal selves, their self-esteem can be negatively affected.[227]

Self-concept refers to beliefs about general personal identity (Seiffert, 2011). These beliefs include personal attributes, such as one's age, physical characteristics, behaviors, and competencies. Children in middle and late childhood have a more realistic sense of self than do those in early childhood, and they better understand their strengths and weaknesses. This can be attributed to greater experience in comparing their own performance with that of others, and to greater cognitive flexibility. Children in middle and late childhood are also able to include other peoples' appraisals of them into their self-concept, including parents, teachers, peers, culture, and media.

Another important development in self-understanding is **self-efficacy**, which is the belief that you are capable of carrying out a specific task or of reaching a specific goal (Bandura, 1977, 1986, 1997). Large discrepancies between self-efficacy and ability can create motivational problems for the individual (Seifert, 2011). If a student believes that he or she can solve mathematical problems, then the student is more likely to attempt the mathematics homework that the teacher assigns.

Unfortunately, the converse is also true. If a student believes that he or she is incapable of math, then the student is less likely to attempt the math homework regardless of the student's actual

[227] Lifespan Development - Module 6: Middle Childhood by Lumen Learning references Psyc 200 Lifespan Psychology by Laura Overstreet, licensed under CC BY 4.0

ability in math. Since self-efficacy is self-constructed, it is possible for students to miscalculate or misperceive their true skill, and these misperceptions can have complex effects on students' motivations. It is possible to have either too much or too little self-efficacy, and according to Bandura (1997) the optimal level seems to be either at, or slightly above, true ability.[228]

As we have seen, children's experience of relationships at home and the peer group contributes to an expanding repertoire of social and emotional skills and also to broadened social understanding. In these relationships, children develop expectations for specific people (leading, for example, to secure or insecure attachments to parents), understanding of how to interact with adults and peers, and self-concept based on how others respond to them. These relationships are also significant forums for emotional development.[229]

Erikson: Basic Trust vs. Mistrust

From Birth to 1 year, Eikson saw the main task that confronted infants as a conflict between basic trust and mistrust. Infants come to understand the world as trustworthy and safe or threatening and unsafe based on how they are treated. Trust comes from being cared for. This is consistent with Bowlby's view of developing an attachment relationship. This is the age of separation as the child undergoes the process of individuation, seeing themselves as a unique person from their parents. The beginnings of the development of an attachment relationship at this age forms the basis of an internal working model of relationships that will be carried forth to subsequent relationships. Because the model is of *relationships* it is a model of both the self and of others – according to Bowlby, it is not possible to separate the child's sense of self from this model of self in relation to others.

Erikson: Autonomy vs. Shame and Doubt

For toddlers ages 1 to 3-years, Erikson saw the main challenge as a conflict between autonomy vs. shame and doubt. Toddlers want to feel that they have some autonomy or control over their environment and their choices. At the same time, they need to experience firm and reasonable control. Children need to feel a sense of self-control, or else they will feel shame and a desire to get away with misbehavior. Development of a sense of autonomy brings feelings of self-determination and pride as the toddler does things for herself. On the overhand, parental overcontrol can create feelings of shame and doubt rather than a sense of independence. Toddlers learn that the can affect the environment (e.g., crying will make dad appear), and grow in their feeling of being capable of

[228] Lifespan Development - Module 6: Middle Childhood by Lumen Learning references Psyc 200 Lifespan Psychology by Laura Overstreet, licensed under CC BY 4.0

[229] Social and Personality Development in Childhood by NOBA is licensed under CC BY 4.0

influencing others and events. Their developing attachment relationships continue to inform the internal working model of relationships and support self-concepts. Self-recognition begins during this age, at about 18-months. Cognitively, children this age are very concrete thinkers and egocentric, and this impacts their view of the self. Toddlers view themselves in physical terms, and self-descriptions are very concrete. The active dimension – the things a child does – is a central part of the self.

Erikson: Initiative vs. Guilt
Psychologist Erik Erikson argues that children in early childhood go through a stage of "initiative vs. guilt." Initiative is enthusiasm for new activities, increasingly governed by conscience. Guilt results when children's efforts result in failure or criticism. If the child is placed in an environment where he/she can explore, make decisions, and initiate activities, they have achieved initiative. On the other hand, if the child is put in an environment where initiation is repressed through criticism and control, he/she will develop a sense of guilt.

The trust and autonomy of previous stages develop into a desire to take initiative or to think of ideas and initiative action. Children may want to build a fort with the cushions from the living room couch or open a lemonade stand in the driveway or make a zoo with their stuffed animals and issue tickets to those who want to come. Or they may just want to get themselves ready for bed without any assistance. To reinforce taking initiative, caregivers should offer praise for the child's efforts and avoid being critical of messes or mistakes. Soggy washrags and toothpaste left in the sink pales in comparison to the smiling face of a five-year-old that emerges from the bathroom with clean teeth and pajamas![230]

During the preschool years, children are typically overly optimistic about their own activities. If you ask a group of younger four-year-olds "who can run the fastest?" they are all likely to raise their hands (even if they have never ran the fastest before). This is because children this age continue to be somewhat egocentric and they are poor at social comparison – utilizing other peers as a basis for comparison. Additionally, preschoolers do not understand that if someone does something with less effort, this means that they are more skilled at the task.

From the ages of 3- to 5-years, children's self concepts focus on external appearance and objects. By age six, children are more likely to identify emotional states, relationships in social groups, and skills in relation to those of others in their self descriptions. There are cultural and socioeconomic differences in the developmental course of young children's self-descriptions, because their sense

---

[230] Children's Development by Ana R. Leon is licensed under CC BY 4.0 (modified by Antoinette Ricardo)

of self develops from life stories.

Summary of developmental changes in self-concept[231]		
From:	To:	Description of change
simple	**differentiated**	Younger children form global concepts; older children make finer distinctions and allow for circumstances Younger: I am clever or I am stupid Older: I am clever at some things and stupid at others. Younger child: I am strong or I am weak. Older child: My arm strength is average; my leg strength is above average.
inconsistent	**consistent**	Younger children are more likely to change their self-evaluation; older children appreciate the stability of the self-concept.
concrete	**abstract**	Younger children focus on external, visible, physical aspects (hair color; height); older children focus on internal, invisible, psychological aspects (honest, kind).
absolute	**comparative**	Younger children focus on self without reference to others; older children describe themselves in comparison with others (social comparison processes)
self-as-public	**self-as-private**	Younger children do not distinguish between private feelings and public behavior; older children consider the private self as the "true self."

Erik Erikson- Industry vs. Inferiority

Erik Erikson proposed that we are motivated by a need to achieve competence in certain areas of our lives. As we've learned in previous chapters, Erikson's psychosocial theory has eight stages of

[231] Schaffer, H. R. (1996). Social development. Oxford, UK: Blackwell Publishers.

development over the lifespan, from infancy through late adulthood. At each stage there is a conflict, or task, that we need to resolve. Successful completion of each developmental task results in a sense of competence and a healthy personality. Failure to master these tasks leads to feelings of inadequacy.

During the elementary school stage (ages 6-12), children face the task of *Industry versus Inferiority*. Children begin to compare themselves to their peers to see how they measure up.

Encouragement increases the child's sense of industry. On the other hand, criticism can result in feelings of inferiority. Children this age attempt to master many skills. They develop a sense of competence or incompetence. They either develop a sense of pride and accomplishment in their schoolwork, sports, social activities, and family life, or they feel inferior and inadequate when they don't measure up.[232]

According to Erikson, children in middle childhood are very busy or industrious. They are constantly doing, planning, playing, getting together with friends, achieving. This is a very active time and a time when they are gaining a sense of how they measure up when compared with friends. Erikson believed that if these industrious children can be successful in their endeavors, they will get a sense of confidence for future challenges. If not, a sense of inferiority can be particularly haunting during middle childhood.[233]

By 4-6 years of age, most children evaluate self-esteem in terms of social acceptance ("Do people like me?") and competence ("I can do _____"). Children this age tend to rate selves extremely high on all aspects. By 7-8 years of age, most children evaluate self-esteem in terms of cognitive/academic competencies (i.e., math, reading), physical prowess (sports), and social self-worth (good person, funny person) and also display a global, overall, sense of self-esteem. Most children show a decline in overall self-esteem at this age because the unrealistically high assessments held earlier are adjusted. In this way, these are more realistic assessments of abilities. As children enter elementary school, there is more social comparison and more feedback from adults. Perceptions of competence tend to decrease across the early elementary school years. After a period of decline, self-esteem rises again.[234]

---

[232] Psychology - 9.2: Lifespan Theories by CNX Psychology is licensed under CC BY 4.0

[233] Sociology: Brief Edition – Explaining Socialization by Steven E. Barkan is licensed under CC BY-NC-SA 3.0

[234] McAfee, O. & Leong, D. (1994). Assessing and guiding young children's development and learning. Boston: Allyn and Bacon.

Growth of a psychological self: In middle childhood, children still describe self in terms of external features. However, they also now include other dimensions. For example, elementary school age children compare their selves to peers, and this comparison becomes a part of their self evaluations. There is a shift toward social comparison, comparing themselves to others. This is in contrast to preschoolers who do not tend to compare themselves to others and describe themselves in absolute terms. For children in middle childhood there is increased focus on their "internal life" as they describe psychological characteristics of their self and define self in terms of internal characteristics. Increasingly, children this age include social aspects in their self-descriptions.

Self-esteem can change. Variations in self esteem are related to development. Preschoolers tend to overestimate their abilities and have very high self-esteem. In fact, low self-esteem is a warning sign for preschoolers because they are typically high. When children enter elementary school there is typically a decline in self-esteem for most children. Children are now using social comparison, and they are also getting more feedback from teachers. For these reasons their self descriptions become more realistic, and their self-esteem lowers from the overly high levels of the preschool years. However, self-esteem is based on perception and not reality. Some children have self-esteems that are lower than one would expect based upon how others rate the child, and some have higher self-esteems than would be expected based upon the perceptions of their peers. For example, children who are bullys and are socially rejected by their peers tend to rate themselves very positively; it is as if they mistakenly believe their peers respect their aggressive behavior and look up to them. A perception is not always a reality.

In middle childhood and into the years of early adolescence, self-concept differentiates into different domains (e.g., academic, athletic, social). Children this age continue to have a global self-concept as well. Although self-perceptions become more realistic, most young adolescents tend to have a positive bias about their abilities.

What Predicts Views of the Self?

Attachment

Other people's esteem

Competence

Big-fish–little-pond effect

Components of Identity

Social identity: the part of self-concept that derives from membership in a group (e.g., gender, ethnic, religious, national, other groups)

Gender identity: a part of self-concept that includes ability to accurately label your sex and your feelings about your gender

Ethnic identity: a part of self-concept that includes a sense of membership in an ethnic group and feelings about that membership

Chodorow and Mothering

Chodorow, a Neo-Freudian, believed that mothering promotes gender stereotypic behavior. Mothers push their sons away too soon and direct their attention toward problem-solving and independence. As a result, sons grow up confident in their own abilities but uncomfortable with intimacy. Girls are kept dependent too long and are given unnecessary and even unwelcome assistance from their mothers. Girls learn to underestimate their abilities and lack assertiveness, but feel comfortable with intimacy.

Both of these models assume that early childhood experiences result in lifelong gender self-concepts. However, gender socialization is a process that continues throughout life. Children, teens, and adults refine and can modify their sense of self based on gender.

Gender Identity, Gender Constancy, and Gender Roles

Another important dimension of the self is the sense of self as male or female. Preschool-aged children become increasingly interested in finding out the differences between boys and girls both physically and in terms of what activities are acceptable for each. While 2 year olds can identify some differences and learn whether they are boys or girls, preschoolers become more interested in what it means to be male or female. This self-identification or **gender identity** is followed sometime later with **gender constanc**y or the knowledge that gender does not change. **Gender roles** or the rights and expectations that are associated with being male or female are learned throughout childhood and into adulthood.

Learning through Reinforcement and Modeling

Learning theorists suggest that gender role socialization is a result of the ways in which parents, teachers, friends, schools, religious institutions, media and others send messages about what is acceptable or desirable behavior as males or females. This socialization begins early-in fact, it may even begin the moment a parent learns that a child is on the way. Knowing the sex of the child can conjure up images of the child's behavior, appearance, and potential on the part of a parent. And this stereotyping continues to guide perception through life. Consider parents of newborns, shown a 7 pound, 20 inch baby, wrapped in blue (a color designating males) describe the child as tough, strong, and angry when crying. Shown the same infant in pink (a color used in the United States for baby girls), these parents are likely to describe the baby as pretty, delicate, and frustrated when crying. (Maccoby & Jacklin, 1987). Female infants are held more, talked to more frequently and given direct eye contact, while male infants play is often mediated through a toy or activity.

Sons are given tasks that take them outside the house and that have to be performed only on occasion while girls are more likely to be given chores inside the home such as cleaning or cooking that is performed daily. Sons are encouraged to think for themselves when they encounter problems and daughters are more likely to be given assistance even when they are working on an answer. This impatience is reflected in teachers waiting less time when asking a female student for an answer than when asking for a reply from a male student (Sadker and Sadker, 1994). Girls are given the message from teachers that they must try harder and endure in order to succeed while boys' successes are attributed to their intelligence. Of course, the stereotypes of advisors can also influence which kinds of courses or vocational choices girls and boys are encouraged to make.

Friends discuss what is acceptable for boys and girls and popularity may be based on modeling what is considered ideal behavior or looks for the sexes. Girls tend to tell one another secrets to validate others as best friends while boys compete for position by emphasizing their knowledge, strength or accomplishments. This focus on accomplishments can even give rise to exaggerating accomplishments in boys, but girls are discouraged from showing off and may learn to minimize their accomplishments as a result.

Gender messages abound in our environment. But does this mean that each of us receives and interprets these messages in the same way? Probably not. In addition to being recipients of these cultural expectations, we are individuals who also modify these roles (Kimmel, 2008). Based on what young children learn about gender from parents, peers, and those who they observe in society, children develop their own conceptions of the attributes associated with maleness or femaleness which is referred to as **gender schemas**.

How much does gender matter? In the United States, gender differences are found in school experiences (even into college and professional school, girls are less vocal in the classrooms and much more at risk for sexual harassment from teachers, coaches, classmates, and professors), in social interactions and in media messages. The **stereotypes** that boys should be strong, forceful, active, dominant, and rational and that girls should be pretty, subordinate, unintelligent, emotional, and gabby are portrayed in children's toys, books, commercials, video games, movies, television shows and music.

In adulthood, these differences are reflected in income gaps between men and women where women working full-time earn about 74 percent the income of men, in higher rates of women suffering rape and domestic violence, higher rates of eating disorders for females, and in higher rates of violent death for men in young adulthood. Each of these differences will be explored further in subsequent chapters.[235]

Gender Identity

The development of gender and gender identity is an interaction among social, biological, and representational influences (Ruble, Martin, & Berenbaum, 2006). Young children learn about gender from parents, peers, and others in society, and develop their own conceptions of the attributes associated with maleness or femaleness (called **gender schemas**). They also negotiate biological transitions (such as puberty) that cause their sense of themselves and their sexual identity to mature.

Table: Sequential understanding of gender[236]

Step	Age of appearance (years)	Sample question asked	Characteristics
1. Identity	1.5 - 2	"Are you a boy or a girl?"	Labels self and others as male or female

---

[235] Lifespan Development - Module 5: Early Childhood by Lumen Learning references Psyc 200 Lifespan Psychology by Laura Overstreet, licensed under CC BY 4.0; Lifespan Development: A Psychological Perspective by Martha Lally and Suzanne Valentine-French is licensed under CC BY-NC-SA 3.0

[236] Source: Schaffer, H. R. (1996). Social development Oxford, UK: Blackwell Publishers

Step	Age of appearance (years)	Sample question asked	Characteristics
2. Stability	3-4	"Will you be a mommy or a daddy when you grow up?"	Understand that people retain the same gender throughout life
3. Constancy	6-7	"If a boy puts on a dress will he be a girl?	Aware gender does not depend on changes in appearance (e.g., hair, clothes)

Age Trends in Gender Identity

Infancy & Toddlerhood: Infants can distinguish between male and female faces. By age two, children label boys and girls, but do so based on appearance. Toddlers begin to pay more attention to objects and activities associated with their own sex. Gender stereotypes about what activities are appropriate for each sex begin to develop.

Early Childhood: Gender constancy emerges – children become aware that gender does not depend on outward appearance. Children tend to become gender-typed in appearance and play and gender stereotypes become more rigid during the preschool years. Many preschoolers are biased toward their own sex, and by four-years-old children are beginning to spend more time in same-sex groups than mixed-sex groups (this will increase as they later transition to elementary school). A few preschoolers are gender-variant or gender nonconforming.

Middle Childhood: A Full understanding of gender constancy emerges. Gender stereotypes intensify during middle childhood, and then begin to wane. Gender segregation peaks as children progress through elementary school. Gender boundaries are often more rigid for boys than for girls.

Adolescence: Comfort with one's gender identity during adolescence predicts adjustment. Most conform to stereotyped activities, but may try out gender-atypical activities.

Each of these examples of the growth of social and emotional competence illustrates not only the interaction of social, biological, and representational influences, but also how their development unfolds over an extended period. Early influences are important, but not determinative, because the capabilities required for mature moral conduct, gender identity, and other outcomes continue to develop throughout childhood, adolescence, and even the adult years.

As the preceding sentence suggests, social and personality development continues through adolescence and the adult years, and it is influenced by the same constellation of social, biological, and representational influences discussed for childhood. Changing social relationships and roles, biological maturation and (much later) decline, and how the individual represents both experience and the self continue to form the bases for development throughout life. In this respect, when an adult looks forward rather than retrospectively to ask, "What kind of person am I becoming?"—A similarly fascinating, complex, multifaceted interaction of developmental processes lies ahead.[237]

Gender Dysphoria

A growing body of research is now focused on Gender Dysphoria, or the distress accompanying a mismatch between one's gender identity and biological sex (American Psychiatric Association, 2013). Although prevalence rates are low, at approximately 0.3 percent of the United States population (Russo, 2016), children who later identified as transgender, often stated that they were the opposite gender as soon as they began talking. Comments such as stating they prefer the toys, clothing and anatomy of the opposite sex, while rejecting the toys, clothing, and anatomy of their assigned sex are criteria for a diagnosis of Gender Dysphoria in children. Certainly, many young children do not conform to the gender roles modeled by the culture and even push back against assigned roles. However, they do not experience discomfort regarding their gender identity and would not be identified with Gender Dysphoria. [238]

Ethnic Identity

Ethnic identity is a part of self-concept that includes a sense of membership in an ethnic group and feelings about that membership. By 9 months, infants distinguish and prefer same-race faces. Most preschoolers can label their racial group but may not understand the label. Around age 6, children use racial features to sort people and begin to understand racism. Around age 10, children recognize broadly held racial stereotypes and stigma. Perceptions of stigma increase through high

[237] Social and Personality Development in Childhood by NOBA is licensed under CC BY 4.0

[238] Lifespan Development: A Psychological Perspective by Martha Lally and Suzanne Valentine-French is licensed under CC BY-NC-SA 3.0

school. Children begin to integrate race and ethnicity in to their self-concept in middle childhood.

There are several components of ethnic identity. First, ethnic self-identification occurs when a child labels her ethnicity. Ethnic constancy occurs when a child realizes that ethnicity is not dependent upon outward, concrete factors. Ethnic knowledge involves the child learning about the culture and / history of her ethnicity. The final stage is the child's development of ethnic feelings and preferences. Jean Phinney (1989) described more specific steps that adolescents go through in the development of ethnic identity. A positive ethnic identity can be a protective factor for children from groups that are marginalized. On the other hand, experiencing racism and discrimination during childhood predicts higher levels of depression and anxiety, lower self-esteem and achievement, increased reports of illness and higher risk of behavior problems, delinquency, crimes, and health risks such as smoking. Children become aware of discrimination as they grow older; the perception of discrimination depends on children's social-cognitive abilities, the obviousness of the discrimination, and the child's personal vigilance toward discrimination.

Stereotype Threat occurs when an individual is concern that their performance will confirm negative stereotypes about their group. This may lead the individual to refuse to engage in the activity out of fear that they might support the stereotypical views of others. For example, when a 3rd-grade girl learned the stereotype that "girls don't do well at math," she began to say "I don't like doing math" and avoided doing math work. Stereotype threat can lead to increased text anxiety as well as lowered test scores.

The word "**micro-aggressions**" refers to subtle behaviors that communicate prejudice, such as: assuming someone who looks "foreign" does not speak English, showing surprise that a person of color has high achievement, or showing surprise that a woman is good at math. Although microaggressions may not be as pronounced as hostile racism, they still communicate negative stereotypes.

Classroom Implications of Gender and Ethnic Identity

Promote positive social identity:

- •Use a multicultural anti-bias curriculum

- •Avoid sex-typed materials

- •Help each student feel valued

- • Hold all learners to high, but reasonable, standards

- • Avoid pushing students to represent their group

- • Avoid microaggressions

- • Be self-reflective about your attitudes toward groups

Reduce prejudice by:

- Using anti-bias training

- Teaching about the history of discrimination

- Encouraging extracurricular activities

Using cooperative learning where different groups:

- Have equal status within the setting

- Share goals

- Cooperate to pursue goals

- Feel support from authority figures like a teacher

MORAL DEVELOPMENT

Conscience consists of the cognitive, emotional, and social influences that cause young children to create and act consistently with internal standards of conduct (Kochanska, 2002). It emerges from young children's experiences with parents, particularly in the development of a mutually responsive relationship that motivates young children to respond constructively to the parents' requests and expectations. Biologically based temperament is involved, as some children are temperamentally more capable of motivated self-regulation (a quality called effortful control) than are others, while some children are more prone to the fear and anxiety that parental disapproval can evoke. The development of conscience is influenced by having good fit between the child's temperamental qualities and how parents communicate and reinforce behavioral expectations.

Conscience development also expands as young children begin to represent moral values and think of themselves as moral beings. By the end of the preschool years, for example, young children develop a "moral self" by which they think of themselves as people who want to do the right thing, who feel badly after misbehaving, and who feel uncomfortable when others misbehave. In the development of conscience, young children become more socially and emotionally competent in a manner that provides a foundation for later moral conduct (Thompson, 2012).

Lawrence Kohlberg's Stages of Moral Development

Kohlberg (1963) built on the work of Piaget and was interested in finding out how our moral reasoning changes as we get older. He wanted to find out how people decide what is right and what is wrong. Just as Piaget believed that children's cognitive development follows specific patterns, Kohlberg (1984) argued that we learn our moral values through active thinking and reasoning, and that moral development follows a series of stages. Kohlberg's six stages are generally organized into three levels of moral reasons. To study moral development, Kohlberg looked at how children (and adults) respond to moral dilemmas. One of Kohlberg's best known moral dilemmas is the Heinz dilemma:

In Europe, a woman was near death from a special kind of cancer. There was one drug that the doctors thought might save her. It was a form of radium that a druggist in the same town had recently discovered. The drug was expensive to make but the druggist was charging ten times what the drug cost him to make. He paid $200 for the radium and charged $2,000 for a small dose of the drug. The sick woman's husband, Heinz, went to everyone he knew to borrow the money but he could only get together about $1,000, about half of what the drug cost. He told the druggist that his wife was dying and asked him to sell it cheaper or let him pay later. But the druggist said: "No, I discovered the drug and I'm going to make money from it." Heinz got desperate and broke into the man's store to steal the drug for his wife. Should the husband have done that? (Kohlberg, 1969, p. 379)[239]

Level One - Preconventional Morality

In stage one, moral reasoning is based on concepts of punishment. The child believes that if the consequence for an action is punishment, then the action was wrong. In the second stage, the child bases his or her thinking on self-interest and reward ("You scratch my back, I'll scratch yours"). The youngest subjects seemed to answer based on what would happen to the man as a result of the act. For example, they might say the man should not break into the pharmacy because the

---

pharmacist might find him and beat him. Or they might say that the man should break in and steal the drug and his wife will give him a big kiss. Right or wrong, both decisions were based on what would physically happen to the man as a result of the act. This is a self-centered approach to moral decision-making. He called this most superficial understanding of right and wrong **preconventional morality.** Preconventional morality focuses on self-interest. Punishment is avoided and rewards are sought. Adults can also fall into these stages, particularly when they are under pressure.

Level Two - Conventional Morality

Those tested who based their answers on what other people would think of the man as a result of his act, were placed in Level Two. For instance, they might say he should break into the store, then everyone would think he was a good husband, or he should not because it is against the law. In either case, right and wrong is determined by what other people think. In stage three, the person wants to please others. At stage four, the person acknowledges the importance of social norms or laws and wants to be a good member of the group or society. A good decision is one that gains the approval of others or one that complies with the law. This he called **conventional morality**, *people care about the effect of their actions on others*. Some older children, adolescents, and adults use this reasoning.

Level Three, post conventional morality, is not included because it focuses on adolescence and adulthood. However, it is in the table below if you'd like an overview of Level Three - Stages 5 and 6.

Table Lawrence Kohlberg's Levels of Moral Reasoning

Preconventional Morality (young children)

Stage	Description
Stage 1	Focus is on self-interest and punishment is avoided. The man shouldn't steal the drug, as he may get caught and go to jail.
Stage 2	Rewards are sought. A person at this level will argue that the man should steal the drug because he does not want to lose his wife who takes care of him.

Conventional Morality (older children, adolescents, most adults)

Stage	Description
Stage 3	Focus is on how situational outcomes impact others and wanting to please and be accepted. The man should steal the drug because that is what good husbands do.
Stage 4	People make decisions based on laws or formalized rules. The man should obey the law because stealing is a crime.

Post Conventional Morality (rare in adolescents, a few adults)

Stage	Description
Stage 5	Individuals employ abstract reasoning to justify behaviors. The man should steal the drug because laws can be unjust and you have to consider the whole situation.
Stage 6	Moral behavior is based on self-chosen ethical principles. The man should steal the drug because life is more important than property.

Although research has supported Kohlberg's idea that moral reasoning changes from an early emphasis on punishment and social rules and regulations to an emphasis on more general ethical principles, as with Piaget's approach, Kohlberg's stage model is probably too simple. For one, people may use higher levels of reasoning for some types of problems but revert to lower levels in situations where doing so is more consistent with their goals or beliefs (Rest, 1979). Second, it has been argued that the stage model is particularly appropriate for Western, rather than non-Western, samples in which allegiance to social norms, such as respect for authority, may be particularly important (Haidt, 2001). In addition, there is frequently little correlation between how we score on the moral stages and how we behave in real life. Perhaps the most important critique of Kohlberg's theory is that it may describe the moral development of males better than it describes that of females (Jaffee & Hyde, 2000).[240]

Motivation as Self-Efficacy

In addition to being influenced by their goals, interests, and attributions, students' motives are affected by specific beliefs about the student's personal capacities. In **self-efficacy theory** the beliefs become a primary, explicit explanation for motivation (Bandura, 1977, 1986, 1997). **Self-efficacy** is the belief that you are capable of carrying out a specific task or of reaching a specific

---

[240] Lifespan Development: A Psychological Perspective by Martha Lally and Suzanne Valentine-French is licensed under CC BY-NC-SA 3.0

goal. As mentioned previously, the optimal level seems to be either at or slightly above true capacity (Bandura, 1997). As we indicate below, large discrepancies between self-efficacy and ability can create motivational problems for the individual.[241]

Motivation

Motivation refers to a desire, need, or drive that contributes to and explains behavioral changes. In general, motivators provide some sort of incentive for completing a task. One definition of a motivator explains it as a force "acting either on or within a person to initiate behavior." In addition to biological motives, motivations can be either intrinsic (arising from internal factors) or extrinsic (arising from external factors).

Extrinsic vs. Intrinsic Motivation

Intrinsic motivation: the desire to pursue an activity for its own sake, not for external reasons; Internal factors such as self-determination, curiosity, challenge, and effort

Extrinsic motivation: the desire to pursue an activity for reasons external to the activity (e.g., getting a reward, avoiding punishment, or earning a grade)

Intrinsically motivated behaviors are performed because of the sense of personal satisfaction that they bring. According to Deci (1971), these behaviors are defined as ones for which the reward is the satisfaction of performing the activity itself. Intrinsic motivation thus represents engagement in an activity for its own sake. For example, if comforting a friend makes a child feel good, they are intrinsically motivated to respond to their friend's distress.

Extrinsically motivated behaviors, on the other hand, are performed in order to receive something from others or avoid certain negative outcomes. The extrinsic motivator is outside of, and acts on, the individual. Rewards—such as a sticker, or candy—are good examples of extrinsic motivators. Social and emotional incentives like praise and attention are also extrinsic motivators since they are bestowed on the individual by another person.

Learned Helplessness and Self-Efficacy

If a person's sense of self-efficacy is very low, he or she can develop **learned helplessness**, a perception of complete lack of control in mastering a task. The attitude is similar to depression, a pervasive feeling of apathy and a belief that effort makes no difference and does not lead to success. Learned helplessness was originally studied from the behaviorist perspective of classical

---

[241] Child Development – Unit 5: Theories (Part II) by Lumen Learning references Educational Psychology by Kelvin Seifert and Rosemary Sutton, licensed under CC BY 4.0

and operant conditioning by the psychologist Martin Seligman (1995). In people, learned helplessness leads to characteristic ways of dealing with problems. They tend to attribute the source of a problem to themselves, to generalize the problem to many aspects of life, and to see the problem as lasting or permanent. More optimistic individuals, in contrast, are more likely to attribute a problem to outside sources, to see it as specific to a particular situation or activity, and to see it as temporary or time-limited. Consider, for example, two students who each fail a test. The one with a lot of learned helplessness is more likely to explain the failure by saying something like: "I'm stupid; I never perform well on any schoolwork, and I never will perform well at it." The other, more optimistic student is more likely to say something like: "The teacher made the test too hard this time, so the test doesn't prove anything about how I will do next time or in other subjects."

What is noteworthy about these differences in perception is how much the more optimistic of these perspectives resembles high self-efficacy and how much learned helplessness seems to contradict or differ from it. As already noted, high self-efficacy is a strong belief in one's capacity to carry out a specific task successfully. By definition, therefore, self-efficacy focuses attention on a temporary or time-limited activity (the task), even though the cause of successful completion (oneself) is "internal."[242]

Further discussion of the role of motivation in academic achievement can be found in the section on individual differences in children's intelligence.

---

[242] Child Development – Unit 5: Theories (Part II) by Lumen Learning references Educational Psychology by Kelvin Seifert and Rosemary Sutton, licensed under CC BY 4.0

Photo: Active exploration is not only important for cognitive development, but it also supports self and emotional development.

13 PEERS, PLAY, AND FRIENDS

Learning Objectives At the completion of this module, students will be able to:	Related Course Objective
13-1 Define social cognition and describe how it relates to social behavior.	1 7
13-2 Describe age trends in prosocial behavior.	1 7
13-3 Describe age trends in aggressive behavior.	1 7
13-4 Explain the role of play and developmental changes in play categories and styles.	1 8
13-5 Describe sociometric popularity with peers, identify sociometric classifications, and give examples of correlates.	1 7
13-6 Describe the importance of friendships and developmental changes in the nature of friendships.	1 7

Social Cognition

Social cognition is the study of how children think about and understand peer relationships. Different models of social cognition have been proposed that describe "on-line" or discrete social cognitive processes. The most well developed of these is Ken Dodge's (1986/1994) Social Information Processing theory. In this theory, Dodge proposes that in a given social interchange children go through a series of steps of processing social information and generating responses. Dodge does not actually believe that children take time to work through each step. Instead, the steps are presented as a model to help understand children's social cognition. The different steps are places where social cognition could "break down."

Steps in Social Information Processing:

●Encoding of Social Cues

●Interpretation of Cues (Attributions)

●Response (Social Strategy) Generation

●Response (Social Strategy) Selection

●Enactment of response

Encoding

When an an individual is in a social exchange they must first attend to and encode the social cues of those they are interacting with. The first step of Dodge's models asks "Does the child encode the social cue?" How much of the relevant information about an interaction do children pick up? This is typically assessed by presenting children hypothetical vignettes of social interactions through video taped or line-drawing based stories. Children are asked to describe the events that were portrayed in the story. Children's descriptions of actions portrayed in hypothetical vignettes are coded for accuracy and the use of social cues presented in the story. Children who are socially aggressive tend to pay more attention to aggressive cues. Children who are socially withdrawn describe fewer cues than other children and their descriptions of the events are more vague.

Attributions of intent

The second stage of information processing involves "How does the child interpret the social cue?" When a social cue has been attended to and encoded, the child must make a determination of what was the intention behind the cue. For example, do children think that an ambiguous provocation is the result of an accident, or that the other person is being hostile or "mean?" For example, imagine that a four-year-old is building a tower with wooden blocks and another child walks through the blocks causing them to fall down. The first child might interpret the actions of the other as accidental – they may conclude that the child didn't mean to do it. A different interpretation is that the other child's actions were benign – the child may believe that the other child was playing or wanting to play when they walked through the blocks. A third interpretation is hostile, that the other child was being mean when they knocked the blocks down.

Children of all ages can make benign attributions, neutral attributions, and hostile attributions about the intentions of others in ambiguous situations. However, there is a developmental trend as well as individual differences. Preschool-age children who are three- and four- as well as 5-year-old kindergartners, tend to make a high proportion of attributions that are hostile. This is due to the egocentrism of the young child, and the assumption that if something bad happened then the other person was being mean. As children enter middle childhood, there is a decline in the proportion of hostile attributions made by children on average.

However, some children continue to make a high proportion of hostile attributions throughout middle childhood and beyond. One of the aspects of peer relations that has been the most well documented by researchers is a hostile attribution bias of aggressive and peer rejected children. Between the ages of 2nd and 8th grade, children who are higher in aggressive behavior and rejected by other children are more likely to attribute hostility in situations in which the intentions of the other are ambiguous.

Response Generation

When a cue has been encoded and interpreted, a child generates a behavioral response. This is sometimes called social problem solving. Response generation is the "script" that children use – their social strategies. For example, if another child knocks down a child's blocks, the child could move to another location, rebuild the blocks, ask the second child to play, or push the child down. Response generation involves the question "How will the child respond to hypothetical social problems?"

Response generation is typically assessed by presenting the child with a hypothetical social story and asking them what they would do next. Researchers code the child's responses to determine if the child's strategies are prosocial, aggressive, or withdrawn. Overall, children's social strategies grow more sophisticated as children grow older. There are also individual differences in the types of strategies children generate. Children who generate strategies that are more prosocial, less aggressive, more engaging and more sophisticated are more likely to be sought out by other children for play or social interaction. Children who display more aggressive behavior are more likely to display more aggressive strategies. Children who display more social withdrawal are more likely to generate strategies that are withdrawing or vague.

In addition, Dodge includes steps for evaluating potential responses and selecting the best, and enacting the chosen response. These steps involve feelings of self-efficacy. By middle childhood, children who display more socially withdrawn behavior are more likely to endorse withdrawn strategies, and children who display more aggressive behavior are more likely to endorse aggressive strategies.

After the child enacts the strategy, their behavior becomes the cue for the other participant to process in turn. Each of these steps in social information processing describe stages at which processing may "break down" and lead to negative social behavior. For example, a child might behave aggressively because she attended to only aggressive cues, or because she interpreted the other's behavior as hostile, or because she generated an aggressive response, or because she believed that an aggressive response was what would work best for her. Thus, the model provides a way to think about a given child's social cognition in order to determine ways to facilitate social behavior for children who have difficulties in social interaction.

Social Behavior

The term "social cognition" refers to how children think about about and understand their interactions with others. The term "social behavior" refers to the actual behavior that children enact during their social interactions. Social behavior impacts the quality of social relationships and peer relations. This section will focus on social behavior. For the sake of organization, social behavior will be divided into two groups: "prosocial" behaviors and "antisocial" behaviors.

Prosocial Behavior

Prosocial behavior is voluntary behavior that benefits others or promotes harmonious relations with others. In simplest terms, it is being helpful, or nice. Altruism is behavior that benefits someone else at the expense of the self without expectation of a gain or reward.

Examples of Prosocial Behavior (5th Grade)

- •Comfort distressed peers

- •Help others

- •Make others smile/laugh

- •Share things

- •Compliment and encourage others

- •Invite others to join in

- •Admit mistakes and apologize

- •Confront those who do wrong, stand up for those who are wronged

- •Use good manners

- •Break up fights and give in to avoid fights

- •Be honest

- •Avoid hurting others' feelings

Age Trends in Prosocial Behavior

Infancy and Toddlerhood

- By 8 months, universal tendency to be helpful and share is apparent

- By 12 months, sharing and cooperating with parents is so common that absence indicates developmental disorders

- By 18 months, children try to help their parents with chores without being asked

- Toddlers express sympathy and comfort others

- By 2 years, self-interest begins to inhibit the impulse to share

Early Childhood

- More selective about prosocial behavior

- Genuinely helpful when others are distressed

- Prosocial children can also be aggressive, lots of positives and negatives

Middle Childhood

- Display a wide variety of prosocial behaviors

- Increasingly share only with familiar others

- Become so skilled at prosocial behavior that they are assigned to take care of younger siblings

Early Adolescence

- Become even more skilled at prosocial behavior

- However, frequency of prosocial behavior does not increase

Why Doesn't Prosocial Behavior Increase? One reason is that adults train children to inhibit prosocial impulses (e.g., "that's the teacher's job"). Another reason is the impact of antisocial models (e.g., in the media). A third is improvement in regulation of emotions and impulse control. Finally, as children grow older the costs of prosocial behavior become clear.

What Predicts Prosocial Behavior?

- Emotional competence and empathy

- Parental responsiveness and attachment

- Parents' values

- Discipline (Use of victim-centered induction)

- Reinforcement (tangible rewards may decrease and praise may increase)

- Practice

Prosocial students are more engaged in the classroom. Students who display more prosocial behavior also have higher achievement levels. Prosocial children are also more likely to promote the achievement of their classmates. This is especially true when the classmates are at risk for poorer academic performance. Thus, it is beneficial to foster prosocial behavior in children. Adults should reinforce prosocial behavior, but not with tangible awards. In fact, using concrete rewards may actually reduce prosocial behavior. Adults also promote prosocial behavior by providing models of prosocial behavior themselves. Adults also promote prosocial behavior through the use of "victim centered induction." This means explaining the reasons behind rules and how a child's behavior can impact others. Here are some other strategies that adults can use to promote prosocial behavior:

- Improve emotional competence (e.g., feel and express gratitude)

- Improve moral reasoning and identity

- Establish warm, secure relationships

- Espouse prosocial values

- Help learners feel responsible for others

- Provide opportunities to practice

- Consider school-based interventions

Aggression, Antisocial Behavior, Bullies, & Victims

ANTISOCIAL BEHAVIOR

Antisocial behavior is behavior that limits further social interaction. One example is aggressive behavior. Aggression is behavior intended to harm or dominate anoither person.There are different types of aggressive behavior.

Instrumental aggression - aggression aimed at obtaining an object, privilege or space with no deliberate intent to harm another person (typical of toddlers). Instrumental aggression declines as children grow older in the early childhood and then middle childhood years, because children develop greater vocabularies and gain more strategies to use in place of the instrumental aggression. However, it does not completely disappear. Instrumental aggression is a type of proactive aggression; the goal is to obtain an object, territory, or privilege, but not to hurt victim

Hostile aggression - Aggression intended to harm another person, such as hitting, kicking, or threatening to beat up someone. The goal of hostile aggression is to harm someone. Hostile aggression can be physical, verbal or relational. Hostile aggression can also be proactive or reactive. Hostile aggression is rare among toddlers but becomes more common during the preschool years and continues into middle childhood.

<u>Physical aggression</u> – Aggression that involves attempting to harm someone through physical contact, such as hitting, slapping, pushing or kicking. Physical aggression is present in both boys and girls but more common in boys.

<u>Verbal aggression</u> - Aggression that attempts to harm others through verbal means. Verbal aggression does not involve physical contact, but is instead a verbal attack, such as name calling or threats.

<u>Relational aggression</u> – Aggression that uses aspects of a relationship to inflict harm, such as gossiping, rumoring, or social exclusion. Relational aggression includes verbal aggression. Relational aggression is observed by four-years-of age. Both boys and girls engage in relational aggression, but it is more common in girls. Relational aggression involves harming others through manipulating their relationships or peer status (e.g., spreading rumors, excluding from a social clique),

<u>Covert aggression</u> – Another term for relational aggression, because relational aggression is often not detected or observed.

<u>Reactive aggression</u> – Aggression in response to a real or imagined threat; a retaliation for provocation. For example, a child believes another child is picking on them so they respond aggressively. Reactive aggression is "hot blooded" because it is expressed in the heat of anger, and usually involves anger and/or frustration.

<u>Proactive aggression</u> – Aggression that is not in response to a real or imagined provocation. Proactive aggression is "cold blooded" because it is not expressed in angry retaliation. The goal of proactive aggression is to achieve personal objectives. Bullying is a type of proactive aggression.

<u>Bullying:</u> a type of proactive aggression; goal is intimidation or dominance over another; occurs repeatedly over time; involves someone of greater power victimizing someone of lower status or power.

<u>Cyberbullying:</u> Bullying that occurs through interactive technologies.

Aggression may be physical or verbal/emotional. Aggression is activated in large part by the amygdala and regulated by the prefrontal cortex. Testosterone is associated with increased aggression in both males and females. Aggression is also caused by negative experiences and emotions, including frustration, pain, and heat. As predicted by principles of observational learning, research evidence makes it very clear that, on average, people who watch violent behavior become more aggressive. Early, antisocial behavior leads to befriending others who also engage in antisocial behavior, which

only perpetuates the downward cycle of aggression and wrongful acts.[243]

Victims of Aggression

As many as 5–20% of students are regularly victimized. There are two general categories of victims. First, *submissive victims* are physically weak, insecure, friendless, cry easily, and are more likely to worry. Second, *aggressive victims*: are children who are poor at emotion regulation, and are described as hot-headed. Aggressive victims provoke a response from bullies. Submissive victims, on the other hand, or sought out by bullies who identify them as perspective targets due to their perceived inability to retaliate.

Age Trends in Aggression and Antisocial Behavior

Infancy and Toddlerhood

- Infants are not capable of aggression, but they are capable of anger

- Aggression toward peers is apparent by 12 months

- Physical aggression increases from 1 to 2 years

- Primarily engage in instrumental aggression

Early Childhood

- Between 2–4 years is most aggressive age

- Around age 3, physical aggression begins decreasing and is replaced with verbal aggression

- Language reduces the need for instrumental aggression

Middle Childhood

- Physical aggression diminishes; becomes rare when adults are present

- Tantrums are typically absent by age 8

- Social aggression becomes more apparent

- Aggression more likely to be hostile rather than instrumental

- Bullying emerges and then declines

Adolescence

- Aggression steadily decreases

- A temporary surge in bullying may occur at transition to middle/junior high school

- Delinquency increases, peaks at 14–15 years, then decreases

- Aggression may be criminal; most crimes are committed in late teens to early adulthood

Clinical Levels of Antisocial Behavior

Oppositional Defiant Disorder (ODD): a clinical diagnosis given to children who are excessively antisocial for at least 6 months

Conduct Disorder (CD): a clinical diagnosis given to youth who are excessively delinquent or aggressive for at least six months

What Predicts CD and ODD?

- Family dysfunction (e.g., parental rejection, harsh discipline, abuse, marital discord, antisocial parents)

- Genetic predisposition

What Predicts Antisocial Behavior?

- Genetic and epigenetics

- Parenting factors

- Coercive family cycle

- Self-esteem

- Social cognition

- Hostile attribution bias

Protective factors correlated with less antisocial behavior

1. Parental warmth. Infants with sensitive, positive parents are likely to be less aggressive into young adulthood.

2. Firm control. For example, parents who do not let children stay up late, or do not let 7th-graders decide whether they can date, have children who are less likely to be antisocial.

3. Parental involvement, such as monitoring, taking interest in, and spending time with children (unless the parent is antisocial).

4. Religiosity. This is also linked to children forgiving aggressors rather than retaliating.

Risk factors correlated with increased antisocial behavior

1. Insecure attachment—at all ages. The effect is weaker for children from two-parent families because stable families are a protective factor.

2. Power assertive discipline, spanking, and authoritarian parenting. These factors undermine self-control and create angry, defiant children, even as early as age 4. Secure attachment may protect children from power assertion.

3. Maternal depression. This is particularly a risk factor for early onset antisocial behavior.

4. Parental smoking.

5. Abuse and domestic violence.

Sources: Barber, Stolz, & Olsen (2005); Blatt-Eisengart et al. (2009); Bowes et al. (2009); Choe, Olson, & Sameroff (2014); Degnan et al. (2008); Goldstein, Davis-Kean, & Eccles (2005); Hay et al. (2011); Joussemet et al. (2008); Kochanska et al. (2009); Lorber & Egeland (2009); Madigan et al. (2015); Michiels et al. (2008); Snyder et al. (2005); Sulik et al. (2015); and Wakschlag et al. (2006).

Bullying and Victims

According to Stopbullying.gov (2016), a federal government website managed by the U.S. Department of Health & Human Services, **bullying** is defined as unwanted, aggressive behavior among school aged children that involves a real or perceived power imbalance. Bullying is verbal or physical behavior intended to disturb someone less powerful. Further, the aggressive behavior happens more than once or has the potential to be repeated. There are different types of bullying, including verbal bullying, which is saying or writing mean things, teasing, name-calling, taunting, threatening, or making inappropriate sexual comments. Social bullying, also referred to as relational bullying, involves spreading rumors, purposefully excluding someone from a group, or embarrassing someone on purpose. Physical bullying involves hurting a person's body or possessions.

A more recent form of bullying is **cyberbullying,** which involves electronic technology. Examples of cyberbullying include sending mean text messages or emails, creating fake profiles, and posting embarrassing pictures, videos or rumors on social networking sites. Children who experience cyberbullying have a harder time getting away from the behavior because it can occur any time of day and without being in the presence of others (Stopbullying.gov, 2016).[244]

Those at Risk for Bullying

The youth most likely affected by bulling are males and younger middle school students. Bullying can happen to anyone but some students are at an increased risk for being bullied, including lesbian, gay, bisexual, transgendered (LGBT) youth, those with disabilities, and those who are socially isolated. Additionally, those who are perceived as different, weak, less popular, overweight, or having low self-esteem, have a higher likelihood of being bullied.

Those Who are More Likely to Bully

Bullies are often thought of as having low self-esteem, and then bully others to feel better about themselves. Although this can occur, many bullies in fact have high levels of self-esteem. You will recall that preschool-age children have very high self-esteem and overestimate their abilities. At the transition to middle childhood, the self-esteem for most children becomes realistic and there is a decline in self esteem. However, this is not the case for many bullies. Instead, these children continue to have an unrealistically high self-esteem. They believe that their peers respect them for

---

[244] Lifespan Development: A Psychological Perspective by Martha Lally and Suzanne Valentine-French is licensed under CC BY-NC-SA 3.0

their bullying behavior. Although some bullies may possess considerable popularity, social power and have well-connected peer relationships, the majority are rejected by their peers. However, these peer rejected children believe that their peers look up to them and respect them. Bullies do not lack self-esteem, and instead lack empathy for others. They like to dominate or be in charge of others.

About a third of bullies were once the victims of bullies themselves when they were younger, but most bullies were not victims themselves. A small number of children are both bullies and victims ("bully-victims") concurrently. For example, a child is a bully when they are with smaller children but a victim when they are with older children. Bullies and victims have a relationship that continue over time, and bullies intentionally pick children who appear to be vulnerable to be their victims. Male bullies are more likely to use physical aggression, and female bullies are more likely to use relational aggression. However, both boys and girls do use both types, and regardless of the type of aggression it has a negative impact on the victims.

Bullied Children

Children who appear vulnerable or who have unusual physical characteristics are more vulnerable to bullying. Ufortunately, most children do not let adults know that they are being bullied. Some fear retaliation from the bully, while others are too embarrassed to ask for help. Those who are socially isolated may not know who to ask for help or believe that no one would care or assist them if they did ask for assistance. Consequently, it is important for parents and teachers to know the warning signs that may indicate a child is being bullied. These include: unexplainable injuries, lost or destroyed possessions, changes in eating or sleeping patterns, declining school grades, not wanting to go to school, loss of friends, decreased self-esteem and/or self-destructive behaviors.

Schools worldwide have bullying problems, and there is a need for intervention programs that reduce bullying. Helping children create friendships is a deterrent to bullying. Having just one friend makes it much less likely that a child will be a victim of bullies. Assertiveness training is also beneficial, both for victims and for bullies. For victims, assertiveness training provides strategies for saying no to bullies. For bullies, assertiveness training provides strategies to replace aggressive strategies. It is beneficial to identify bullies and victims early s that social skills training in assertiveness can improve their behavior. Other programs that have been found to be successful in reducing bullying include:

- Older peers act as monitors; intervene

- Create/post school-wide rules and sanctions

- Include anti-bullying message/program in other community activities for adolescents

- Encourage parents to reinforce/model positive behaviors and interactions

- Parents: contact professional to help with child's bullying behavior or victimization

- Parents get involved in school programs

Classroom Implications for Reducing Bullying & Aggression:

- Avoid using retention in grade

- Eliminate hunger and tiredness

- Be thoughtful about what behavior you reinforce

- Build academic skills

- Establish warm teacher-student relationships

- Promote positive school & classroom climate

- Avoid power-assertive discipline

- Involve all learners in lessons

- Do not accept bullying

- Teach witnesses to stand up for victims

- Provide supervision, especially in places where bullying is most common

- Screen for behavior problems early

Play is the business of childhood

Play can be defined as "pleasurable activities engaged in for their own sake." Have you ever seen a puppy or a kitten play? What sorts of behaviors did the puppy or kitten engage in? Why did you think of the behavior as "play?" Have you ever seen a film of wild animals, such as wolf cubs or lion cubs engaging in play? Clearly, play isn't something that only domesticated animals have learned from interacting with humans. But why would animals engage in play? They are using energy in a way that the energy seems to be "wasted." Survival of the fittest would suggest that animals who waste energy would be less likely to survive. This suggests that there must be some purpose or value to the play. Ethologists believe that one of the functions of play is to prepare the organism for behaviors that promote survival in adulthood. For example, wolf clubs playing together are working their muscles, developing strength and endurance, and improving the coordination of their perception with their motor movements. These skills will help them during hunts when they are older. Moreover, the wolf cubs are learning skills about interacting and communicating with each other while they engage in play together. These skills will help them work together as a pack when they are adults. Thus, in this view, there are biological benefits of play, and play is an activity that organisms are biologically programmed to engage in.

What about humans? What functions would play serve for children? Freud saw play as a means for children to release pent-up emotions and to deal with emotionally distressing situations in a more secure environment. Today, children benefit from a variety of different play therapy techniques conducted by trained therapists. Emotional well-being seems to be one benefit of play.

Vygotsky and Piaget saw play as a way of children developing their intellectual abilities (Dyer & Moneta, 2006). Piaget believed that children actively construct knowledge through hands-on exploration. In this view, play becomes the "business of childhood," as children engage in activities through which they build knowledge. Play is how children learn. Piaget created stages of play that correspond with his stages of cognitive development. These stages are:

Table - Piaget's Stages of Play[245]

Stage	Description
Functional Play	**Exploring, inspecting, and learning through repetitive physical activity.**

---

[245] Cognitive and Social Types of Play (n.d.). Retrieved from https://groundsforplay.com/cognitive-and-social-forms-play

Stage	Description
Symbolic Play	The ability to use objects, actions, or ideas to represent other objects, actions, or ideas and may include taking on roles.[246]
Constructive Play	Involves experimenting with objects to build things[247]; learning things that were previously unknown with hands on manipulations of materials.
Games with Rules	Imposes rules that must be followed by everyone that is playing; the logic and order involved forms that the foundations for developing game playing strategy[248]

While Freud, Piaget, and Vygostsky looked at play slightly differently, all three theorists saw play as providing positive outcomes for children. Today, experts value play for the benefits in cognitive, language, social, emotional and physical development. Play is not frivolous, it is a necessary and beneficial part of childhood.

Mildred Parten (1932) observed two to five year-old children and noted six types of play. These categories are designed to be exhaustive (they covered everything that the children could be doing during the observations) and mutually exclusive (the children's behavior at a given time could only be described by one category and not others). Three types she labeled as non-social (unoccupied, solitary, and onlooker) and three types were categorized as social play (parallel, associative, and cooperative). The table below describes each type of play. Younger children engage in non-social play more than those who are older; by age five associative and cooperative play are the most

---

[246] Symbolic Play (n.d.). Retrieved from https://www.pgpedia.com/s/symbolic-play

[247] Constructive Play (n.d.). Retrieved from https://www.pgpedia.com/c/constructive-play

[248] Games with Rules (n.d.). Retrieved from https://www.pgpedia.com/g/games-rules

common forms of play (Dyer & Moneta, 2006). [249]

Table - Parten's Classification of Types of Play[250]

Category	Description
Unoccupied Play	Children's behavior seems more random and without a specific goal. This is the least common form of play. In this category, the child is not engaging in "play" as commonly understood; for example, they might stand in one spot.
Solitary Play	Children play by themselves, do not interact with others, nor are they engaging in similar activities as the children around them. They are occupied, though – the child plays alone, independently of others.
Onlooker Play	Children are observing other children playing. They may comment on the activities and even make suggestions, but will not directly join the play.
Parallel Play	Children play alongside each other, using similar toys, but do not directly act with each other. The Child plays separately from others, but in aa manner that mimics their play. This is a form of A form of limited social participation in which the child plays near other children with similar materials but does not interact with them.
Associative Play	Children will interact with each other and share toys, but are not working toward a common goal. Although there is social interaction, there is little or no organization. This is a form of true social participation in which children are engaged in separate activities, but they interact by exchanging toys and commenting on one another's behavior.
Cooperative Play	Children are interacting to achieve a common goal. Children may take on different tasks to reach that goal. There is a sense of organized activity in the

[249] Lifespan Development - Module 5: Early Childhood by Lumen Learning references Psyc 200 Lifespan

[250] Psychology by Laura Overstreet, licensed under CC BY 4.0

Category	Description
	social participation. This is a form of true social participation in which children's actions are directed toward a common goal (e.g., working together on a block structure, or acting out a make-believe theme together).

There is a developmental tendency in these stages, but the stages do not have hard boundaries based upon age. By this I mean, there is not one day that a child moves, for example, from n being a parallel player to being an associative player. Rather, children are more likely to participate in a particularly gar type of play at a given age, but these types of play never completely go away. For example, older infants and younger toddlers tend to spend the highest proportion of their play time engaging in solitary play. As they move into older toddlerhood and the younger preschool years, the amount of time spent in solitary play decreases, and there is increasing time spent in parallel play. But solitary play doesn't completely go away – even adults may spend time in solitary play engaging in a puzzle of game of solitaire. But, for most children, the amount of time spent in solitary play decreases between the ages of two and three.

Sometimes adults wonder if they should be concerned about children three and older who engage in solitary play. For this reason, it is helpful to distinguish between types of solitary play. One type is solitary-active play. This is solitary play involving functional or pretense play, while alone. This can be a red flag for poor social skills, if a child plays pretend or functional play alone when others are available to play with. The second type is solitary-passive play. This is solitary play involving construction or exploring objects while alone. These are activities typically done alone and are not necessarily a cause for concern.

It is common for older two-year-olds and younger three-year-olds to spend a substantial amount of time in onlooker play. These children are actively observing the ongoing play of others. There is a look of interest and concentration on their faces, and sometimes they will even mouth words while they watch. It is common for adult observers to believe that the child wishes to engage and to attempt to help the child to enter the ongoing play. However, at this age of younger three, it is developmentally appropriate for children to be onlookers, they are actively constructing knowledge through their observations. However, onlooker behavior declines during the third year, and by age four a large proportion of time spent in onlooker behavior can indeed be a sign that the child could benefit in support entering groups.

For most children, parrallel play becomes the predominate form of play during the second year of life. Two-year-olds engage in parallel play when they play alongside other children and engage with similar materials. Parallel play does not go completely away, but associative play becomes the predominate play type for children from ages three to four, and for 4-year-olds, cooperative play becomes most common. There also are individual differences in the proportion of time spent in different types of play from child to child. For example, some 4-year-olds spend a greater proportion of time engaged in cooperative play than do other 4-year-olds.

Rough-and-Tumble Play vs. Aggression

Rough-and-tumble play is emotionally arousing physical play. It is different from aggression. Rough-and-tumble play can involve soft, open-hand hitting or play hitting. It also can involve pushing, chasing, teasing and wrestling. When engaging in rough-and-tumble play children will stop and help anyone who appears to be hurt. Aggression, on the other hand, involves actual hard hits, shoving and kicking and results in someone being hurt. There are also differences in displayed emotions. In rough-and-tumble play children are smiling or laughing. During aggression, children are frowning or scowling. It is the difference of looking like one is happy and having fun versus looking like one is angry or hostile. There are differences in the outcomes or results of the types of behavior. Rough-and-tumble play results in continuing shared activities, participants stay together afterword. Following aggression, on the other hand, participants separate. Finally there are differences in the intentions of the participants. In rough-and-tumble play the goals of the participants are to have fun, to play, to share an exciting time and to express affection. During aggression, the intentions may be instrumental - to obtain materials or space – or hostile, to inflict harm.

Adults are typically able to distinguish between rough-and-tumble play and aggressive behavior through observation of the children's social cues. Both men and women are equally skilled in being able to distinguish between the two. However, adult males are more likely to tolerate rough-and-tumble play and allow it to continue, whereas adult females are more likely to discourage rough-and-tumble play although the recognize it as "only playing." Rough-and-tumble play provides an essential opportunity for children to develop and practice skill in emotion regulation. It is only through experience in emotionally arousing situations that children are able to recognize their own emotional cues and learn strategies for self-regulation that work for them. It is preferable to allow children to engage in rough-and-tumble play but to place limits on the time and place where it can occur. More importantly, rough-and-tumble play most often turns into aggression when a child who did not want to play is included in the play. For example, imagine two kindergartners playing a chase game. While one chases the other, the pass a third child. This third child does not want to play, and so begins to run away from the two children who are playing chase. The children playing chase interpret this running as the child entering the play frame, and the chaser now catches the child who didn't want to play and begins to drag him to the pretend jail. This unfortunate situation can end in negative behaviors It is important for adults to teach children signals – at a group level so that all children understand the signal the same way – for children to indicate that there are not a part of the play. For example, teaching children to freeze and say "I'm on base" if they do not want to engage in a chase game, and teaching all children to recognize that this signal means that child is "off limits." With this sort of strategy, adults can manage rough-and-tumble play without eliminating it. This allows children the opportunity to engage in this normative type of play that is important for their development.

Conflict and aggression can occur during children's play. By age four, conflict during play is most typically solved through negotiation. There are gender differences in aggressive behavior during play by ages four to five. As you will remember from the section on aggressive behavior, boys are more likely to engage in physical aggression and girls in relational aggression (although both boys and girls engage in both physical and relational aggression to some degree).

Benefits of play

Play is associated with cognitive abilities and academic achievement (e.g., intelligence, verbal ability, visual-spatial ability, problem solving ability, creativity). Play also is associated with social and emotional competence (e.g., self-control, theory of mind, prosocial behavior, happiness). This highlights the importance of play for children's development. It is important for adults to support children's play, but to remember that the value of play comes from its self-directed, open-ended nature. Therefore, it is important that adults "set the stage" for play but do not overly direct the content of the play itself. Adults should value play as a support to learning, and provide materials to support it.

Adults should provide props, space and time for children to engage in pretend and sociodramatic play. Children should also have access to board games and puzzles. It is through the sorts of hands-on activities that children develop math and spatial skills. For example, a child playing a board game rolls three on the dice and counts 1-2-3 spaces. Eventually, the child just moves three spaces as a block. When rolling two dice, they count 1-2-3 spaces for the first die and 1-2-3 for the second. They will then begin to add the dice as one number of "six." Through this type of real experience, children construct a sense of number that is more concrete than just the label of the number. They come to understand properties of the number, and to understand one-to-one correspondence (every number represents one unit).

For older preschoolers and elementary schoolers, games for "drill and practice" can benefit the encoding of strategies and content knowledge. Teachers can provide play centers that have games and materials intentionally selected to promote specific learning. For example, on a given day a first-grade classroom might include a science center with a microscope and slides of insects, a writing center with paper and pencils and writing prompts, a reading center with books on a selected topic, and manipulative centers for hands-on reinforcement of mathematical concepts. Especially with older students, teachers should encourage mind-play in lessons, especially with older students. Adults also can use educational electronic games (serious games) as appropriate.

One unfortunate circumstance is that sometimes adults do not recognize the value of play. Adults who do not understand how children develop and learn may view play as frivolous and a waste of time that could be spent "working." This view is sometimes exacerbated by stress that is placed on the adults in terms of outcomes on required standardized tests. The adults may believe that in order to improve the test scores they must maximize the time spent on academic drill. In some schools, this has led to a reduction in the time allowed for recess. This is a very unfortunate circumstance because children need recess in order to be mentally prepared for other learning activities. In Tennessee, for example, state laws require a minimum of 130 hours of physical activity per week in elementary schools

Play and Symbolic Thought

A major advancement in the preschool years is the acquisition of symbolic thought—a type of thinking in which symbols or internal images are used to represent objects, persons, and events that are not present. Examples of symbolic thought are pretend play, drawing, writing, and speaking.

Sociodramatic play is complex pretend play that includes other children and involves sophisticated enactments and intricate themes and story lines. Sometimes sociodramatic play themes may be based on concrete, real experiences that children have shared. For example, common sociodramatic play themes include playing the roles of a doctor at a doctors office, or playing the roles encountered in a restaurant or grocery store. Other times sociodramatic play is based upon real situations that children have not directly experienced, such as piloting a jet airliner. Other times sociodramatic play is even more fanciful, such as going to the moon, pirates on a ship, or knights in a castle.

There is a developmental trend in sociodramatic play in terms of complexity, duration, use of language, social interaction, and the degree to which concrete connections are necessary. Toddlers engage in sociodramatic play of events they have directly observed or experienced. For example, a toddler may pretend to cook while stirring a toy pot, or rock a baby doll. Sociodramatic play at this age is not social, requires very realistic props, and is of short duration.

As children grow older they can use props that are less and less realistic – and so, require more and more pretense. For example, in order to pretend to talk on a phone, a toddler needs a realistic toy phone. By age four, children can use displacement to pretend that a wooden block is a phone. A kindergartner no longer even needs the block and pretend to talk on a phone by holding nothing but their hand to their ear.

Sociodramatic play requires the the ability to symbolically represent events, people, and objects in one's mind. Thus it depends upon – and gives opportunities to practice with – symbolic thought. As children grow older, the social interaction in sociodramatic play increases. Children progress through parallel play in sociodramatic play – in which they are playing in the same area with the same sorts of props, but each child is in their own pretend world – to cooperative play in sociodramatic play – paying together, sharing the pretend play frame and goals. This level of social interaction necessitates high-level thinking, such as planning and negotiation. It also provides practice with using language. Children negotiate roles and plans with each other as they engage in play. They will sometimes "step out of the play frame" momentarily to check in on the other's status, reach agreements, and give instructions. This helps to maintain the play over time. In contrast to the fleeting sociodramatic play of toddlers, sociodramatic play in four-year-olds can continue across days and different locattions.

Sociodramatic play is a means by which intelligence, language, and creativity grow and enhance one another. Sociodramatic play has been found to relate to both intellectual ability and language ability. Children with high intellectual ability engage in more complex sociodramatic play. Sociodramatic play appears to enhance problem-solving skills. Sociodramatic play also is related to higher IQ and higher performance on Piagetian tasks. Language ability and sociodramatic play are closely related. Vygotsky believed this was because both rely on symbolic thought. Consider, for example, 4-year-old children playing in a pretend grocery store. Toy food and empty food boxes can be collected to be used as props. Not only are children learning socially by interacting with each other to set up the store, but they are also supporting their emergent literacy skills as they "read" the labels on the boxes and packages. They gain in numeracy skills as they make play money and count out change. They may use invented spelling to write signs to place throughout the store. As you can see, sociodramatic play allows for hands-on construction of knowledge in a variety of domains.

When preschoolers engage in sociodramatic play—the enactment of make-believe roles—much symbolizing can be observed. Children use objects to stand for things that are completely different, and they transform themselves into pretend characters. Adults should create sociodramatic play centers to encourage children to pretend. Include realistic props related to themes and topics in the children's experience. For example, a teacher might have a prop box for doctor's office that includes lab coats, a stethoscope, clean medicine bottles annd toy syringes. Another example could be a restaurant prop box that includes menus and toy dinner ware and logoed items from local eateries. Adults also should include some nonrealistic items in the area to encourage the symbolic leaps required to transform such an object into something else.

Adults can "enter the play frame" to support sociodramatic play, but it is important that adults do not take over the play and direct it. Instead, adults should scaffold their involvement to promote contined social interaction and greater symbolization, and back away when their support is not needed. Adults can encourage children to take on diverse and highly imaginative roles, to transform objects, and to invent make-believe situations will enhance symbolic thought. Adults can help less socially skilled children enter ongoing play frames by helping children adapt their behavior to fit that of the play. For example, if children are playing the doctor's office, they are likely to rebuff and ignore a child who comes up and asks "can I play?" This is because the child is breaking down the pretend play frame and that can disrupt the ongoing play. The child is much more likely to be accepted in to the play frame if they adjust their behavior to match that of the play. Adults can demonstrate this skill to children, for example, by introducing the child to the doctor's office by saying "Doctor, my friend is sick – can you help her?" This helps to align the child's behavior with those of the group and to enter the ongoing play without disrupting it.

Play and Culture

Some researchers have reported that children of low socioeconomic status or those from nontechnological societies play less often and less well. However, many of these findings are likely due to children's disinterest in typical classroom toys that may have little to do with their own experiences, or the inability of researchers to capture sociodramatic play in the group because the researcher is using a narrow, Euro-centric definition. There are cultural differences in emphasis on social interaction and symbolic use of objects in play.

Play can include a wide range of objects and activities other than toys. Play-work integrates play and family chores, including child care. From an early age, children imitate the tasks of parents as they prepare for adult roles. Non-toy play involves interaction with others, with little or no focus on objects. Children may play using objects other than commercial toys, or with video and computer games that nonetheless require symbolic though. Embedded play involves engaging in make-believe play while also performing other types of play. Some children exhibit more sociodramatic play outdoors or in areas besides the designated "sociodramatic play" area.

Work-play, non-toy play, and embedded play, which researchers may be less likely to spot, are more common among certain groups. Work-play is more prevalent among low-SES families and children in nonindustrialized societies. The play of African American children tends to be more people-centered and less object-oriented. Puerto Rican children have been found to engage in ample sociodramatic play… in the music center and outdoors, but not always in designated sociodramatic play areas.

Play, including sociodramatic play, is different in different cultures. Traditional measures of play often don't accurately capture the symbolism that is present in sociodramatic play among children from other cultures. It is important for adults who work with young children to understand and appretciate the cultural differences in children's play. Adults should observe carefully to find pretend elements in children's non-play activities. Also, adults should strive to create culturally sensitive dramatic play centers that include elements such as dolls of different races, from themes relating to children's lives, and toys, games, and objects that are familiar to children in the group.

Play and differences in abilities

Challenging conditions can impact children'ssociodramatic play, and classroom environments and interactions may be adapted to address these limitations. For example, a visual impairment can make it hard for a child to distinguish between fantasy and reality in play without the help of visual cues. Adults can adapt interactions by giving children with visual impairments regular tactile tours of the classroom, through rehearsing pretend play with new props and toys, and by helping children interpret the make-believe of peers using other senses.

Similarly, children with hearing impairments can not always participate actively in the social negotiations and complex verbal communication that accompany most sociodramatic play. Adults may adapt interactions by adapt interactions by assisting children with hearing impairments in communicating their ideas to peers during sociodramatic play, and by using sign language or exaggerated voice to help children with hearing impairments understand the input of their peers.

For children with intellectual disabilities, imaginative play is present but may be delayed. Young children with intellectual disabilities may perform sociodramatic play a level typical of peers of a younger age, and there may be more repetition of play behaviors. Children with intellectual disabilities are likely to use less language in their sociodramatic play than there same age peers, and they benefit from simple, concrete play themes of familiar events with realistic props. Adults can adapt sociodramatic play for children with intellectual disabilities by modeling and prompting play entry strategies (such as the example above of "Doctor, my friend is sick."), and by suggesting appropriate make-believe roles that children can successfully accomplish. Adults may also support children with intellectual disabilities by interpreting and explaining the make-believe behavior of other children.

Consider this observation made by the author in a 4-year-old pre-K classroom. The father of a boy in the classroom was suffering from terminal cancer. He was receiving care at home, and a hospital bed had been set up in the home. The teacher had provided the classroom with props associated with the doctors office, including scrub outfits, a cot, a stethoscope and so on. The boy had responded to these props by wanting to lay in the cot and be treated by the or playing the role of doctor. After a few days, most of the peers of the boy had grown tired of the game and had begun to ignore the boys overtures to play. The exception was a girl in the class who had Down Syndrome. She played the role of doctor and "took care" of the boy during center time every day for weeks.

Autism severely limits sociodramatic play. Children with autism are more likely to use toys in a repetitive action than to engage with them symbolically. Children with autism may have difficulty with sociodramatic play because they may have limited theories of mind or limited intersubjectivity (ability to share common understanding of a subject with others). Adul cts can adapt play interactions to support children with autism by intervening actively to guide and encourage pretend play when possible. Adults can create opportunities for functional activities in the context of dramatic play. Finally, adults can prompt peers to engage classmates with autism in their dramatic play.

Peers

Relationships within the family (parent-child and siblings) are not the only significant relationships in a child's life. Peer relationships are also important. Social interaction with another child who is similar in age, skills, and knowledge provokes the development of many social skills that are valuable for the rest of life (Bukowski, Buhrmester, & Underwood, 2011). In peer relationships, children learn how to initiate and maintain social interactions with other children. They learn skills for managing conflict, such as turn-taking, compromise, and bargaining. Play also involves the mutual, sometimes complex, coordination of goals, actions, and understanding. For example, as preschoolers engage in pretend play they create narratives together, choose roles, and collaborate to act out their stories. Through these experiences, children develop friendships that provide additional sources of security and support to those provided by their parents.

Peers are individuals near the same age or maturity level. Peers help children learn reciprocity, fairness, justice. Children are able to learn these through peer relationships because the relationships are more "horizontal" - the members have about equal power and status. It is not possible to learn these through social interactions with parents or other adults because these sorts of relationships are more "vertical" - the adult always has more power and knowledge, and thus is a source of "authority." When interacting with an adult, a young child assumes that what the adult says is "right" because they have the authority in that relationship. It is only through interacting with peers that children learn about equity, fairness, and that rules can be negotiated by members to maintain justice, rather than being set by an outside authority.

However, peer relationships can be challenging as well as supportive (Rubin, Coplan, Chen, Bowker, & McDonald, 2011). Negative influences of peers are possible. Being accepted by other children is an important source of affirmation and self-esteem, but peer rejection can foreshadow later behavior problems (especially when children are rejected due to aggressive behavior).

Peer relationships require developing very different social and emotional skills than those that emerge in parent-child relationships. They also illustrate the many ways that peer relationships influence the growth of personality and self-concept.[251]

Social Understanding

As we have seen, children's experience of relationships at home and the peer group contributes to an expanding repertoire of social and emotional skills and also to broadened social understanding. In these relationships, children develop expectations for specific people (leading, for example, to

---

[251] Children's Development by Ana R. Leon is licensed under CC BY 4.0

secure or insecure attachments to parents), understanding of how to interact with adults and peers, and developing self-concept based on how others respond to them. These relationships are also significant forums for emotional development.

Remarkably, young children begin developing social understanding very early in life. Before the end of the first year, infants are aware that other people have perceptions, feelings, and other mental states that affect their behavior, and which are different from the child's own mental states. Carefully designed experimental studies show that by late in the preschool years, young children understand that another's beliefs can be mistaken rather than correct, that memories can affect how you feel, and that one's emotions can be hidden from others (Wellman, 2011). Social understanding grows significantly as children's theory of mind develops.

How do these achievements in social understanding occur? One answer is that young children are remarkably sensitive observers of other people, making connections between their emotional expressions, words, and behavior to derive simple inferences about mental states (e.g., concluding, for example, that what Mommy is looking at is in her mind) (Gopnik, Meltzoff, & Kuhl, 2001). This is especially likely to occur in relationships with people whom the child knows well, consistent with the ideas of attachment theory discussed above.

Growing language skills give young children words with which to represent these mental states (e.g., "mad," "wants") and talk about them with others. Thus in conversation with their parents about everyday experiences, children learn much about people's mental states from how adults talk about them ("Your sister was sad because she thought Daddy was coming home.") (Thompson, 2006b).

Developing social understanding is based on children's everyday interactions with others and their careful interpretations of what they see and hear. There are also some scientists who believe that infants are biologically prepared to perceive people in a special way, as organisms with an internal mental life, and this facilitates their interpretation of people's behavior with reference to those mental states (Leslie, 1994).

Here is a table of social and emotional milestones that children typically experience during early childhood.

Table - Social and Emotional Milestones[252]

Typical Age	What Most Children Do by This Age
3 years	• Copies adults and friends • Shows affection for friends without prompting • Takes turns in games • Shows concern for a crying friend • Dresses and undresses self • Understands the idea of "mine" and "his" or "hers" • Shows a wide range of emotions • Separates easily from mom and dad • May get upset with major changes in routine
4 years	• Enjoys doing new things • Is more and more creative with make-believe play • Would rather play with other children than by self • Cooperates with other children • Plays "mom" or "dad" • Often can't tell what's real and what's make-believe • Talks about what she likes and what she is interested in
5 years	• Wants to please friends • Wants to be like friends • More likely to agree with rules • Likes to sing, dance, and act • Is aware of gender • Can tell what's real and what's make-believe • Shows more independence • Is sometimes demanding and sometimes very cooperative

Friendships, Peers, and Peer groups

Parent-child relationships are not the only significant relationships in a child's life. Friendships take on new importance as judges of one's worth, competence, and attractiveness. Friendships provide the opportunity for learning social skills such as how to communicate with others and how to negotiate differences. Children get ideas from one another about how to perform certain tasks, how to gain popularity, what to wear, say, and listen to, and how to act. This society of children marks a transition from a life focused on the family to a life concerned with peers. Peers play a key role in a child's self-esteem at this age as any parent who has tried to console a rejected child will tell you. No matter how complimentary and encouraging the parent may be, being rejected by

---

[252] Developmental Milestones by the CDC is in the public domain

friends can only be remedied by renewed acceptance.[253]

Children's conceptualization of what makes someone a "friend" changes from a more egocentric understanding to one based on mutual trust and commitment. Both Bigelow (1977) and Selman (1980) believe that these changes are linked to advances in cognitive development. Bigelow and La Gaipa (1975) outline three stages to children's conceptualization of friendship[254].

Table - Three Stages to Children's Conceptualization of Friendship[255]

Stage	Descriptions
Stage One	In stage one, reward-cost, friendship focuses on mutual activities. Children in early, middle, and late childhood all emphasize similar interests as the main characteristics of a good friend.
Stage Two	In stage two, normative expectation, focuses on conventional morality; that is, the emphasis is on a friend as someone who is kind and shares with you. Clark and Bittle (1992) found that fifth graders emphasized this in a friend more than third or eighth graders.
Stage Three	In stage three, empathy and understanding, friends are people who are loyal, committed to the relationship, and share intimate information. Clark and Bittle (1992) reported eighth graders emphasized this more in a friend. They also found that as early as fifth grade, girls were starting to include the sharing of secrets and not betraying confidences as crucial to someone who is a friend.

A *reciprocated friendship* means that both children nominate each other as a friend. On the other hand, a *unilateral friendship* occurs when child nominates another as a friend, but the reverse is not true. Not all friendships are created equal, and not all friendships are reciprocal. A *clique* is a tightly knit group of about 2–10 friends, usually of same sex and age. Cliques become a more important aspect of children's peer relations at the transition from elementary to middle school.

---

[253] Lifespan Development - Module 6: Middle Childhood by Lumen Learning references Psyc 200 Lifespan Psychology by Laura Overstreet, licensed under CC BY 4.0

[254] Lifespan Development - Module 6: Middle Childhood by Lumen Learning references Psyc 200 Lifespan Psychology by Laura Overstreet, licensed under CC BY 4.0

[255] Lifespan Development - Module 6: Middle Childhood by Lumen Learning references Psyc 200 Lifespan Psychology by Laura Overstreet, licensed under CC BY 4.0

Children base friendship choices on similarity. *Homophily* is the tendency to prefer and bond with similar others. There are developmental differences though. Toddlers and younger preschoolers tend to spend more time with peers who are similar to them in outward, physical characteristics. Preschoolers tend to spend more time with peers who engage in similar activities and have similar activity levels (e.g., a child who prefers quiet activities spends more time with another child who prefers quiet activities, whereas a child who prefers loud and boisterous activities spends more time with peers who prefer these sorts of activities). By elementary school, children continue to select friends based on similar activity interests, but are also beginning to select friends based upon personal qualities. This continues into adolescence as friendship qualities become more and more based on internal characteristics such as attitudes and beliefs. In general, this is a transition in similarity in more concrete to more abstract characteristics. Similarities in behavior and demographics also are important in forming friendships.

This basis of similarity accounts for some of the gender segregation that becomes apparent in children's groups. Toddlers and preschoolers will spend time in both same-sex and mixed-sex groups, but, due to concrete similarities, begin to prefer peers of the same gender. By preschool, children show a preference for their own gender. Although preschoolers continue to engage in mixed-gender groups, when given a choice, boys affiliate with other boys and girls with other girls. This is due to similarity in activity choices.

By elementary school, this gender segregation has become more pronounced. In fact, boys and girls spend so much time in separate groups in elementary school and gender segregation is so common that some researchers have suggested a "Two cultures theory." This is the idea that the social worlds of boys and girls are so different that they represent very different peer experiences. This view predicts that children will have very different experiences, based on their gender. There is mixed support for this view. It does seem that there are different rules for boys and girls groups in middle childhood. Girls tend to interact in smaller groups that are in locations closer to adults. Boys interact in larger groups that are further from adults. Imagine, for example, an elementary school playground during recess. There might be a large group of primarily boys engaging in a game with rules, such as kick ball. There also are smaller groups, primarily of girls, engaging in different activities. The activities of the predominantly girl groups are based more on conversation, negotiation, and a communication style that is based on relationship development. The activities of groups of boys are based more upon rules based, organized games in which there are clearly defined roles and known expectations. There is less negotiation of roles than in the girl's groups. The communication in the boys groups is characterized as "report talk" in which the boys pass information. The communication in the girl's groups is characterized as "rapport talk" that is based more on self-disclosure and relationship building.

However, some researchers do not believe that the interaction styles of boys and girls becomes so different that it can be thought of as "two cultures." They point out that, although most children at elementary school age spend predominantly more time in single-sex groups, both boys and girls continue to participate in mixed-sex groups throughout the elementary school years. In addition, both boys and girls engage in both report talk and rapport talk. Both boys and girls are more likely to engage in report talk in more structured situations and rapport talk when in smaller, informal groups. Thus, the differences observed in communication styles may be a factor that boys spend more times larger, rule-based groups and girls in smaller groups, but both sexes are able to adapt their communication style to the needs of the situation.

In addition, there are some children who spend more times in opposite-sex sex activities. For example, there are some girls who will participate in the more formal games of boys, and there are some girls that will engage with the smaller groups of girls. However, this behavior may have negative impact for the children among their same-sex peers, and they may be more likely to be excluded from activities by their same-sex peers. This may constitute a type of *peer pressure;* friends can exert pressure on each other to conform to group norms. In general, peer pressure is typically positive, but can be negative.

There also are gender differences in conceptualizations of friendships. Across ages, males and females generally stress different qualities as being important in friendships. Males tend to emphasize the importance of engaging in activities together, whereas females tend to emphasize sharing intimacy and emotional closeness as important in friendships.

Friendships are very important for children. Gary Ladd suggested six functions that friendships serve for children. First, friends provide companions, somteone to spend time with and engage in activities with. Second, friends provide stimulation – activities with friends provide cognitive and emotional excitement and interest. Third, friends provide physical support. Remember, for example, that children with at least one friend are less likely to be the victims of bullies. Fourth, friends provide ego support, meaning that they make us feel better about ourselves and give us positive feedback. Fifth, friends provide opportunities for social comparison. As children begin utilizing social comparisons in their self-concepts, friends provide an important context for these. Finally, friends are a source of Intimacy and affection. Researchers who study friendship describe intimacy as self-disclosure, someone to share personal information and secrets with.

The quantity and quality of friendships is predicted by several factors. First, children's overall social competence predicts friendships – inversely, children who display greater levels of aggressive behavior on average have fewer friendships. Parenting factors, such as coaching children in social skills and providing opportunity for peer interaction, predicts friendships, as well as the quality of parent-child attachment. Children whose parents parents model positive social skills through their own high-quality friendships and marriages are likely to have higher quality friendships. Parents also provide benefit by intentionally teaching and coaching friendship skills.

Remember, though, that not all friendships and not all friends are equal, and so not all friendships serve all of these functions equally well. There are other benefits of friendships though. The social interaction with another child who is similar in age, skills, and knowledge provokes the development of many social skills that are valuable for the rest of life (Bukowski, Buhrmester, & Underwood, 2011). In these relationships, children learn how to initiate and maintain social interactions with other children. They learn skills for managing conflict, such as turn-taking, compromise, and bargaining. Play also involves the mutual, sometimes complex, coordination of goals, actions, and understanding. Through these experiences, children develop friendships that provide additional sources of security and support to those provided by their parents.[256]

Five Stages of Friendship from Early Childhood through Adulthood[257]

Selman (1980) outlines five stages of friendship from early childhood through to adulthood.
- In stage 0, **momentary physical interaction**, *a friend is someone who you are playing with at this point in time.* Selman notes that this is typical of children between the ages of three and six. These early friendships are based more on circumstances (e.g., a neighbor) than on genuine similarities.
- In stage 1, **one-way assistance**, *a friend is someone who does nice things for you*, such as saving you a seat on the school bus or sharing a toy. However, children in this stage, do not always think about what they are contributing to the relationships. Nonetheless, having a friend is important and children will sometimes put up with a not so nice friend, just to have a friend. Children as young as five and as old as nine may be in this stage.
- In stage 2, **fair-weather cooperation**, children are very concerned with fairness and reciprocity, and thus, *a friend is someone who returns a favor*. In this stage, if a child

---

Five Stages of Friendship from Early Childhood through Adulthood

does something nice for a friend there is an expectation that the friend will do something nice for them at the first available opportunity. When this fails to happen, a child may break off the friendship. Selman found that some children as young as seven and as old as twelve are in this stage.

- In stage 3, **intimate and mutual sharing**, typically between the ages of eight and fifteen, *a friend is someone who you can tell them things you would tell no one else.* Children and teens in this stage no longer "keep score," and do things for a friend because they genuinely care for the person. If a friendship dissolves in this stage it is usually due to a violation of trust. However, children in this stage do expect their friend to share similar interests and viewpoints and may take it as a betrayal if a friend likes someone that they do not.
- In stage 4, **autonomous interdependence**, *a friend is someone who accepts you and that you accept as they are.* In this stage children, teens, and adults accept and even appreciate differences between themselves and their friends. They are also not as possessive, so they are less likely to feel threatened if their friends have other relationships or interests. Children are typically twelve or older in this stage.

There are developmental changes in friendships. Infants clearly prefer attachment figures in their social interactions. By the age of 1, infants who participate in play groups with other infants have regular playmates in their social groups. Young toddlers tend to have just one friend, who is equally likely to be of opposite sex as of the same sex. In group settings, toddlers tend to spend more time with other toddlers who are most similar to them in outward, physical characteristics. Toddlers begin to show a preference for same-sex peers beginning about 2.5 years of age. Older toddlers may have more friends than younger toddlers.

During the preschool years, children who are older and are more socially skilled more likely to have friends. Parents play a role in helping children develop social skills and friendships, by providing opportunities for peer interaction and through direct coaching and teaching of social skills. By the preschool years, interactions among friends are different than interactions among nonfriends. Friendships provide preschoolers opportunities to practice social skills and foster the acquisition of social skills. At 3–4 years of age, children use the word "friend" but may not really understand the meaning of "friendship." Instead, preschoolers are likely to call anyone they have the opportunity to play with their friend. About 30% of 3- to 7-year-olds may have imaginary friends, and in some ways "actual" friendships of preschoolers are similar to "imaginary" friendships – the child may view their "friend" as more of who they imagine them to be than who they really are. Friendships at this age are very "one-sided" However, by the preschool years there are friendships that are enduring and can last for years.

Friendships grow more psychological at the transition to middle childhood and elementary school. Friends at this age usually share a number of similarities. Provide companionship and support, but there can be negative aspects such as fighting. There are many individual differences in friendships, for example the amount of gender segregation. However, on average friendships and friendship groups at this age become very gender segregated and the impact of homophily becomes stronger. Many children this age actively avoid opposite-sex peers (flirting with opposite sex at a young age is not a sign of maturity). More children have friends at this age – as many as 85% of middle childhood age children report having a friend. Time with peers increases compared to time with adults.

By adolescence, most (80–90%) have reciprocal friends, homophily continues to increase and the total amount of time with peers continues to increase. At the transition to middle school, groups of friends called "cliques" become an important part of the social structure.

Peer Groups

Peer relationships can be challenging as well as supportive (Rubin, Coplan, Chen, Bowker, & McDonald, 2011). Being accepted by other children is an important source of affirmation and self-esteem, but peer rejection can foreshadow later behavior problems (especially when children are rejected due to aggressive behavior). With increasing age, children confront the challenges of bullying, peer victimization, and managing conformity pressures. Social comparison with peers is an important means by which children evaluate their skills, knowledge, and personal qualities, but it may cause them to feel that they do not measure up well against others. For example, a boy who is not athletic may feel unworthy of his football-playing peers and revert to shy behavior, isolating himself and avoiding conversation. Conversely, an athlete who doesn't "get" Shakespeare may feel embarrassed and avoid reading altogether.

Also, with the approach of adolescence, peer relationships become focused on psychological intimacy, involving personal disclosure, vulnerability, and loyalty (or its betrayal)—which significantly affect a child's outlook on the world. Each of these aspects of peer relationships require developing very different social and emotional skills than those that emerge in parent-child relationships. They also illustrate the many ways that peer relationships influence the growth of personality and self-concept.[258]

---

[258] Lifespan Development: A Psychological Perspective by Martha Lally and Suzanne Valentine-French is licensed under CC BY-NC-SA 3.0

Peer Relationships

Most children want to be liked and accepted by their friends. Some popular children are nice and have good social skills. These popular-prosocial children tend to do well in school and are cooperative and friendly. Popular-antisocial children may gain popularity by acting tough or spreading rumors about others (Cillessen & Mayeux, 2004). Rejected children are sometimes excluded because they are shy and withdrawn. The withdrawn-rejected children are easy targets for bullies because they are unlikely to retaliate when belittled (Boulton, 1999). Other rejected children are ostracized because they are aggressive, loud, and confrontational. The aggressive-rejected children may be acting out of a feeling of insecurity. Unfortunately, their fear of rejection only leads to behavior that brings further rejection from other children. Children who are not accepted are more likely to experience conflict, lack confidence, and have trouble adjusting.

One method to assess peer relationships is a Sociogram, which is a social map of the classroom. Sociograms are produced by observing the group and noting which children interact with whom. Another way that peer relationships are studied is using **sociometric assessments** (which measure attraction between members of a group). The sociometric method asks children through interviews or self reports which classmates they like, or prefer to play or work with, and which they dislike. Children are asked to mention the three children they like to play with the most, and those they do not like to play with. The number of times a child is nominated for each of the two categories (like and do not like) is tabulated. Based on those tabulations, children are categorized into the following:

Table - Categories in Peer Relationships[259]

Category	Description
Popular Children	Receive many votes in the "like" category, and very few in the "do not like" category.
Rejected children	Receive more unfavorable votes, and few favorable ones.

---

[259] Lifespan Development: A Psychological Perspective by Martha Lally and Suzanne Valentine-French is licensed under CC BY-NC-SA 3.0

Category	Description
Controversial children	Mentioned frequently in each category, with several children liking them and several children placing them in the do not like category.
Neglected children	Rarely mentioned in either category.
Average children	Have a few positive votes with very few negative ones.

Children rated as sociometrically popular are sought out for play by other children. They are more likely than other children to have social strategies that are active and engaging – they have a lot of fun ideas and lead play. These children are viewed as leaders by their peers. Other children look at them more often, and adults rate pictures of these children as more physically attractive. Popular children are "nice" and have good social skills. They also have larger vocabularies and better overall verbal skills, and are more likely to do well in school and on academic tasks. They are more outgoing, friendly and cooperative.

By middle childhood, we begin to see a second group of children who receive many like most nominations and are rated as popular. This smaller group does not display more prosocial behavior and instead may gain popularity by acting tough or spreading rumors with others. This group may overlap to some degree with the children rated as sociometrically controversial. These children, who we begin to see in middle childhood, receive a high number of both like most and like least nominations. This is a smaller group of children and are less studied than other groups, but they appear to be children who can bully one group of children and another group of children finds it funny.

Sociometrically neglected children receive few like most or like least nominations. When observed, they typically play alone. There are two groups of neglected children. The first group rarely interacts with other children but does not care and is not bothered by this. These children have low motivation for social interaction. The second group, on the other hand, recognizes that they do not play with other children but would like to. These children have low self-efficacy. They believe that if they tried to interact with others it would not work out for them. They may have social anxiety and feel nervous trying to interact. These children have social strategies that are more vague, less sophisticated and more withdrawing. Their behavior is more shy and withdrawing. By first grade, these children report feeling more loneliness, and these children are at greater risk for internalizing disorders such as anxiety and depression. Additionally, these children also interact with adults less than other children do. They can "slip through the cracks" with teachers because they do not draw attention to themselves. Neglected children are one of the two groups (along with controversial) most likely to change classification across time. Some neglected children will become actively rejected by peers and will enter the group of withdrawn rejected children. Others will enter the group of sociometrically average children, while some will remain in the neglected group.

Rejected children are actively rejected by their peers. The largest group, who we begin to see in the preschool years, are children who are aggressive. These children are on a pathway for becoming bullies and have a faulty perception that the way to feel powerful is through aggressive behavior. These children have faulty self-perceptions and believe that they are popular and well liked by their peers. You will remember that at the transition to elementary school, the self-esteem of most children drops from the overly high self-esteem of the preschool years to a more realistic level. The aggressive peer rejected children are the exception to this. Rejected-aggressive children think they are more popular than they are. They believe that their peers look up to them and respect their aggressive behavior, although the peers are in actuality rejecting them. Between the ages of 2nd to 8th grade there is a well documented hostile attribution bias among these aggressive peer-rejected children – they are more likely than other children to attribute hostility to the actions of others in ambiguous situations. Aggressive rejected children are at greater risk for externalizing problems as they grow older. They are at risk for aggression, delinquency and violence. Peer rejection also predicts low academic achievement. Rejected children are least likely to change classification across time.

There is a second group of peer rejected children that becomes detectable in the elementary school years. These are non-aggressive children who are rejected by their peers because they engage in some sort of behavior that is reputationally damaging. Rejected-withdrawn children see themselves as socially incompetent. Rejected children who are shy and withdrawn and are easy targets for bullies because they are unlikely to retaliate when belittled. These children begin to fear being rejected by their peers. Unfortunately for rejected children, their fear of rejection only leads to behavior that brings further rejection from other children. Peers treat this group of children differently than the neglected children. Neglected children are often left out of social interaction because they do not attempt to enter. The withdrawn rejected children are actively excluded by other children. Other children will tell them o go away or rebuff their attempts at interaction. Children who are not accepted are more likely to experience conflict, lack confidence, and have trouble adjusting. (Klima & Repetti, 2008; Schwartz, Lansford, Dodge, Pettit, & Bates, 2014).[260] Peer rejection predicts psychological distress (victimization, loneliness, low self-esteem, and depression).

Prosocial behavior predicts higher levels of peer acceptance, and aggression predicts peer rejection. Social withdrawal (such as being shy even among familiar peers) and lower levels of social skills predicts neglected and withdrawn-aggressive sociometric classifications. Parents impact children's peer acceptance in three broad ways. First, parents make about the child's peer world, and provide opportunities for children to engage in peer relationships, such as taking young children to play dates and birthday parties. Second, parents may actively teach or coach children's social skills. Finally, there are indirect relationship variables – parents who have warm, predictable, responsive relationships with their children have children who are doing better with peer relations. On the other hand, there are parenting risk factors for peer relations. Marital conflict and divorce are associated with more difficulty in children's peer relations, as are parental use of harsh and power-assertive discipline. Father's negativity while playing with his children is associated with peer relation difficulties, as are parental maltreatment and abuse.

Teachers and other helping adults can help support peer rejected children by teaching the children to reduce aggression and increase prosocial behavior. This can be encouraged by teaching focusing on the children's social cognitive skills and by helping students develop better emotion regulation. Adults also support children's peer relations by capitalizing on children's strengths and promoting skills in non-social areas, such as academic skills. Children who are struggling with peer relations benefit when adults provide opportunities for them to engage with peers. Although it may seem like a good idea to pair a child with another who is doing well socially, this can have a negative impact if the other child becomes bored with the child who is struggling and reinforces the child's negative self-perceptions. Instead, it is a better strategy to pair the child who is struggling with a younger peer who will have more equal social ability. This gives the child opportunities to practice peer interaction skills in a setting in which they may be more successful.

---

[260] Lifespan Development: A Psychological Perspective by Martha Lally and Suzanne Valentine-French is licensed under CC BY-NC-SA 3.0

14 The Child in Context: Family Structure, Child Care, and Media.

Learning Objectives At the completion of this module, students will be able to:	Related Course Objective
14-1 Articulate how family structure influences children, create classrooms that support learners from all family structures, and promote parent involvement.	1 2
14-2 Differentiate the complex experiences and outcomes linked to maternal employment and child care for various learners..	1 2
14-3 Recognize signs of emotional distress and child abuse in children.	11
14-4 Evaluate how media positively and negatively influences learners, and analyze how to help learners minimize negative influences.	1 2

Family Systems

Remember that a family is a system. The family system is made up of subsystems defined by gender, generation, and role. Systems contain as few as two people in a relationship (called dyadic systems) or they include three or more people in relationships (called polyadic systems). Every member of a system impacts every other member. For example, consider the transition of a dyadic system of romantic couple to a polyadic system with the birth of a baby. The mother and father continue to impact each other as a dyadic systetm within this more complex system. The system also contains two new dyadic systems. First there is a dyadic system between mother and the baby. The mother impacts the baby and in return the baby impacts the mother. The father is a member of the entire polyadic family system, but not this particular dyadic sub-system. However, this mother-infant system has an impact on the father. There is an additional dyadic system that includes the father and the infant. This system impacts the mother and is impacted by the mother. The triadic system – mother, father and infant – is also a system in this family.

Within and between systems there are indirect and direct influences from marital relations, parenting, and infant behavior. In our example, suppose that the infant is colicky and the parents are not getting adequate sleep. The result could be that the quality of the relationship between mother and father declines as they take out their frustrations on each other. Thus, the infant had an impact upon the mother-father system. The reverse can also be an indirect impact on the infant – if the mother-father have a quality relationship this can "trickle down" to the infant through the generally happier mood that the parents bring to their interactions. On the other hand, if there is a high level of conflict between mother and father, the increased stress can spill over and impact the quality of the interactions between each parent and the infant.

You will remember that in the unit about theories of child development we discussed Bronfrenbrenner's model of ecological systems. This is a good time to review the levels of systems in that model.

Family Life
Relationships between parents and children continue to play a significant role in children's development during early childhood. We will explore two models of parenting styles. Keep in mind that most parents do not follow any model completely. Real people tend to fall somewhere in between these styles. And sometimes parenting styles change from one child to the next or in times when the parent has more or less time and energy for parenting. Parenting styles can also be affected by concerns the parent has in other areas of his or her life. For example, parenting styles tend to become more authoritarian when parents are tired and perhaps more authoritative when they are more energetic. Sometimes parents seem to change their parenting approach when others are around, maybe because they become more self-conscious as parents or are concerned with

giving others the impression that they are a "tough" parent or an "easy-going" parent. And of course, parenting styles may reflect the type of parenting someone saw modeled while growing up.

Baumrind

Baumrind (1971) offers a model of parenting that includes four styles. The first, **authoritarian**, is the traditional model of parenting in which parents make the rules and children are expected to be obedient. Baumrind suggests that authoritarian parents tend to place maturity demands on their children that are unreasonably high and tend to be aloof and distant. Consequently, children reared in this way may fear rather than respect their parents and, because their parents do not allow discussion, may take out their frustrations on safer targets-perhaps as bullies toward peers.

Authoritarian parents are High on control and low on acceptance. Rules not negotiated or discussed – the parent has the attitude of "my way or the highway." Discipline tends to be punitive and use power-assertive discipline techniques. If asked to explain the reason behind rules parents would say "because I said so." Authoritarian parenting is associated with child outcomes in which the child is somewhat obedient in situations where they feel that they are being monitored (this is called situational compliance). Children with authoritarian parents tend tho show adequate achievement (although this is associated with high levels of achievement among Asian-American families). Children with authoritarian parents tend to show a lack of self-confidence. Authoritarian parenting is linked to more behavior problems and lower achievement, compared to authoritative parenting, for all children.

However, these effects are weaker for Black or Asian children than for White and Latino children. Why would there be differences in the impact of authoritarian parenting? One possibility is that authoritarian parenting may be interpreted differently in some cultures–for example, as a sign of caring instead of rejection. It also is the case that the same behavior can have different meanings in different cultures. In many Asian-American cultures, for example, parents teach that training leads to improvement in academic ability. In contrast, many middle class white Americans endorse the belief that differences in academic ability are individual traits. Thus, the impact of authoritarian parenting on children's academic achievement may be different in Asian-American families due to the differences in underlying beliefs about training and academic ability.

Permissive parenting involves holding expectations of children that are below what could be reasonably expected from them. This is sometimes called an indulgent parenting style. Children are allowed to make their own rules and determine their own activities. Parents are warm and communicative, but provide little structure for their children. Children fail to learn self-discipline and may feel somewhat insecure because they do not know the limits. Permissive parents are low on control and high on acceptance. These parents establish few expectations for behavior and few rules, and they seldom discipline their children. However, these parents do display warmth and support for their children. Permissive parenting is associated with child outcomes that include low self-control and low levels of achievement. Children of permissive parents are more likely to engage in delinquency during adolescence. On the other hand, children of permissive parents are typically socially skilled and self-confident and are described as peer-oriented

Authoritative parenting involves being appropriately strict, reasonable, and affectionate. Parents allow negotiation where appropriate and discipline matches the severity of the offense. A popular parenting program that is offered in many school districts is called "Love and Logic" and reflects the authoritative or democratic style of parenting just described. Authoritative parents are high on control and also are high on acceptance. These parents have firm expectations for their child's behavior and have rules, but they support the child's quest to develop autonomy. Authoritative parents give reasons for rules and decisions – this is called induction or "inductive discipline." Authoritative parenting is the style associated with the most positive outcomes for children. Children with authoritative parents are high in self-control and show the highest levels of achievement, social competence and self-esteem. Authoritative parenting is associated with a secure parent-child attachment.

Uninvolved parents (also referred to as rejecting/neglecting or indifferent style) are disengaged from their children. They do not make demands on their children and are non-responsive. These children can suffer in school and in their relationships with their peers (Gecas & Self, 1991). Uninvolved parents have few rules and show little affection or responsiveness to their children. They have little interest in their child's activities. Children of uninvolved parents show low levels of self-control and low levels of achievement. These children are at greater risk of high levels of delinquency.

CHILD DEVELOPMENT
Control and Demandingness

	Low	High
Low	**Indifferent**	**Authoritarian**
High	**Indulgent**	**Authoritative**

Acceptance and Responsiveness (vertical axis label)

Lemasters and Defrain

Lemasters and Defrain (1989) offer another model of parenting. This model is interesting because it looks more closely at the motivations of the parent and suggests that parenting styles are often designed to meet the psychological needs of the parent rather than the developmental needs of the child.

The **martyr** is a parent who will do anything for the child; even tasks that the child should do for himself or herself. All of the good deeds performed for the child, in the name of being a "good parent", may be used later should the parent want to gain compliance from the child. If a child goes against the parent's wishes, the parent can remind the child of all of the times the parent helped the child and evoke a feeling of guilt so that the child will do what the parent wants. The child learns to be dependent and manipulative as a result.

The **pal** is like the permissive parent described previously in Baumrind's model. The pal wants to be the child's friend. Perhaps the parent is lonely or perhaps the parent is trying to win a popularity contest against an ex-spouse. Pals let children do what they want and focus mostly on being entertaining and fun and set few limitations. Consequently, the child may have little self-discipline and may try to test limits with others.

The **police officer/drill sergeant** style of parenting is similar to the authoritarian parent described by Baumrind. The parent focuses primarily on making sure that the child is obedient and that the parent has full control of the child. Sometimes this can be taken to extreme by giving the child tasks that are really designed to check on their level of obedience. For example, the parent may require that the child fold the clothes and place items back in the drawer in a particular way. If not, the child might be scolded or punished for not doing things "right". This type of parent has a very difficult time allowing the child to grow and learn to make decisions independently. And the child may have a lot of resentment toward the parent that is displaced on others.

The **teacher-counselor** parent is one who pays a lot of attention to expert advice on parenting and who believes that as long as all of the steps are followed, the parent can rear a perfect child. "What's wrong with that?" you might ask. There are two major problems with this approach. First, the parent is taking all of the responsibility for the child's behavior-at least indirectly. If the child has difficulty, the parent feels responsible and thinks that the solution lies in reading more advice and trying more diligently to follow that advice.

Parents can certainly influence children, but thinking that the parent is fully responsible for the child's outcome is misguided. A parent can only do so much and can never have full control over the child. Another problem with this approach is that the child may get an unrealistic sense of the world and what can be expected from others. For example, if a teacher-counselor parent decides to help the child build self-esteem and has read that telling the child how special he or she is or how important it is to compliment the child on a job well done, the parent may convey the message that everything the child does is exceptional or extraordinary. A child may come to expect that all of his efforts warrant praise and in the real world, this is not something one can expect. Perhaps children get more of a sense of pride from assessing their own performance than from having others praise their efforts.

So what is left? Lemasters and Defrain (1989) suggest that the **athletic coach** style of parenting is best. Before you draw conclusions here, set aside any negative experiences you may have had with coaches in the past. The principles of coaching are what are important to Lemasters and Defrain. A coach helps players form strategies, supports their efforts, gives feedback on what went right and what went wrong, and stands at the sideline while the players perform. Coaches and referees make sure that the rules of the game are followed and that all players adhere to those rules. Similarly, the athletic coach as parent helps the child understand what needs to happen in certain situations whether in friendships, school, or home life, and encourages and advises the child about how to manage these situations. The parent does not intervene or do things for the child. Their role is to provide guidance while the child learns firsthand how to handle these situations. And the rules for behavior are consistent and objective and presented in that way. So, a child who is late for dinner might hear the parent respond in this way, "Dinner was at six o'clock." Rather than, "You know good and well that we always eat at six. If you expect me to get up and make something for you now, you have got another thing coming! Just who do you think you are showing up late and looking for food? You're grounded until further notice!"

The most important thing to remember about parenting is that you can be a better, more objective parent when you are directing your actions toward the child's needs and while considering what they can reasonably be expected to do at their stage of development. Parenting is more difficult when you are tired and have psychological needs that interfere with the relationship. Some of the best advice for parents is to try not to take the child's actions personally and be as objective as possible.

Cultural Influences on Parenting Styles

The impact of class and culture cannot be ignored when examining parenting styles. The two models of parenting described above assume that authoritative and athletic coaching styles are best because they are designed to help the parent raise a child who is independent, self-reliant and responsible. These are qualities favored in "individualistic" cultures such as the United States, particularly by the white middle class. African-American, Hispanic and Asian parents tend to be more authoritarian than non-Hispanic whites.

In "collectivistic" cultures such as China or Korea, being obedient and compliant are favored behaviors. Authoritarian parenting has been used historically and reflects cultural need for children to do as they are told. In societies where family members' cooperation is necessary for survival, as in the case of raising crops, rearing children who are independent and who strive to be on their own makes no sense. But in an economy based on being mobile in order to find jobs and where one's earnings are based on education, raising a child to be independent is very important.

Working class parents are more likely than middle class parents to focus on obedience and honesty when raising their children. In a classic study on social class and parenting styles called Class and Conformity, Kohn (1977) explains that parents tend to emphasize qualities that are needed for their own survival when parenting their children. Working class parents are rewarded for being obedient, reliable, and honest in their jobs. They are not paid to be independent or to question the management; rather, they move up and are considered good employees if they show up on time, do their work as they are told, and can be counted on by their employers. Consequently, these parents reward honesty and obedience in their children.

Middle class parents who work as professionals are rewarded for taking initiative, being self-directed, and assertive in their jobs. They are required to get the job done without being told exactly what to do. They are asked to be innovative and to work independently. These parents encourage their children to have those qualities as well by rewarding independence and self-reliance. Parenting styles can reflect many elements of culture.[261]

Spanking

Many adults can remember being spanked as a child. This method of discipline continues to be endorsed by the majority of parents (Smith, 2012). Just how effective is spanking, however, and are there any negative consequences? After reviewing the research, Smith (2012) states "many studies have shown that physical punishment, including spanking, hitting and other means of causing pain, can lead to increased aggression, antisocial behavior, physical injury and mental health problems for children" (p. 60).

Spanking is linked to antisocial behaviors and associated with increased aggression. This is more pronounced when the punishment is severe, and strong emotional support of parents reduces the link. Spanking is associated with immediate compliance but long-term noncompliance and "sneaky" behavior. This is because spanking is associated with lower levels of morality. The child sees the source of "right and wrong" as the external parent, rather than developing an internal sense of right and wrong. Their behavior choices are made to reduce avoid punishment, not because of what is "right" or kind or fair. If the child does not believe that they will be caught, there is nothing to prevent them from engaging in the behavior.

Gershoff, (2008) reviewed decades of research and recommended that parents and caregivers make every effort to avoid physical punishment and called for the banning of physical discipline in all U.S. schools. Gershoff and Grogan-Kaylor (2016) completed another metanalysis that looked at research over 160,927 children. They found increased risk for negative outcomes for children who are spanked and that effects of spanking were similar to that of physical abuse.

In a longitudinal study that followed more than 1500 families from 20 U.S. cities, parents' reports of spanking were assessed at ages three and five (MacKenzie, Nicklas, Waldfogel, & Brooks-Gunn, 2013). Measures of externalizing behavior (aggression and rule-breaking) and receptive vocabulary were assessed at age nine.

---

[261] Lifespan Development - Module 5: Early Childhood by Lumen Learning references Psyc 200 Lifespan Psychology by Laura Overstreet, licensed under CC BY 4.0

Spanking

Reasons to avoid physical punishment use include the long term negative consequences, more sneaky behavior, less internalized sense of right and wrong, poorer grades and social interaction, and increased aggressive behavior. Sometimes, physical discipline, especially combined with parents experiencing high levels of stress and low levels of social support, can lead to physical abuse. Of course, not all physical discipline leads to physical abuse. On the other hand, all parents who physically abuse their children use physical discipline.

Most US parents use it at least occasionally with their 3- and 4-year-olds. Overall, 57% of mothers and 40% of fathers engaged in spanking when children were age 3, and 52% of mothers and 33% of fathers engaged in spanking at age 5. Maternal spanking at age 5, even at low levels, was associated with higher levels of aggression at age 9, even after an array of risks and earlier child behavior were controlled for. Father's high-frequency spanking at age 5 was associated with lower child receptive vocabulary scores at age 9. This study revealed the negative cognitive effects of spanking in addition to the increase in aggressive behavior.

Internationally, physical discipline is increasingly being viewed as a violation of children's human rights. Thirty countries have banned the use of physical punishment, and the United Nations Committee on the Rights of the Child (2014) called physical punishment "legalized violence against children" and advocated that physical punishment be eliminated in all settings.

Alternatives to spanking are advocated by child development specialists and include:
- Praising and modeling appropriate behavior
- Providing time-outs for inappropriate behavior
- Giving choices
- Helping the child identify emotions and learning to calm down
- Ignoring small annoyances
- Withdrawing privileges

Changing Families in a Changing Society

The sociology of the family examines the family as an institution and a unit of socialization. Sociological studies of the family look at demographic characteristics of the family members: family size, age, ethnicity and gender of its members, social class of the family, the economic level and mobility of the family, professions of its members, and the education levels of the family members.

Currently, one of the biggest issues that sociologists study are the changing roles of family members. Often, each member is restricted by the gender roles of the traditional family. These roles, such as the father as the breadwinner and the mother as the homemaker, are declining. Now, the mother is often the supplementary provider while retaining the responsibilities of child rearing. In this scenario, females' role in the labor force is "compatible with the demands of the traditional family." Sociology studies the adaptation of males' role to caregiver as well as provider. The gender roles are increasingly interwoven.

Parents in any family structure can be sensitive and authoritative. Permissive, authoritarian, and uninvolved parenting styles also can be found in any parenting structure. Children fare better in any family structure with high-quality parenting.

Diverse Family Forms

A **single parent family** usually refers to a parent who has most of the day-to-day responsibilities in the raising of the child or children, who is not living with a spouse or partner, or who is not married. The dominant caregiver is the parent with whom the children reside the majority of the time. If the parents are separated or divorced, children live with their custodial parent and have visitation with their noncustodial parent. In western society in general, following separation a child will end up with the primary caregiver, usually the mother, and a secondary caregiver, usually the father. There is a growing community of **single parent by choice** families in which a family is built by a single adult (through foster care, adoption, donor gametes and embryos, and surrogacy).

Cohabitation is an arrangement where two people who are not married live together in an intimate relationship, particularly an emotionally and/or sexually intimate one, on a long-term or permanent basis. Today, cohabitation is a common pattern among people in the Western world. More than two-thirds of married couples in the U.S. say that they lived together before getting married.

Gay and lesbian couples are categorized as **same-sex relationships**.[262] After a Supreme Court ruling in 2015, all 50 states in the U.S. must recognize same-sex marriage, there are still some counties in several states that will not issue a marriage license to a same-sex couple.[263]

Sibling Relationships

Siblings spend a considerable amount of time with each other and offer a unique relationship that is not found with same-age peers or with adults. Siblings play an important role in the development

---

[262] Children's Development by Ana R. Leon is licensed under CC BY 4.0

[263] Same-sex marriage by Wikipedia is licensed under CC BY SA 3.0

of social skills. Cooperative and pretend play interactions between younger and older siblings can teach empathy, sharing, and cooperation (Pike, Coldwell, & Dunn, 2005) as well as negotiation and conflict resolution (Abuhatoum & Howe, 2013). However, the quality of sibling relationships is often mediated by the quality of the parent-child relationship and the psychological adjustment of the child (Pike et al., 2005). For instance, more negative interactions between siblings have been reported in families where parents had poor patterns of communication with their children (Brody, Stoneman, & McCoy, 1994). Children who have emotional and behavioral problems are also more likely to have negative interactions with their siblings. However, the psychological adjustment of the child can sometimes be a reflection of the parent-child relationship. Thus, when examining the quality of sibling interactions, it is often difficult to tease out the separate effect of adjustment from the effect of the parent-child relationship.

While parents want positive interactions between their children, conflicts are going to arise, and some confrontations can be the impetus for growth in children's social and cognitive skills. The sources of conflict between siblings often depend on their respective ages. Dunn and Munn (1987) revealed that over half of all sibling conflicts in early childhood were disputes about property rights. By middle childhood this starts shifting toward control over social situations, such as what games to play, disagreements about facts or opinions, or rude behavior (Howe, Rinaldi, Jennings, & Petrakos, 2002). Researchers have also found that the strategies children use to deal with conflict change with age, but that this is also tempered by the nature of the conflict.

Abuhatoum and Howe (2013) found that coercive strategies (e.g., threats) were preferred when the dispute centered on property rights, while reasoning was more likely to be used by older siblings and in disputes regarding control over the social situation. However, younger siblings also use reasoning, frequently bringing up the concern of legitimacy (e.g., "You're not the boss") when in conflict with an older sibling. This is a very common strategy used by younger siblings and is possibly an adaptive strategy in order for younger siblings to assert their autonomy (Abuhatoum & Howe, 2013). A number of researchers have found that children who can use non-coercive strategies are more likely to have a successful resolution, whereby a compromise is reached and neither child feels slighted (Ram & Ross, 2008; Abuhatoum & Howe, 2013).

Sibling relationships can be both pleasant and aggressive. Siblings treat children different than parents treat them. Some level of conflict is typical among siblings. However, extensive conflict between siblings is linked to poor outcomes.

Birth order affects sibling relationships. Firstborn siblings may receive more attention but also more pressure from parents. Firstborns tend to be more adult-oriented, helpful, anxious, conforming, and to show higher levels of self-control. It is often the case that parents are less demanding of later-born siblings as parents gain experience in the parenting role. Later-born siblings also are influenced by their older siblings. There is more variety in the characteristics displayed by later-born siblings.

In previous generations, there were many stereotypes of children who did not have siblings, or "only children." There is some research supporting that only children are more independent, more self-centered, and show lower self-control. Only children may also be more achievement-oriented. The only child may have a more intense and positive relationship with their parents. However, there is no evidence that peer skills or social relationships are deficient in only children.

With the birth of a sibling, interactions with the mother change and this can lead to whiny behavior in the older sibling. It is very common for children to be toddlers or younger preschoolers when a younger sibling is born. Sometimes children can show "regression" to behavior of a younger age, and may not continue to display behaviors they had mastered. A part of this is due to young children's inability to understand that they can experience multiple emotions at the same time, and the feelings of happiness, excitement, jealousy and fear can be difficult for the child to process.

Sibling relationships are more positive than negative for most siblings living in overall harmonious family environments. When children are treated with considerable warmth, and when parents are happy in their marriage, sibling relationships are more positive. However, some conflict among siblings is inevitable. Siblings may perceive differential amounts of parental attention or treatment or may feel threatened in issues of space or resources. On the other hand, siblings also serve as playmates. Sibling relationships are a very special type of peer relationship because they carryover time and space. Not surprisingly, friendly relationships with siblings often lead to more positive interactions with peers. The reverse is also true. A child can also learn to get along with a sibling, with, as the song says "a little help from my friends" (Kramer & Gottman, 1992).[264]

Social Emotional Theories of Development
Child and the Family

The reason we turn out much like our parents, for better or worse, is that our families are such an important part of our socialization process. When we are born, our primary caregivers are almost always one or both of our parents. For several years we have more contact with them than with any other adults. Because this contact occurs in our most formative years, our parents' interaction with

---

[264] Lifespan Development: A Psychological Perspective by Martha Lally and Suzanne Valentine-French is licensed under CC BY-NC-SA 3.0

us and the messages they teach us can have a profound impact throughout our lives. During middle childhood, children spend less time with parents and more time with peers. Parents may have to modify their approach to parenting to accommodate the child's growing independence. Using reason and engaging in joint decision-making whenever possible may be the most effective approach (Berk, 2007).[265]

Family Atmosphere

One of the ways to assess the quality of family life is to consider the tasks of families. Berger (2005) lists five family functions:

- Providing food, clothing and shelter

- Encouraging learning

- Developing self-esteem

- Nurturing friendships with peers

- Providing harmony and stability

Notice that in addition to providing food, shelter, and clothing, families are responsible for helping the child learn, relate to others, and have a confident sense of self. The family provides a harmonious and stable environment for living. A good home environment is one in which the child's physical, cognitive, emotional, and social needs are adequately met. Sometimes families emphasize physical needs but ignore cognitive or emotional needs. Other times, families pay close attention to physical needs and academic requirement, but may fail to nurture the child's friendships with peers or guide the child toward developing healthy relationships. Parents might want to consider how it feels to live in the household. Is it stressful and conflict-ridden? Is it a place where family members enjoy being?[266]

The Family Stress Model

Family relationships are significantly affected by conditions outside the home. For instance, the **Family Stress Model** describes how financial difficulties are associated with parents' depressed moods, which in turn lead to marital problems and poor parenting that contributes to poorer child

---

[265] Sociology: Brief Edition is licensed under CC BY-NC-SA 3.0

[266] Lifespan Development: A Psychological Perspective by Martha Lally and Suzanne Valentine-French is licensed under CC BY-NC-SA 3.0

adjustment (Conger, Conger, & Martin, 2010). Within the home, parental marital difficulty or divorce affects more than half the children growing up today in the United States. Divorce is typically associated with economic stresses for children and parents, the renegotiation of parent-child relationships (with one parent typically as primary custodian and the other assuming a visiting relationship), and many other significant adjustments for children. Divorce is often regarded by children as a sad turning point in their lives, although for most it is not associated with long-term problems of adjustment (Emery, 1999).

Family Forms

As discussed previously in chapter 9, the sociology of the family examines the family as an institution and a unit of socialization. Sociological studies of the family look at demographic characteristics of the family members: family size, age, ethnicity and gender of its members, social class of the family, the economic level and mobility of the family, professions of its members, and the education levels of the family members.

Currently, one of the biggest issues that sociologists study are the changing roles of family members. Often, each member is restricted by the gender roles of the traditional family. These roles, such as the father as the breadwinner and the mother as the homemaker, are declining. Now, the mother is often the supplementary provider while retaining the responsibilities of child rearing. In this scenario, females' role in the labor force is "compatible with the demands of the traditional family." Sociology studies have examined the adaptation of males' role to caregiver as well as provider. The gender roles are becoming increasingly interwoven and various other family forms are becoming more common.

Here is a list of some of the diverse types of families:

Families Without Children
Singlehood family contains a person who is not married or in a common law relationship. He or she may share a relationship with a partner but lead a single lifestyle.

Couples that are **childless** are often overlooked in the discussion of families.

Families with One Parent
Single parent families are a diverse and sizable group – about 37% of children in the U.S. live in a single-parent family. A single parent family usually refers to a parent who has most of the day-to-day responsibilities in the raising of the child or children, who are not living with a spouse or partner, or who is not married. The dominant caregiver is the parent with whom the children reside

for the majority of the time; if the parents are separated or divorced, children live with their custodial parent and have visitation with their noncustodial parent. In western society in general, following a separation a child will end up with the primary caregiver, usually the mother, and a secondary caregiver, usually the father. The majority of single-parent families are headed by a mother, although there is a smaller group headed by fathers.

Single parent by choice families refer to a family that a single person builds by choice. These families can be built with the use of assisted reproductive technology and donor gametes (sperm and/or egg) or embryos, surrogacy, foster or kinship care, and adoption. The number of children in single-parent by choice families has risen, but this group is a small portion of the total number of children of single-parents. The fastest growing group of unmarried mothers consists of employed, college-educated women. When stress levels are low, children in these single-parent homes display levels of adjustment comparable to children in two-parent families.

There has been an increase in single-parent families due to increase in births to unmarried women. Although all single-parent families are different, children raised in single-parent homes, as a group, are more likely to live in poverty than other children. Of course, this is not the case for all children in single-parent homes. It is most likely when the mother is herself a teen and when the mother has lower levels of education. With young mothers, there may be other issues (such as the mother's own developmental task of establishment of personal identity). It is least likely when the mother is older and has higher levels of education. Nonetheless, as a group, children in single-parent families, especially those with teen mothers, are at increased risk for behavior problems, alcohol or drug use, special education placement, retention in grade, dropping out of school, lower test scores. Children of teen single-parents are also at increased risk of becoming teen parents themselves. Infants born to teen mothers are more likely than other infants to be born premature, and to be medically fragile infants with low birth weight. This factor also puts these children at increased risk.

There are several reasons why children in intact two-parent families (the term "nuclear families" is used to refer to intact two-parents families with the two biological parents) may generally fair better than children in single-parent families. First, on average parents in nuclear families have higher levels of education than single parents. Nuclear families have more residential stability and have fewer moves in home. This provides more neighborhood, school and community stability for their children. Research shows that there is greater parent–child closeness in nuclear families, better parent-child relationships and less abuse. This is probably due to nuclear families having less financial strain due to the extra income, as well as an extra person for resources. Father presence is a protective factor for children. There also may be less conflict experienced by children in intact families than in divorced or separated families.

Two Parent Families

The nuclear family is often referred to as the traditional family structure. It includes two married parents and children. While common in industrialized cultures (such as the U.S.), it is not actually the most common type of family worldwide.[267] It also has not been the most common type of family through all of U.S. history – extended families were more common during the generations when the U.S. was primarily an agriculturally-based nation.

Cohabitation is an arrangement where two people who are not married live together in an intimate relationship, particularly an emotionally and/or sexually intimate one, on a long-term or permanent basis. Today, cohabitation is a common pattern among people in the Western world. More than two-thirds of married couples in the U.S. say that they lived together before getting married.

Gay and lesbian couples with children have **same-sex families**. While now recognized legally in the United States, discrimination against same-sex families is not uncommon. According to the American Academy of Pediatrics, there is "ample evidence to show that children raised by same-gender parents fare as well as those raised by heterosexual parents. More than 25 years of research have documented that there is no relationship between parents' sexual orientation and any measure of a child's emotional, psychosocial, and behavioral adjustment. Conscientious and nurturing adults, whether they are men or women, heterosexual or homosexual, can be excellent parents. The rights, benefits, and protections of civil marriage can further strengthen these families."[268]

Among same-sex couples, 33% of men and 22% of women are rearing at least one child. These children develop in much the same ways that other children do. Sexual orientation has not been found to be an important factor in parenting quality.

There are three myths about children in same-sex families that are sometimes repeated in our society. The first of these is that children in gay/lesbian households will have more negative outcomes. Research has found this is not true. A second myth is that other children will make fun of them. Research does not support this. Finally, a third myth is that these children will be more

---

[267]Types of Families by Lumen references Cultural Anthropology/Social Institutions/Family by WikiEducator, which is licensed under CC0

[268]Same-sex marriage by Wikipedia is licensed under CC BY-SA 3.0

likely to be gay when they grow up. This is not the case.

The American Academy of Child & Adolescent Psychiatry in 2013: "Current research shows that children with gay and lesbian parents do not differ from children with heterosexual parents in their emotional development or in their relationships with peers and adults" and they are "not more likely than children of heterosexual parents to develop emotional or behavioral problems."

https://www.aacap.org/AACAP/Families_and_Youth/Facts_for_Families/FFF-Guide/Children%20with%20Lesbian,%20Gay-Bisexual-and-Transgender-Parents-092.aspx

The American Academy of Pediatrics (AAP) in 2013: "A growing body of scientific literature demonstrates that children who grow up with one or two gay and/or lesbian parents fare as well in emotional, cognitive, social, and sexual functioning as do children whose parents are heterosexual."

https://www.aap.org/en-us/about-the-aap/aap-press-room/Pages/American-Academy-of-Pediatrics-Supports-Same-Gender-Civil-Marriage.aspx

The American Psychological Association (APA) in 2005: "same-sex couples are remarkably similar to heterosexual couples, and that parenting effectiveness and the adjustment, development and psychological well-being of children is unrelated to parental sexual orientation." "beliefs that lesbian and gay adults are not fit parents have no empirical foundation."

https://www.apa.org/pi/lgbt/resources/parenting

Blended families describe families with mixed parents: one or both parents remarried, bringing children of the former family into the new family[269]. Blended families are complex in a number of ways that can pose unique challenges to those who seek to form successful stepfamily relationships (Visher & Visher, 1985). These families are also referred to as stepfamilies. There will be more information about Blended families below.

Families That Include Additional Adults
Extended families include three generations, grandparents, parents, and children. This is the most common type of family worldwide.[270]

---

[269] Family by Wikipedia is licensed under CC BY SA 3.0

[270] Types of Families by Lumen references Cultural Anthropology/Social Institutions/Family by WikiEducator, which

Almost 10% of U.S. children below the age of 18 live in a household in which a grandparent is present. These children represent a diversity of experiences. Over one million children (2002) live with custodial grandparent who has primary legal custody of them. Female African-American non–high school graduates are most likely to take custodial roles with grandchildren. Other children live with a single-parent, perhaps a teen parent, in their grandparent's home. The single-parent is the custodial parent of these children. Other children live with their parents and their grandparents in their parents home – the parents are taking care of their older parents. Also, sometimes older single and dual-parent families "move back in" to a grandparents home after job loss or a financial setback. All children who live in extended family settings with grandparents present experience benefits, such as close bonding and family connections that span multiple generations. Children who live with custodial grandparents, though, do face some special challenges and are at increased risk. Children living with custodial grandparents are more likely to be poor, and less likely to have health insurance.

What Are Some Parent-Child Issues and Societal Changes in Families?

When parents are not of the same ethnicity, they build interracial families. Until the decision in Loving v Virginia in 1969, this was not legal in the U.S. There are other parts of the world where marrying someone outside of your race (or social class) has legal and social ramifications.[271] These families may experience issues unique to each individual family's culture.

Families by choice are relatively newly recognized. Popularized by the LGBTQ community to describe a family not recognized by the legal system. It may include adopted children, live-in partners, kin of each member of the household, and close friends. Increasingly family by choice is being practiced by those who see benefit to including people beyond blood relatives in their families.[272]

While most families in the U.S. are **monogamous**, some families have more than two married parents. These families are **polygamous**.[273] Polygamy is illegal in all 50 states, but it is legal in

is licensed under CC BY-SA

[271]Interracial marriage by Wikipedia is licensed under CC BY-SA 3.0

[272]Types of Families by Lumen references Cultural Anthropology/Social Institutions/Family by WikiEducator, which is licensed under CC BY-SA

[273]Family by Wikipedia is licensed under CC BY SA 3.0

other parts of the world.[274]

Additional Forms of Families

Kinship families are those in which the full-time care, nurturing, and protection of a child is provided by relatives, members of their Tribe or clan, godparents, stepparents, or other adults who have a family relationship to a child. When children cannot be cared for by their parents, research finds benefits to kinship care.[275]

When a person assumes the parenting of another, usually a child, from that person's biological or legal parent or parents this creates **adoptive families.** Legal adoption permanently transfers all rights and responsibilities and is intended to affect a permanent change in status and as such requires societal recognition, either through legal or religious sanction. Adoption can be done privately, through an agency, or through foster care and in the U.S. or from abroad. Adoptions can be closed (no contact with birth/biological families or open, with different degrees of contact with birth/biological families). Couples, both opposite and same-sex, and single parents can adopt (although not all agencies and foreign countries will work with unmarried, single, or same-sex intended parents).[276]

Children living in foster care are particularly vulnerable. First, children are in foster care often due to neglect or parent drug use. This means that many children in foster care have experienced negative life events prior to entering foster care. Foster homes tend to be in low-SES, high-risk neighborhoods. A high proportion of foster homes are with single or cohabiting caregivers.

More than 1.5 million children in the U. S. are adopted. This includes those adopted domestically and internationally. Children adopted as infants experience outcomes similar to those in intact families. Children adopted at older ages, though, can face some special challenges. These older adopted children are at greater risk for emotional and behavioral problems, but the magnitude of differences is not large. Adopted children have high rates of insecure attachment and avoidance. A minority of adopted children (12%) have substantial behavior problems. Adjustment is better for those who are adopted compared to those in foster homes or institutional environments.

In 1989, 170,000 children were discovered neglected and malnourished in Romanian orphanages. Many of these children were adopted by families in America and Europe. Study of these children

---

[274] Legality of polygamy by Wikipedia is licensed under CC BY-SA 3.0

[275] About Kinship Care by the Child Welfare Information Gateway is in the public domain

[276] Adoption by Wikipedia is licensed under CC BY-SA 3.0

revealed that those who were adopted younger than six months of age developed a typical attachment relationship with their adopted parents. Those were adopted after six months of age made substantial gains, but some problems remained. The longer the children's institutionalization, the worse their brain development. See https://www.apa.org/monitor/2014/06/neglect

Changes in Families - Divorce

The tasks of families listed above are functions that can be fulfilled in a variety of family types— not just intact, two-parent households. Harmony and stability can be achieved in many family forms and when it is disrupted, either through divorce, or efforts to blend families, or any other circumstances, the child suffers (Hetherington & Kelly, 2002). Changes continue to happen, but for children they are especially vulnerable. Divorce and how it impacts children depends on how the caregivers handle the divorce as well as how they support the emotional needs of the child.

Divorce

A lot of attention has been given to the impact of divorce on the life of children. The assumption has been that divorce has a strong, negative impact on the child and that single-parent families are deficient in some way. However, 75-80 percent of children and adults who experience divorce suffer no long-term effects (Hetherington & Kelly, 2002). An objective view of divorce, repartnering, and remarriage indicates that divorce, remarriage and life in stepfamilies can have a variety of effects.[277]

Factors Affecting the Impact of Divorce

As you look at the consequences (both pro and con) of divorce and remarriage on children, keep these family functions in mind. Some negative consequences are a result of financial hardship rather than divorce per se (Drexler, 2005). Some positive consequences reflect improvements in meeting these functions. For instance, we have learned that a positive self-esteem comes in part from a belief in the self and one's abilities rather than merely being complimented by others. In single-parent homes, children may be given more opportunity to discover their own abilities and gain independence that fosters self-esteem. If divorce leads to fighting between the parents and the child is included in these arguments, their self-esteem may suffer.

The impact of divorce on children depends on a number of factors. The degree of conflict prior to the divorce plays a role. If the divorce means a reduction in tensions, the child may feel relief. If the parents have kept their conflicts hidden, the announcement of a divorce can come as a shock

---

[277] Lifespan Development - Module 6: Middle Childhood by Lumen Learning references Psyc 200 Lifespan Psychology by Laura Overstreet, licensed under CC BY 4.0

and be met with enormous resentment. Another factor that has a great impact on the child concerns financial hardships they may suffer, especially if financial support is inadequate. Another difficult situation for children of divorce is the position they are put into if the parents continue to argue and fight—especially if they bring the children into those arguments.

Divorce is actually a series of events, not a single event. The characteristics of the series of events influence children's outcomes. For example, children's outcomes are associated with the amount of stress, amount of conflict, change in structure and home environment, change in family finances and SES.

There are several factors that affect children's response to divorce. The first is age. The easiest adaptation is for infants, whereas the hardest is for preschoolers and middle childhood. Child temperament is also important – some children are more impacted by change than others. The most important factor is quality of parenting.

Intervention of the legal system is also correlated with children's outcomes. Sometimes court system intervention is necessary and this is linked with more negative outcomes, on the other hand, divorce mediation is linked with more positive outcomes. These findings could be because there is more conflict in couples when there is court intervention, and less with mediation. Experiencing multiple divorces poses greater risks for children.

Socially mature, responsible children show fewer behavioral problems. Less-competent children have lower self-esteem, and display more behavior problems.

Short-term consequences: In roughly the first year following divorce, children may exhibit some of these short-term effects:

- **Grief over losses suffered**. The child will grieve the loss of the parent they no longer see as frequently. The child may also grieve about other family members that are no longer available. Grief sometimes comes in the form of sadness but it can also be experienced as anger or withdrawal. Older children may feel depressed.

- **Reduced Standard of Living**. Very often, divorce means a change in the amount of money coming into the household. Children experience new constraints on spending or entertainment. School-aged children, especially, may notice that they can no longer have toys, clothing or other items to which they've grown accustomed. Or it may mean that there is less eating out or being able to afford cable television, and so on. The custodial parent may experience stress at not being able to rely on child support payments or having the same level of income as before. This can affect decisions regarding healthcare, vacations, rents, mortgages and other expenditures. And the stress can result in less happiness and relaxation in the home. The parent who has to take on more work may also be less available to the children.

- **Adjusting to Transitions**. Children may also have to adjust to other changes accompanying a divorce. The divorce might mean moving to a new home and changing schools or friends. It might mean leaving a neighborhood that has meant a lot to them as well.

- All children suffer some negative impact from divorce. However, for most the issues decline after 2-years following the divorce. 25% of children from divorced families show serious emotional problems compared to only 10% of children from intact, never divorced families.

Long-Term consequences: Here are some effects that go beyond just the first year following divorce.

- **Economic/Occupational Status**. One of the most commonly cited long-term effects of divorce is that children of divorce may have lower levels of education or occupational status. This may be a consequence of lower income and resources for funding education rather than to divorce per se. In those households where economic hardship does not occur, there may be no impact on economic status (Drexler, 2005).

- **Improved Relationships with the Custodial Parent** (usually the mother): Most children of divorce lead happy, well-adjusted lives and develop stronger, positive relationships with their custodial parent (Seccombe and Warner, 2004). Others have also found that relationships between mothers and children become closer and stronger (Guttman, 1993) and suggest that greater equality and less rigid parenting is beneficial after divorce (Steward, Copeland, Chester, Malley, and Barenbaum, 1997).

- **Greater emotional independence in sons**. Drexler (2005) notes that sons who are raised by mothers only develop an emotional sensitivity to others that is beneficial in relationships.

- **Feeling more anxious in their own love relationships.** Children of divorce may feel more anxious about their own relationships as adults. This may reflect a fear of divorce if things go wrong, or it may be a result of setting higher expectations for their own relationships.

- **Adjustment of the custodial parent**. Furstenberg and Cherlin (1991) believe that the primary factor influencing the way that children adjust to divorce is the way the custodial parent adjusts to the divorce. If that parent is adjusting well, the children will benefit. This may explain a good deal of the variation we find in children of divorce.[278]

Child outcomes linked to divorce:

Prediction of these outcomes is consistent but the effect size is generally small:

Insecure attachment

Externalizing disorders (e.g., aggression, drug use, teen parenthood)

Internalizing disorders (e.g., depression, anxiety)

Medical problems and illnesses

Academic problems (e.g., low achievement)

Adult relationship problems (e.g., divorce)

Blended Families

Child outcomes linked to single-parent and stepfamilies are similar to outcomes associated with divorce. However, children may only have these problems if they have other risk factors as well (e.g., depressed mother, negative family).

Step fathers are most common role in US blended families, because the most typical pattern for custody is placement with biological mothers. The step mother role is more vaguely defined by society. On one hand, society sees stepmothers as interlopers with another women's children (the wicked queen), on the other hand society expects that because stepmothers are women they should be able to automatically step in and care for children naturally (Mary Poppins). Because of these different pressures, step mothers may have a difficult time defining role.

In both nuclear and blended families, fathers and step-fathers have ore time spent in playing with the children and less time in caregiving than mothers. When the time in play is closely examined,

---

[278] Lifespan Development - Module 6: Middle Childhood by Lumen Learning references Psyc 200 Lifespan Psychology by Laura Overstreet, licensed under CC BY 4.0

fathers spend more time in emotionally arousing rough-and-tumble play. High levels of paternal engagement are related to positives outcomes for children. On the other hand, fathers also are more likely to encourage use of sex-stereotyped toys.

A large percentage of non-custodial fathers have little or no contact with children, especially when children are born out of wedlock. Unmarried teen parents form especially fragile families that are less likely to endure over time. Unmarried fathers, especially teen father, who do not spend time with the infant immediately after birth are unlikely to ever have contact with the child. When asked by interviewers, noncustodial fathers cited these obstacles for their lack o contact with the children. The most common obstacle was the mother (conflict, interfering, bad mouthing). The second was personal reasons (jobs, substance abuse). Third, they stated that older children had no time for them. Finally they stated pragmatic issues such as long distance to travel and their own lack of resources due to lower SES.

Noncustodial father involvement after divorce

Divorced less than 2 years: 43% of fathers have regular contact with their children

Divorced 3-5 years: 33% had regular contact

Divorced 6-10 years: 19% had regular contact

Divorced 11 years or more: 31% had no contact at all

(Selter, 1991 as cited on http://www.hec.ohio-state.edu/famlife/divorce/dmo.htm)

Usually, the quality of life for stepchildren is thought to be enhanced when their biological mother remarries. This is because of the SES benefits of an extra wage earner coming in to the family. Studies show that children in step families exhibit similar adjustment problems to children in single-parent families and more problems than children in original two-parent families.

Stepchildren/stepsiblings

Following parents' remarriage, many children of all ages show initial increases in problem behavior and disruptions with other family members. Behavioral, social, emotional, and learning problems are higher for stepchildren than for children in non-divorced families. Both boys and girls in blended families display more externalizing behaviors. However, not all children exhibit negative behavior in response to remarriage. A negative response is most likely for girls during adolescence. Even for those children who have negative initial reactions, a large percentage adapt to stepfamily over time. Younger children adjust in 2-3 years, but for older children adjustment may take longer than two years.

Factors associated with children's adjustment in stepfamiliesSibling relationships are more complex when stepfamilies involve children of both partners. Rivalry and jealousy between siblings and step-siblings can be more intense and coalitions may develop. Rivalry, disengagement and hostility are more likely to occur than positive, mutually supportive behavior. However, strong relationships with mutual support can develop over time. Step-sisters more likely to be positive and supportive. Many step-siblings find they have better quality relationships as adults who are no longer living in the same home competing for resources.

Factors associated with children's adjustment in stepfamilies include the marital adjustment of husband and wife. When the husband and wife report higher levels of satisfaction with the marriage, the adjustment is better for the children. Another factor associated with positive adjustment is authoritative parenting – including warmth, support, involvement, and monitoring. On the other hand, parental coercion, conflict and negativity are associated with more difficulties in adjustment. Children with more social support have more positive adjustment to stepfamilies. Another factor associated with children's adjustment to step families is the children's adjustment from previous transitions. Especially for boys, conflict, the mothers' number of dating partners and the courtship length and timing can impact their adjustment.

Family impact on children's other systems

During middle childhood, children spend less time with their parents than they did during early childhood. However, families are the most important part of the 6 to 11-year-old's life. However, peers and friendships become more and more important to the child in middle childhood. This trend will continue through adolescence as children spend more time with peers and less time with parents.

Parent involvement in education is predictive of school success. Academic socialization: parents communicating educational goals and expectations to their children and linking schoolwork with future success.

There has been a concern over the past two generations that an increased number of working mothers – in both intact and single-parent homes – could negatively impact children. However, many researchers find no detrimental effects of maternal employment. There is a greater risk of problems if the mother's work stress spills into home. For example, if the mother has a bad day at work and that impacts her interaction with the children at home. There also continues to be concern of negative impacts when the mother works in the child's first year. Effects of maternal employment may be negative when mothers work during the child's infancy, work more than 30 hours per week, must work night shift or irregular schedules, or have a low-pay, no-benefit job. The effects of maternal employment may be positive when mothers receive pay that helps the family leave poverty, are single, enjoy their work and believe their employment is good for their children, and make sure they spend time with their children after work hours.

Media and Child Development

Children from preschool to high school spend a great deal of time using media. Some TV and computer programs are educational or prosocial, but children spend much more time with antisocial media

A great deal of violent content is available on television, video games, computers, mobile devices and streaming media. Although television violence is only one of many factors linked to increase aggression, years of research documents that there is a link between television and aggressive behavior. The National Institute of Mental Health has documented these conclusions:

- Children may become less sensitive to the pain and suffering of others.
- Children may be more fearful of the world around them.
- Children may be more likely to behave in aggressive or harmful ways toward others.

Increased viewing of violent TV during early childhood predicts aggression in adulthood. Huesmann and Eron (1986) found that the individuals who had watched a lot of TV violence when they were 8 years old were more likely to be arrested and prosecuted for criminal acts as adults. Children who watch aggressive content are more aggressive. TV viewing is weakly associated with attentional problems.

Children use other forms of video entertainment, including computers and video games. Many video games have violent content. Higher exposure is linked to higher aggression levels. A 2010 review by psychologist Craig A. Anderson and others concluded that "the evidence strongly suggests that exposure to violent video games is a causal risk factor for increased aggressive behavior, aggressive cognition, and aggressive affect and for decreased empathy and prosocial behavior."

Prosocial shows and games are also available . For example, Seseme Street was designed to give a boost in vocabulary to children living in poverty. Programs such as Dora the Explorer were made with close attention to the curriculum that the show was based upon.

During infancy through early childhood, 40% of U.S. children live in homes where a TV is on most of the day as "background." Toddlers watch about 2 hours a day of TV on average, and mostly watch shows designed for adults. The American Academy of Pediatrics has long recommended parents discourage all screen exposure for children under two; this recommendation has been updated to no screen time for children younger than 18-months and discouraged screen exposure for children under two. There is growing concern that screen time may be particularly harmful for older infants and toddlers because they are "receptive" of the content and do not have a proactive way to engage.

Media use increases during elementary school and seems to peak at ages 11–14. Entertainment TV watched by children in middle childhood tends to be violent.

By adolescence, teens watch 1–2.5 hr/day of TV, but there is an increased use of computer and social media and especially smart phones. Among adolescents, 93% use the Internet. Most have their own cell phones, and spend an average of 1.5 hr/day texting. In 2015, 71% of adolescents used Facebook, but each wave of teens tends to prefer the own methods of social media, from snapchat and instragram to tick tock and so on. Higher media use is associated with a lack of physical activity, bad eating habits, and disrupted sleep. Children and teens are also impacted by the media's glamorized use of drugs, alcohol, tobacco and vaping. There also may be pressure to be sexually active, and media can promote promiscuous attitudes and behavior.

Higher television viewing is associated with lower academic achievement, unless the content is educational TV. Moderate computer use is linked to higher academic achievement. Watching television results in poor executive functioning. In terms of emotional development, media use can lead to desensitization of violence, increased anxiety, fear, and a "mean world" view. In terms of social development, increased viewing of aggressive media is linked to increased aggression, whereas increased viewing of porsocial media is linked to increased prosocial behavior.

On average, girls use more social media than boys, and boys are more likely to play video games. Of course, though, boys use social media and girls play games. Low-SES youth watch more TV and play more video games than high-SES youth. African American and Latino children spend about 4.5 hours a day more watching TV, playing video games, and listening to music as compared to Asian American or White children.

Child Care

According to the U.S. Census Bureau in 2011, over sixty percent of families with children under five relied on regular child care arrangements. Around a quarter of those families used organized child care facilities as their primary arrangement.[279] (see https://www.census.gov/prod/2013pubs/p70-135.pdf). A 2016 report from the National Center for Education Statistics revealed similar numbers; 60% of children age 0-5 experienced nonparental care, spending an average of 24 hours a week in center-based arrangements, 27 hours a week in non-relative informal arrangements, and 23 hours a week being cared for by a relative (see https://nces.ed.gov/nhes/tables/ECPP_HoursPerWeek_Care.asp).

Child care involves supervising a child or children, usually from infancy to age thirteen, and typically refers to work done by somebody outside the child's immediate family. Child care is a broad topic covering a wide spectrum of contexts, activities, social and cultural conventions, and institutions. The majority of child care institutions that are available require that child care providers have extensive training in first aid and are CPR certified. In addition, background checks, drug testing, and reference verification are normally required.

It is traditional in Western society for children to be cared for by their parents or their legal guardians. In families where children live with one or both of their parents, the child care role may also be taken on by the child's extended family. If a parent or extended family is unable to care for the children, orphanages and foster homes are a way of providing for children's care, housing, and schooling.

Child Care in the United States

Formal child care options include **center-based care** and **family child care homes**. Each state has different regulations for licensing child care centers, including teacher requirements. In some states, teaching in a child care center requires an associate's degree in child development. States with quality standards built into their licensing programs may have higher requirements for support staff, such as teacher assistants. **Head Start** (a federally funded child care program for income qualified families) lead teachers must have a bachelor's degree in Early Childhood Education. States vary in other standards set for daycare providers, such as teacher to child ratios.

---

[279] Who's Minding the Kids by the U.S. Census Bureau is in the public domain

Child Care Concerns

About 77.3 percent of mothers of school-aged and 64.2 percent of mothers of preschool-aged children in the United States work outside the home (Cohen and Bianchi, 1999; Bureau of Labor Statistics, 2010). Most young children (about 60%) receive regular nonmaternal care during early childhood. Infants and toddlers are the most likely to spend time in home-based care arrangements.Preschoolers are more likely to be in center-based care arrangements.. Seventy-five percent of children under age 5 are in scheduled childcare programs. Others are cared for by family members or friends. Older children are often in after school programs, before school programs, or stay at home alone after school once they are older.

Of the children who will ever be in child care, about one quarter enter care by 5-months of age. About 50% will enter by age 2.5. Initially, likely to be part-time and in home based care.

After age 3, more likely to be in center-based care. Just prior to kindergarten, 83% of children are in some kind of care, from a few hours a week to full time.

School is the primary source of child care after age 6. Children may be in after-school programs or self-sibling care or self-care after school. Many people continue to express concern about school-age children who lack supervision during the day because both parents are employed. Such children are known as latchkey children.

Latchkey children report that they are often lonely, and they may have a significantly greater number of behavior and delinquency problem than children who are supervised before and after school. Large communities and cities usually have extensive recreational programs for school-age children. The cost of participating in these activities is usually minimal.

The type of care does not seem related to outcomes. Instead, the quality of family relationships are the most important variable in predicting children's outcomes. The quality of the care is a more important predictor than the quantity of care. Quality childcare programs can enhance a child's social skills and can provide rich learning experiences. But long hours in poor quality care can have negative consequences, especially for young children.

Quality of Care

What determines the quality of child care? Some aspects of high quality care are "regulable." This means that we can make laws and regulations that define the minimum requirements. For example, one consideration is the **teacher/child ratio**. States specify the maximum number of children that can be supervised by one teacher. In general, the younger the children, the more teachers required for a given number of children. The lower the teacher to child ratio, the more time the teacher has for involvement with the children and the less stressed the teacher may be so that the interactions can be more relaxed, stimulating and positive. There are regulations for both the number of adults perr child and the total number of children allowed in groups. Larger group sizes present challenges to quality as well. The program may be more rigid in rules and structure to accommodate the large number of children in the facility.

Ratios for Daycare Centers in Tennessee

Age of Children	Child: Staff Ratio	Max Group Size
6 weeks	4:1	8
9 months	4:1	8
18 months	6:1	12
27 months	7:1	14
3 years	9:1	18
4 years	13:1	20
5 years	16:1	20
6 years	20:1	NR
7 years	20:1	NR
8-9 years	20:1	NR
10 years and older	20:1	NR

Age Ranges in Tennessee	Ratios for Large Family Child Care
Total Number of Children Allowed:	8-12; Plus 3 School-Age Children (SAC)
Ratio of Children to One Provider:	12:1 For 3+-yrs 15:1 For 3+-yrs, with at least 3 SAC
Provider's Own Children Counted:	Yes; If under age 9

Age Ranges in Tennessee	Ratios for Small Family Child Care
Total Number of Children Allowed:	5-7
Maximum Number of Children to One Provider:	7
Provider's Own Children Counted:	Yes; If under age 9
Maximum Number of Infants/Toddlers to One Provider:	4; Under 2-yrs

In high quality programs, the **physical environment** should be engaging, clean, and safe. The **philosophy** of the organization and the **curriculum** available should be child-centered, positive, and stimulating. Providers should be trained in early childhood education. A majority of states do not require training for their childcare providers. And while formal education is not required for a person to provide a warm, loving relationship to a child, knowledge of a child's development is useful for addressing their social, emotional, and cognitive needs in an effective way.

By working toward improving the quality of childcare and increasing family-friendly workplace policies such as more flexible scheduling and perhaps childcare facilities at places of employment, we can accommodate families with smaller children and relieve parents of the stress sometimes associated with managing work and family life.[280]

There are other aspects of high-quality care that are non-regulable. For example, regulations can be

[280] Lifespan Development - Module 5: Early Childhood by Lumen Learning references Psyc 200 Lifespan Psychology by Laura Overstreet, licensed under CC BY 4.0

set for educational requirements for early childhood teachers and care givers – both education in child development and experience working with children make independent contributions to care quality. In contrast, personal characteristics of the caregivers are non-regulable. However these characteristics are essential elements of quality. High-quality care involves caregivers who are sensitive and warm, who use rich language, and who teach emergent literacy and informal math. Moreover, high quality care is associated with caregivers that are stable. Unfortunately, due to the difficult economic model of early child care, wages are low and so turnover in teachers and staff tends to be high.

Child care in a home setting may be licensed and regulated, or it may be unlicensed and informal. State legislation may regulate the number and ages of children allowed before the home is considered an official family child care program and subject to licensing regulations. Often the nationally recognized Child Development Associate credential is the minimum standard for the individual leading this home care program.

In addition to these licensed options, parents may also choose to find their own caregiver or arrange childcare exchanges/swaps with another family. This care is typically provided by nannies, au pairs, or friends and family. The child is watched inside their own home or the caregiver's home, reducing exposure to outside children and illnesses. Depending on the number of children in the home, the children utilizing in-home care can enjoy the greatest amount of interaction with their caregiver and form a close bond.

There are no required licensing or background checks for this type of in-home care, making parental vigilance essential in choosing an appropriate caregiver. The cost of in-home care is the highest of childcare options per child, though a household with many children may find this the most convenient and affordable option.[281]

Early Child Care and Child Outcomes

The National Institutes of Child Health and Human Development began the largest longitudinal study of the impact of child care on children's adjustment in 1991. The study included 1300 children from ten different locations in the U.S. who were followed from birth through high school. Findings from this study suggest that children who attended more high-quality care, and especially center-based care, were later rated by their school teachers as being more advanced academically and with language. On the other hand, the more out-of-home care that children

---

[281] Lifespan Development - Module 4: Infancy by Lumen Learning references Psyc 200 Lifespan Psychology by Laura Overstreet, licensed under CC BY 4.0

experienced, regardless of type or quality, the more likely their teachers were to later describe them as aggressive with peers or defiant to adults (but not a t clinical level). In the following paragraphs I will summarize research from the NICHD study and other studies of child care on outcomes for children.

Low-quality and unstable care is linked to insecure attachment; this is especially true for less sensitive mothers, and the impact of poor quality care can be buffered by increased maternal sensitivity. In addition, a higher amount of time in nonmaternal care is linked to linked to insecure attachment, and again this is especially the case when mothers are less sensitive. No associations have been found between the type of care and attachment; however, overall home care for infants was rated in the NICHD study as being higher in quality for infants than center-based care.

Researchers have examined stress levels in children by measuring the level of a hormone called cortisol in their saliva. Cortisol levels are high even in high-quality care, but are highest in low-quality care. Cortisol levels are higher in larger-group care.

For child social outcomes, high-quality care is linked to better social abilities than low quality care. This effect is strongest for children from low SES homes. After age 3, center-based care is more strongly associated with better social skills than is home-based care. High quality after school programs are linked to better social ability for school age children, and thiis effect is also strongest for children from low SES homes. In general, the quality of care is a more important predictor. Low-quality care is linked to long term social behavior problems and aggressive behavior. High-quality is linked to better social skills. In the NICHD study, long hours attending even high quality care was linked to higher rates of aggression at the transition to kindergarten, but this was a smaller effect than low-quality care.[282]

The amount of care is linked to negative social outcomes. Greater than 10 hours per week has been linked to poor social skills and behavior problems, especially if care began in infancy. More time in center-based care also has been linked to behavior problems. The amount of time spent in self- or sibling- care is linked to antisocial behavior, especially if the amount is greater than 10 hours per week. Finally, high-quality care is associated with more complex peer play than that found in low-quality care, and center-based care is associated with more complex peer play than found in home-based child care.

Early Childhood Education

---

[282]https://www.nichd.nih.gov/research/supported/seccyd/overview

Providing universal preschool has become an important lobbying point for federal, state, and local leaders throughout our country. In his 2013 State of the Union address, President Obama called upon congress to provide high quality preschool for all children. He continued to support universal preschool in his legislative agenda, and in December 2014 the President convened state and local policymakers for the White House Summit on Early Education (White House Press Secretary, 2014).

However, universal preschool covering all four-year olds in the country would require significant funding. Further, how effective preschools are in preparing children for elementary school, and what constitutes high quality early childhood education have been debated.

To set criteria for designation as a high quality preschool, the National Association for the Education of Young Children (NAEYC) identifies 10 standards (NAEYC, 2016). These include:

- Positive relationships among all children and adults are promoted.

- A curriculum that supports learning and development in social, emotional, physical, language, and cognitive areas.

- Teaching approaches that are developmentally, culturally and linguistically appropriate.

- Assessment of children's progress to provide information on learning and development.

- The health and nutrition of children are promoted, while they are protected from illness and injury.

- Teachers possess the educational qualifications, knowledge, and commitment to promote children's learning.

- Collaborative relationships with families are established and maintained.

- Relationships with agencies and institutions in the children's communities are established to support the program's goals.

- The indoor and outdoor physical environments are safe and well-maintained.

- Leadership and management personnel are well qualified, effective, and maintain licensure status with the applicable state agency.

Parents should review preschool programs using the NAEYC criteria as a guide and template for asking questions that will assist them in choosing the best program for their child.

Selecting the right preschool is also difficult because there are so many types of preschools available. Zachry (2013) identified Montessori, Waldorf, Reggio Emilia, High Scope, Creative Curriculum and Bank Street as types of early childhood education programs that focus on children learning through discovery. Teachers act as facilitators of children's learning and development and create activities based on the child's developmental level. Here is a table summarizes characteristics of each type of program.

Table - Types of Early Childhood Education Programs[283]

Program	Founder	Characteristics
Montessori	Dr. Maria Montessori	• Refers to children's activity as work (not play); children are given long periods of time to work • Focus on individual learning • Features child-sized furniture and defined work areas • Materials are carefully chosen and introduced to children by teacher • Features mixed-aged grouping • Teachers should be certified
Waldorf	Rudolf Steiner	• Focus on whole child • Features connections to nature, sensory learning, and imagination • Provides large blocks of time for play • Delay formal academic instruction • Environment protects children from negative

[283] Gordon, A. M., & Browne, K. W. (2016). Beginning essentials in early childhood education. (3rd ed.). Cengage: Boston.

Program	Founder	Characteristics
		influences
		• Relationships are important so groupings last for several years (**looping**)
		• Teachers should be certified
Reggio Emilia	Loris Malaguzzi	• Teachers and children co-construct the curriculum
		• Teachers are researchers
		• Environment is the third teacher and features beauty and order
		• Children's learning is documented through the multiple methods (100 languages of children)
		• Have atelier (art studio) with an atelierista (artist) to instruct children
		• Believe children are competent and capable
		• Children stay together for 3 years
		• Parents partner with teachers
		• Community is extension of school
High Scope	David Weikart	• Features defined learning areas
		• Has 8 content areas with 58 key developmental indicators
		• Consistency of daily routine is important
		• Uses plan-do-review sequence in which they make a plan, act on it, and then reflect on the results

Program	Founder	Characteristics
		• Teachers are partners and use the Child Observation Record (COR) to help assess children and plan curriculum • Utilizes 6 step process to teach children conflict resolution
Bank Street	Lucy Sprague Mitchell	• Also referred to as the Developmental-Interactionist Approach • Environment is arranged into learning centers • Focus on hands-on experience with long periods of time given • Teacher uses questions to further children's exploration • Blocks are primary material in the classroom • Field trips are frequently used
Creative Curriculum	Diane Trister Dodge	• Focus on children's play and self-selected activities • Environment is arranged into learning areas • Large blocks of time are given for self-selected play • Uses projects as basis for curriculum • Is researched based and includes assessment system

Head Start

For children who live in poverty, Head Start has been providing preschool education since 1965 when it was begun by President Lyndon Johnson as part of his war on poverty. It currently serves nearly one million children and annually costs approximately 7.5 billion dollars (United States Department of Health and Human Services, 2015). However, concerns about the effectiveness of Head Start have been ongoing since the program began. Armor (2015) reviewed existing research on Head Start and found there were no lasting gains, and the average child in Head Start had not learned more than children who did not receive preschool education.

A recent report dated July 2015 evaluating the effectiveness of Head Start comes from the What Works Clearinghouse. The What Works Clearinghouse identifies research that provides reliable evidence of the effectiveness of programs and practices in education, and is managed by the Institute of Education Services for the United States Department of Education. After reviewing 90 studies on the effectiveness of Head Start, only one study was deemed scientifically acceptable and this study showed disappointing results (Barshay, 2015). This study showed that 3- and 4-year-old children in Head Start received "potentially positive effects" on general reading achievement, but no noticeable effects on math achievement and social-emotional development.

Nonexperimental designs are a significant problem in determining the effectiveness of Head Start programs because a control group is needed to show group differences that would demonstrate educational benefits. Because of ethical reasons, low income children are usually provided with some type of pre-school programming in an alternative setting. Additionally, Head Start programs are different depending on the location, and these differences include the length of the day or qualification of the teachers. Lastly, testing young children is difficult and strongly dependent on their language skills and comfort level with an evaluator (Barshay, 2015).[284]

Applications to Early Education

Understanding how children think and learn has proven useful for improving education. Activities like playing games that involve working with numbers and spatial relationships can give young children a developmental advantage over peers who have less exposure to the same concepts.

---

[284] Lifespan Development: A Psychological Perspective by Martha Lally and Suzanne Valentine-French is licensed under CC BY-NC-SA 3.0

Mathematics

Even before they enter kindergarten, the mathematical knowledge of children from low-income backgrounds lags far behind that of children from more affluent backgrounds. Ramani and Siegler (2008) hypothesized that this difference is due to the children in middle- and upper-income families engaging more frequently in numerical activities, for example playing numerical board games such as Chutes and Ladders. Chutes and Ladders is a game with a number in each square; children start at the number one and spin a spinner or throw a dice to determine how far to move their token. Playing this game seemed likely to teach children about numbers, because in it, larger numbers are associated with greater values on a variety of dimensions. In particular, the higher the number that a child's token reaches, the greater the distance the token will have traveled from the starting point, the greater the number of physical movements the child will have made in moving the token from one square to another, the greater the number of number-words the child will have said and heard, and the more time will have passed since the beginning of the game. These spatial, kinesthetic, verbal, and time-based cues provide a broad-based, multisensory foundation for knowledge of numerical magnitudes (the sizes of numbers), a type of knowledge that is closely related to mathematics achievement test scores (Booth & Siegler, 2006).

Playing this numerical board game for roughly 1 hour, distributed over a 2-week period, improved low-income children's knowledge of numerical magnitudes, ability to read printed numbers, and skill at learning novel arithmetic problems. The gains lasted for months after the game-playing experience (Ramani & Siegler, 2008; Siegler & Ramani, 2009). An advantage of this type of educational intervention is that it has minimal if any cost—a parent could just draw a game on a piece of paper.

Reading

Cognitive developmental research has shown that phonemic awareness—that is, awareness of the component sounds within words—is a crucial skill in learning to read. To measure awareness of the component sounds within words, researchers ask children to decide whether two words rhyme, to decide whether the words start with the same sound, to identify the component sounds within words, and to indicate what would be left if a given sound were removed from a word. Kindergartners' performance on these tasks is the strongest predictor of reading achievement in third and fourth grade, even stronger than IQ or social class background (Nation, 2008). Moreover, teaching these skills to randomly chosen 4- and 5-year-olds results in their being better readers years later (National Reading Panel, 2000).

Warning Signs of Child Abuse

Below are indicators of child abuse and neglect, please note that the signs in each category may pertain to one or more types of abuse or neglect. If you suspect abuse, please call the Tennessee toll-free at 1-877-237-0004

- Soreness or bruising, pain or itching in genital or anal areas
- Sexually transmitted diseases
- Nightmares or bedwetting
- Unexplained loss of appetite
- Becoming isolated or withdrawn
- Excessive masturbation or sexual play
- Abuses children, animals or pets
- Attaches very quickly to strangers or new adults in their environment
- Obsession with pornography or viewing sexually explicit photos
- Repeated runaway or suicide attempts
- Self-destructive behavior/self-injury/cutting, risky or delinquent behavior
- Substance abuse

- History or presence of emotional, sexual, or other physical abuse
- Sexually transmitted diseases
- Evidence of homelessness; no identification and runaway
- Inexplicable appearance of expensive gifts, clothing, or other costly items
- Presence of an older boy-/girlfriend
- Evidence of drug use
- Possesses multiple phones and hotel room cards
- Repeated statement of urgent need to leave or get back home

- Unexplained fractures or injures
- Previous injuries in various healing stages
- Patterned injuries consistent with objects of abuse (cigarettes, belt, hands)
- Burns on extremities, buttocks or genitals
- Frightened of or shrink at approach of adult caregiver

- Emotional turmoil (anxiety, depressed, suicidal); developmental delays
- Self-isolation or undue aggression
- Fear of going home; many school absences
- Abuses animals or pets

- Anxiety, depression or humility
- Constant belittling, shaming, and humiliation
- Developmental delays; failure to thrive

- Abandonment or reports that there is no one at home to provide care
- Constant hunger or begs or steals food for money; signs of malnutrition
- Abuses alcohol or drugs
- Lacks sufficient clothing for the weather or clothes are filthy
- Neglected personal hygiene (body odor, matted hair)
- Consistent lack of supervision
- Untreated medical issues

In Tennessee, everyone is legally mandated to report suspected child abuse and neglect. For more information, please visit https://www.sworps.utk.edu/children or https://www.tn.gov/dcs.html This project is funded through an agreement with the state of Tennessee.

Resilience

Unfortunately, much of the research about child development is based upon a "deficit approach." This means that researchers and theorists, interested in improving outcomes for children, have searched for "things that may make development difficult," with the idea that by identifying "risk factors" that are associated with negative outcomes, we can try to prevent children from experiencing those.

Today, the phrase "**childhood adversity**" has gained currency. This is the idea that adverse events in childhood, such as high stress, child abuse and neglect, poverty and exposure to violence and can impact development in ways that influence behavior and adjustment through adulthood. This is a continuation of the deficits approach.

Remember that risk factors or "childhood adversity" do not *guarantee* that a child is on a path to negative outcomes. Instead, these are factors that are correlated with negative outcomes. This means that negative outcomes might be more likely. However, we can not use risk factors to make predictions about any given individual child. The statistics that risk factors are based upon assume that we are examining the links between risk factors and outcomes at a group level. They may "improve our odds at making a bet" about percentages at a group level, but they do not apply to predictions about individuals.

One demonstration of this is that there are many children who have experienced multiple risk factors who will "turn out just fine" or who will excel. Many children encounter stress and difficulty. An opposite approach to examining deficits is to search for protective factors that are associated with resilience. These are factors that "buffer" the child from the impact of negative factors. For example, for children from marginalized groups, having a strong sense of ethnic identity is a protective factor from the negative impacts of racism.

Resiliency is the ability to overcome challenges and to bounce back. Many individuals overcome risk factors. Many factors contribute to resiliency. Some that have been identified by research include a warm secure parental relationship, supportive teachers, a strong self-concept, and peer friendships.

Research shows that having just one adult that they can count on can change a child's life. You will have impact on children's lives, and sometimes you will have impacts that you never even know about. Please remember that, and make sure that you are having impacts for the good. Thank you for reading.

Made in the USA
Middletown, DE
08 January 2025

69121152R00236